THE BEST AMERICAN

# NONREQUIRED
# READING
## 2004

THE BEST AMERICAN

# NONREQUIRED
# READING

## 2004

■

EDITED BY
## DAVE EGGERS

INTRODUCTION BY
VIGGO MORTENSEN

HOUGHTON MIFFLIN COMPANY
BOSTON ▪ NEW YORK
2004

Visit our Web site: www.houghtonmifflinbooks.com.

ISSN 1539-316X
ISBN 0-618-34122-6
ISBN 0-618-34123-4 (pbk.)

Printed in the United States of America

MP 10 9 8 7 6 5 4 3 2 1

# CONTENTS

# FOREWORD

IT'S HARD to imagine that it was just a year ago that we were finishing up last year's *Best American Nonrequired Reading*! Then again, doing last year's collection last year, as opposed to this year, seems to have been the right way to go. We took a gamble on that decision, and I think it paid off.

Like last year, our *Best American* mailbag is full of letters, written in crayon and blood and begging to be answered. Let us begin.

*What is this collection again? You told me last year, but I spaced. —*
*Dominique, Santa Monica, CA*

Thank you for your question, Dominique, which I am happy to answer in much the same fashion as I did last year, when you first asked. The purpose of this book is to collect good work of any kind — fiction, humor, essays, comics, journalism — in one place, for the English-reading consumer. The first edition of the book could also be used as a low-frequency ham radio, but this feature has been discontinued.

*Is this book a benefit of some kind? — Steve I. Setter, Milwaukee, WI*

It's funny you should ask, Steve. It's not that your question is funny, but it's funny that you are speaking, when from what we know, you are not a human but a dog. That a dog, an Irish setter, no less, is asking us a question is very funny to us. Ha ha, we say.

The answer: The editors' portion of the proceeds for this book goes directly to 826 Valencia, a San Francisco nonprofit that provides students with free tutoring, college scholarships, workshops, SAT prep, and mentoring, and is housed behind a shop that sells supplies to the working buccaneer. To learn more, visit us at www.826Valencia.com, or stop by anytime; we're between Nineteenth and Twentieth streets in San Francisco's Mission district. We direct you also to our sister nonprofit in Brooklyn, which performs much the same functions, while differing only in that it's housed not behind a pirate store but in the rear of the Brooklyn Superhero Supply Co. More information can be found at www.826NYC.com.

*Who are these "826 All-Stars" who are credited with co-editing this book? — Dan and Becky, Newport, R.I.*

The 826 All-Stars is a moniker for a student committee, stalwart and true, that sifts through virtually everything published in the United States in a given year and from this morass — did we say *morass?* We meant to say *bounty* — finds the best twenty-five or so writings that work together and don't include references to bestiality or John Ashcroft or both. The student committee goes by these names: Kevin Feeney, Alison Cagle, Jeremy Ashkenas, Alexei Wajchman, Juliet Linderman, Adrienne Mahar, Antal Polony, Francesca Root-Dodson, Sabrina Ramos, and Jennifer Florin. They are all high school students from the San Francisco Bay area.

*I must know more about these students. Is more information available? Should I go online? I have heard that the information on the Internet is vast and invariably correct. — Brent Hoff, New York, NY*

Here is what we know, although the bios are written by the committee members and thus completely unreliable:

Jeremy Ashkenas was born in Berkeley and still lives there. He has brownish eyes, massive thighs, and shaved his head only minutes ago. His little sister helped him with the tricky spots. The razor buzzed hot and now he's clean and fresh and bald. It's a steamy day today; he opened every window in the house. And so when he showered with cool water and the wind came blowing through the curtains it felt like ice snakes coiling up on his scalp skin. It's a new feeling. He will attend college out East in the fall.

*Antal Polony* lives in Oakland, went to school at Berkeley High, and next year is going to Tulane University in New Orleans. He was very glad to get in. He gives credit to his piano playing and a bona fide recommendation by Dave the editor.

*Kevin Feeney* just graduated from Saint Ignatius College Prep in San Francisco. He is the editor of *Thought* magazine and is also this year's recipient of the 826 Valencia Young Author's Scholarship. In the fall he will attend a very impressive college in Boston.

In the fall of 2004, the youngest committee member, *Alison Cagle*, will be a junior at a coastal high school with an ocean view of possibilities. Through teachers, mentors, friends, and colleagues she's gained valuable insight into the many cultures of the San Francisco Bay Area, i.e. the world, and all places between Motown and Cold Comfort Farm. She loves the study of outer space but at the moment concentrates on peace on earth.

*Alexei Wajchman* is a graduating senior from San Francisco's School of the Arts high school. He plays clarinet, saxophone, and guitar, sings, and is the leader of a folk/blues/bluegrass/old-time/traditional band, The Blind Willies. In addition, The Big A is a very handsome man.

*Adrienne Mahar* is eighteen years old. She graduated from the San Francisco School of the Arts in June 2004 as a music major (oboe). She looks forward to attending Reed College [get it? Oboe? Reed? Oh, forget it. — Ed.] in Portland, Oregon, in the fall as an English or anthropology major, and also plans to participate in creative writing and journalism on campus.

*Juliet Linderman* attended Lowell High School, the largest public high school in San Francisco and probably anywhere else. She will matriculate in the fall of 2004 at New York University.

*Francesca Root-Dodson* is a young lady who lives in San Francisco and will be attending UC Berkeley in the fall. She generally tries to be the best that she can be.

*Sabrina Ramos* lives in San Francisco, in an apartment off Haight-Ashbury with her mother, and attended Lick-Wilmerding High School. There she studied statistics and photography, but all that is about to change next fall, when she leaves for college in Providence, Rhode

Island. She is a moody person who spends too much time courting free chocolate samples at See's and not enough time applying herself.

*Jennifer Florin* will be a senior at Lowell High School. She enjoys writing, reading, and getting angry at her elected leaders.

*How are the pieces selected? I have heard the editors do most of the work while rowing.* — *Adrienne Barbeau, Phoenix, AZ*

It is true that the editors do quite a bit of rowing, and that much of the discussions of the work in this book are done whilst rowing. But make no mistake: there is much discussion on land, too! Over the course of about six months, the committee and I met once a week, during which time we would discuss what we'd read, look through new work, and talk about the overall shape of the book. Sometimes Alexei, who likes zombies, would suggest the inclusion of fiction about, or essays by, zombies, and always the committee would talk him down. Francesca had her own obsessions: comics about highway patrolmen, and something called poetry. When she would suggest the inclusion of such things, we would put her back into the small cage we keep for her in the back room. The cage, which we have named Francesca's Cage, has a nice rug inside, and we feed her steak and chitlins.

Generally speaking, the members of the committee seek out back issues of periodicals, make copies of things they like, and bring them in for everyone to read. This is an increasingly organized process, with each member required to write his or her comments on the back of the copies. Those pieces that garnered positive comments from a majority of readers would make it into the final round. During the final round, special outfits are worn, mats are distributed over the floor, and there is much wrestling done. At the end of all the wrestling, the collection is finished and we all go back to rowing.

*What sorts of things were eligible? Work from any periodicals at all?* — *Dorsetta Cagle, Pacifica, CA*

It's nice to hear from you, Dorsetta. The answer to your question is yes, as long as these periodicals are American and not

about stereos or zombies or poetry. We always make a very con-
certed effort to include work from lesser-known magazines and
quarterlies and Web sites, and we did find some great things in
some small-circulation publications — we did a better job of including such work this year than ever before. You should be very
proud of your daughter.

*Why is Viggo Mortensen writing an introduction to this book? You
would think he would have better things to do. Was this part of some
kind of work-release program or what?* — Lucy Hackett, Medfield, MA

This collection's mission, if there is one — and there isn't — is
to bring new writing to new audiences. We hope that people will
pick up this book after seeing the name or names of a few writers
they like and then become exposed to other good people who
write. Viggo has been associated with 826 Valencia for some time,
having helped us with fundraising and such. He is also a noted
poet and artist, and thus the perfect ambassador for this collection, bringing, we hope, new people to some great contemporary
writing. We can only hope that this introduction-writing business
takes off for him, given how lucrative it is and how much glory attends it.

*I appreciate the questions thus far, but it seems that no one is willing to
ask the most obvious one, which is: How do the Koreans feel about the
Germans, and vice versa?* — Rasheed Wallis and Tanya Tucker,
Nashville, TN

What a weird coincidence. I was wondering about this the other
day, and thus wrote the following short-short story, which doesn't
ultimately answer your question.

## How Do the Koreans Feel About the Germans?

You are sitting in a movie theater, waiting for the previews to start,
exploring a scratchiness at the back of your throat that makes you
feel both feline and distressed. You are plumbing your throat as
best you can with the heel of your tongue, and while doing so, you

are wondering how the Germans feel about the Koreans, and vice versa. You know generally how Americans feel about Germans (it's complicated) and how Americans feel about Koreans (we don't have such pronounced views), but you don't have any idea how the Germans feel about the Koreans, and how the Koreans feel about the Germans. You first surmise that they probably don't think too much of each other either way. Then you remind yourself that everyone has opinions about Germany, so you deduce that the Koreans probably have more distinct ideas about the Germans than the other way around. But do the Germans think much about the Koreans? You want to ask a German, but you don't really know any Germans. Not well enough to call on the phone, for sure. In college there was Sabine, who was from Frankfurt, in the United States on a tennis scholarship. She was beautiful and broad-shoul-dered, and didn't, even distantly, think of you in a romantic way. After a few weeks of friendship, in the way you have assumed thereafter is common to all Germans, she told you of her complete disinterest in clear and unvarnished language. But beyond Sabine, do you know any Germans that you could ask about the Koreans? Perhaps you could call an embassy. But it's after nine p.m., and you need to know now. You need to know now how the Germans feel about the Koreans before the previews start. You turn to the older couple behind you, he with a beard and she with a small goi-ter, and you ask them about this, about how the Germans feel about the Koreans. The man says, "That's an odd question," and goes back to eating a sandwich he has brought with him. The woman, however, gives the question some thought and says, "I would imagine the Germans would feel the same way we all feel about all of the so-called foreign peoples of the world: we wish them freedom and safety and hope. And besides, are we all that different? Aren't we all getting more alike? Aren't the people of the world heading toward some kind of giant amalgam, a human Pangaea, if you will? Wouldn't that be interesting — the conti-nents drift apart, the universe expands, but at the same time, peo-ple become ever more the same, all whirled together by th— " And at that point you lose track of what the goiter-woman is saying, because the previews have begun. Man, that Garry Marshall seems to have done it again!

*That was odd and unsettling: such a short story about such a subject. I can't decide if I feel completely unsatisfied or simply angry. Can you provide me with more examples of these sorts of very short story-essays, allowing me to form more concrete negative views about the form? — Dr. James Benton, Jr., and family, Lake Bluff, IL.*

*Example 1: You'll Have to Save That for Another Time*
    You are at dinner and you want to tell your wife about how you beat your brother, who is four inches taller than you, at basketball. You have just remembered to tell her this. You beat him earlier in the day — it was so sunny and windless — and you forgot to tell her sooner but now you will tell her, as soon as she is done telling her story about the pregnant friend who slept with her ex-husband on a boat, with her current husband on the boat, too. When she is done with this story and you have commented on the story, because it is a good story, you will tell her about beating your brother at basketball. You haven't beaten him in years — since his height shot past yours when he was sixteen and he became more skilled at basketball and just about every sport — and you feel that having beaten him will improve your virility in her eyes. Finally, her story is winding down. There is some mention of the police being called in to intercede between the friend and husband and ex-husband, on the dock, in what became a very vocal squabble, and your wife is laughing her full-throated laugh about it all. You are getting ready to tell your own news from the day, which in its small way means that you are not irreversibly getting older and slower and less capable of notable physical achievements, that perhaps the course you are on is not one of steady decline, but of dips and spikes, a descent less dramatic and laughable. And just as she is finishing her story and you are about to begin your own, as your mouth is actually open, forming the first words of your account, you realize that you didn't, in fact, beat your brother at basketball today. You were ahead for a while, and then eventually lost. But it

was while you were ahead that you thought about how great it would be to tell your wife about beating him.

*Example 2: The Definition of Reg*

The man, named Reg, works in a small office. He is twenty-seven years old. There are three people in Reg's office: Reg, an older woman named Bea, and a man named Stu, who is about forty. They all get along well, and talk often during and after work, about a wide range of subjects. One Friday, when their boss has encouraged all of them to dress more casually if they so choose, Reg comes to work in a short-sleeved polo shirt and khaki pants. Stu, who is married and straight, comments on what Reg is wearing. "I didn't know you were so buff!" Stu says. Reg is standing about four feet from Stu, removing a new dry-erase board from its packaging, and Stu is looking him over. "I always thought you were kind of skinny," Stu says, "but you're well built, man! Like a jock! Do you work out?" Reg shrugs and tells Stu that he doesn't work out, but sometimes plays lacrosse, a sport he played in college. Stu is still looking him over. "Well, you should wear stuff like that more often. That shirt's good on you. Chicks would dig that, I bet. You gotta show off those pipes," he says, now pointing to Reg's arms. Reg is hoping he is not blushing, and Stu is not finished: "You've got nice shoulders, Reg. You swim?" Reg admits that he did a bit of swimming as a young man. "Looks like it," Stu says. "Man, you think you know a guy, then he comes to work like some kind of Adonis!" There is a long pause as Reg wonders if Stu is finished commenting on his body and while Stu continues to examine Reg, deciding if there is any more commenting that needs to be done. Finally Stu's phone rings, and he turns to answer it and the moment is over. Reg returns to his desk and tries to work. How can he work? He feels touched, massaged. He feels as if he's been slathered with peanut butter and that Stu has licked it off. Reg is straight and knows that Stu is straight and that he doesn't mean anything sexual by his comments, but still Reg wonders, briefly, what it would be like to kiss Stu. He imagines the bristles of Stu's goatee against his own chin. He wonders if Stu's tongue, if men's tongues generally, are thicker than women's. He tries to work but finds he cannot concentrate. Is he in love with Stu or in love with his own body now that it has been immortalized by Stu's gorgeous words? He cannot sit still. He goes to the bathroom and flexes his arms. He pushes his sleeves up a bit to reveal more bicep. He jogs in place. He returns to his desk and writes down Stu's exact words. He daydreams of spending more time with Stu, basking in his approval, being appreciated this way. All Reg has ever wanted, he now realizes, is this kind of thing: to be gazed at, to be admired. It electrifies every part of him; it's more pleasing to him than the affirmation of any work he's ever done or could do, and he wants more of it. He wants it always, and he finds himself wondering how far — into a different lifestyle, as a gay man, as a young man dating an older man, as a seducer, as a home wrecker — he would be willing to go to get it. But first he wonders how to tell Stu that if this is going to work, Stu will need to lose some weight, because right now he looks like a goddamned heifer.

*Example 3: You Know How to Spell Elijah*

You are at the airport, airless, and sitting in a black faux-leather chair near your departure gate. There is a girl, about twelve, sitting in a similar chair, across the wide, immaculate aisle, and she wants to know how to spell Elijah. She is working on a crossword in *Teen* magazine, and is squinting at it, chewing her inner mouth. She is flanked by her parents and soon appeals to them for help. Her father is burly and bearded, her mother tall and thin. Her mother, who reminds you of a praying mantis, answers her daughter's question this way: "It's easy, Dakota: E-L-I-S-H-A." And though you have your own things to do, your own *Boating Week* to read and your bagel to eat, you can no longer concentrate on anything but this young girl's crossword puzzle, quickly being polluted by the advice of these people she calls her parents. (And the young girl is working not in pencil — fool! — but in pen.) You are burning to tell her the truth about the young actor's name spelling but fear you would embarrass or undermine her mother, which you don't want to do. Besides, you think, the girl's father will surely correct the mother; isn't that the beauty of the two-parent system? Indeed it is, for here he is now, leaning over, inspecting the crossword like a good dad. And now he is putting on his glasses even, and finally he tells her, "No, Sharon. I'm pretty sure it's A-L-I-G-A." Good lord! You let out a quick, desperate cough. These people, you think, cannot be serious. This poor girl, stuck forever in a dim, ill-spelling world, nowhere to turn. She'll never know the spelling of Elijah, or Enrique, or even Justin or J.C. Should you intervene? Isn't it your duty? Don't those who know the truth have a responsibility to stop the dissemination of untruths? Standing idly by is tantamount to complicity, a partnership in ignorance! You must step in. You can do so good-naturedly. You can do so without upsetting the family unit, the sanctity thereof. But you're eighteen feet away, making it impossible to do without implying that you were paying much too much attention to the girl's crossword than would seem casual or proper. They'll assume you have an unhealthy interest in *Teen* magazine and its cover boys. And, really now, what were you doing listening in to her spelling request? Why had you directed your attention her way? What's wrong with you, anyway? Isn't your own life complicated enough? Is your own existence so free of mistakes that you need to seek them out in strangers at airports, inserting yourself into the life of a twelve-year-old with a crush on a hobbit-playing actor? No wonder you're on your way to a spa in Palm Desert. You damn well need the rest.

*Example 4: On Making Someone a Good Man by Calling Him a Good Man*

Stuart has the face of a Scottish warrior. He has been told this, though he is unsure if this means he has a historically accurate and fierce Highlands look or that he simply looks like a particular actor from *Braveheart*. Stuart has been friends with Margaret since they were very small. Margaret, soft in every way, recently married

Phillipe, who is an idiot. Stuart feels no jealously toward Phillipe, for he and Margaret were never romantic, and he actually wanted to like Phillipe — from the start he tried to like Phillipe — but Phillipe has always made this difficult because Phillipe is a moron. Phillipe does not work, or does not work often, and feels no guilt at all about allowing Margaret to pay for food, for car repairs that he makes necessary, and for rent. When he has his own money, he goes on sportfishing vacations without Margaret. As we said, he is an idiot. Is he charming? He is not. Is he handsome? Passably. What, then, is his appeal? The narrator is not sure. Anyway, one day, Stuart and Phillipe were standing near each other at one of the many birthdays, bar mitzvahs, and christenings at which they find themselves. As they were talking about sportfishing, which at least means Phillipe will not talk about the ineffectiveness of the UN, Phillipe noticed, at the corner of the building, a young boy being taunted by three others. Before Stuart could react, Phillipe sprinted toward the scrum, chased away the offenders, and was soon consoling the young boy, who after a few minutes was laughing at Phillipe's jokes. When Phillipe returned to the gathering, Stuart, who had seen the entire scene unfold, patted Phillipe on the back and said, "Phillipe, you're a good man." Stuart said this very seriously, because he was very impressed by Philippe's heroics and because the words "good man" are used with the utmost sincerity in his family. In fact, the primary aspiration of the men in Stuart's family is to be called, by their father or grandfather or great-uncle Alastair, a "good man." So Stuart called Phillipe a good man, and though he felt initially that he might have jumped the gun, that one decent act doesn't necessarily define a man, Stuart was surprised to see that over the next weeks and months, Phillipe seemed to change. He stood straighter; he showed up on time. He was kind to, even chivalrous to, Margaret, and began a steady job. He sent her and two of her friends to a weekend spa, and fixed the broken door to her closet. Phillipe never said a word about being called a good man, and Stuart couldn't be sure that the words had any effect on him. But the change in him was clear: he was becoming what Stuart had called him, a good man, and Stuart wondered if we, all or any of us, are so easily improved. If all we need is this kind of semantic certainty. If to be named is to be realized. If once something like that is settled — I am a good man! — we no longer need to struggle, to guess, to err.

*Example 5: When She Started Saying "Appreciate It" After "Thank You"*

She was fifty years old when she began to do this, to say "I appreciate it" each time she said "Thank you." She said these words during interactions with clerks, bus drivers, cabbies, cashiers, bellhops, telephone operators. While for the first four or so decades of her life it seemed enough to say "Thank you" or "Thanks" or "Thanks a lot," now she seems invariably to add "I appreciate it," or more accurately, " 'Preciate it," to her Thank yous. She can't pinpoint when this happened, but it's now involuntary, it's constant, and the odd thing, the strange twist, is that she damn well means it every time. She really does appreciate it when people do kind things for her, no matter how trivial, no matter how expected the service might be given the person's line of work. She is thankful when any human interaction goes off without a hitch, so thankful that her heart gets down on its knees in gratitude and her mouth translates this into words: " 'Preciate it." Has she had so many ugly interactions in her life that she feels thankful for those that go smoothly? Perhaps. At her age, they have added up — the tussles with congenitally angry people, the random misunderstandings, the clashes with the uncompromising or the crazy. All she wants now is to pass through days without rancor. Days without rancor! She should engrave that on her door, tattoo it on her chest. Does she fear people? She does not. Is she affected when her meeting of a new person, in any context, goes poorly? She is devastated. For days she carries with her the sneers of surly pharmacy counter-persons, the inexplicable rage of the woman whose long-leashed dog got caught up in her legs and who somehow blamed her, the entangled! These conflicts affect her too much, she knows. Every one brings her close to a precipice from which she seems destined to fall into a two-day funk, and thus when instead of being pushed over she is pulled back and embraced, even the slightest amount — is extended the most basic human courtesy — she finds herself soaring. Seeing her life as a series of potential skirmishes, she appreciates, damn well 'preciates, peace of any kind.

*Example 6: Woman Waits, Seething, Blooming*

She is a single mother and has no interest in any men but her son, who is fifteen and has not called. It is 2:33 a.m. and he hasn't phoned since 5:40 that evening, when he said he'd be eating dinner out. And now she is watching *Elimidate,* drinking red wine spiked with gin, and picturing hitting her only son with a golf club. She is picturing slapping him flat and hard across his face and is thinking that the sound it would make would almost make up for her worry, her inability to sleep, the many hundreds of dire thoughts that have torched her mind these past hours. Where is he? She doesn't even know where he would go, or with whom. He's a loner, an eccentric. He is, she thinks, the sort of teenager who gets involved with deviants from the Internet. And yet somehow she knows that he is safe, that he is fine but has for whatever reason been unable to call, or has not even given it much thought. He is testing his boundaries, perhaps, and she will remind him of the consequences of such thoughtlessness. And when she thinks of what she will say to him, and loudly she will say it, she feels a strange kind of pleasure. The pleasure is like that enjoyed when a body overwhelmed with irritation is passionately scratched. Giving herself up to that scratching, everywhere and furious — which she did only a month earlier when she'd contracted poison oak — was the most profound pleasure she had ever known. And now, waiting for her son and knowing how righteous will be her indignation, how richly justified will be anything she yells into his irresponsible face, she finds herself awaiting his arrival in the way the ravenous might await a meal. She is nodding her head. She is tapping her foot. She tries to order her thoughts, tries to decide where to start with him. How general should her criticisms be? Should they be specific only to this night, or should this be the door through which they pass to talk about all of his failings? Oh, the possibilities! She will have license to go anywhere, to say anything! She pours more gin into her tumbler of merlot, and when she looks up, at 2:47, his headlights are drawing chalk across the front window. This will be good, she thinks. This will be so good. It will be florid, glorious; she will scratch and scratch. She runs to the door, for she simply can't wait for it to begin.

*Are you finished? — Mark Hadley, Guam*
　Am I finished with what?

*With all of those short-short story thingies. — Mark Hadley, Guam*
　I can be. Are you suggesting that I finish?

*I think so. I kind of think it would be nice if we just stopped all this and got into the good part of the book. No offense. — Mark Hadley, Guam*
　One thing before we go: I would like to take the opportunity to congratulate and thank and lushly praise the student committee. Most of the group has been together for about two years now, and I have to say that I've never seen a more inspiring group of young people. They almost make you sick with their intelligence, charm, cohesiveness, divisiveness, astuteness, brilliance, and dedication. It was with great pride that I heard about their college plans, all of them impressive to no end, and it is with a heavy heart that we say goodbye to them. As of June, we are now but three members, our committee, and are in the process of putting together our new group. By the time you read this, we will have assembled a new panel, ideally one without misguided obsessions with zombies and, we hope, inclusive of at least one member who will fit into the cage we used to keep for Francesca. On their behalf, I hope you enjoy this collection, and that you fulfill your ham radio needs elsewhere, if you have them.

DAVE EGGERS

# INTRODUCTION

I SHARE WITH many people, especially men, the tendency to stub-
bornly resist being given directions or having to read any and all
user guides or assembly manuals. I like to believe that at least
some of my assiduous avoidance of preparatory instruction comes
from a sincere and positive desire to get the word first — to get to
it, to see and sound it out for myself in relative ignorance, to dive
in with a minimum of preconception. Judgments will be formed
almost instantly anyway, as rapidly and effortlessly as conjunctivitis jumped from my right eye to my left the day before yesterday.
Usually, when I pick up a book, I turn to a first page and already,
without consciously reading a single syllable, there are paper, ink,
font, letter size, and any number of other factors about which I'll
inevitably leap to conclusions. I don't need or want to be taken by
the hand, don't want to be prepared for the written contents of any
book, because this somehow makes the words that follow any introduction someone else's — claimed before I've had a chance to
weigh and dissect their combinations myself. If I've liked reading
a book, however, I'll sometimes subsequently read its introduction
out of curiosity.

Therefore, I don't consciously refer to anything in this book,
directly or indirectly, do not seek in the slightest way to prepare
you for the selections made by others for *The Best American Nonrequired Reading 2004*. I do not even recommend that you read any

of this book, especially not a single additional word of mine beyond this one. Put the book down, if you like. Give it away, dump it, cut it into little pieces and eat it, burn it — apply any anarchic means or action you can invent to dispose of it, to put it out of your thoughts. Or, read on. Read some, read randomly, backwards, over a period of years, retain none of it, mock it, misapply it, write to the publisher about its defects in content and professional presentation — particularly this nonrequired introduction, if you wish — or about how your life was for the slightest instant disrupted or detoured for the better by reading this book. As far as I know, none of those sample reactions is illegal at this point. We are still free to read or not read (unless this book of nonrequired reading is required by someone you wish to obey), and still free to make up our own minds about what we have or have not read.

I value words. I am curious about the way words sound, how they draw pictures and provoke unexpected emotional reactions. A single disconnected word or phrase can stop you cold, give you a new world to live in. I like reading unauthorized excerpts of the minutes of private meetings. I like reading photo album captions, want ads, my son's homework, Chinese AIDS-prevention pamphlets, laundry lists, foreign phone books, obituaries, awkward subtitles, road maps, lost-pet fliers fading on streetlight poles, old and forgettable books, instruction manuals I do not need but have found torn out of publications or removed from the packaging of the obsolete product concerned — useless information that I imagine having discovered or saved from extinction. I enjoy reading how people wrote in another time about what I do not understand.

As a boy I would read under a blanket using a flashlight long after my parents, grandmother, or others thought I was asleep. Now I find the same secret enjoyment in reading whatever interests me, and still do so long after the lights should be out. There is no need to hide with a flashlight anymore, and the only one tricked is me — out of precious rest. To this day, I resist reading what others recommend and am attracted to reading what is unpromoted, unnoticed, discarded, perhaps unnecessary.

That's why "Nonrequired" is what stands out for me, what gets my attention in the title of this book. Not being required to understand or explain words appeals to me. It feels better not to be in a hurry to take ownership of or pervert the essence of words with a critical eye, but instead to trust inspiration in reading or writing to come as notions, impulses, or lives that already had shape and were waiting to be perceived long before I stumbled over them. Better to recognize than to decide what words mean to me personally. Write something down and it is dead; writers are murderers. Some writers do kill more gracefully, inflicting less pain than others. Nevertheless, any word written is dead. It can be revived only by being rewritten or reread, by being given successively different meanings.

People whose occupation it is to judge writing and recommend how it should or should not be read often seem to require a tidiness of language, a measurable consistency in the arrangement of words. There might be an understandable assumption involved in school instruction — an expectation of self-regulation of content and style on the part of the student — that takes for granted that certain rules and restrictions have always provided starting points or blueprints for writers and readers alike. A lot is to be said for learning rules and skills, born of practical experience and study, before dismissing them. Nonetheless, it seems worth remembering that words do exist — with or without academic pruning and judgment — as sounds or emotional reference points and will always invite spontaneous, subjective reactions.

Did you ever read or write a sentence without a thought for the origin or reason of any of the words from first to last, simply because you felt like doing so? Don't you snatch words impulsively or intuitively from road signs, songs, newspapers, magazines, television shows, Web sites, overheard sotto voce disagreements — from your own decaying, hodgepodge record of all that happens? Individual words and phrases can stand alone and satisfy a reader in even the longest story, regardless of context. When we read willingly, we can get lost in the beauty and rhythm of words before we look for any satisfaction in the significance of their ordering. Maybe we can understand or feel the "rightness," the tone of words, before we embrace or reject the story they might tell, before we concern ourselves with the logic of their sequence. Our expectation of coherence and, eventually, of resolution in any piece of writing does, of course, grow as we become familiar with the quality of its wordplay, when we begin to guess what line of thought or even which phrase might or ought to come next. Perhaps one of the toughest challenges a writer faces, aside from getting started, is how to remain personally interested in words to come, involved in where the story might go. If there are no surprises along the way for the writer, no happy chance of discovery regardless of how well planned or structured the work sets out to be, it is unlikely to be of memorable interest for the reader.

I recently had the unfortunate experience of losing practically everything I'd written during the last three years. As I was in the process of moving from one house to another, my car was loaded with boxes of books, clothes, kitchen utensils, and all the usual household appliances and sacks of hurriedly packed scraps of letters, papers, drawings, photos, soaps, music, hood ornaments, lucky sticks and stones, spurs, superfluous combs, and outdated to-do lists. While I was carrying some of this debris into the new house, someone broke into the passenger-side window of my car and grabbed the backpack containing several notebooks I'd filled, since early 2001, with handwritten stories and poems.

The backpack also contained a couple of journals, two screenplays, my passport, and two half-read books. The hardest losses were the stories and poems in the notebooks. I had been looking forward, in particular, to reviewing and fine-tuning hundreds of pages of, for me, uncharacteristically long and unguarded poetry that had been written during a series of very quiet nights spent in the Sahara Desert in late 2002. During that time, for various reasons, I had begun writing extended pieces using a lot of abstract imagery and fragmented recollections from my childhood, combined with the rush of sensory impressions I was receiving while living and working in Morocco. The thick white pages of the notebooks from that time were grimy, stained red from the dust near Ouarzazate, yellow from Erfoud and Merzouga, brown and gray from my hands and the ashes of campfires and cigarettes, dog-eared, black with grease. They held sandstorms, camel gargles, vultures, Arabic songs, calls to prayer, prayer rugs, tea, coffee, tent flaps. They reeked of diesel, were alive with flies, fossils, heat waves, goats, soldiers, scorpions, unseen women, donkeys, date palms, doves, hawks, vipers, new or decaying gardens, graveyards, city walls, mosques, stables, wells, fortresses, and schools. This was the start of a long-overdue cataloging of buried memories of plants and their names, horses, car accidents, lightning, pet lizards, parts of arguments between my parents, illnesses, sheep; of fish caught, lost, released, cleaned, cooked, spied in rivers, ponds, lakes, eaten, rotting, struggling, dying, or dead. In those notebooks could be found faces of teachers I've had, of policemen, children, and old people suffering, giggling, sleeping, or otherwise lingering in emergency rooms, bus stations, on street corners, walking or standing on traces of roads or tracks through harsh deserts, prairies, icescapes, or urban wastelands. Here were all the toy soldiers, ineffective windshield wipers, first tastes of chocolate, wine, asparagus, venison, trout, chalk, ants, a Big Mac, dirt, dandelion stem, unsweetened yerba mate, duck, beer, snow, blood . . .

As the world was girding itself for the obviously imminent invasion of Iraq by the U.S.-led "coalition of the willing," a growing sense of urgency could be felt even out there in the idyllic stillness of the North African dunes under ridiculously starry skies. That, as well as the effects of working all day in the sun on horseback with Moroccan, Spanish, French, English, and American colleagues, probably put me in an unusual state of mind each night as I sat eagerly scribbling in relative silence and welcome isolation. I'm not trying to go into travel diary mode, just trying to briefly describe a place and time that I was lucky to be in and that provided me with a lot of energy and inspiration. Words were everywhere I looked, filling dreams, giving me names for everything. It was all I could do to keep up with them, catch a few as they drifted through me, fell now and then from clouds, from my eyes to the table, onto my lap or became tangled in horses' manes. Most of the words got away, as they usually will, but at night I regularly managed to gather them in bunches. The many handwritten poems that came out of that experience were what I most was looking forward to tackling in my new home back in California. That is why the backpack containing those notebooks was on the top of the carload of belongings, leaning against the passenger-side window, in plain view for any potential passing thief. Out of my sight for perhaps five minutes, and then gone forever.

I spent a lot of time and effort in the following weeks scouring my part of town, looking through trash cans and alleyways, offering no-questions-asked rewards, doing anything I could think of to find what was irreplaceable for me and probably completely useless to whoever had stolen it. Finally, I let most of it go, knowing I would never be able to recreate what had been written far from home in that exhausted but uniquely productive state of mind. It does not matter where any of it was written, or whether any of it was as valuable as I remember it being. What had taken its place was the painful sense of losing ideas, forgetting unlikely swervings, unexpected matings and applications of words. Just as I've recently had the scary but hopefully temporary experience of not being able to see very clearly — because of the conjunctivitis — I now was faced with the alarming reality that newly captured and arranged impressions were gone. Patches of recorded feeling vanished, irretrievable. There is no point in trying to remember and rebuild the word houses, word hills, word dams, or word skeletons like some sort of archeology project. There may be pieces I recall or inadvertently retell, but every word will be new, will go somewhere, will die no matter what I might do to tame or hold it.

You have, for whatever reason, continued to read up to this point in spite of the clearly presented options to do something else with your time many words ago. This nonrequired introduction has no doubt become so predictable, so obviously overstated in its meandering, that it might as well be required. Before I get any more entangled in this trap, I'll leave you with the following from the writer Paul la Cour:

"Being a poet is not writing a poem, but finding a new way to live."

Viggo Mortensen

THE BEST AMERICAN

# NONREQUIRED READING

2004

CHIMAMANDA NGOZI ADICHIE

■

# Half of a Yellow Sun

FROM *Zoetrope: All-Story*

(Editor's note: This story was originally workshopped at the Zoetrope Virtual Studio and originally published by the Virtual Studio member Beverly Jackson in her stellar online literary magazine *Literary Potpourri*.)

*The Igbo say that a mature eagle feather will always remain spotless.*

It was the kind of day in the middle of the rainy season when the sun felt like an orange flame placed close to my skin, yet it was raining, and I remembered when I was a child, when I would run around on days like this and sing songs about the dueling sun and rain, urging the sun to win. The lukewarm raindrops mixed with my sweat and ran down my face as I walked back to my hostel after the rally in Nsukka. I was still holding the placard that read RE-MEMBER THE MASSACRES, still marveling at my new — at our new — identity. It was late May, Ojukwu had just announced the secession, and we were no longer Nigerians. We were Biafrans.

When we gathered in Freedom Square for the rally, thousands of us students shouted Igbo songs and swayed, riverlike. Somebody said that in the market outside our campus, the women were dancing, giving away groundnuts and mangoes. Nnamdi and I stood next to each other and our shoulders touched as we waved green dogonyaro branches and cardboard placards. Nnamdi's placard read SECESSION NOW. Even though he was one of the student leaders, he chose to be with me in the crowd. The other leaders were in front carrying a coffin with NIGERIA written on it in white chalk. When they dug a shallow hole and buried the coffin, a cheer rose and snaked around the crowd, uniting us, elevating us, until it was one cheer, until we all became one.

I cheered loudly, although the coffin reminded me of Aunty Ifeka, Mama's half sister, the woman whose breast I sucked because Mama's dried up after I was born. Aunty Ifeka was killed during the massacres in the north. So was Arize, her pregnant daughter. They must have cut open Arize's stomach and beheaded the baby first — it was what they did to the pregnant women. I didn't tell Nnamdi that I was thinking of Aunty Ifeka and Arize again. Not because I had lost only two relatives while he had lost three uncles and six cousins. But because he would caress my face and say, "I've told you, don't dwell on the massacres. Isn't it why we seceded? Biafra is born! Dwell on that instead. We will turn our pain into a mighty nation, we will turn our pain into the pride of Africa."

Nnamdi was like that; sometimes I looked at him and saw what he would have been two hundred years before: an Igbo warrior leading his hamlet in battle (but only a fair battle), shouting and charging with his fire-warmed machete, returning with the most heads lolling on sticks.

I was in front of my hostel when the rain stopped; the sun had won the fight. Inside the lounge, crowds of girls were singing. Girls I had seen struggle at the water pump and hit each other with plastic buckets, girls who had cut holes in each other's bras as they hung out to dry, now held hands and sang. Instead of "Nigeria, we hail thee," they sang, "Biafra, we hail thee." I joined them, singing, clapping, talking. We did not mention the massacres, the way Igbos had been hunted house to house, pulled from where they crouched in trees, by bright-eyed people screaming *Jihad,* screaming *Nyamiri, nyamiri.* Instead, we talked about Ojukwu, how his speeches brought tears to our eyes and goose bumps to our skin, how easily his charisma would make him stand out among other leaders — Nkurumah would look like a plastic doll next to him. *"Imakwa,* Biafra has more doctors and lawyers than all of Black Africa!" somebody said. "Ah, Biafra will save Africa!" another said. We laughed, deliriously proud of people we would never even know.

We laughed more in the following weeks — we laughed when our expatriate lecturers went back to Britain and India and America, because even if war came, it would take us only one week to crush Nigeria. We laughed at the Nigerian navy ships blocking our ports, because the blockade could not possibly last. We laughed as we gathered under the gmelina trees to discuss Biafra's future foreign policy, as we took down the UNIVERSITY OF NIGERIA, NSUKKA sign and replaced it with UNIVERSITY OF BIAFRA, NSUKKA. Nnamdi hammered in the first nail. He was first, too, to join the Biafran Army, before the rest of his friends followed. I went with him to the army enlistment office, which still smelled of fresh paint, to collect his uniform. He looked so broad-shouldered in it, so capable, and later I did not let him take it all off; I held on to the grainy khaki shirt as he moved inside me.

My life — our lives — had taken on a sheen. A sheen like patent leather. We all felt as if liquid steel, instead of blood, flowed through our veins, as if we could stand barefoot over red-hot embers.

I heard the guns from my hostel room. They sounded close, like thunder funneling up from the lounge. Somebody was shouting outside with a loudspeaker. Evacuate now! Evacuate now! There was the sound of feet, frenzied feet, in the hallway. I threw things into a suitcase, nearly forgetting my underwear in the drawer. As I left the hostel, I saw a girl's stylish sandal left lying on the stairs.

*The Igbo say who knows how water entered the stalk of a pumpkin?*

The air in Enugu smelled of rain and fresh grass and hope and new anthills. I watched as market traders and grandmothers and little boys hugged Nnamdi, caressed his army uniform. Justifiable heroism, Obi called it. Obi was thirteen, my bespectacled brother who read a book a day and went to the Advanced School for Gifted Children and was researching the African origin of Greek civilization. He didn't just touch Nnamdi's uniform, he wanted to try it on, wanted to know exactly what the guns sounded like. Mama invited Nnamdi over and made him a mango pie. "Your uniform is so *debonair,* darling," she said, and hung around him as if he were her son, as if she had not muttered that I was too young, that his family was not quite "suitable," when we got engaged a year ago.

Papa suggested Nnamdi and I get married right away, so that Nnamdi could wear his uniform at the wedding and our first son could be named Biafrus. Papa was joking, of course, but perhaps because something had weighed on my chest since Nnamdi entered the army, I imagined having a child now. A child with skin the color of a polished mahogany desk, like his. When I told Nnamdi about this, about the distant longing somewhere inside me, he pricked his thumb, pricked mine, and, although he was not usually superstitious, we smeared our blood together. Then we laughed because we were not even sure what the hell that meant exactly.

*The Igbo say that the maker of the lion does not let the lion eat grass.*

I watched Nnamdi go, watched until the red dust had covered his boot prints, and felt the moistness of pride on my skin, in my eyes. Pride at his smart olive uniform with the image of the sun rising halfway on the sleeve. It was the same symbol, half of a yellow sun, that was tacked onto the garish cotton tie Papa now wore to his new job at the War Research Directorate every day. Papa ignored all his other ties, the silk ones, the symbol-free ones. And Mama, elegant Mama with the manicured nails, sold some of her London-bought dresses and organized a women's group at St. Paul's to sew for the soldiers. I joined the group; we sewed singlets and sang Igbo songs. Afterward, Mama and I walked home (we didn't drive, to save petrol), and when Papa came home in the evenings, during those slow months, we would sit on the veranda and eat fresh anara with groundnut paste and listen to Radio Biafra, the kerosene lamp casting amber shadows all around. Radio Biafra brought stories of victories, of Nigerian corpses lining the roads. And from the War Research Directorate, Papa brought stories of our people's genius: we made brake fluid from coconut oil, we created car engines from scrap metal, we refined crude oil in cooking pots, we had perfected a homegrown mine. The blockade would not deter us. Often we ended those evenings by telling each other, "We have a just cause," as if we did not already know. Necessary affirmation, Obi called it.

It was on one of those evenings that a friend dropped by to say that Nnamdi's battalion had conquered Benin, that Nnamdi was fine. We toasted Nnamdi with palm wine. "To our future son-in-law," Papa said, raising his mug toward me. Papa let Obi drink as much as he wanted. Papa was a cognac man, but he couldn't find Rémy Martin even on the black market, because of the blockade. After a few mugs Papa said, with his upper lip coated in white foam, that he preferred palm wine now: at least he didn't have to drink it in snifters. And we all laughed too loudly.

*The Igbo say the walking ground squirrel sometimes breaks into a trot, in case the need to run arises.*

Enugu fell on the kind of day in the middle of the harmattan when the wind blew hard, carrying dust and bits of paper and dried leaves, covering hair and clothes with a fine brown film. Mama and I were cooking pepper soup — I cut up the tripe while Mama ground the peppers — when we heard the guns. At first I thought it was thunder, the rumbling thunder that preceded harmattan storms. It couldn't be the Federal guns because Radio Biafra said the Federals were far away, being driven back. But Papa dashed into the kitchen moments later, his cotton tie skewed. "Get in the car now!" he said. "Now! Our directorate is evacuating."

We didn't know what to take. Mama took her manicure kit, her small radio, clothes, the pot of half-cooked pepper soup wrapped in a dish towel. I snatched a packet of crackers. Obi grabbed the books on the dining table. As we drove away in Papa's Peugeot, Mama said we would be back soon anyway, our troops would recover Enugu. So it didn't matter that all her lovely china was left behind, our radiogram, her new wig imported from Paris in that case of such an unusual lavender color. "My leather-bound books," Obi added. I was grateful that nobody brought up the Biafran soldiers we saw dashing past, on the retreat. I didn't want to imagine Nnamdi like that, running like a chicken drenched by heavy rain. Papa stopped the car often to wipe the dust off the windscreen, and he drove at a crawl, because of the crowds. Women with babies tied to their backs, pulling at toddlers, carrying pots on their heads. Men pulling goats and bicycles, carrying wood boxes and yams. Children, so many children. The dust swirled all around like a translucent brown blanket. An exodus clothed in dusty hope. It took a while before it struck me that, like these people, we were now refugees.

*The Igbo say that the place from where one wakes up is his home.*
  Papa's old friend Akubueze was a man with a sad smile whose greeting was "God bless Biafra." He had lost all his children in the massacres. As he showed us the smoke-blackened kitchen and pit latrine and room with the stained walls, I wanted to cry. Not because of the room we would rent from Akubueze, but because of Akubueze. Because of the apology in his eyes. I placed our raffia sleeping mats at the corners of the room, next to our bags and food. But the radio stayed in the center of the room, and we walked around it every day, listened to it, cleaned it. We sang along when the soldiers' marching songs were broadcast. *We are Biafrans, fighting for survival, in the name of Jesus, we shall conquer, hip hop, one two.* Sometimes the people in the yard joined us, our new neighbors. Singing meant that we did not have to wonder aloud about our old house with the marble staircase and airy verandas. Singing meant we did not have to acknowledge aloud that Enugu remained fallen and that the War Research Directorate was no longer paying salaries and what Papa got now was an "allowance." Papa gave every note, even the white slip with his name and ID number printed in smudgy ink, to Mama. I would look at the money and think how much prettier than Nigerian pounds Biafran pounds were, the elegant writing, the bold faces. But they could buy so little at the market.
  The market was a cluster of dusty, sparse tables. There were more flies than food, the flies buzzing thickly over the graying

pieces of meat, the black-spotted bananas. The flies looked healthier, fresher, than the meats and fruits. I looked over everything, I insisted, as if it were the peacetime market and I still had the leisure that came with choice. In the end, I bought cassava, always, because it was the most filling and economical. Sickly tubers, the ones with grisly pink skin. We had never eaten those before. I told Mama, half teasing, that they could be poisonous. And Mama laughed and said, "People are eating the peels now, honey. It used to be goat food."

The months crawled past and I noted them when my periods came, scant, more mud-colored than red now. I worried about Nnamdi, that he would not find us, that something would happen to him and nobody would know where to find me. I followed the news on Radio Biafra carefully, although Radio Nigeria intercepted the signal so often now. Deliberate jamming, Obi called it. Radio Biafra described the thousands of Federal bodies floating on the Niger. Radio Nigeria listed the thousands of dead and defecting Biafran soldiers. I listened to both with equal attention, and afterward, I created my own truths and inhabited them, believed them.

*The Igbo say that unless a snake shows its venom, little children will use it for tying firewood.*

Nnamdi appeared at our door on a dry-aired morning, with a scar above his eye and the skin of his face stretched too thin and his worn trousers barely staying on his waist. Mama dashed out to the market and bought three chicken necks and two wings, and fried them in a little palm oil. "Especially for Nnamdi," she said gaily. Mama, who used to make coq au vin without a cookbook.

I took Nnamdi to the nearby farm that had been harvested too early. All the farms looked that way now, raided at night, raided of corn ears so tender they had not yet formed kernels and yams so young they were barely the size of my fist. Harvest of desperation, Obi called it. Nnamdi pulled me down to the ground, under an ukpaka tree. I could feel his bones through his skin. He scratched my back, bit my sweaty neck, held me down so hard I felt the sand pierce my skin. And he stayed inside me so long, so tightly, that I felt our hearts were pumping blood at the same rhythm. I wished in a twisted way that the war would never end so that it would always have this quality, like nutmeg, tart and lasting. Afterward, Nnamdi started to cry. I had never even considered that he could cry. He said the British were giving more arms to Nigeria, Nigeria had Russian planes and Egyptian pilots, the Americans didn't want to help us, we were still blockaded, his battalion was down to two men using one gun, some battalions had resorted to machetes and cutlasses. "Didn't they kill babies in the north for being born Igbo, eh?" he asked.

I pressed my face to his, but he wouldn't stop crying. "Is there a God?" he asked me. "Is there a God?" So I held him close and listened to him cry, and listened to the shrilling of the crickets. He said goodbye two days later, holding me too long. Mama gave him a small bag of boiled rice.

I hoarded that memory, and every other memory of Nnamdi, used each sparingly. I used them most during the air raids, when the screeching *ka-ka-ka* of the antiaircraft guns disrupted a hot afternoon and everybody in the yard dashed to the bunker — the room-size hole in the ground covered with logs — and slid into the moist earth underneath. Exhilarating, Obi called it, even though he got scratches and cuts. I would smell the organic walls and floor, like a freshly tilled farm, and watch the children crawl around looking for crickets and earthworms, until the bombing stopped. I would rub the soil between my fingers and savor thoughts of Nnamdi's teeth, tongue, voice.

*The Igbo say let us salute the deaf, for if the heavens don't hear, then the earth will hear.*

So many things became transient, and more valuable. I savored a plate of cornmeal that tasted like cloth, because I might have to leave it and run into the bunker, because when I came out a neighbor might have eaten it or given it to one of the children.

Obi suggested that we teach classes for those children, so many of them running around the yard chasing lizards. "They think bombings are normal," Obi said, shaking his head. He picked a cool spot under the kolanut tree for our classroom. I placed planks across cement blocks for benches, a wooden sheet against the tree for a blackboard. I taught English, Obi taught mathematics and history, and the children did not whisper and giggle in his classes as they did in mine. He seemed to hold them somehow, as he talked and gestured and scrawled on the board with charcoal (when he ran his hands over his sweaty face, they left black patterns like a design).

Perhaps it was that he mixed learning and playing — once he asked the children to role-play the Berlin Conference. They became Europeans partitioning Africa, giving hills and rivers to each other although they didn't know where the hills and rivers were. Obi played Bismarck. "My contribution to the young Biafrans, our leaders of tomorrow," he said, glowing with mischief.

I laughed, because he seemed to forget that he too was a future Biafran leader. Sometimes even I forgot how young he was. "Do you remember when I used to half-chew your beef and then put it in your mouth so it would be easier for you to chew?" I teased. And Obi made a face and said he did not remember.

The classes were in the morning, before the afternoon sun turned fierce. After the classes, Obi and I joined the local militia — a mix of young people and married women and injured men — and went combing, to root out Federal soldiers or Biafran saboteurs hiding in the bush, although all we found were dried fruits and groundnuts. We talked about dead Nigerians, we talked about the braveness of the French and Tanzanians in supporting Biafra, the evil of the British. We did not talk about dead Biafrans. We talked about anti-kwash too, how it really worked, how many children in the early stages of kwashiorkor had been cured. I knew that anti-kwash was absolute nonsense, that those leaves were from a tree nobody used to eat; they filled the children's bellies but gave no nourishment, definitely no protein. But we *needed* to believe stories like that. When you were stripped down to sickly cassava, you used everything else fiercely and selfishly — especially the discretion to choose what to believe and what not to believe.

I enjoyed those stories we told, the lull of our voices, until one day, we were at an abandoned farm wading through tall grass when we stumbled upon something. A body. I smelled it before I saw it, an odor that gagged me, suffocated me, left me light-headed. "Hei! He's a Nigerian!" a woman said. The flies rose from the bloated body of the Nigerian soldier as we gathered around. His skin was ashy, his eyes were open, his tribal marks were thick, eerie lines running across his swollen face. "I wish we had seen him alive," a young boy said. "*Nkakwu*, ugly rat," somebody else said. A young girl spat at the body. Vultures landed a few feet away. A woman vomited. Nobody suggested burying him. I stood there, dizzy from the smell and the buzzing flies and the heat, and won-dered how he had died, what his life had been like. I wondered about his family. A wife who would be looking outside, her eyes on the road, for news of her husband. Little children who would be told, "Papa will be home soon." A mother who had cried when he left. Brothers and sisters and cousins. I imagined the things he left behind — clothes, a prayer mat, a wooden cup used to drink kunu.

I started to cry.

Obi held me and looked at me with a calm disgust. "It was people like him who killed Aunty Ifeka," Obi said. "It was people like him who beheaded unborn babies." I brushed Obi away and kept crying.

*The Igbo say that a fish that does not swallow other fish does not grow fat.*

There was no news of Nnamdi. When neighbors heard from their sons or husbands on the front, I hung around their rooms for days, willing their good fortunes to myself. "Nnamdi is fine," Obi said in a tone so normal I wanted to believe him. He said it of-ten during those months of boiled cassava, months of moldy yams, months when we shared our dreams of vegetable oil and fish and salt.

Because of the neighbors, I hid what little food we had, wrapped in a mat and stuck behind the door. The neighbors hid their own food, too. In the evenings, we all unwrapped our food and clustered in the kitchen, cooking and talking about salt. There was salt in Nigeria; salt was the reason our people were crossing the border to the other side, salt was the reason a woman down the road was said to have run out of her kitchen and torn her clothes off and rolled in the dirt, wailing. I sat on the kitchen floor and listened to the chatter and tried to remember what salt tasted like. It seemed surreal now, that we had a crystal saltshaker back home. That I had even wasted salt, rinsing away the clumpy bottom before refilling the shaker. Fresh salt. I interspersed thoughts of Nnamdi with thoughts of salty food.

And when Akubueze told us that our old pastor, Father Damian, was working in a refugee camp in Amandugba, two towns away, I thought about salt. Akubueze was not sure; stories drifted around about so many people being in so many places. Still, I suggested to Mama that we go and see Father Damian. Mama said yes, we would go to see if he was well, it had been two long years since we saw him. I humored her and said it had been long — as if we still paid social calls. We did not say anything about the food Caritas Internationalis sent to priests by secret night flights, the food the priests gave away, the corned beef and glucose and dried milk. And salt.

Father Damian was thinner, with hollows and shadows on his face. But he looked healthy next to the children in the refugee camp. Stick-thin children whose bones stuck out, so unnaturally, so sharply. Children with rust-colored hair and stomachs like balloons. Children whose eyes were swallowed deep in their faces. Father Damian introduced Mama and me to the other priests, Irish missionaries of the Holy Ghost, white men with sun-reddened skin and smiles so brave I wanted to tug at their faces and see if they were real. Father Damian talked a lot about his work, about the dying children, but Mama kept changing the subject. It was so unlike her, something she would call "unmannered" if somebody else did it. Father Damian finally stopped talking about the children, about kwashiorkor, and he looked almost disappointed as he watched us leave, Mama holding the bag of salt and corned beef and fish powder he had given us.

"Why was Father Damian telling us about those children?"

Mama shouted as we walked home. "What can we do for them?" I calmed her down, told her he probably just needed to talk to someone about his work and did she remember how he used to sing those silly, off-tune songs at church bazaars to make the children laugh?

But Mama kept shouting. And I too began shouting, the words tumbling out of my mouth. Why the hell did Father Damian tell us about those dying children, anyway? Did we need to know? Didn't we have enough to deal with?

Shouting. A man walked up the street, beating a metal gong, asking us to pray for the good white people who were flying food in for the relief center, the new one they set up in St. Johns. Not all white people were killers, *gong, gong, gong,* not all were arming the Nigerians, *gong, gong, gong.*

At the relief center, I fought hard, kicking through the crowds, risking the flogging militia. I lied, cajoled, begged. I spoke British-accented English to show how educated I was, to distinguish myself from the common villagers, and afterward I felt tears building up, as if I only had to blink and they would flow down. But I didn't blink as I walked home, I kept my eyes roundly open, my hands tightly wrapped around whatever food I got. When I got food. Dried egg yolk. Dried milk. Dried fish. Cornmeal.

Shell-shocked soldiers in filthy shirts roamed around the relief center, muttering gibberish, children running away from them. They followed me, first begging, then trying to snatch my food. I shoved at them and cursed them and spat in their direction. Once I shoved so hard one of the men fell down, and I didn't turn to see if he got up all right. I didn't want to imagine, either, that they had once been proud Biafran soldiers, like Nnamdi.

Perhaps it was the food from the relief center that made Obi sick, or all the other things we ate, the things we brushed blue mold from, or picked ants out of. He threw up, and when he was emptied, he still retched and clutched at his belly. Mama brought in an old bucket for him, helped him use it, took it out afterward. I'm a chamber-pot man, Obi joked. He still taught his classes but he talked less about Biafra and more about the past, like did I remember how Mama used to give herself facials with a paste of honey and milk? And did I remember the soursop tree in our backyard, how the yellow bees formed columns on it? Mama went to Albatross Hospital and dropped the names of all the famous doctors she had known in Enugu, so that the doctor would see her before the hundreds of women thronging the corridors. It worked, and he gave her diarrhea tablets. He could spare only five and told her to break each in two so they would last long enough to control Obi's diarrhea. Mama said she doubted that the "doctor" had even reached his fourth year in medical school, but this was Biafra two years into the war, and medical students had to play doctors because the real doctors were cutting off arms and legs to keep people alive. Then Mama said that part of the roof of Albatross Hospital had been blown off during an air raid. I didn't know what was funny about that, but Obi laughed, and Mama joined in, and finally I did too.

Obi was still sick, still in bed, when Ihuoma came running into our room. Her daughter was lying in the yard, inhaling a foul concoction of spices and urine that somebody said cured asthma. "The soldiers are coming," Ihuoma said. She was a simple woman, a market trader, the kind of woman who would have had nothing in common with Mama before Biafra. But now she and Mama plaited each other's hair every week. "Hurry," she said. "Bring Obi to the outer room — he can hide in the ceiling!" It took me a moment to understand, although Mama was already helping Obi up, rushing him out of the room. We had heard that the Biafran soldiers were conscripting young men, children really, and taking them to the front, that it had happened in the yard down our street a week ago, although Obi said he doubted they had really taken a twelve-year-old. We heard too that the mother of the boy was from Abakaliki, where people cut their hair when their children died, and after she watched them take her son, she took a razor and shaved all her hair off.

The soldiers came shortly after Obi and two other boys climbed into a hole in the ceiling, a hole that had appeared when the wood gave way after a bombing. Four soldiers with bony bodies and tired eyes. I asked if they knew Nnamdi, if they'd heard of him, even though I knew they hadn't. The soldiers looked inside the latrine, asked Mama if she was sure she was not hiding anybody, because that would make her a saboteur and saboteurs were worse than Nigerians. Mama smiled at them, then used her old voice, the voice of when she hosted three-course dinners for Papa's friends, and offered them some water before they left. Afterward, Obi said he would enlist when he felt better. He owed it to Biafra, and besides, fifteen-year-olds had fought in the Persian War. Before Mama left the room, she walked up to Obi and slapped his face so hard I saw the immediate slender welts on his cheek.

*The Igbo say that the chicken frowns at the cooking pot, and yet ignores the knife.*

Mama and I were close to the bunker when we heard the antiaircraft guns. "Good timing," Mama joked, and although I tried, I could not smile. My lips were too sore; the harmattan winds had dried them to a bloody crisp during our walk to the relief center, and besides, we had not been lucky: we got no food.

Inside the bunker, people were shouting *Lord, Jesus, God Almighty, Jehovah.* A woman was crumpled next to me, holding her toddler in her arms. The bunker was dim, but I could see the crusty ringworm marks all over the toddler's body. Mama was looking around. "Where is Obi?" she asked, clutching my arm. "What is wrong with that boy, didn't he hear the guns?" Mama got up, saying she had to find Obi, saying the bombing was far away. But it wasn't, it was really close, loud, and I tried to hold Mama, to keep her still, but I was weak from the walk and hunger and Mama pushed past me and climbed out.

The explosion that followed shook something inside my ear loose, and I felt that if I bent my head sideways, something hard-soft, like cartilage, would fall out. I heard things breaking and falling above, cement walls and glass louvers and trees. I closed my eyes and thought of Nnamdi's voice, just his voice, until the bombing stopped and I scrambled out of the bunker. The bodies strewn about the street, some painfully close to the bunker entrance, were still quivering, writhing. They reminded me of the chickens our steward used to kill in Enugu, how they flapped around in the dust after their throats had been slit, over and over, before finally lying quiet. Dignity dance, Obi called it. I was bawling as I stared at the bodies, all people I knew, trying to identify Mama and Obi. But they were not there. They were in the yard, Mama helping to wash the wounded, Obi writing in the dust with his finger. Mama did not scold Obi for his earlier carelessness, and I did not rebuke Mama for dashing out like that either. I went into the kitchen to soak some dried cassava for dinner.

Obi died that night. Or maybe he died in the morning. I don't know. I simply know that when Papa tugged at him in the morning and then when Mama threw herself on him, he did not stir. I went over and shook him, shook him, shook him. He was cold. "*Nwa m anwugo,*" Papa said, as if he had to say it aloud to believe it. Mama brought out her manicure kit and started to clip Obi's nails. "What are you doing?" Papa asked. He was crying. Not the kind of manly crying that is silence accompanied by tears. He was wailing, sobbing. I watched him, he seemed to swell before my eyes, the room was unsteady. Something was on my chest, something heavy like a jerry can full of water. I started to roll on the floor to ease the weight. Outside, I heard shouting. Or was it inside? Was it Papa? Was it Papa saying *Nwa m anwugo, nwa m anwugo?* Obi was dead. I grasped around, frantic, trying to remember Obi, to remember the concrete things about him. And I could not. My baby brother who made wisecracks, and yet I could not remember any of them. I could not even remember anything he said the night before. I had felt I would have Obi for a long, long time and that I didn't need to notice him, really notice him. He was there, I believed he would always be there. With Obi, I never had the fear I had with Nnamdi, the fear that I might mourn someday. And so I did not know how to mourn Obi, if I could mourn Obi. My hair was itching and I started to tear at it, to feel the warm blood on my scalp. I tore some more and then more. With my hair littering our floor, I wrapped my arms around myself and watched as Mama calmly filed Obi's nails.

There was something feverish about the days after Obi's death, something malarial, something so numbingly fast it left me free not to feel. Even Obi's burial in the backyard was fast, although Papa spent hours fashioning a cross from old wood. After the neighbors and Father Damian and the crying children dispersed, Mama called the cross shabby and kicked it, broke it, flung the wood away.

Papa stopped going to the War Research Directorate and dropped his patriotic tie into the pit latrine, and day after day, week after week, we sat in front of our room — Papa, Mama, and me — staring at the yard. The morning a woman from down the street dashed into our yard I did not look up, until I heard her shouting. She was waving a green branch. Such a brilliant, wet-looking green. I wondered where she got it; the plants and trees around us were scorched by January's harmattan sun, blown bare by the dusty winds. The earth was sallow.

The war is lost, Papa said. He didn't need to say it though; we already knew. We knew when Obi died. The neighbors were packing in a hurry, to go into the smaller villages because we had heard the Federal soldiers were coming with truckloads of whips. We got up to pack. It struck me how little we had, as we packed, and how we had stopped noticing how little we had.

*The Igbo say that when a man falls, it is his god who has pushed him down.*

Nnamdi clutched my hand too tightly at our wedding. He did everything with extra effort now, as if he were compensating for his amputated left arm, as if he were shielding his shame. Papa took photos, telling me to smile wider, telling Nnamdi not to slouch. But Papa slouched himself, he had slouched since the war ended, since the bank gave him fifty Nigerian pounds for all the money he had in Biafra. And he had lost his house — our house, with the marble staircase — because it was declared abandoned property and now a civil servant lived there, a woman who had threatened Mama with a fierce dog when Mama defied Papa and went to see her beloved house. All she wanted was our china and our radiogram, she told the woman. But the woman whistled for the dog.

"Wait," Mama said to Papa, and came over to fix my hat. She had made my wedding dress and sewn sequins onto a secondhand hat. After the wedding we had pastries in a café, and as we ate, Papa told me about the wedding cake he used to dream about for me, a pink multilayered cake, so tall it would shield my face and Nnamdi's face and the cake-cutting photo would capture only the groomsman's face, only Obi's face.

I envied Papa, that he could talk about Obi like that. It was the year Obi would have turned seventeen, the year Nigeria changed from driving on the left-hand side of the road to the right. We were Nigerians again.

DANIEL ALARCÓN

# City of Clowns

FROM *The New Yorker*

WHEN I GOT TO the hospital that morning, I found my mother mopping floors. My old man had died the day before and left an outstanding bill for her to deal with. They'd had her working through the night. I settled the debt with an advance the paper had given me. I told her I was sorry, and I was. Her face was swollen and red, but she wasn't crying anymore. She introduced me to a tired, sad-looking black woman. "This is Carmela," she said. "Your father's friend. Carmela was mopping with me." My mother looked me in the eye, as if I were supposed to interpret that. I did. I knew exactly who the woman was.

"Oscarcito? I haven't seen you since you were this big," Carmela said, touching the middle of her thigh. She reached for my hand, and I gave it to her reluctantly. Something in that comment bothered me, confused me. When had I ever seen her? I couldn't believe that she was standing there in front of me.

At the *velorio,* I picked out my half brothers. I counted three. For twelve years I had insulated myself from my old man's other life — since he left us, right after my fourteenth birthday. Carmela had been his lover, then his common-law wife. Petite, cocoa-colored, with blue-green eyes, she was prettier than I had imagined. She wore a simple black dress, nicer than my mother's. We didn't say much, but she smiled at me, glassy-eyed, as she and my mother took turns crying and consoling each other. No one had foreseen the illness that brought my father down.

Carmela's sons were my brothers, that much was clear. There

was an air of Don Hugo in all of us: the close-set eyes, the long arms and short legs. They were a few years younger than me, the oldest maybe seventeen, the youngest about eleven. I wondered whether I should approach them, knew, in fact, that as the oldest I should. I didn't. Finally, at the insistence of our mothers, we shook hands. "Oh, the reporter," the oldest one said. He had my old man's smile. I tried to project some kind of authority over them — based on age, I guess, or the fact that they were black, or that I was the *real* son — but I don't think it worked. My heart wasn't in it. They touched my mother, with those light, careless touches that speak of a certain intimacy, as if she were a beloved aunt, not the supplanted wife. Even she belonged to them now. Being the first-born of the real marriage meant nothing at all; these people were, in the end, Don Hugo's true family.

At the paper the next day, I didn't mention my father's death to anyone but the obituary guy, whom I asked to run a notice for me, as a favor to my mother. "Is he a relative?" he asked, his voice non-committal.

"Friend of the family. Help me out, will you?" I handed him a scrap of paper:

> Hugo Uribe Banegas, native of Cerro de Pasco, passed into eternal life this past February 2nd at the Dos de Mayo Hospital in Lima. A good friend and husband, he is survived by Doña Marisol Lara de Uribe. May he rest in peace.

I left myself and my brothers out of it. Carmela, too. They could run their own obituary if they wanted, if they could afford it.

In Lima, those who die in phantasmagoric fashion, violently, spectacularly, are celebrated in the fifty-cent papers beneath appropriately gory headlines: "DRIVER GETS MELON BURST" or "NARCO SHOOTOUT, BYSTANDER EATS LEAD." I don't work at that kind of newspaper, but if I did I would write those headlines too. Like my father, I never refuse work. I've covered drug busts, homicides, fires at discos and markets, traffic accidents, bombs in shopping centers. I've profiled corrupt politicians, has-been soccer

players, artists who hate the world. But I've never covered the unexpected death of a middle-aged construction worker in a public
hospital. Mourned by his wife. His child. His other wife. His other
children.

My father's dying was not news. I knew this, and there was no
reason for it to be surprising or troubling. It wasn't, in fact. At the
office, I typed my articles and was not bothered by his passing. But
that afternoon Villacorta sent me out to do research on clowns, for
a Sunday feature on street performers that he'd assigned me a few
weeks earlier. It may have been the mood I was in, but the idea of
it made me sad: clowns with their absurd and artless smiles, their
shabby, outlandish clothes. I'd walked only a few blocks when I
felt, inexplicably, assaulted by loss. In the insistent noise of the
streets, in the cackling voice of a DJ on the radio, in the glare of the
summer sun, it was as if Lima were mocking me, ignoring me,
thrusting its indifference at me. A heavy woman sold wigs from a
wooden cart. A tired clown rested on the curb, a cigarette between
his lips, and asked me for a light. I didn't have the heart to interview him. The sun seemed to pass straight through me. My tiny
family had been dissolved into another grouping, one in which I
had no part.

In Lima, my father had settled on construction. He built offices,
remodeled houses. He was good with a hammer, could paint and
spackle, put up a wall in four hours. He was a plumber and a lock-
smith. A carpenter and a welder. When offered a job, he always answered in the same way. "I've done it many times," he'd reassure a
contractor, while examining a tool he'd never seen before in his
life. As a child, I admired him and his hard work. Progress was
something you could measure in our neighborhood: how fast the
second floor of your house went up, how quickly you acquired the
accoutrements of middle-class life. During the week, he worked
on other people's houses; on weekends, he worked on ours. Hard
work paid off. We inaugurated a new stereo with a Hector Lavoe
tape. We watched the '85 Copa América on a fancy color television.

It was not all that transparent, of course. My father was *vivo*, quick to understand the essential truth of Lima: if there is money to be made, it must be bled from these concrete city blocks. Some win and some lose, and there are ways to tilt the odds. He was charming, and he did good work, but he was always, always looking out for himself.

He'd been too restless to survive back home. Pasco, where he and my mother and I were born, is, oddly, neither city nor country. It is isolated and poor, high on an Andean puna, but in a very specific way it is urban: its concept of time is mechanized, and no one is spared by capitalism's ticking clock. A mining town, Pasco is not pastoral or agricultural. Men descend into the earth for ten-hour shifts. Their schedule is monotonous, uniform. They emerge — in the morning, the afternoon, or the evening — and start drinking. The work the men do is brutal and dangerous, and in time their life aboveground begins to resemble life below: they take chances, they drink, they cough and expel a tarry black mucus. *The color of money,* they call it, and buy another round of drinks.

My old man wasn't suited to those rituals. Instead, he found work driving trucks to the coast and into the city. He was twenty-nine when he married my mother, nearly a decade older than his young wife. He'd spent most of his twenties working in the city, coming back only once every three or four months. Somehow a romance had blossomed on those visits home. By the time they married, they'd been a couple for five years already, most of that time spent apart. I was born six months after the wedding. My father went on coming and going for years, making a home for himself in Lima, in the district of San Juan de Lurigancho. When my mother could no longer tolerate being left alone, he brought us there too.

That was, I think, the only good thing he did for us. Or for me. When I remember Pasco, that cold high plain, its thin air and sinking houses, I'm grateful to be here. I grew up in Lima. I went to university here and landed a respectable job. There is no future in Pasco. Kids don't study and, anyway, are taught almost nothing. They inhale glue from brown paper bags or get drunk in the weak morning light before school.

I was eight when we moved. My father was a stranger, it seemed, even to my mother. They held hands on the bus to Lima, and I slept in her lap, even though I was too old for that. It was early January; we left Pasco iced over, the syncopated drumming of hail falling on its metal roofs. We watched the speckled orange lights fade behind us, and when I woke up it was dawn and we were pulling into the station in Lima. "There are bad people here," my old man warned us. "Be *mosca*, Chino. You're an *hombrecito* now. You have to take care of your mother."

I'd been to the city before, two years earlier, though I scarcely remembered it. My father had come home to Pasco one day and carried me off for three weeks. He'd led me through the city, pointing out the important buildings; he'd shown me the movement of the streets. I remember my mother telling me that at age six I was already more traveled than she was. Now she held my hand as the world swirled around us, and I watched my old man push his way through a thicket of men at the open door of the bus's baggage hold. They elbowed and pushed one another, the crowd swelling this way and that, and my father, who was not tall or particularly strong, disappeared into the center of it. My mother and I waited. I stared down a mustachioed man who was circling us, his greedy eyes tugging at the red woolen bag my mother had wedged between us. Then there was yelling: one man pushed another, accusing him of trying to steal his package. The accuser had a foot planted firmly on top of his box. It was taped, a name and address printed on one side.

"*Oye, compadre, que chucha quieres con mis cosas?*"

"Ah? *Perdón, tío*, my mistake."

The second man was my father. It was an accident, he protested. Packages look alike. My father's long arms were bent, palms up, a charmless shrug. But the older man was furious, his face red and his fists clenched. "*No mierda, aquí no hay errores*. Thief!" The other men pulled them apart; in the blur of it, my father grinned at me, and I realized that we'd brought only bags, no boxes.

In front of the Congress, along Avenida Abancay, a protest had spilled off the sidewalk, and traffic was stalled for five city blocks.

The protesters were construction workers or telephone workers or obstetricians. Social movements, like all predators, sense weakness: the president was teetering; half his cabinet had resigned. But on the street it still looked like Lima, beautiful, disgraced Lima, unhappy and impervious to change. I'd been to a press conference in the suburbs and was on a bus headed back to the city. The air was sticky and as thick as soup. A svelte policewoman in a beige uniform directed cars east, through the miniature streets of Barrios Altos, where cramped *quintas* fell in on each other, where kids laced up their cheap sneakers, scanning the slow-moving traffic for an opportunity. The day before, there had been robberies, entire busloads shaken down at a red light, and we were all tense, bags clutched tightly against our chests. It was the first week of carnival, and everyone from age five to fifteen (which, in Barrios Altos, is nearly everyone) was in the streets with water balloons, menacing, eager. The dilemma we faced was which way to suffer.

"*Oye, chato.* Close the window."

"*Estás loco.* It's too hot."

The tug-of-war began: between those who were willing to accept the risk of theft or pranks in order to counter the oppressive heat, and those who were not. The driver strained against his homemade seat belt. Windows opened and closed, pulled and pushed from all sides, and on the sidewalks youths salivated, hands in buckets, kneading water balloons as if they were their best friend's girlfriend's tits. Then it came from everywhere at once: from the narrows between crumbling buildings, and from the roofs as well, kids tossing overhand and underhand, unloading balloons two at a time. Water splashed through the cracked windows. The sidewalks glistened, littered with the exploded insides of red and green and white balloons. The primary target, I soon realized, was not our bus, or any bus, or, as is often the case, a young woman in a white shirt. Instead, on the sidewalk, dodging water balloons, there was a clown.

He was a vendor, a traveling salesman, a poor working clown. He'd stepped off a bus and found himself in the crosshairs of a hundred children. He was struggling to get his bearings. He tucked his chin into his chest so that his multicolored wig bore the brunt of the attack, strands of pink and red sagging beneath the soaking. He had nowhere to go: a step forward, a step back, a step to the wall, a step to the curb — he danced clumsily in his big clown shoes, the balloons raining down on him. There was laughter on our bus, laughter that built community; passengers emerged from their private meditations to point and laugh and ridicule. Then the ticket collector, moved by pity, opened the door and pulled the clown in.

We fell silent. The clown dripped on the corrugated-metal floor of the bus, his white face paint running, crinkled pink hairs sticking to his cheeks. He made me want to cry, this poor clown, this pathetic specimen of *Limeño. Hermano! Causa!* The bus didn't move, and then it did. The volley of balloons receded. And, in the uncomfortable silence, disheveled though he was, the clown went to work. He reached into an inside pocket and took out a large bag of mints. Tiny drops of water slid off the bag. "*Señores y Señoras, Damas y Caballeros,*" he proclaimed. "I'm here today to offer you a new product, a product you may never have seen before. Developed with the newest and most refined technology in European mint processing . . ."

We could hear the protest still, on the west side of the congressional building. Wooden spoons against pots, a dull metallic complaint, rhythmless, the thick voice of the people and their unfocused rage. The clown, with his plastic clown voice, tried to sell us mints, his smile a force of will.

The newsroom swarmed with activity; a presidential pronouncement on the economy had set everyone to work. There were rumors: some cabinet members had fled. I didn't pay much attention. I left the office early and went to San Juan to see my mother. I took a copy of the paper to show her the obituary, a peace offering of sorts.

San Juan, my old street: the same crooked tree casting thin shadows in the vanishing light of dusk. I'd been living downtown for six years, but I recognized some faces. Don Segundo, from the restaurant, who had fed me for free a hundred times when we were short. Señora Nelida, from the corner, who would never give our ball back if it landed on her roof. Our old neighbor Elisa was there too, sitting, as she always did, on a wooden stool in front of her store. One of its legs was shorter than the others. She'd repaired it with a phone book, wedged between the ground and the offending leg.

"*Vecina,*" I said.

We spoke for a minute, the exchange easy and familiar. What I was doing. My work at the paper. How proud they were of me in the neighborhood when they saw my name in print. I knew this last part wasn't true, at least not among the people my age. I'd seen how my old friends looked at me: aware, perhaps, that I had once existed as a part of their world, but dismissive of every claim I had of belonging there still. We were disappearing fragments of one another's history, fading tracers against a clear night sky.

Finally, Elisa said, "Your mother's not home, Chino."

The streetlights had come on, and I noticed with some surprise that they crawled up the mountainside now. The neighborhood was still growing. New people arrived every day, as we once had, with bags and boxes and hopes, to construct a life in the city. We'd been lucky. Our new house had been small but well built. Everyone had welcomed us. Our street was overflowing with children, and within a week I'd forgotten about Pasco, about the friends I'd left there. My mother found work as a maid in San Borja, four days a week at the Azcárates', a friendly couple with a son my age. Her employers were generous, kind, and understanding to a fault, especially after Don Hugo left us. They lent us money, and helped pay for my studies when my old man abandoned that responsibility as well. They never kept my mother late — so where was she?

Elisa looked at me somewhat sheepishly. "You know, Chino, she's been staying with *la negra.* With Carmela's family, in La Victoria."

"How long?"

"Since your father got sick, Chino."

Elisa motioned for me not to leave while she sold a kilo of sugar to an elderly woman in a light green dress. I'd rolled the newspaper with the obituary into a tight baton. Now I tapped it against my thigh. I considered Elisa's news, what it meant. The scope of my mother's weakness, her astounding lack of pride. How could the arrangement work on either side, especially now, with the man who connected the two women dead? Carmela ran a dress shop, an enterprise she'd begun with my father's investment. With *my* money, probably, which should have been spent on *my* books, on *my* schooling. The business had succeeded, but was it enough, I wondered, to support the grief of two widows and three children — two of whom, at least, were still in school?

Elisa turned to me again as her customer shuffled down the street.

"Does she come here, then? Ever?" I asked.

"Your mother? Sometimes. I saw her a few days ago. I don't ask so much, you know. She's embarrassed. She's afraid of what you'll think."

"She knows exactly what I think."

Elisa sighed. "She didn't want you to know."

"Then you shouldn't have told me."

Elisa leaned back against the metal gate in front of the store. "Oscar."

"I'm sorry, *vecina*." I looked down at my feet like a misbehaving child, and stamped out the prints of my sneakers in the dusty earth. "Anyway, thank you."

"I'll tell her you came by when I see her. Or, you know, Chino, if you want you could —"

"Thank you, *vecina*."

It was late. From my old street, I used to cut across the field behind the market at any hour, fearlessly, but now it seemed an unnecessary hazard. The addicts would be out. In the firelight flicker of their ritual, I might have recognized an old friend, ashen, lost. I walked the long way out to the avenue.

I tried to picture my mother in her new home, sleeping in a guest bed or on a cot in the living room that she put away each morning. She and Carmela, sharing stories and tears, forgiving the old man in a nostalgic widows' duet. What could they have in common? Carmela was *Limeña,* a businesswoman; she knew how the city worked. My mother had been just a girl when she met my old man, barely fifteen. In Lima, he had learned to dance salsa. To drink and smoke, to fight, fuck, and steal. My mother had learned none of this. She had waited for Hugo to come home and propose. Even now, she still had her mountain accent. For years she had known only one bus line — "the big green bus," she called it — that took her to the Azcárates' home. What could Carmela and my mother share besides a battleground? My mother had capitulated. It gave me vertigo: it was the kind of humiliation only a life like hers could prepare you for.

On Saturdays, when we first moved to the city, she would take me to the Azcárates' house with her. We rode that big green bus, my mother tense, watching the streets pass in gray monotony, afraid of missing her stop. As a child and not an employee, I was able to cross certain lines. The Azcárates were permissive with me, and I never felt out of place in their home. I'd lay out my books on the table in the garden and do my homework, humming songs to myself. Sometimes their son, Sebastián, and I would wage war, setting up epic battles with swarms of plastic soldiers.

My mother liked everything about being in that house. She liked the order of it. She liked the plush of the golden brown carpet. She even liked the books, though she couldn't read them, for the progress they represented. If I was bothering her in the kitchen, she always shooed me away: "Go grab a book, Chino. I'm busy right now."

I was sitting with her in the kitchen one day when I asked her why we had moved. In the comfort of that kitchen, I knew that *this* was better than *that,* but, the way my mother spoke of Pasco sometimes, one might picture a wide fertile valley instead of the poor and violent town it really was. Lima frightened her. She felt safe in only two places: our house and the Azcárates' house.

"We had to move, Chino. Your father was here." She was baking a cake and she stirred the mix with a spatula. "Do you miss Pasco?"

I didn't have to think about it. "No," I said. "Do you miss it, Ma?"

"Of course," she said.

"Why?"

Her face fell. "Your grandparents are there! I grew up there! Chino, how can you ask such a thing?"

"I don't know," I said, because I didn't. She was a mystery to me, romanticizing the life we'd left behind. "It's cold there."

"If you lived away from me, wouldn't you miss me?" she asked.

"Of course, Ma."

"That's how I feel."

"Papi doesn't miss Pasco."

She smiled. It was true, of course. Lima was his backyard, the place where he could become what he'd always imagined himself to be. "He," she said finally, "is different. And you, Chino," she added, "you're just like your father."

I sat on the Jirón, watching Lima pass by. A pedestrian mall of roast chicken joints and tattoo parlors, of stolen watches and burned CDs. Colonial buildings plastered over with billboards and advertisements. A din of conversations and transactions: dollars for sale; slot machines; English tapes announcing, "*Mano*" — pause, pause — "Hand." Blind musicians singing songs. Pickpockets scoping tourists. The city inhaling. A cop took a bribe in the privacy of a recessed doorway. A nun tried to pin a ribbon on me, for a donation. I dodged her with my most polite smile. Then I felt, like an electric current, the street convey a message. From the Plaza San Martín, the whole world appeared to be running toward me, and past me, toward the Plaza Mayor. Metal gates closed with clangs and crashes all along the Jirón. Businesses were shuttered with customers inside. The cop disappeared. I imagined the worst: a drunken mob of soccer fans wrecking and looting, raping and robbing. I ran to the end of the block and watched the people scatter. Then the Jirón was empty, and it was one of the strangest things I'd ever seen.

Fifteen shoeshine boys.

The children walked in rows of three, dressed in secondhand clothes, sneakers worn at the heels, donated T-shirts with American logos. Some were so young that they were dwarfed by their kits. One dragged his wooden box behind him, unconcerned as it bumped and bounced along the cobblestones. All were skinny, fragile, and smiling. As they marched toward me, they were led by a clown on stilts, twice their height, dancing elegantly around them in looping figure eights, arms extended like the flapping wings of a bird.

I watched in amazement as the protest strode past me, the children whispering their demands, the panic subsiding. Had it been a drill? A joke of some sort? Storeowners and customers emerged from their bunkers, relieved and confused. Lima was playing tricks again.

I was twelve when I learned that my old man had another angle. The scheme went like this: You put in a new bathroom, or tile a kitchen, or add a third floor to a house in Surco or La Molina. You are a model worker, always polite and respectful. You don't play your music too loud. You wipe your feet and clean up after yourself. All the while, you do your real work with your eyes. Television, *check*. Stereo, *check*. Computer, *check*. Jewelry, *check*. Anything electric can be sold — kitchen appliances, even wall clocks. Nice clothes, too, especially women's. You scout for windows without locks, flimsy doors, back entrances. You keep track of schedules: When the husband is at work, when the wife is at the salon. When the kids come home from school. When the maid is there alone.

My father and his crew were smart. They could wait a few months or as long as a year. Sometimes the neighborhood security guard was in on it too; for a small fee, he'd tell them when a family was out of town. Other times, the maid got the worst of it: the fright, and often the blame.

I remember one evening at our house. They were planning, or, perhaps, celebrating. There were six of them, and I knew some so well that I called them *tío*. They came around a lot, to drink with my old man, to play soccer on Sundays. And they sat close together, talking in low voices, bubbling now and then into laughter.

I was called to bring more beer from the fridge. I passed a cold bottle to my father, who took it without looking, intent on what his partner, Felipe, was saying. I listened too. "I always try to smack the maid real good," Felipe said proudly. "And I try to break something — just so the family doesn't think she was in on it." Everyone cheered this perverse generosity. My father too. Standing at the edge of the circle of men, I thought of my own mother falling to the floor.

Villacorta was asking for his article. I was avoiding him. The government had not fallen, and the protests continued. A group of unemployed textile workers burned tires and looted in El Agustino. There was talk of the president not returning from his next state trip. I was counting on the story to snowball, to crowd my clown feature out of the news section the following Sunday. An extra week would help.

I worked and slept and worked, and thought as little as possible about my old man, my mother, Carmela. I thought about clowns. They had become, to my surprise, a kind of refuge. Once I'd started looking for them, I found them everywhere. They organized the city for me: buses, street corners, plazas. They suited my mood. Appropriating the absurd, embracing shame, they transformed it. *Laugh at me. Humiliate me. And, when you do, I've won.* Lima was, in fact and in spirit, a city of clowns.

The February heat smothered the city, even after dark, and in the evenings I rarely made it farther than the bar downstairs. The overhead fans whirled, stirring the warmth. I listened to the hum of a dozen separate conversations, to the clink of glasses, to cheerful applause in the back room. It made me feel less alone.

One night, a clown stood at the counter next to me. I recognized him. He worked mornings in front of San Francisco, for the children who went there on school trips. I knew the red and orange plaid of his suit. Usually he had a partner, but he was alone now, tired, halfway out of costume, headed for home. Like me, he probably wanted a drink to help him sleep. I should have let him go on his way, but before I realized it I'd blurted out, "You're a clown."

He turned, puzzled, and looked me in the eye. "You asking me or telling me, *causa?*"

"Asking, friend."

"And who the fuck are you?" His frown was very unclownlike, the kind of look that would frighten a child. There was white greasepaint ground into the wrinkles at the edges of his mouth.

"Oscar Uribe," I said. "I write for *El Clarín.*"

"The newspaper?" He turned away, back to the business of ordering a drink. I pulled out two chairs at a table by the bar and moved my bottle of red wine.

"*Maestro!*" I called to the waiter. "Another glass, please!" The waiter acknowledged me with a wave. I looked back at the clown, motioning to the empty chair. He shrugged and sat down.

His name was Tonio, he said, and he didn't have all night.

But I kept the wine coming. I found myself telling him about my mother, about my old man. About Pasco and San Juan. He listened and drank. Then he told me about his hometown, in the north, about arriving in Lima penniless. He said that he'd lived under the Santa Rosa Bridge for a time. And clowning? "It's work, brother. Better than some, worse than others," he said. "I'm not good at much else. It's either this or stealing."

"Amen," I said.

He told me how good it felt to be someone else for a living, to be out in the streets on a clear day. He said that the children had sweet faces and it touched him to see them happy. He complained about having to compete with every unemployed nobody selling candy on the buses.

"Does it pay the bills?"

"I don't need much," he said, nodding. "No wife. No kids."

"How did you settle on this line of work?"

He smiled then, so unexpectedly that I thought he'd misunderstood me. It was a wonderful smile, a real clown smile. With his thumb, he rubbed at the paint still hiding in the creases of his face. "No, *causa,*" he said, shaking his head. "It's like this: You wake up one morning, and *boom!* You're a clown."

\*

Señor Ingeniero Hubert Azcárate opened the door. He shook my father's hand, patted me on the head, and waved us both in. I wiped my feet three times, back and forth against the thick doormat. I'd been there many more times than my father had. He was watching my every move. There were three stairs, and at the bottom of the landing the room opened up into a wide, airy space full of light. An L-shaped sofa and a leather armchair were positioned around a wooden coffee table. Built-in shelves along the walls held hundreds of books. The windows opened onto a garden terrace with trees and grass and flowers sprouting in warm colors.

"Mari!" Señor Azcárate called out. "Your husband is here, with Chino!"

My mother appeared from the kitchen, a little shocked to see us. Her maid's uniform was a pristine white. She kissed us both, and then asked, concerned, "What are you doing here?"

Señor Azcárate had already made his way to his comfortable leather chair, and he sat now, observing us with an air of patrician benevolence. "Oh, don't worry, Mari," he said. "Your husband only wanted to speak with me. It's no problem at all."

"Go on back to the kitchen," my father said. "We'll come say goodbye before we leave."

My father sat down. He began by recounting the reasons that we were grateful to Señor and the Azcárate family. The generosity, the solidarity, the understanding. "Things haven't always been easy, but I tell Mari, I tell her every day, God was smiling on us the day she got this job."

I had never heard my father invoke God for any reason other than to explain the weather.

Señor Azcárate nodded, *yes, yes, yes,* savoring my father's gratitude. He was a thin man whose pale blue eyes had become even more prominent as his hair receded. He often squinted when he spoke, as if we were drifting away and he might lose sight of us. "Please, please, Hugo. Go on."

"Señor Ingeniero, at Chino's new school," my father continued, "everyone will have money." I was about to start at a private school in San Isidro, where the Azcárates had arranged a scholarship.

"Are you worried about the tuition?" Señor Azcárate asked. "I explained to Mari that everything is covered except the uniforms."

"No, no, it's not that." My old man searched for the right words. "You know, Señor Ingeniero, I'm a builder. I work almost every day — I should say, every day that I can." He put his arm around me. "We're so proud of Chino. I always knew that he was a smart one. But, you know, we struggle to pay for this, to pay for that. There isn't always work, that's the thing . . . I'm embarrassed to even ask, after all you've done for us."

"No, no, ask, Hugo, please." Señor Azcárate leaned toward my father. My father's silence was studied. "How long has Marisol worked with us?" Azcárate asked. "I'll tell you: long enough that she's family." He smiled, then turned to me, speaking as if to a child of five. "You're family, Chino, you know that? Your father, he's family too."

I nodded, perplexed. Finally, my old man spoke, and this time he went straight to the point. "I was hoping, if it's possible, if anyone from Chino's new school would be doing work on their house . . ."

"I really couldn't say."

"No, but, if they were, could you put in a word for me? For my business?"

It was Don Hubert Azcárate's favorite kind of favor, the kind he could fulfill. The kind that confirmed his own charity. He was a nice man, he really was. He promised that he would. My father smiled happily. "Thank Señor Azcárate, Chino," he told me. I shook the engineer's veiny hand. Then the two men embraced. "You don't know what this means to me," my old man said.

All my life, I've been Chino. In Pasco, in Lima. At home, in my neighborhood. The way some people are Chato or Cholo or Negro. I hear those two syllables and look up. There are thousands of us, of course, perhaps hundreds of thousands, here and everywhere that Spanish is spoken. No nickname could be less original. There are soccer players and singers known as Chino. One of our crooked presidents lived and died by his moniker: *chino de mierda*.

Still, it is my name, and always was my name. Until I started at Peruano Británico, that is. There, I was called Piraña.

Piranhas were already a phenomenon in Lima by the time I started high school. The authorities had ordered investigations and organized police sweeps. There were news reports and shocking images. A city on the brink. In packs of fifteen or twenty, they would swarm a car and swiftly, ruthlessly undress it. Hubcaps, mirrors, lights. The crawling commute held the prey in place — the owner of the car, helpless, honking his horn frantically, aware perhaps that the wisest thing was to do nothing at all. To wait for them to pass. But that was an option only for a while. More audacious crews started breaking windows, taking briefcases, cell phones, watches, sunglasses, radios. *Full service*, people joked darkly. A new kind of crime, sociologists called it. And an astute observer — of the kind who traffic in phrases — named them piranhas.

At morning roll call in the courtyard of my new school, my class lined up in single file. I found my place in the order of last names, Uribe, almost at the back. Ugaz in front of me. Ventosilla behind me. My uniform was neat and pressed, and I looked, from a distance, just like all the others. The teacher called us off, and one by one we marched to our new classroom. It wasn't until recess that afternoon that my classmates sought me out. "*Oye*, you play?" The kid held a soccer ball in his hands. He kicked it to me. I passed it back, making sure I used good form. I introduced myself as Oscar or Chino. "César," he answered. We formed a team. We grabbed a kid with glasses and put him in goal. We played. We scored and were scored on. We yelled and sweated and cursed and then, when I took the ball from a kid on the other team, he called a foul, dropped to the ground, and held his ankle, grimacing. In San Juan, I would have called him a pussy, and that would've been that. But he yelled, "*Oye! Oye!*" and we stopped. "That's a foul here, *huevón*," he said, frowning. "Where the hell are you from?"

I didn't have to respond, but I did. I could have said any place in the city, but I didn't. "San Juan de Lurigancho," I answered.

Of course, eventually they would have found out where I was from. They would have seen me walking to the Avenida Arequipa to catch the bus home. They would have known that I didn't live in La Molina or Surco. But perhaps if they hadn't learned this detail on the very first day, if they had known me better, they wouldn't have associated me with the criminal reputation of my district.

"San Juan?" he said, breaking into a cruel smile. "Ooooohh . . . *Habla piraña!*"

I met Tonio at eight-thirty the next morning in front of San Francisco. He was already painted and dressed. I was still shaking off sleep and a red-wine headache. He introduced me to his partner, a yellow-faced clown named Jhon.

"You're the reporter?" Jhon asked suspiciously.

"Be nice," Tonio said.

He pulled an oversize polka-dot suit from his backpack. It was white with green dots. It fit me like a garbage bag. Tonio declared it perfect. Jhon agreed. A pair of green shoes was next; I wiggled my feet into them. They were twice the length of my forearm. Then Tonio handed me a mirror and three plastic canisters of face paint, each the size of a roll of film. "You take care of that," he said, holding out a thin brush.

I felt outside of myself; the details of the previous night's conversation were so hazy and wine-soaked that I couldn't recall exactly how I had ended up there or what commitments I had made. In the mirror, I watched myself transform. I put red circles on my cheeks. Jhon passed me a nose. It was an oversize red Ping-Pong ball cut in half and threaded by a rubber band. Finally, Tonio pulled a worn jester's hat from the bottom of his bag, the colors faded, the pointy edges falling limply in my face. It would have to do.

Walking through the city, one third of a trio of clowns, I was surprised to find how relaxed I was, and how invisible. You'd think the world's gazes would have converged on us, on our loud costumes and painted smiles, but most people simply ignored us, walked past without a glance; only the children smiled and pointed, sometimes waved. Jhon and Tonio chatted about soccer; I watched and listened in a daydream.

We let a few buses pass because they were too empty. "It's bad

luck at the beginning of the day," Tonio explained. Finally, he nodded as a more crowded bus approached. We pushed past the ticket
collector and were instantly onstage, all eyes on us. "*Señores y
Señoras, Damas y Caballeros!*" We stood in a row, Tonio in the center, yelling over the asthmatic rattle of the engine. "I am not here
asking for charity! In fact, I am a rich man! This is my bus! This is
my driver! And *this*," Tonio bellowed, pointing to the ticket collector, hanging halfway out the door of the bus, calling the route, "*this*
is my mascot!"

Jhon was the chorus, echoing every pronouncement Tonio
made, in the stereotypical voice of a drunk lifted from a Rubén
Blades song. He pretended to fall, and Tonio made sheepish apolo-
gies for his drunken partner, who had spent the night before "celebrating the purchase of a new three-story home in San Borja!"

I felt useless. I flashed my dumb clown smile and tapped my
fingers against my chest. I could feel my face paint drying to an
uncomfortable film, affixing an unnatural contortion to the muscles of my face. I was dazed, almost seasick, as the bus sped along
the avenue. Tonio was wrapping up. "My humble servant — God
bless the poor deaf-mute — will be passing by your seats now to
collect your fare." He bowed low, and then nodded at me.

We weren't selling anything; this was a bold conceit that Tonio
had devised to cut costs. It was *our* bus; I simply passed down the
aisle collecting everyone's fare. "*Pasajes, pasajes a la mano,*" I mur-
mured, just as a ticket collector would. Some passengers, nap-
ping, barely opening their eyes, handed me a coin without thinking. Some dropped loose change in my hand; some even thanked
me. Most ignored me, looking away, even men and women who
had watched the act and smiled.

I collected a total of 4.20 *soles*. The bus stopped. "Ladies and
gentlemen, good day!" Tonio shouted. We stepped off into the
morning sun. The whole thing had taken five minutes.

I put a coin in the slot and dialed the number for Elisa's bodega. It
was early afternoon. Tonio and Jhon sat in a café across the street,
sharing a cup of tea. We were back downtown, taking a break.

We'd been thrown off buses, had change tossed at us, been spat at. But we'd made money. A good day, Tonio assured me, better than usual. They seemed content.

The phone rang and rang in San Juan, and then she answered. She asked me how I was.

I looked at the busy street, the people meandering homeward or workward, lost in their own lives. "I'm at the office, *vecina*. I can't talk long." I asked her if she'd seen my mother.

"At the funeral, Chino. Why weren't you there?"

"I had to work. I couldn't make it. Did she say anything?"

"She misses you, Chino." I heard Elisa sigh. "She said that everything is good with Carmela. That she might sell the house."

I didn't say anything.

"Chino, are you there?"

"I'm here."

"Are you going to visit her?"

Tonio and Jhon were paying with change, haggling for a little extra hot water. They counted the money out in ten-cent coins. The waitress tried to hold back a smile. Jhon leaned over the counter and blew her a kiss. They were charming clowns. "Thank you, *vecina*," I said, and hung up the phone.

My new nickname both labeled me as dangerous and emasculated me. I was never scary to them. I was a joke. A nerdy kid from the ghetto. I was too skinny. Too weak. Even when I played well or ran fast, they hurled insults at me. In San Juan, we'd joked about how I would beat up these *pitucos*, but the reality was different. They wielded their power carelessly, sometimes unconsciously. They could cut me out with a comment or simply with silence.

"It's time for you to start working," my father announced.

It was my second year at Peruano Británico. I was almost fourteen. In more than a year, I'd never been invited to a classmate's home. Each day, I rode the bus from San Juan to San Isidro in silence.

I'd given my father's line of work a lot of thought. I'd examined it under the rules of ethics and law. It was wrong. Certainly. But when he told me it was time for me to work my mind gathered a year of scattered insults and wove them together. I savored those injuries, imagined what a delight it would be to go through one of those boys' houses, to exchange smiles and handshakes. To work there, and then to *steal*. I began to understand my old man, or to think I did. But I wanted to be sure.

"I want to work," I said.

"Of course you do. Every man wants to work."

"Pa, are we going to break in to this house?"

He sat back. Frowned. He'd misread me. "Have people been saying things?"

I nodded.

"And what do you think about what they say?" He seemed poised to smile at the slightest hint of approval.

"I believe them."

"Well, Chino," he said, and stopped.

I wanted to take it back. To add to it: *I believe what they say, but it's all right with me.* I wanted to tell him that those rich fucks could complain to God if they didn't like it. That they could move to Miami and become American. That, if they wanted to call me Piraña, then they'd better be good and fucking ready when I came in and repossessed all their treasures.

He ran a finger through his hair and winked. His large black eyes were set close, his mouth was small, comically so, but his broad smile evened everything out, organized the jumble of his features. He kept his black hair meticulously combed back. At rest, he was a caricature of an Indian. In laughter, he was a mestizo Clark Gable. So he laughed and smiled and made that smile the linchpin of his personality. Now he met my gaze, his son — I believed, his only son. "Chino, we're just men who work. You and I both. Crazy things happen in the city." He snapped his fingers and laughed. He hugged me. "Okay?"

The wife had a good eye for color. She had decorated the house herself, she told us. She walked us through the expansive suburban mansion — my father, Felipe, and me — pointing out renovations and design touches: a wall they'd knocked down, leaving only painted beams. "See how this adds space to the room? Gives it another feel?" she asked. The three of us nodded, our eyes wide and observant. There were skylights, balconies, a garden with blossoming trees, but we focused on what could be taken away: a computer, a stereo, even a dishwasher. The husband was an executive at a bank, an old friend of Señor Azcárate's. They wanted to remodel the second floor, to add a television room, she said. It wouldn't be a lot of work, maybe three or four weeks. Some painting. New carpet. A couple of new windows and light fixtures.

I worked on Saturdays, and I saw my father more on those days than I ever had at home. During the week, he was mostly gone. His youngest son was still in diapers, and my mother must have known about Carmela by then. When he was home they argued, but I didn't know why. The construction on our own house had stalled, the second floor still open air, a thick plastic sheet tied at the corners of three walls. When they were fighting, I retreated there and watched the ridges of the hills draw lines against the sky.

The family we were working for had a son, Andrés, who was in the class above me at Peruano Británico. At his house, he ignored me. At school, he let it be known that I had crossed the line. I felt the stares, the judgment. By the time he woke up on Saturdays, I had already been working for three or four hours. His weekends, as far as I could tell, took the shape of an extended yawn. I placed tiles in the hallway. He ate cereal. I sanded down corners and measured for bookshelves. He spoke on the phone, loud enough for me to hear. "Yeah, Piraña's here. You bet I'm watching my shit, *huevón*." He made no attempt to hide his disdain for me. I listened to him speculate as to which girl would be the first to let him seduce her in the new room we were building. How far she would spread her legs. With a long phone cord dragging behind him, he paraded through the work area, complained of the dust, asked his mother to tell us that the sanding was hurting his ears. He put on a show of power. I bowed my head at the appropriate times and pretended not to hear.

One Saturday, when we were almost done, the entire family was getting ready for a wedding. The mother flitted about, changing her dress three times. The father came in to tell us that we'd have to leave a little early because they all had to go. We were hurrying our work along, trying to finish, when Andrés called out to his mother, "Mami, tell Piraña to stop with the hammering! I can't even think!"

He stepped out into the hallway, wearing a gray wool suit and a red tie, still unknotted. He glared at me.

"What did you call him, Andrés?" his mother said sharply, coming into the room. Her hair was styled in a hard, gelled bob. She stood in front of him, waiting for him to speak.

"Piraña," Andrés muttered.

"What?" she said, surprised, embarrassed. "Why would you call him that?" She turned to me. "Son, what's your name?"

"Oscar, Señora."

"Your mother works with the Azcárates, doesn't she?"

I felt myself turning red. "Yes, Señora."

"And what year are you in?"

"Third, Señora."

Andrés watched this exchange with practiced condescension. In his elegant suit he was transformed, ready to be photographed for Lima's society pages. He was taller than me, and more handsome, bathed at that moment in superiority, profound and harsh. I wore my work clothes, worn at the knees and splattered with paint.

"Andrés," his mother said, "this is Oscar. This young man is a student at your school. He is friends with Sebastián Azcárate. Now shake his hand and introduce yourself like a gentleman."

His eyes steeled, and his hand too. He held it out.

"Andrés," he said.

"Oscar."

We shook. *No, you were right,* I thought. *Piraña concha tu madre. That's my fucking name.* I glared at him and held his hand, perhaps a moment too long. I squeezed.

"That's enough, boys," his mother said, and they both turned to leave.

"Good afternoon, Señora," I called.

\*

We played to passengers in Santa Anita, Villa Maria, and El Agustino. We rode through Comas, Los Olivos, and Carabayllo. Three days. Lima on display, in all her grandeur, the systems of the city becoming clear to me: her cells, her arteries, her multiple beating hearts. We collected laughs and coins until the money weighed heavy in my suit pocket. I was a secret agent. I saw six people I knew: among them, an ex-girlfriend, two old neighbors from San Juan, and a woman from the university. Even a colleague from the paper. Exactly zero recognized me. I was forgetting myself too, patrolling the city, spying on my own life. I had never felt this way: on display, but protected from the intruding eyes of strangers and intimates.

I watched the ex-girlfriend chew the nail of her pinkie. When we were together, she'd seemed to me the type who would flower, grow into herself, become more attractive each year. But she was twenty-seven now and still not beautiful. I looked her in the eye as she handed me a coin, felt a shock when her finger grazed my open palm. She had no idea who I was.

My old man had paid off the security guard. He'd given us a time and a day. The whole family was out of town. I'd been waiting six months for this. I was a good student and they hated me. I was a good soccer player and they mocked me. I didn't understand a thing about them, or why they were the way they were.

We rode in Felipe's windowless van. They tossed me over the wall. I opened the garage and they backed the van in. The rest was easy. The television, the VCR, the computer, the stereo — each was carried out and packed carefully into the van. We moved nimbly through the dark house, carrying the wares as if they were works of art. And they were. A sleek cordless phone meant thirty *soles*. A blender, fifteen, if you knew where to sell it. It was so ordered and efficient, it didn't seem like stealing at all.

My father told me once that in Lima anything can be bought and sold. We were walking through the market in San Juan, past the fruit stalls, flies buzzing around the meat and fish. A woman sold clothes piled in high, disordered mounds. Fake Barcelona jerseys. Stolen car parts and bags and watches. An old man stood by his cart of hardware: hammers, pliers, and nails, bent, rusty, unmistakably used. My old man found it pathetic. "Used nails!" he cried out. "For the love of God, are we this poor?"

I did a last run through the house. We were almost done. It was my first time out, my old man's way of saying he trusted me. I wanted in because I trusted him. We were going to be okay. I knew it. We would have money again. We would finish the second story of our house, and my mother would be happy again. They would both be happy. I had no idea that he was preparing to leave us.

I lingered at the top of the stairs, looking at the room we'd built. It was really something, even with the gaping hole where the television had been. I was proud of my work. A few steps down the hall, along the tiles I'd laid myself, was Andrés's room. I wasn't looking for anything in particular. We'd already taken his boom box and alarm clock. I turned on the lamp. In the closet, there were half a dozen pairs of shoes and button-down shirts in white and blue. I touched them all. I ran my fingers along the rack and found it: his gray wool suit. I'd just pulled it from the closet when my father walked in.

"What the fuck are you doing?" he hissed. "Turn that goddamn light off!"

"I'm sorry," I said. We were in darkness again.

"We're leaving. Put that back," he said. "We can't sell that."

"We could."

"We're in a hurry, Chino. Let's go."

"It's for me," I said.

"This isn't a department store. You don't need it."

He was right. I didn't need it, wouldn't need it. Not until I wore it for my interview at *El Clarín*, seven years later. I knew it would take me a year or two to grow into it, if I grew into it at all. It was a dull, shapeless longing, but it was real. "I want this," I said, "for my birthday."

I could barely see him in the purple shadows.

"Your birthday?" my father said. He'd forgotten. His voice softened. "Well, then, take it."

*

I rode around the city in my green and white suit and thought about my mother. I put my article in an envelope, sealed it, and dropped it in the mail. I didn't see Villacorta, or check the paper to see if he'd published it. I broke away from Tonio and Jhon, paid them twenty *soles* for the suit and the shoes and the memories. I thanked them from the very bottom of my new clown heart. And I didn't do their act, or any act. I spent my savings. I put on the polka-dot suit and stepped into the unwieldy shoes. I painted my face in the dim reflection of the hallway mirror. I placed the red Ping-Pong ball over my nose, felt the tight pull of the rubber band against my hair. And I rode the buses, paying my fare like any other passenger, except that I was unlike any other passenger. I knew that I would see her. This was our city, hers and mine.

I rode to La Victoria, where the corner kids eyed me, wondering if it was worth their trouble to mug a clown. I walked the narrow streets, my shoes flopping on the crumbling sidewalks. I sat on a bench in front of Carmela's house and waited. My black brothers came and went to their schools, to their jobs. They didn't even shoot me a glance. I was part of the architecture. A cop stopped and asked if I was all right.

"Just resting, chief," I said.

Was I from around here?

"I'm Don Hugo's kid."

"Carmela's Hugo?" he asked. Then he left me alone.

Carmela came home, carrying dresses, and smiled at me because she smiled at everyone. Her door swung open wide, and from my bench I peered into her world, my mother's new world. And then things came at me in waves: the street, the house. *I haven't seen you since you were this big,* Carmela had said at the hospital. I remembered. When I was six, Don Hugo had taken me to see his mistress. I'd never seen a black person before. I cried and said she looked burnt. He hit me and told me to be nice to my *tía.* She grinned and pinched my cheek. Now I couldn't bring myself to ring the doorbell. I knew that she'd be kind, even with me dressed this way. As kind as she was to my mother. She'd answer my questions and tell me how she met my father, how she fell for him, the sweet things he'd told her. Carmela and my mother must have spoken of all this already. What revelations did I have for them, anyway? They had worked out the details of their parallel heartbreaks: who had him when, who had him first, who was innocent, who was guilty. And they'd forgiven him, and that was the most astounding thing of all.

Why were you always forgiving him, Ma? He told *her* everything first — about you, about me, about the work he did and planned to do. He let you swim in darkness, and wonder at the vacant spaces, and ask yourself what mistakes you'd made. And then he left us. And you forgave him, Ma. You forgave him.

After we broke in to Andrés's house, the loot was split, but my mother and I saw none of it, except the gray wool suit. The next week, I found myself on my knees again, burnishing the lacquered floorboards of another house. Another Saturday, and then another. I went on three jobs with my father and his crew. I understand now that money must have been tight. He had four sons to support. We'd just finished a two-week job when Felipe came by with the van. I remember thinking it was strange that they hadn't given the place time to cool. I thought I understood the hustle. I asked my father about it.

"Shut up," he said. "Don't ask questions."

We drove through the dark streets of the city. I sat in the back, felt the van swaying. I had no idea where we were going, but when I got out I knew immediately where I was. I looked at my father, horrified, expecting some kind of explanation, but he just shrugged. *Crazy things happen in the city.* They boosted me over the wall, into the garden where I'd played as a child. I could see through the glass window, the high bookshelves against the far wall, the elegant leather sofas.

They were too rich and too trusting. Their watchman was asleep in a rickety wooden chair. I opened the garage door from the inside, and the man woke with a start. My father stepped in and broke his jaw. Felipe dragged him into the garden and tied him to a tree. The watchman sat there, blindfolded and gagged and bleeding, while we disassembled the house. Their possessions were so familiar that it was like stealing from myself.

It was terrifying and logical: the riskiest hit of all. I led Felipe and my father around the house like a tour guide: Don't forget the microwave and the blender my mother loves so much. And, in here, the old engineer's nifty calculator and the television with its remote control. There was something beautiful about our silent artistry. Everyone would be a suspect. The gardener, my mother, my father, me. Whichever members of the crew had worked on the house. And the watchman tied to the tree, bleeding into a rag.

The van was full. It was time to go. The watchman's chin was slumped into his chest, his breathing heavy. I felt the conviction that he too was one of us, and it disgusted me. It could have been anything: a stray light that shone on him, or a spasm in his face that made me think he was smiling. I kicked him. He snapped to attention, seeing only his blindfold. He struggled against the tree. I hocked something viscous and unclean on his forehead. *The color of money.*

My father called me, and we disappeared.

She left Carmela's and I followed her. She got on the bus at Manco Cápac. She wore her uniform, as clean and as white as a high summer cloud. She didn't notice me behind her, sat across from me innocently, not even looking in my direction. I closed my eyes, felt the rumble of the bus along the potholed avenue. The ticket collector sang the route: La Victoria, San Borja! La Victoria, San Borja! Between the standing passengers, I could still catch glimpses of her. No one sat in the empty seat beside me. Then she stood. She got off, and I followed.

I knew the way, of course, to the Azcárates' house, where I once kept my mother company and did my homework in the garden. The house my father and I had violated, nearly sacrificing her livelihood. But she had always been safe there. And, worse, I had too. They'd welcomed me into their looted house, consoled me when I cried. *You're too old for that, Chino. Look, they didn't steal the books.* The old engineer with his generous heart, trying to make me feel better.

I trailed half a block behind her now, an expert in my clumsy green shoes, marching down the very center of an empty street. "Ma!" I shouted. "Ma!" She half turned, and then sped up at the sight of me. I rushed to keep pace with her. "Ma!" I shouted again. "Ma, it's Oscar! It's Chino!"

She stopped beneath a flowering tree. "*Hijo?*" she said. "Is that you?"

I hadn't seen her since the *velorio*. I had left her to bury the old man without me. She had held his hand and watched him die. She had put him in the earth and covered him.

"It's me, Ma."

"Chino! You scared me!"

"I'm sorry, Ma."

"Your nose, Chino?"

I pulled off my red nose, let it drop to the ground.

"And your shoes? What's all this?"

I stepped out of the clown shoes and kicked them toward the sidewalk. "I'm writing a story, Ma. For the paper."

She nodded, not understanding.

"I'm sorry," I repeated.

"Where have you been, Chino?"

"Here and there," I said. I took off my jester's hat. "I'm here now."

She took me in her arms and stroked my hair. She kissed my forehead and wiped the paint from my cheeks. "Are you all right?"

"I came to Carmela's, but I didn't knock."

"You should have," she said. "Will you?"

"I don't know," I said. "Did he ask about me?"

It was a travesty, my wanting to know, but I did. She held me tighter. My face paint was running, coming off in white streaks on the sleeve of my suit. "He missed you, Chino," she said.

I felt the warm salty wet of her cheek against mine, and it was good to be held.

"I missed you too," my mother said.

"I won't leave you again," I told her. But a shiver passed over me. I knew in my heart that the clown was lying.

DAVID BENIOFF

■

# Zoanthropy

FROM *Tin House*

WHENEVER A LION WAS spotted prowling the avenues, the authorities contacted my father. He had a strange genius for tracking predators; he made a lifelong study of their habits; he never missed an open shot.

There is a statue of him in Carl Schurz Park, a hulking bronze. He stands, rifle slung casually over his shoulder, one booted foot atop a dead lion's haunches. A simple inscription is carved on the marble pedestal: MACGREGOR BONNER / DEFENDER OF THE CITY. The statue's proportions are too heroic — no Bonner ever had forearms like that — but the sculptor caught the precise angle of my father's jaw line, the flat bridge of his nose, the peacemaking eyes of a man who never missed an open shot.

In the old days, the media cooperated with the authorities — nobody wanted to spark a panic by publishing news of big cats in the streets. That attitude is long gone, of course. Every photographer in the country remembers the *New York Post*'s famous shot of the dead lion sprawled across the double yellow lines on Twenty-third Street, eyes rolled white, blood leaking from his open jaws, surrounded by grinning policemen, below the banner headline: "BAGGED!" My father was the triggerman; the grinning policemen were there to keep the crowds away.

So it's sacrilege to admit, but I always rooted for the cats' escape. A treasonous confession, like a matador's son pulling for the bull, and I don't know what soured me on my father's business. A reverence for exiled kings, I suppose, for the fallen mighty. I wanted the lions to have a chance. I wanted them to live.

All good stories start on Monday, my father liked to say, a line he inherited from *his* father, a Glasgow-born minister who served as a chaplain for the British troops in North Africa and later moved to Rhodesia, where my father was born. For my grandfather, the only story worth reading was the holy one, King James version. My father rejected the God of the book in favor of empirical truth. He never understood my obsession with fictions, the barbarians, starships, detectives, and cowboys that filled the shelves of my childhood room. He purged his mind of fantasy only to watch his lone child slip back into the muck.

This story starts on Tuesday. I was twenty years old. On bad afternoons I sometimes found myself where I had not meant to go: lying on the dead grass in Bryant Park with a bottle of celery soda balanced on my chest; inside a Chinese herb store breathing exotic dust; riding the subway to the end of the line, Far Rockaway, and back. The bad days came like Churchill's black dogs; they paced the corridor outside my bedroom, raking the carpet with their claws. The bad days chewed the corners. When my corners got too chewed for walking, I took a taxi to the Frick museum, stood in front of Bellini's Saint Francis, waited for the right angles to return.

On this bad Tuesday I stared at Saint Francis and Saint Francis stared into the sky, hands open by his side, head tilted back, lips parted, receiving the full favor of the Lord. Bellini shows the man at the moment of his stigmatization, the spots of blood sprouting from his palms. I don't think I'm being vulgar or inaccurate when I say that the saint's expression is orgasmic — the rapture of divine penetration. The animals are waiting for him, the wild ass, the rabbit, the skinny-legged heron — they want to have a word with him, they see that Francis is in ecstasy and they're concerned. From the animal perspective, I think, nothing that makes you bleed is a good thing. The rabbit, especially, watches the proceedings with extreme skepticism.

After an hour things inside my brain had sorted themselves out, the thoughts began to flow with relative order, my bladder swelled painfully. I went to the restroom, stopping on the way to take a photograph for a honeymooning German couple who thanked me effusively and gave me a business card from their bookstore in Düsseldorf. In the toilet stall I locked the door, did my business, closed the seat and sat down for a smoke.

The stall door was scrawled with names and dates, a worldly graffiti: Rajiv from London, Thiago from Saõ Paulo, Sikorsky from Brooklyn. I leaned forward, the cigarette gripped between my teeth, the smoke in my lungs, pulled a ballpoint pen from my hip pocket, wrote my name in boxy capitals: MACKENZIE ALASTAIR BONNER, and then, in lieu of a hometown, LIVES!

Someone rapped on the door. "Occupied," I said.

"You'll have to put out the cigarette, sir. No smoking in the museum."

I took a final long drag, stood, lifted the toilet seat, and flushed the butt. When I opened the stall door the guard was still standing there, a tired-looking kid about my age, batwing-eared, narrow-shouldered, his maroon blazer two sizes too large. He stared at me sadly, hands in his pockets.

"You smoke Lucky Strikes," he said. "I could smell them from the hallway. They used to be my brand." He spoke with a forlorn air, as if the real meaning of his words was *You slept with Cindy. She used to be my girlfriend.* "Hey," he added, smiling, "the Saint Francis man."

I squinted at him and he nodded happily.

"You're the guy that always comes and stands by that Saint Francis painting. What's the matter, you don't like the other stuff?"

"I like *The Polish Rider.*"

I was spending too much time in this place. The Frick made for a cheap afternoon with my student discount — I had dropped out of NYU after a term and kept my ID — but I hated the idea that people were watching me. Perhaps I had grown too dependent on Saint Francis. I walked over to the sink to wash my hands.

"Me too, I like that one. Well, listen, sorry about busting you. It's pretty high school. Detention! But I've only been working here a couple weeks and, you know."

He held the door open for me and I thanked him and exited the bathroom, drying my hands on the seat of my corduroys. The guard followed me, walking with a bowlegged strut as though he had six-guns strapped to his waist. "The thing about Lucky Strikes, they have this sweetness, this . . . I don't know how to describe it."

"You're not from New York, are you?"

"Huh?"

"Where are you from?"

He grinned, jangling the heavy key ring dangling from his belt. "Bethlehem, Pennsylvania. What, I have hay in my hair?" His "Bethlehem" had two syllables: *Beth-lem*.

We were in the garden courtyard now, a beautiful pillared room with an iron trelliswork skylight and a fountain in the center where stone frogs spitting water flanked a giant marble lily pad. I sat down on a bench and watched the frogs. The guard stood behind me, fiddling with his black tie. He seemed lonely. Or gay. Or both.

"So you're an artist?" I asked him. "You're in school here?"

"Nah. I don't think I could look at paint after being in this place all day. Nope, not for me."

"Actor?"

"Nope, nothing like that. It's —"

We both saw the lion at the same time, padding below the colonnade on the far side of the courtyard, yellow eyes glimmering in the shadows, claws click-clacking on the floor. He rubbed his side back and forth against a pillar before limping to the fountain. The lion looked unwell. His mane was tangled and matted down; an open red sore marred one shoulder; his ribs seemed ready to poke through his mangy fur. He stared at us for several seconds before dipping his muzzle to the water and drinking, huge pink tongue lapping up the frog spit. His tail swayed like a charmed cobra. After satisfying his thirst he looked at us again, and — I swear — winked. He left the same way he came.

"Lion," said the guard. What else could he say?

Neither of us moved for a minute. We heard screams from the other rooms. People ran through the courtyard in every direction, hollering in foreign languages. A small girl in a dress printed with giant sunflowers stood alone beneath the colonnade, hands covering her ears, eyes clenched shut.

They closed the museum for the remainder of the afternoon and all of us witnesses had to answer questions for hours — the police, the Park Service rangers, the television and newspaper reporters. I was interviewed on camera and then stood to the side, listening to the other accounts. A group of schoolchildren and chaperones from Buffalo had seen the lion walk out the museum's front door, search the sky like a farmer hoping for rain clouds, and walk slowly east. A bicycle courier spotted the lion on Park Avenue and promptly pedaled into a sewer grate, flipping over the handlebars and smashing his head against the curb. He spoke to the reporters while a paramedic wrapped gauze bandages around his forehead. After Park Avenue, the lion seemed to disappear. A special police unit had scoured the surrounding blocks and found nothing. New Yorkers were being advised to stay indoors until further notice, advice that nobody took.

After all the interviews were over, the guard found me sitting on the bench by the frog fountain. "That was something," he said. "I need a beer. You want to get a beer somewhere?"

"I do," I said. "I really do."

We went to the Madison Pub, a dark old speakeasy where the gold-lettered names of long-dead regulars scrolled down the walls. We didn't say much during the first beer, didn't even exchange names until the food came.

"Louis Butchko," I said, repeating the name to help me remember it. My father had taught me that trick.

"Mmm." He was chewing on a well-done cheeseburger. "Most people call me Butchko."

"He winked at us. Did you notice that? The lion, he winked."

"Hmm?"

"I'm telling you, I saw him wink. He looked right at us and winked."

"Maybe. I didn't see it. One thing's for sure," he said, licking his lips, "they didn't mention lions when I applied for the job. Mostly they're afraid of people touching the paintings."

"He winked."

"I thought maybe a lunatic splashing yellow paint on the Titians, something like that, but lions? I ought to get, what do they call it, danger pay? Hazard pay?"

The bartender, an old Cypriot with dyed black hair who had worked in the pub since my father first took me there as a child, rubbed down the zinc bar top with a rag and a spray bottle. He whistled a tune that I could not place, a famous melody. It was maddening, the simple, evasive music.

"How long have you been here?" I asked Butchko.

"New York? Nine months. Down on Delancey."

"I like that neighborhood. You mind if I ask what you're paying?"

He took the pickle off his bun and offered it to me. It was a good pickle. "One-fifty."

"One-fifty? What does that mean?"

"One hundred and fifty dollars. A month."

I stared at him, waiting for an explanation.

"Come over and see the place sometime. I got a great deal. I met the superintendent and we worked it out. You know, New York is very expensive."

"Yes," I said.

"I didn't really have the money to move here, but it's one of the requirements. As a title holder."

"What title?" I examined his scrawny neck, his small white hands. "You're not a boxer?"

"Nope." He smiled, bits of blackened beef on his lips, in his teeth. "Nothing like that."

"You're going to make me guess? You're Anastasia, daughter of the czar?"

"It's something I kind of have to keep a low profile about. No publicity."

I sighed and waited.

"All right," he said, "all right. But you can't go around telling people. It's part of the deal; I have to keep it undercover. I'm the Lover," he said, beaming a little in spite of himself.

"Okay," I said. "Whose lover?"

"No, *the* Lover. Capital L."

"Right," I said, finishing my beer. The bartender, quartering limes, kept whistling his one song. "You're a porn star."

"No," he said, offended. "Nothing like that." He looked around the shadowy barroom, making sure nobody was within hearing distance. "The Lover of the East Coast. I'm the Greatest Lover on the East Coast. Not counting Florida — they're independent."

I smiled at him happily. The great thing about New York is that no matter how insane you are, the next man over is bound to be twice as bad.

"What is there," I asked him, "a tournament?"

"It's not something you compete for," said Butchko. "It's more like the poet laureate. The last guy, Gregory Santos, he lives up in the Bronx, near Mosholu Parkway. Really nice guy. He took me out for drinks when I got the title, told me how to handle certain situations. He said it would change my whole life. The pressure is — I mean, women have *expectations* now. It's like being the New York Yankees."

I was pondering that for a while. The New York Yankees? No other customers remained in the pub, just the two of us and the bartender whistling. I imagined the Cypriot coming to work on the subway, head buried in the newspaper, while a small black-eyed girl sitting next to him whistled notes she heard at breakfast from her father's razor-nicked lips, notes her father heard the night before as he stood in the crowded elevator and watched the lighted floor numbers count down.

I concentrated on Butchko's sallow face, the purple blooms below his eyes. Studying a face will keep things quiet for a while. I tried to imagine that this was the man millions of East Coast women fantasized about while doodling in the margins of crossword puzzles. I tried to imagine him mounting bliss-faced seductees from the northern tip of Maine to Georgia, whispering in their ears, making them go all epileptic, their skin stretched so tight over rioting nerves that one touch in the right place would send them ricocheting around the room like an unknotted balloon.

I could picture the rapturous women because I had read about them in novels, had seen them in movies, but I had never held one in my arms. I had not touched a naked breast since the day my mother weaned me. The only contact I had with women was incidental: the brush of a supermarket clerk's fingers as she handed me my change, or an old lady tapping my shoulder, asking me to move aside so she could step off the bus. Like my beloved Saint Francis, I was a virgin.

"So what happened," I asked Butchko, "your high school girlfriend said you were the greatest?" I was trying to figure the origins of his fantasy.

He seemed mystified by the question. "Well, yeah."

There was something appealing about him. His delusions had originality, at least. All the other New York immigrants think they're the greatest actor, artist, writer, whatever — it was nice to meet the greatest lover.

The whistling Cypriot would never quit. Verse chorus verse chorus verse. If there was a bridge, the man didn't know it. I dug my knuckles into the corners of my eye sockets and breathed deeply.

"Mackenzie? You okay?"

"This *song,*" I whispered. "What is this song he's whistling?"

"'Paper Moon,'" said Butchko. He sang to the Cypriot's accompaniment: *"Say, it's only a paper moon, sailing over a cardboard sea, but it wouldn't be make-believe, if you believed in me."* Butchko's voice was gorgeous, a pitch-perfect tenor, and for a moment I believed everything, all of it, the cities, towns, and countrysides full of quivering women sloshing about their bathtubs, moaning his name, *Butchko, Butchko,* wetting a thousand tiled floors in their delirium.

"Lion," he said, plowing the ketchup on his plate with the tines of his fork. "My first lion."

As soon as I got home I began preparing the house for my father, transferring six steaks from the freezer to the refrigerator, vacuuming the carpet in the master bedroom, winding each of the antique clocks, stacking the logs and kindling in the library's fireplace, arranging the ivory chess pieces in their proper formations. I knew that he would have heard about the lion, that he would be on a plane crossing the Atlantic. We lived in a turn-of-the-century brownstone, the façade adorned with wine-grape clusters and leering satyrs. My room was on the top floor, beneath a skylight of pebbled glass. After the house was made ready for its master, I locked myself in my bedroom and turned off the lights.

Not counting the skylight, there was only one window in my room, as small and round as a porthole, facing south. Next to this window, mounted on a tripod, stood a brass telescope that my father had given me for my twelfth birthday. The telescope had once belonged to the Confederate general Jubal Early; his monogram was stamped into the brass below the eyepiece. Our house stood on the highest hill in Yorkville and the vista must have been pretty before the surrounding apartment towers rose up to steal the sunlight. The resultant view was of the building directly south of us, a redbrick Goliath of forty stories. The upper floors made for poor spying — I could only see into the apartments nearly level with my own room. Humbled telescope: once employed to track Union troop movements in the Shenandoah Valley, now trained on the cramped quarters of New Yorkers: a red-haired woman watching television with a thermometer in her mouth; four young girls sitting cross-legged on the living room rug, folding origami cranes; an old man, bare-chested, arms folded on the windowsill, looking over me to Harlem; two women, one old, one young, slow-dancing in the kitchen; a small boy with a bowl haircut, wearing Superman pajamas, lying in bed reading a book.

I was watching the night this boy's mother first brought him home from the hospital, bundled in blue blankets. I was watching when he learned to crawl, took his first steps, met his new puppy on Christmas morning. It sounds sinister, I know, the spying. It sounds creepy. Believe what you will, I cannot stop you, but the truth is, I loved that boy as a baby brother. I've always been a coward but I would have been ferocious in his defense. Night after night I would look in on him, to make sure he slept safely, the

Babar night-light glowing in his doorway, a cup of water by his bedside. When his mother held her hand against his damp forehead, I would feel the fever surge in sympathy through my own body.

I focused on the cover of the boy's book. *The Count of Monte Cristo*. He was awfully bright, this kid; he devoured novels in the nighttime while his parents slept. A real prodigy, making me proud. I watched over him until he switched off the light, and then I swept over the other rooms of the apartment to make sure everything was safe. Sometimes I half hoped to see smoke pouring from the toaster oven so that I could call the fire department and watch the snorkel truck raise its boom to the little boy's window, watch the fireman pluck him from danger. Sinister, creepy, I won't defend myself. I was lonely. If there is a witness to my soul, He knows the truth, and I am calm in that judgment.

When I was satisfied that the boy was safe I capped the telescope's lens and eyepiece, undressed, climbed into bed. It was a marvelous bed, with four tall cedar wood posts and handwoven mosquito netting from the Ivory Coast. There weren't many mosquitoes in the brownstone, but I loved how the netting endlessly swayed in the air conditioner's breeze, pale lungs inhaling and exhaling.

Rain pounded the pebbled glass of my skylight, the hoof steps of a cavalry brigade heard from a great distance. It was almost dawn. The house was less empty than it had been. I pulled on a pair of green plaid pajamas and walked downstairs, knocked on the door of the master bedroom.

"Come in," called my father.

I opened the door. He sat cross-legged on the floor, the parts of his rifle disassembled, gleaming and oiled, on a spotted towel thrown over his steamer trunk. He wore his undershirt and a grass-stained pair of khakis; wire-framed glasses; a black steel wristwatch with a nonreflective face, the gift of a Ugandan general.

If you are sitting in your home, late at night, alone, strange noises echoing down the hallways, disturbing your mind, and if you look out across the street, look through the window of a stranger's apartment, the apartment lit only by the television's static, and the stranger's room glows a cool and eerie blue — that was the exact color of my father's eyes.

He wiped his hands clean on a corner of the towel, stood up, walked over, and clasped my shoulders, kissed me on the forehead. "You look thin."

"I was sick for a while. I'm okay."

"You're eating?" He watched me carefully. I was never able to lie to my father. I mean, I was able to lie to him but I never got away with it.

"I forget sometimes." That was the truth. On bad days the idea of food, of eating, seemed somehow ridiculous, or indulgent.

He walked over to his desk, a gorgeous roll-top of luminous mahogany that had supposedly belonged to Stonewall Jackson. Hanging on the wall above the desk were four masks — carved wood embellished with feathers and shredded raffia — that my father had bought in Mali. Each represented a figure from the old Bambaran saying: *What is a crow but a dove dipped in pitch? And what is a man but a dog cursed with words?*

My father pulled a sheaf of fax papers from his desktop and looked through them. "I saw your name in here. You were one of the witnesses?"

"He winked at me."

My father continued reading through the papers, holding them at arm's length because his prescription was too weak and he never bothered to get reexamined. Being farsighted had little effect on his aim, though. I remember reading a profile of my father in a glossy hunting magazine; accompanying the article was a photograph of a silver dollar that had been neatly doughnutted by a high-caliber bullet. The caption below the picture read: "SHOT BY MACGREGOR BONNER AT 400 YARDS IN THE TRANSVAAL (PRONE POSITION)." My father had bet a drunk Johannesburg socialite one thousand dollars that he could make the shot; when the woman paid up she told him, "I hope I never make you angry, Bonner."

My father read through the fax papers and I said again, "He

winked at me. The lion. He was staring right at me and then he winked and then he walked away."

My father removed his glasses and hung them, by one stem, from the neck of his undershirt. He pinched the bridge of his nose for a moment and then laughed.

"All mammals blink, Mackenzie. It keeps the eyeballs from drying out."

"Wink, not blink. He winked at me."

"Okay, he winked at you. Why don't you go back to sleep for a while. I'll make us a big brunch later on."

I went to my room and burrowed deep beneath the sheets, listened to my own breathing and the morning rain. In the strange space between sleeping and waking I imagined myself lionized. I paced the avenues, mane dreadlocked by city dirt. I met my stone brothers on the public library's steps; I sat with them and watched the beat cop pass, orange poncho clad, walkie-talkie chattering on his hip. I went underground, below the sidewalks, prowled the subway tunnels. The big-bellied rats fled when they smelled my hide. I curled up beside a soliloquizing madman, a filthy bundle of piss-damp rags, once a babe in a cradle, a shiny possibility. I licked the tears from his face and he buried his head in my mane. Soon he slept, and it was the first good sleep he'd had in years. Nothing could hurt him now; he was safe between the lion's paws.

Nobody saw the lion for the next five days. Wildlife experts on television speculated on his disappearance and proposed various possibilities for his whereabouts, but nobody knew anything. My father met with the chief of police and the mayor to coordinate the hunt. He inspected the sites where the lion had been seen and carefully studied all the eyewitness reports. In the terse interviews he gave to carefully chosen members of the press, he urged the public to remain cautious. He believed that the lion was still on the island of Manhattan.

Six days after I first saw the lion, on a humid afternoon — the kind when every surface is wet to the touch, as if the city itself were sweating — Butchko called and invited me to come over. I had forgotten that I gave him my number, and at first I was reluctant to go all the way downtown in the miserable August heat. But I had nothing better to do and I was curious to get a look at his $150 apartment.

I met him on the stoop of his building. Before I could speak he raised a finger to his lips and motioned me to sit beside him. The hysterical dialogue of a Puerto Rican soap opera spilled from the open window of the first-floor apartment. I let the language wash over me, the rolling *r*'s, the sentences that all seemed to rhyme. Every few minutes I'd recognize a word and nod. *Loco! Cerveza! Gato!*

"*Te quiero,*" said Butchko, practicing the accent during a commercial break. "*Te quiero, te quiero, te quiero.*"

"You speak Spanish?"

"I'm learning. Gregory Santos said bilinguality is one of the seven steps to the full-out shudders."

Bilinguality? "What's the full-out —"

The soap opera came on again and Butchko hushed me. We listened to a hoarse-voiced man calm a distraught woman. A swell of violins and cellos seemed to signal their reconciliation and I imagined the kiss, the woman's eyes closed, tears of happiness rolling down her face as the darkly handsome man wrapped her in his arms. Butchko nodded solemnly, stroking his chin. When the show ended he led me into the brownstone and up a poorly lit staircase, pointing out various obstacles to avoid: a dog-shit footprint, a toy car, broken glass. At the top of the last flight of stairs he pushed open a graffiti-tagged door and led me onto the tarpapered roof. A water tower squatted on steel legs alongside a shingled pigeon coop.

"You hang out up here?" I asked.

"This is home," he said, closing the door behind me and securing it with a combination lock. "Look," he said, pointing. "That's a pigeon coop."

"I know it's a pigeon coop."

"Ask me why it has two doors."

The coop was windowless and low-slung, narrow and long,

hammered together of weathered gray boards. Splits in the wood had been stuffed with pink fiberglass insulation. A yellow door hung crooked in its frame on one end; I circled around the coop and found an equally crooked red door on the opposite end.

"Why does it have two doors?"

"Because if it had four doors it would be a pigeon sedan."

He was so happy with the joke his face turned bright red. He opened up his mouth and shined his big white Pennsylvania teeth at me. "Oh, Mackenzie. You walked right into that one."

I opened the red door and stepped inside. There were no pigeon cubbies, just a green sleeping bag, patched in places with electrical tape, rolled out on the bare wood flooring; a space heater, unplugged for the summer; a clock radio playing jazz; a blue milk crate stacked with paperbacks; an electric water boiler; and a pyramid of instant ramen noodles in styrofoam cups. The wires ran into a surge protector connected to a thick yellow extension cord that snaked down a neatly bored hole in the floor.

"The super sets me up with electric," said Butchko, standing in the doorway behind me. We had to stoop to fit below the steeply canted ceiling. "Pretty good deal, I think."

"Don't you get cold up here?" Even with the space heater at full blast, the coop could not be good shelter in the depths of winter.

Butchko shrugged. "I don't sleep here most nights, you know?"

I picked a paperback off the top of the pile. *The Selected Poetry of Robert Browning*. I read a few lines, then returned the book to its brothers. "There's a toilet somewhere?"

"Down in the basement. And a shower, too. If I need to pee I just go off the roof, see how far I can get. Here, look at this." He ushered me out of the converted coop to the edge of the roof. We leaned against the parapet and looked at the brick wall of the building opposite us. "See the fire escape? I hit it the other day. What do you think, twenty feet across?"

With my eyes I followed the ladders and landings of the fire escape down to the alley below, deserted save for a blue Dumpster overflowing with trash.

"It's just rats down there anyway," said Butchko. "They don't mind a little pee. Or maybe they do, but screw 'em, they're rats. And then, here, this is the best part. Come over here."

In the cool shadow of the water tower he grabbed a canteen off the tarpaper and began climbing the steel rungs welded onto one of the tower's legs. I walked back into the sunlight to watch his ascent. At the upper lip of the tower he turned and waved to me, thirty feet below, before pulling himself over the edge and disappearing from view. A minute later he started climbing down. He jumped with five feet to go and hit his landing perfectly.

"Here," he said, offering me the canteen. I drank cold water.

"There's a tap up there for the inspectors. They come twice a year and check things out, make sure there's no bacteria or whatnot floating around."

I handed him back the canteen and watched him drink, watched his heavy Adam's apple bob in his throat.

"Are you ever going to tell me what the full-out shudders are?"

Butchko grinned. "Come on, Mackenzie, you've been there."

"Where?"

He capped the canteen and laid it down in the shade of the tower. "The shudders are reality," he said, and by the way he said it I knew he was quoting. "The shudders are the no-lie reality. Listen, women are very different from men."

"Oh! Ah!"

"Well, okay, it sounds obvious, but it's important. For a man, sex is simple. He gets in and he gets off. But it's not automatic for a woman."

It wasn't automatic for me, either, but I kept my mouth shut.

"The thing is, women are more sensitive than men. They don't want to hurt our feelings."

"Ha," I countered.

"In general," he said. "So they act, sometimes. They pretend. Now, for me, given my circumstances, it's very important that I know exactly what works and what doesn't. And I can't rely on what she's saying, or the groaning, the moaning, the breathing, none of that. Arching the back, curling the foot, biting the lip — none of that is a sure thing. Only the shudders. There's no faking the full-out shudders. You see those thighs start to quiver, I mean *quiver,* you know you found the pearl. Oysters and pearls, Mackenzie. Everybody knows where the oyster is — finding the pearl is what makes a good lover."

I stared at the water tower looming above us. The kid was a genuine lunatic, but I liked him.

"I'll tell you the first thing I learned, living in the city," said Butchko. "Puerto Rican women are excellent lovers."

"All of them?"

"Yes," he said. "All of them."

I smoked Lucky Strikes on the rooftop and talked with Butchko about women and lions until he told me he had to get ready for his date. Twenty minutes later I was riding the First Avenue bus uptown. "Air conditioner's broken," the driver told me before I stepped on. "There's another bus right behind me." He said the same thing to everyone, and everyone besides me grunted and waited for the next bus, but I paid the fare and sat in the back row. My decision displeased the driver. I think he wanted to drive his hot empty bus at high speeds, slamming on the brakes at red lights with no passengers to complain. I wouldn't have said a word. He could have cruised up the avenue at ninety miles per hour, swerving around the potholes; it didn't matter to me. I was easy.

When we passed under the Queensboro Bridge I saw the lion. I shouted, a wordless shout, and the driver looked at me in his mirror and hit the brakes, as simple as that, as if he were used to riders shouting when they wanted to get off. I shoved through the heavy double doors at the rear of the bus and ran back to the bridge, under the shadowy barrel vault.

It could be that I read too much in a wink, and I wouldn't have been the first, but it seemed to me that the lion knew who I was. I believed that. I believed that the lion had a message for me, that the lion had come Lord knows how many miles in search of me, had evaded countless hunters in order to deliver his intelligence. Now he was here and my father had been hired to kill him. The lion would never make it back to Africa.

He waited for me on the sidewalk below the bridge. Flies crawled in the tangles of his mane. He watched me with yellow eyes. His hide sagged over his bones; the sore on his shoulder was inflamed, graveled with white pustules. His belly was distended, bloated from hunger. I thought of how far he was from home, how many thousands of miles he had traveled, so far from the zebras and wildebeests, the giraffes and antelopes of his native land, his nourishment. Here there were only people to eat. I could not imagine this lion stooping to devour the neighborhood mutts or the blinkered carriage horses.

I wondered how long it would take him to gobble me down, and how much it would hurt, the long white teeth, the massive jaws, how long, and would he strip me to the wet bone or leave some meat for the pigeons to peck at, would he spit out my knuckles and watch them roll like gambler's dice, would he chew through my spine and suck out the marrow, would he look up from my carcass, his muzzle painted red, watch the taxis race by like stray gazelles frantic for their herd?

"Speak to me," I pleaded, hungry for revelation. "Speak to me."

If you have ever stood near a lion, you understand humility. Nothing that lives is more beautiful. A four-hundred-pound lion can run down a thoroughbred, can tear through steel railroad car doors with his claws, can hump his mate eighty times in one day.

The lion rose to all fours and walked closer, until his whiskers were nearly brushing against my shirt. I closed my eyes and waited. The carnivorous stink of him, the low purr of his breathing, the mighty engine of him — I was ready. I got down on my knees on the sidewalk, below the Queensboro Bridge, and the lion's breath was hot as steam in my ear.

When I opened my eyes the lion was gone and I was shivering in the August heat. I hailed a taxi and directed the turbaned driver to the Frick museum, but when I got there the front doors of the old robber baron's mansion were bolted shut. It was Monday, I remembered. The museum was closed. That's why Butchko was home. It was the worst possible time to be Monday, and I imagined that all days would now be Monday, that we would suffer through months of Mondays, that the office workers would rise day after day and never come closer to the weekend, they would check the newspaper each morning and groan, and the church-goers would find themselves, perpetually, a day too late for the Sabbath.

I needed Bellini's Francis. I needed to stand with the virgin saint and experience the ecstasy, to feel the rapture driven through my palms, my feet. I needed to understand the language of animals, the words of the beasts, because when the lion whispered in my ear it sounded like nothing but the breath of a big cat. I needed translation.

I walked all the way home. The house was empty, every clock ticking solemnly until — in the space of a terrifying second — they yodeled the hour in unison. Whenever my father was in Africa I would quit winding the clocks; in every room their dead hands would mark the minute the pendulum stopped swinging. He always synchronized them the day he came home.

In my bedroom I uncapped the telescope's lens and eyepiece and studied the apartments across the street. My little brother was away — at a baseball game, I imagined. He rooted for the Mets and had their pennant on his wall. In the next apartment over, the old man leaned against his windowsill, gazing toward Harlem. The redhead one floor below him seemed healthier; she lay belly down on her carpeted floor, propped on her elbows, chewing a pencil, still working on Sunday's crossword. Behind her, on the television, Marlon Brando smooched Eva Marie Saint. The red-head never turned the TV off — not when she was away at work, not when she was sleeping. I understood — voices comforted her, even strangers' voices.

These people were my friends, my comrades. I cared about them, but I wanted that building to slide aside for the afternoon. I wanted a clear prospect of the entire city. I was looking for a lion and a blue-eyed hunter.

The redhead finished her crossword and began checking her answers against the solution in Monday's paper. The television behind her flashed an urgent graphic: BREAKING NEWS. A reporter wearing a safari hat and sunglasses began speaking into his microphone, gesturing to the crowd surrounding him. I tried to read his lips. Bored of the game, I was about to swing the telescope away when I saw the lion, *my* lion, staring into the camera. He sat by a fountain, a great round fountain with a winged angel standing above the waters.

I ran. Down the stairs, out the door, west on Eighty-fourth Street, dodging the street traffic, dashing across the avenues, York First Second Third Lexington Park Madison Fifth, into Central Park, panting, sweat pouring into my eyes. All the way to Bethesda Terrace, at least a mile, farther than I had run in years. When I got there the crowd bulged way back to the band shell, hundreds of yards from the fountain. A man with a pushcart sold Italian ices and sodas. A news helicopter circled above us.

I shoved and sidled my way to the front lines, ignoring the dirty looks, the muttered heys, watchits, and yos. Blue police sawhorses barricaded the way, a cop stationed every ten feet. Two curving stone staircases flanked by balustrades swept down to the terrace. The lion sat patiently by the angel fountain. Behind him was the stagnant pond where paddleboating tourists typically photographed the bushes and collided with each other and cursed in every language known to man. They had all been evacuated. I saw my father, halfway down the steps, on one knee, holding his rifle. Two Park Service rangers stood next to him, high-powered dart guns aimed at the lion. Police sharpshooters ringed the terrace.

At the back of the crowd people yelled and whistled and laughed, but up close, in view of the lion, there was cathedral silence. My father gave the order and the rangers pulled their triggers. Darts fly far slower than bullets; I could trace their black flight from gun barrels to lion shoulder.

The lion roared. His jaws swung open and he roared. All the birds sitting in the trees burst from their branches and squawked skyward, a panicked flight of pigeons and sparrows. Everyone leaning against the barricades fell back, the entire crowd retreating a step as instincts commanded: *run, run, run! A* lion's roar can be heard for five miles in the emptiness of the savanna. Even in Manhattan his protest echoed above the constant squall of car alarms and ambulance sirens, above the whistles of traffic cops and the low rumble of subway trains. I imagine that sunbathers in the Sheep Meadow heard the roar, and tourists in Strawberry Fields; that bicyclists squeezed their hand brakes and stood on their pedals, squinted through their sunglasses in the direction of the noise; that old men, piloting their remote-controlled miniature schooners across the algae-filmed water of the Boat Pond, looked north, leaving their ships to drift; that dog walkers watched their charges go rigid, prick up their ears, then bark madly, until all the dogs in the borough were howling; that every domestic cat sitting on a windowsill stared heartlessly toward the park and licked its paws clean.

The lion stood unsteadily, blinking up at the sun. He began to walk, headed for the staircase, but stumbled after a few paces. Everyone in the crowd inhaled at the same moment. My father gave another command and two more darts pierced the lion's hide, releasing their tranquilizers. The rangers cradled their guns in their arms and waited; four darts were enough to put a rhino to sleep.

The lion charged. He reached the steps so quickly that none of the sharpshooters had time to react; he bounded up the broad stone stairs, white fangs bared, while the rangers fumbled with their guns and the cops standing near me said *Jesus Christ* and backed into the sawhorses and mothers in the crowd covered their children's eyes.

In midleap the lion seemed to crash into an invisible wall; he twisted in the air and landed heavily on his side, front paws two steps above his hind paws. The rifle shot sounded as loud and final as a vault door slamming shut. My father ejected the spent shell and it glittered in the air before bouncing off the balustrade and into the vegetation below. I ducked under the sawhorse, evading the dazed policemen, and ran down the stairs. My father saw me coming and shouted my name, but I was past him before he could stop me. I knelt down beside the lion and held his furred skull in my palms, my forearms buried in his dirty mane. He seemed smaller now, shrunken. The blood puddling beneath him began to drip down the steps.

"Tell me," I begged him, looking into his yellow eyes. My father was coming for me. I lowered my head so that my right ear rested against the lion's damp muzzle. "Tell me."

A series of violent spasms ran down the length of his outstretched body. Each breath exited his lungs with an unnerving whistle. His jaws slowly parted. I closed my eyes and waited. He licked my face with his mighty tongue until my father collared me and dragged me aside. I did not watch the mercy shot.

Hours later, when I stood in the shower and let the hot water beat down on me, I picked three blue splinters from my palms. It took me a while to figure out that they came from gripping the police sawhorse by Bethesda Terrace. After the shower I toweled myself dry, pulled on my pajamas, climbed the stairs to my bedroom, locked the door behind me, and switched off the lights. A pale moon shone weakly through the pebbled glass. I tried to remember how many miles away she was, how many cold miles of sky I would need to climb. It seemed impossible to me that men had ever walked there, had ever cavorted in her loose gravity.

When I was young I had known the number, known her distance to the mile. I had known her diameter, her weight in metric tons, the names of her major craters, the precise duration of her orbit around the earth. I forgot everything.

I uncapped General Early's telescope and scanned the apartments opposite. Whatever the old man was looking for in Harlem, he had quit for the night — the lamps were all out and the shades drawn. My little brother was awake. He sat beneath his sheets with a flashlight — a one-boy tent — furtively reading when he was supposed to be sleeping. I watched him for an hour, until I felt the calm blood return, flowing through the arteries and capillaries, delivering peace and oxygen to every living cell.

I checked the other rooms in my customary search for fire, and this night I found it. Not in the boy's apartment but one flight down, candles burning atop the stereo speakers and bookshelves, the coffee table and turned-off television, the windowsill and mantel. The redhead, naked, straddled a man on her sofa, her hands resting on his narrow shoulders. In the candlelight her flanks were mapped with copper trails of sweat. She rose and fell like a buoy in the sea, bobbing with the waves. Before I turned away, to give them their privacy, the woman flung her head back and stiffened for an instant, her hands falling from Butchko, her fingers spread wide. Her mouth opened but I'm sure no words came out, no words at all, nothing but ecstasy.

CHRISTOPHER BUCKLEY

∎

# We Have a Pope!

FROM *Atlantic Monthly*

RICK RENARD DOES NOT normally write about his clients. I'm a PR guy. I do not go in for titles like "strategic communicator," as do many of my colleagues in the Washington, D.C., spindustry. At any rate, writing about clients in a national magazine is not part of the job. The idea, greatly boiled down, is to make them look good. But since there's been so much in the media recently about my role in trying to help elect an American pope, the record could use a little, shall we say, straightening.

Two months ago I was in my office on K Street, this being where my professional ilk tend to have their offices, brainstorming how to persuade a Senate subcommittee to grant one of my clients a tax deduction for his herd of buffalo, on the grounds that they emit less methane than cows, when my assistant, LaMoyne, buzzed to inform me that Bernard Baroom was on the phone.

"*The* Bernard Baroom?" I said. LaMoyne sighed. "No, the *other* Bernard Baroom." LaMoyne — he's not French, he's from Indiana — is capable of attitude, but he is efficient and more or less runs Renard Strategic Planning International, that being the name of my company. We have mailboxes in Toronto, Geneva, and Kuala Lumpur, which makes us international. We're planning to expand. At any rate, I took the call from Bernard Baroom.

He dispensed with the usual pleasantries. It's my experience of billionaire financiers — not that I have had nearly enough experience of them — that they come right to the point, time being money. His car would pick me up in ten minutes. He didn't bother to inquire whether I was available. A billionaire financier expects a PR man to be available at any time, even if you are in the middle of sex or a Botox injection.

LaMoyne was impressed. He'd seen the Baroom mansion in Upperburg, Virginia, featured in the pages of *Opulent Domicile* magazine.

"Twelve pages," he said. "A bit baronial for my *goût*."

"Goo?"

"*Goût*. Taste."

He does this, LaMoyne, which drives me nuts; but as I say, he's efficient. "Private chapel. Don't see many of *those* anymore. Bet there's a dungeon too. Strange duck, that one."

"He's the fourteenth richest duck in the United States, according to *Forbes*. Call the mink ranchers and tell them I've been summoned to a meeting at the White House." That always impresses them.

The Minnesota Mink Ranchers Association was a client. The anti-fur people were sneaking in at night and shaving the minks. I was gearing up a media campaign to highlight just how awful minks really are. Nature doesn't come redder in tooth and claw, as the saying goes, than mink. Vicious little devils. This is the part of the job I really enjoy — the learning about different things.

Baroom's Cadillac Sixteen was waiting for me. You know you're off to a good start when they send a quarter-million-dollar chauffeur-driven car for you.

It was an hour's ride to the Baroom abode, the last ten minutes spent going up the driveway. Bernard Baroom had started out with condom dispensers in public men's rooms and was now the chairman of three companies listed on the stock exchange. His private secretary was English. "Ah, Mr. *Renard*, Mr. *Baroom* is expecting you." Recently rich Americans love that. Well, I suppose all Americans are recently rich, more or less.

Mr. *Baroom* was in his study — one of those walnut and mahogany jobs with this very solemn feeling to it, as if it were designed to deliver grave news in. There were these religious-themed paintings on the walls: Madonnas, a Saint Sebastian — the one stuck full of arrows who provided inspiration for all those Italian paint-ers. Above him was one showing Jesus driving the moneychang-ers from the Temple. The nameplate on it said EL GRECO, which is Spanish for "Ten Million." My kind of client.

Baroom did not rise from his chair. The very rich are different from you and me, as the late F. Scott Fitzgerald observed: they don't bother to get up when you walk into the room.

He was reading a thick file marked RENARD. He said without looking up, "You used to work for Nick Naylor."

Nick Naylor, of course, is a legend. It was Nick who mounted the final public relations battle on behalf of the tobacco industry. It was a magnificent last stand, the Little Bighorn of that war. Nick went down, but gloriously. After he got out of prison, he moved to California and now represents movie stars. Not my goo, but who could blame him? He'd earned his lounge chair by the pool. A lot of people in Washington pretend they never knew him. Not Rick Renard. I learned a lot from Nick. More or less everything, really, when you come right down to it. I'm proud to have worked for him.

"Well," I said, "that was a long time ago."

He closed the file and shook his head. "Maybe that explains why I can't find a single instance in your entire curriculum vitae where you let something as trivial as principle get in the way."

I figured that Bernard Baroom had not sent his $250,000 to fetch me so that he could lecture me on ethics. A smile spread across his face like lard melting in a skillet.

"Mr. Renard, I have made a lot of money in my life. A tremen-dous amount of money."

I wasn't quite sure how to respond. "That's just great, sir!" didn't feel quite right.

"Now I want to give something back."

Aha. I do a little teaching on the side, at Martha Washington University School of Strategic Planning, and I tell my graduate students, "When the really rich announce that they want to give something back, be there, with buckets."

"How can I help, sir?"

"The pope isn't expected to live out the week. I want the next pope to be an American."

I also tell my graduate students, "Don't expel your beverage through your nostrils when the really rich demand the impossible. There's a fortune's worth of billable hours between 'What an interesting idea' and 'Well, we tried.'"

"Do you follow the cardinals, Mr. Renard?"

I was about to reply that I'd once lost five hundred dollars on the World Series when I realized he was talking about the College of Cardinals, not St. Louis.

"More or less."

"My sources say it's going to be Arooba, the Nigerian. Or that Mexican." He grunted with evident displeasure. "What are you hearing?"

*Improvise, Renard,* I said to myself. I managed to cough up some ambiguous gargle about how "the Filipino is showing surprising strength." There had to be at least one Filipino cardinal, I figured. Very Catholic country, the Philippines.

"God forbid they should elect a pope from a country that's solved the problem of indoor *plumbing,*" he said. "It's like the UN." He leaned back with a squeak of expensive leather. "The French want it, you know. So bad they can taste it. They're already in there maneuvering, cutting their deals. Their little cheesy *deals.* Can you imagine a *French* pope?"

"Mr. Baroom," I said, "I don't even want to think about that. But, sir, these recent, uh, developments . . ." I thought "developments" sounded better than "widespread pedophile scandals." "How do you see that, that is, in the context of electing an American pope? Give me the benefit of your input here." I tell my graduate students that this is a way of saying to the client, *Were you on drugs, or just drunk, when you came up with this idea?*

He glowered at me. "You saying that Saint Peter, the first pope, was perfect?"

"Well —"

"Didn't he deny knowing Jesus three *times?*"

"You have me there."

"'Thou art Peter, and upon this rock I will build my church.' Matthew 16:18."

"Beautifully quoted, sir. But paying hush money to — well, I'm not a theologian."

"These scandals give us an advantage going in."

"I hadn't thought of that."

*Just Because He Shuffled Pedophiles Around and Paid Hush Money Doesn't Mean He Wouldn't Make a Fabulous Pope.* It wasn't sticking to my bumper.

"It's the last thing anyone would expect. You know the saying: 'He who enters a conclave *papabile* leaves a cardinal.'"

That old chestnut. Of course. I gave a sort of low chuckle by way of pretending that I knew exactly what he was talking about. Later I learned that *papabile* is not a kind of pasta but means "pope-able." That is, electable. Whatever.

"I want to show you something." Baroom pressed a hidden switch and a panel slid back, revealing a stone staircase going down. I thought, *Uh-oh.* I followed him, my hand inside my pocket nervously gripping my cell phone, ready to dial 911 at the first sign of someone wearing a hood.

It turned out to be his relic room. I'd bet you that not many billionaire homes have a relic room. It wasn't included in the *Opulent Domicile* spread. He had accumulated quite the collection: Saint Theresa of Ávila's toenail; a lock of Saint Francis of Assisi's hair; enough bones to make three skeletons, including a femur that once belonged to Saint Jerome of Illyria. Also Saint Tatiana's knuckle.

"She's more venerated in the East," he explained, "but I always had a sweet spot for her." The pièce de résistance was Mary Magdalene's tooth. "Third molar," he pointed out. You could barely see the tooth for all the gold and rubies and diamonds it had been mounted on, by some czar of the fifteenth century mainly famous for impaling several thousand recalcitrant peasants on stakes.

I had a *Beam me up, Scotty* moment.

Back in his study and badly in need of a drink, I said thoughtfully, "Mr. Baroom, this isn't going to be easy." I tell my graduate students this is a tactful way of saying *I'm going to want a lot of money.*

He took a fountain pen and scribbled on a piece of paper and slid it across the table. It was an impressive number, with a beautiful string of zeros, like a strand of pearls. It was a number that you could retire on. I found myself thinking, *You know, maybe it is time that we had a pope.*

"This would be the fee for a successful outcome?" I asked.

He took back the piece of paper and drew a line through a few of the pearls. "Your retainer. Make it happen and I'll add those zeros back."

"There will be expenses, of course."

"Look, Mr. Renard," he said in that annoyed-billionaire way, "that's just not a problem. You get to work. Once the Holy Father passes, there's only a couple weeks before the conclave. There's no time to waste."

On the way down the driveway I looked back and saw white smoke coming out the chimney of his study. That's what they send up the chimney of the Sistine Chapel to announce that they've elected a new pope.

Back at the office LaMoyne said, "So?"

"You were right about the dungeon."

"I knew he was kinky."

"You have no idea."

Baroom had given me the name of a contact at the AAPC — the American Association of Princes of the Church, one of Washington's more elite trade associations. You have to be a cardinal to belong.

There was a man standing outside the AAPC headquarters with a sign that said HANDS OFF THE ALTAR BOYS!

It's always a challenge when your candidates for pope are being picketed for sex offenses with minors. Monsignor Murphy had told me over the phone to go in the back way. I was tempted to say something, but didn't. I tell my graduate students, "Don't tease the client about sex scandals until you've established a good working relationship."

Monsignor Murphy was the executive director of the AAPC. He was in his mid-fifties, pudgy, with an Irish accent and intense black eyes. A chain smoker. He didn't look like he'd slept much lately.

"So you've met Bernard," he said, exhaling a lungful of unfiltered cigarette smoke. "Did he show you Saint Tatiana's knuckle?"

"Very impressive."

"He's on to a dealer in Istanbul who claims to have part of Saint Paul's pelvis. He's like a boy in his enthusiasms, bless his heart. So, we're going to have an American pope, are we? Well, splendid, splendid."

I got the feeling that Monsignor Murphy wasn't a hundred percent on board.

"I should explain one or two particulars," he said. "First and very foremost, my cardinals aren't to have knowledge of this, em, operation."

"Monsignor, this is going to be enough of a challenge as it is."

"One doesn't *campaign* for the office, Mr. Renard. It's not the New Hampshire primary. The princes must be above politics. Church law is quite specific on the matter. I, on the other hand, am not in the running for the office. If you follow. Can I offer you a drink, Mr. Renard? I'm guessing you're a scotch rather than a brandy man. I don't normally take a drink at mid-afternoon, but these are times that try a man's soul."

He fired up another cigarette. "My princes have been through rather a lot lately." Indeed. One of them had been led off in handcuffs just a week before. I'd scratched his name off my *papabile* list. "I can't say that any of us will look back on this time with nostalgia. It would be grand for morale all 'round if you could manage this miracle. All we seem to do now is depositions, with expensive lawyers."

"Can I ask what's the connection between you and Baroom?"

He blew out another lungful. "Well, it's rather an old-fashioned sort of connection, isn't it? I'm his confessor."

"Confessor?"

"Yes. When he makes his confession, which Catholics should, and sometimes actually do, he comes to me. So there you have it."

"Three Hail Marys and two Our Fathers — that sort of thing?"

"Em," he said, looking uncomfortable, "that sort of thing. Now, I've prepared some background for you on the princes." He pointed to a cardboard box that looked heavy.

"Who do we like? Any front-runners?"

"Well, they're all grand in their own way. Whelan of Houston has perhaps the strongest personality. He's the one who stood up to the federal marshals who wanted to arrest the illegal Mexicans in his cathedral basement. It was the one bit of fortunate television we've had in the past year. Tierney of Pittsburgh. Stickler for procedure. Martinez of Miami. Floated over from Havana as a child. I won't say he goes out of his way to discourage the miraculous aspect of it. Durkin of New York. Got into a bit of warm water over the annulments, but what I wouldn't give for that kind of scandal these days. Vaghi of Washington, fluent in nine languages, four of them dead. There's the new one — Kanu of Los Angeles, handsome as a movie star, deft at the outreach to the various communities."

"Is he the one who surfs?"

"The same. Bunbergler of Chicago. Genius at the fundraising, which isn't easy these days, let me tell you, with all the unpleasantness. Linquist of Minnesota, a pillar, theologically speaking, very close to Rome, though I wouldn't necessarily say Charisma is his middle name. I think what we're hoping for, Mr. Renard, is generally to promote the *idea* of an American pontiff in the world community. If we could just do that much, get people thinking about the princes in a different context, well, that would be accomplishment enough. You'll have earned your place in heaven." He smiled. "At the least your retainer."

He looked at his watch. "I'm afraid I must be off. Archbishop Gurk is being deposed."

The deathwatch was on at the Vatican. Once the pope died, the clock would begin ticking. There would be little sleep at Renard Strategic Planning in the days ahead. Normally I would have ordered up some polling data and let the buzz develop organically. But this was no ordinary product launch.

I knew from the get-go that I was probably going to have to "go negative." I generally try to be positive, but sometimes there's just no substitute for cutting the other person off at the knees, harsh as that may sound. The American birds — cardinals, that is — may have all been good, even holy, men in their own way, but a Dream Team they were not, *papabile*-wise. Except maybe for this Dwayne Cardinal Kanu of L.A., the surfer. Pope John Paul II had gotten some very good ink in his day for being a skier. I think people are reassured to know that their pope favors an athletic lifestyle, that he's not going to just sit on a throne all day talking Latin and handing down papal decrees about keeping women out of the priesthood.

I saw from Monsignor Murphy's — I must say CIA-quality — dossiers on the leading foreign cardinals that the front-runner was this Kojo Cardinal Arooba of Nigeria, an extremely impressive fellow, I'll be the first to admit, the Colin Powell of the College of Cardinals. He'd been converted from some African religion called animism to Catholicism by Irish missionaries. Meanwhile, Felix Cardinal Verguenza of Honduras, the other front-runner, had denounced the United States for training Latin American dictators at the School of the Americas. I'm not saying he was wrong. I'd probably feel the same way if I were a Honduran cardinal whose family had been wiped out by a military junta. He was also continually demanding that U.S. Banana do something about the snakes and spiders that were constantly biting its workers. Apparently, poisonous snakes and spiders love bananas. Again, this is the part of the job I enjoy, the learning about different cultures. At any rate, this gave me something to work with.

It was my mentor, Nick Naylor, who pioneered the field of product placement among opinion makers. Until then product placement had been confined to paying film and TV producers to "place" your "product" in their movies and shows. It hadn't occurred to anyone to pay talking heads (I won't name any names) who go on TV. These folks don't make huge salaries from their newspaper columns and what have you. They're usually happy to slip in a reference to your client's continuing efforts to reduce harmful pollutants, or the nifty new jet fighter that a couple of

Luddite congressmen are holding up in Appropriations. They're more than happy to receive in return a small token of appreciation — in the form of, say, a new German sports car or a Rolex watch or a two-week cruise — along with a note saying "Great appearance on Larry King!" Is this quote unquote ethical? I say, Let him who is without spin cast the first stone.

But I didn't want this to be just a top-down campaign. Ultimately, in any campaign you've got to have the "little people" on your side. Since LaMoyne was working full-tilt on oppo (that is, opposition research), I put Lorraine on this. Lorraine had been one of my more promising grad students. She'd done her master's thesis on the California prune industry's campaign to reposition its product as "dried plums." Lorraine took it to the next level, proposing that rotten fruit could successfully be packaged and sold as a "pre-softened" high-fiber food for seniors. I was just blown away. I hired her immediately as a junior associate. I sent her paper to Nick, in California. He wrote back, "A natural. She'll go FAR!!!"

I said to Lorraine, "It takes a miracle to produce a miracle." I didn't have to explain further. It's a pleasure to work with someone who "gets it" right away. Also, she was Catholic. And she could provide me with a "woman's perspective" on the whole business of a 2,000-year-old self-perpetuating male hierarchy. Lorraine was only in her mid-twenties, but she still dressed like a Catholic schoolgirl, and quite fetchingly, I must say, in the blazer, pleated skirt, dark stockings, and black pumps. That said, I make it a rule not to get romantically involved with junior associates. For one thing, it makes it very difficult to fire them.

It wouldn't have been seemly to roll out the campaign while the present Holy Father was on his deathbed. But we were able to hit the ground running the moment he started to cool. I don't mean that disrespectfully. He was huge, absolutely a giant. It would have been a piece of cake getting him elected.

At any rate, the morning after he finally expired (and, I'm certain, breezed through the Pearly Gates like a motorist with an E-Z Pass), the first public-service announcements appeared, sponsored by the Upon This American Rock Foundation: "Two Thousand Years. Isn't It Time *We* Had a Pope?"

"Upon This Rock" is, of course, a reference to what Jesus said to Peter, who was the first pope, when he said that he was going to make Peter the foundation of the Church. Lorraine informed me that it has a double meaning, because the Latin word for rock is *petra*. Up to then I thought it was the name of an expensive French wine. It's full of amazing stuff like this, the Bible. You can see why people study it. At any rate, the first call came while I was still in the shower, which I didn't take as a good sign, since my name didn't appear anywhere in the ad. (The address listed at the bottom was a Catholic-sounding P.O. box in Chicago.) Sure enough, it was my old nemesis, Lloyd Grove, of the *Washington Post.*

"So, Rick Renard is behind this?"

"If you're asking am I 'behind' the idea of the United States having at least some input into the administration of a major world religion, the answer is 'Hell, yes.'"

Perhaps this was not an ideal choice of words, but I hadn't slept in three days and I was dripping wet. The more pressing question was, Who leaked it to Grove? I had hoped to low-key my involvement with Upon This American Rock.

I reached Murf on his cell. I heard chanting. He was in the middle of saying mass with some archbishops. He said he'd have to call me back. I said, "Don't call me back, just plug the leak in your shop, because this certainly didn't come from my shop." You can't spell *discreet* without the *d* in Renard. I was cheesed. You'd think that an organization that has been around for two thousand years would be a little more disciplined. But we were off and running.

That night three of my, shall we say, cash-encouraged talking heads were on separate TV shows, yakking it up about how it was high time there was an American pontiff. One of them, a former White House speechwriter, even suggested that the French might try to "steal" the election. Another suggested that the Chinese were "up to their usual mischief." Brilliant, and entirely their own spin. It's a pleasure to work with real pros. I included flowers along with their cash envelopes. Phase One was complete.

The next day Upon This American Rock, of which I was now officially the "executive director" (what the hell), released the results of a poll showing overwhelming support for the idea among

American Catholics. To be sure, the sampling error, at 48 percent, was a little higher than the normal plus or minus 4 percent, but the important thing was to get the poll "out there." The media love polls and will report anything you give them. By the time they get around to noticing that your "respondents" consisted of two cab-drivers and a bartender, your poll has already made headlines. Phase Two complete.

Lorraine called from Los Angeles to report that she had an elderly woman who, in return for an all-expenses-paid cruise to Alaska, was prepared to call the *L.A. Times* and say that she had been miraculously cured of a very nasty case of psoriasis by Dwayne Cardinal Kanu.

"Psoriasis?" I said. "Can't we do better than a skin condition? Cancer, leukemia, a heart condition — anything would be more dramatic than itching."

"I can ask." She sounded a bit dubious. This was really her first time out "in the field." I've seen this happen before. They're great on paper, but when it comes time to get down there in the trenches, they get all squirrelly.

"Hey — is this the same Lorraine who came up with the idea of selling rotten fruit to seniors, at a significant markup?"

"I'll try."

"How often do you get a chance to help elect the next pope? We're making history here."

She called back to report that Mrs. Garcia, who would now be going on a round-the-world cruise, had been miraculously cured not of psoriasis but of something called alopecia.

"Sounds awful," I said.

"It is."

"*Now* you're cooking," I told her. I was genuinely proud. I thought back to my first assignment for Nick Naylor: calling up reporters to tell them that our client's rival burger-chain operation was using kangaroo meat. One headline said, "WHOPPER OR HOPPER? BURGER BOY DENIES KANGAROO MEAT ALLEGATION." I got misty-eyed thinking of it. At any rate, Phase Three complete. On to Rome!

LaMoyne went into the mother of all funks when I told him he would have to stay in dull old D.C. and run things from the office.

"It's the Eternal City," I said. "It's not going anywhere."

"Like me."

Sometimes I think half the job is keeping the people who work for you inspired. It's not easy being pope.

I took to Rome like a Visigoth. For someone in my profession it's inspiring to be in a city that has been doing the Big Spin for thousands of years. Here, I felt, I could be myself. Walking around those historical stones felt weirdly familiar, as though I'd been there in earlier times, advising Roman road builders on how to package their bids for the Appian Way, or even the emperor on how to get maximum credit for providing bread and circuses to the low-income.

Walking into Saint Peter's Basilica for the first time, I was in awe. I imagined advising various popes on how to handle Luther and Henry VIII and Galileo. In the first instance, I would have told Pope Leo X to not-so-quietly get the word out about the fact that Luther had had several nervous breakdowns. And what kind of monk goes around nailing pieces of paper to the doors of cathedrals? Some vow of obedience *he* took.

With Henry, I would have said to Popes Clement VII and Paul III, Look, this isn't about religion; this isn't about the quote unquote Real Presence of Christ in the communion; this is about control. Everyone's acting like an alpha gorilla. Get him down here for a weekend at Castel Whatever, fill him up on your best wine, tell him he's the best King Henry that England has ever had, including Henry V. Then have Cardinal Sinatra find a loophole in the annulment law and *give him his divorce.* Look at the big picture. We're losing Germany because of that nutball monk, now you want to lose England, all that monastic land? Over this? Would you want to sleep with Catherine of Aragon? *No, gracias!*

With Galileo, I would have said to Pope Urban VIII, Before you start with the hot pokers, stop and ask yourself: do you really want to torture an old man — who, by the way, seems to be on to something here — just for looking through a telescope and saying, *Whoa, we're revolving!* Burning heretics at the stake is satisfying in the short run, and wonderful entertainment for the people, but how's it going to look in a couple of centuries, when they start sending up the Hubble telescope? I would have told him, Progress happens. Make it work *for* you. Embrace it. Go up there on the balcony and announce, Yo, everyone, Galileo is working for *us!* We love this man! We're going to put an observatory right here in Saint Peter's!

Standing there on the spot where they crucified poor old Saint Peter, I thought, *The man ends up here in rags and chains, upside down on a cross, to make up for those three denials, and two thousand years later he's got* this *for a tomb and one billion followers.* Whatever faith you believe in, you have to hand it to Peter and Paul. Talk about spinergy. At any rate, these were my thoughts as I wandered around the basilica. I couldn't remember when I had felt so pumped about a client.

I set up my war room in a little *pensione* — Italian for "cheap hotel" — off the Spanish Steps, not far from the cheap hotel where the English poet Keats died, of TB, in 1821. Very historical, Rome. Everywhere you turn, someone famous died there or was horribly executed. On Bernard's budget I could have rented the top floor of the Hilton, but my presence here was strictly unofficial. Murf set me up with a man we'll call Angelo, who was hot-wired into the Vatican press corps. I suspected from the diamond rings and the $1,800 suit and $800 shoes that Angelo was on about five different payrolls, but at least you know you're not going to waste time hand-wringing over ethics. I laid an eyeball-widening brick of Bernard's crisp $100 bills on the table and told him what I needed, and his attitude was *Pronto, Signor Renardo!* My kind of people, Italians.

The next day *L'Osservatore Romano,* which is to the Vatican what the *Daily Racing Form* is to horse racing, ran a page-one, above-the-fold piece saying don't count the Americans out. The jump included a nice mention of Cardinal Kanu and Lorraine's alopecia woman.

The cardinals, some of whom apparently themselves suffered from alopecia — what luck! — were now starting to arrive. They were technically forbidden — by papal decree, no less — access to any kind of media: television, radios, newspapers, and such. The previous pope, God rest him, had spelled out the rules for electing his successor in a document called *Universi Dominici Gregis*. I read it — twenty-four single-spaced pages of regs, with footnotes. Violate any one of them and it was into the eternal darkness with you.

The cardinals would be housed in a new $20 million Vatican guesthouse — the Domus Sanctae Marthae, built for them by a rich American from Pittsburgh. The birds weren't allowed to speak to anyone outside, and no one was allowed to talk to them. No phones, cell phones, or fax machines. They weren't even allowed to engage in politicking among themselves. This must have made for very dull conversation around the Domus water cooler. You'd think there would be some pretty furious horse trading going on: *Vote for me — I'll put you in charge of all L.A. annulments*, that sort of thing. But technically this is called simony. I had to look it up: "buying or selling ecclesiastical preferment." And anyone who engages in it gets excommunicated. Good thing I'm not Catholic.

No chance, either, of sneaking in and distributing campaign literature. This was a terrible shame, inasmuch as there had been some terrific stuff lately on Dwayne Cardinal Kanu. One of the tabloid papers had nicknamed him "The Big Kanuna," and the History Channel had devoted an entire hour to the history of popes and outdoor sports, including some incredible footage of then Monsignor Kanu executing a truly divine "cheater five" on his longboard at Oceanside Pier.

The guesthouse and the Sistine Chapel, where the voting takes place, would be swept regularly for listening devices. The whole place would be sealed off by the Swiss Guard — and the Swiss, whatever else they may be, are old hands when it comes to borders.

I asked Lorraine how she was coming with the Nostradamus predictions — Nostradamus being the sixteenth-century French (figures) astrologer who wrote that book that appeals to a certain element of the public. She was here with me in Rome — a source of some resentment on the part of LaMoyne. She looked tired. Well, we were all tired. She said she couldn't find anything in Nostradamus.

"*Lorraine.*"

"Rick. There's just nothing in here about a surfing American cardinal who cures alopecia getting elected pope in the early part of the twenty-first century. I'm *sorry.*"

It wasn't that I expected the *New York Times* to pick up a Nostradamus "prediction," but this sort of thing helps with the supermarket-tabloid-reading set, and you need them.

"Fudge," I said.

"Fudge?"

"*Fudge.* Do I have to do everything?"

She finally cobbled together some mumbo jumbo about "a man of the West" who would "walk on water" to the "East." "Perfect," I said. "Start faxing." She looked like she was about to cry. I took her out to Tullio, off the Piazza Barberini, for a nice dinner. It seemed to cheer her up. Afterward we walked over to the Palazzo Barberini, this being the palace of an Italian family that produced a pope and a number of prelates. Their symbol was a bee, the emphasis being on the stinger more than the honey. If you look at the base of the twisty bronze columns around the main altar in Saint Peter's, you'll see the bee symbol. The Barberinis melted down the bronze from plates they took from the Pantheon. They were the Sopranos of the papacy, you might say. But then, a lot of building in Rome consisted of plundering from other sites, just like the construction business in New Jersey. I said to Lorraine, "Someday there will be little American motifs in Saint Peter's if we do our job right." She seemed pleased by the idea.

I called Bernard to give him a progress report and got the English private secretary on the phone. "Mr. Ba*room* is with the *law*-yers. He *cahn't* come to the *phone.*" I said, "Well, tell Mr. Ba*room* it's going very *swimmingly,* you can positively *feel* the groundswell."

That night I had this vision. It might have been from the high levels of potassium in the artichokes at Tullio. In Italy you can eat the entire artichoke, and they were so good I ate five. At any rate, I immediately called Murf, in Washington, who was getting ready to come over with his prince delegation, and said to him, "Is there any way your birds can arrive by boat? Peter was a fisherman, and I think it would be appropriate, and a fabulous visual, to have them come up the Tiber River — I'll check on the depth — by boat. A torchlight procession up the steps from the river at Castel San Angelo, with a choir singing 'The Battle Hymn of the Republic.' We'll get Placido Domingo — better yet, Stevie Wonder." *Mine eyes have seen the glory!* Sometimes I think I'm really a frustrated impresario.

"Em," Monsignor Murf said, "it's a lovely idea, Rick. But I'm not sure my princes will go for it."

"Every time I turn on the TV, I see another dreary cardinal at Fiumicino" — the Rome airport — "rolling his own suitcase or schlepping his garment bag. They look like flight attendants. If these guys are princes, they need to start acting like princes. Let's get some *majesty* going here. In the old days, they arrived in jeweled carriages to the sound of trumpets."

"I'll get back to you." You hear this all the time in Washington. Basically, it means no. He did, however, say that he might have something useful for me when he got to Rome.

The Media Center was in a building that was once used to torture people who didn't believe in the Holy Trinity. I'd installed Lorraine there, along with a half-dozen worker bees (we called them our Barberinis), as a credentialed correspondent for *Working Pontiff* magazine. Her real job was to monitor the media. Cardinal Arooba had arrived in Rome that morning. She showed me the video of it. Half of Rome had turned out to meet him, people grabbing to kiss his hand. Catholics just can't seem to get enough of hand-smooching the higher-ups. Cardinals must walk around with permanently damp hands. I don't mean it as a criticism. At any rate, I'll be the first to admit that Arooba was radioactively charismatic. A regular Catholic Bishop Tutu. Shoo-in of the Fisherman. You could just see him in that white soutane on the balcony, bestowing his first papal blessing on a million swooning Catholics. Ladbrokes, the London oddsmakers, had him at even money. Verguenza was at 6:1. Dwayne Cardinal Kanu they had at 112:1. There being 112 cardinals, this was not what you would call encouraging.

Time to go negative. Let me state for the record: I don't like to go negative, but as my mentor, Nick, used to say, "At least you can say you considered *not* going negative."

I laid another brick of Franklins in front of Angelo. The next day my favorite Vatican rag ran a page-one story on animism, from which the Irish missionaries in Africa had converted Cardinal Arooba, along with a killer quote — from someone identified as one of the world's "ultimate authorities" on animism — about how animists believe that the spirits of dead animals live on and can even be dangerous. The quote continued, "Not that Cardinal Arooba still adheres to these stern beliefs, so far as we are aware." Bull's-eye, Angelo.

"Get this out to every reporter and producer here," I said to Lorraine.

I'd flown over a couple of tame talking heads with passable credentials as Vaticanisti — that is, Vatican-watchers. You pick up a lot of local lingo in this job. The next morning they were on the U.S. talk shows saying that Cardinal Arooba was a wonderful man who would "probably not" suddenly start sacrificing goats on the altar and casting spells. Of course, they were careful to add, there was no hard data available on the recidivism rate among former animists. There's nothing more satisfying than building a good, solid media campaign. It's meat and potatoes, basically. You just get the information out there so that people can make an informed choice. At any rate, things were going well.

That afternoon I was in my room at the Pensione Tiberculosi, on the phone to the head of the Knights of Columbus back in the States, who was about to take off for Rome on a chartered 747 with four hundred of his top Knights. There was a knock on my door. Two suits with U.S. State Department ID.

"Richard Renard? The ambassador would like to see you."

I said, "Well, I'm a little busy right now."

"Now, please. *Sir.*"

I wasn't sure what the jurisdiction issue was, but never let it be said that Rick Renard isn't patriotic. The suits were not what you would call conversational, which gave the trip up the Via Peoria to the U.S. Embassy to the Holy See the aroma of a forced march.

The American ambassador didn't look pleased to see me. Her aide went into instant buttlock when he saw me, and then he disappeared, as though being in the same room with me might retard his chances of becoming deputy chief of mission to Ulan Bator.

"Mis-ter Renard," she said, making "Mister" sound like a fifty-fifty proposition. "And what brings *you* to Rome?"

"I'm on a pilgrimage," I said. "Yourself?"

Rick Renard does not normally insult U.S. ambassadors on first meeting, but I was a little *formaggio*ed at being hauled onto her carpet in this brusque manner. Her Excellency's qualification for the job, aside from being a fabulously wealthy Catholic widow, the sister of a powerful U.S. senator, and a major contributor to the current president's election campaign, was — well, I'll have to get back to you on that. I don't mean to imply that being U.S. ambassador to the smallest nation in the world (0.2 square miles — Central Park is bigger) is anything to sneeze at, but let's just say we didn't send Henry Kissinger there. Maybe we will when the Vatican gets the bomb. At any rate, I was in no mood to kowtow to Madam Ambassador.

"I'm here to look after our country's interests," she said, ice forming on her tongue. "Which includes preventing U.S. *mercenaries* from disrupting papal elections."

Who had sold me out? Murf ran a tight shop. Angelo. Had to be Angelo.

"I'm only helping to make it a level playing field," I said.

"Are you Catholic, Mr. Renard?"

"Not technically, though I'm very impressed with what I've seen so far. It's definitely an option, spiritual-wise."

"If you were, you'd be excommunicated. Placing your soul in mortal danger might not worry you, Mr. Renard, but any Catholic involved in this — this *sinister* operation of yours — is also automatically excommunicated. Am I getting through to you?"

"Excuse me, but what's so quote unquote sinister about an American pope? I thought you were looking out for our interests here."

"Do you have any idea," she said, "how catastrophic this could be? Trying to influence the election of the Roman *pope?*"

"Unlike influencing the election of the U.S. president?"

"Mr. Renard, the pope is above politics! He is a *holy* figure!"

"Well, our president is no saint, I'll grant you."

The interview didn't go uphill from there. She threatened to have me deported.

"Where?" I said. "To the other side of the Tiber? I'll walk and save you the trouble."

Unfortunately, she took me up on my offer. And just try to find a cab in Rome during a papal conclave. I had to walk back to my *pensione.* I was as steamed as Tullio *carciofi* when I got back to the Tiberculosi.

I said to Lorraine, "Turns out Angelo is no angel. He's working for the bad guys."

"Who are the bad guys? I'm confused."

"Us. As usual. Typical bureaucratic small-mindedness. You'd think she'd have offered to help."

"So are we closing up shop?"

"Of course not. Reinforcements are on the way."

At this exact moment the phone rang. It was Bernard. "A quarter million dollars to charter a 747?" He didn't sound at all pleased. This happens. The client tells you money is no object, and suddenly he's going over every bill with an electron microscope.

"Mr. Baroom," I explained, "the Knights of Columbus are our foot soldiers in this campaign." It took ten minutes of strenuous client mollification to calm him down.

"I thought he was rich," Lorraine said when I hung up. "He wasn't sounding very rich."

"He'll feel better when he sees the TV coverage of the Knights pouring into Saint Peter's. Where do we stand with the crucifixes?"

"They should get here tomorrow, by FedEx." We'd ordered thousands of crosses made from miniature longboards. They'd be distributed to followers of Cardinal Kanu to wear. If you're going to start a cult, you need gear. These would definitely get all the brahs amped, as they say in surfing circles.

Everything was coming together nicely, but I was concerned that the U.S. embassy might expose our operation. I conceived a plan. As the toast goes, "Confusion to the enemy."

On the drive out to Fiumicino to greet the Knights, I said to Lorraine, "Listen closely." This is another part of the job I enjoy — the mentoring process. It's satisfying to help bring young people along.

I dialed Angelo. "Angelo," I said in my best conspiratorial voice, "I've just heard from my people. There's a change of plan. They've cut a deal. The operation is off. I repeat, off. Canceled. We're throwing our support to Verguenza, from Honduras."

"*Bene,*" Angelo said. One thing about the Italians: they don't question violent changes of allegiance. For them it's normal.

"In return for our support," I continued, "Verguenza will cease putting pressure on U.S. Banana and that military college where we train the Latino dictators. Anyway, our operation to elect an American *papa* is off. *Finito, cancellato.* We're most appreciative of your efforts. I'll be sending you a nice token of our appreciation."

"*Bene.*"

"Is that true?" Lorraine asked as I hung up.

"Not a word of it. I just wish I could be there when he tells Madam Plenipotentiary that our cardinals are throwing their support behind the most anti-American prelate in the Western Hemisphere." I permitted myself a low chuckle. "Oh, the phones are going to be ringing *tonight.*"

That evening four hundred Knights of Columbus processed into the Piazza San Pietro carrying red, white, and blue Glo-stick "torches" and signs proclaiming VIVA IL PAPAMERICA! I thought the Italian would give it a more local flavor.

Standing there watching, I got choked up to think that after two thousand years we might finally have an American pontiff. I understand that, technically speaking, America has existed for only one tenth of that period of time. I'm more talking about the idea. At any rate, the TV coverage, as you probably saw for yourself, was spectacular. CNN slugged it "The Night of the Knights." The impact back home was tremendous. For years American Catholics had been waking up every morning to stories about sex scandals. Now they saw this triumphant procession into the front yard of their faith. Rick Renard is not one to bang his own drum, but at times like this I am tempted to say, "Not bad for an old hack." This was no time for complacency, however. The conclave would start the next day.

Murf's princes had been sealed off in the Domus Sanctae Marthae, the papal guesthouse.

"I've got something for you," Murf called to say. "But I can't discuss it over the telephone."

We met at a trattoria in Trastevere. I hadn't seen Murf since D.C. He looked exhausted — but then, monsignors in charge of cardinals don't get much sleep before a papal conclave. His eyes were dartier than ever.

"One of my princes, he's the chaplain to the U.S. Armed Forces, intimately well connected in Washington. He received a call from a certain person of importance there asking him was it true that the American princes were supporting Cardinal Verguenza. You wouldn't know anything about this?"

I told him about planting the disinformation with his man Angelo in order to throw the embassy off my trail and get it to work on taking out Verguenza.

"Jaysus, Rick. You should check with me first before doing such a thing. It's awkward for my prince. He had to deny the whole thing. Anyway, Angelo's no spy. I know the man well. I've heard his confession. He may not be a saint, but he's loyal, I can vouch."

"Well, someone sold me out to the embassy. It had to be Angelo. The ambassador sent goons for me and threatened to deport me."

"Bit of a dragon, isn't she? The princes refer to her in private as 'The Holy Mother.' But she's a dragon without teeth. I wouldn't worry about her. But don't be spreading any more of this. I won't have my princes needing to deny they're part of a cabal to elect a communist pope."

"Whatever — but I won't be using Angelo again."

"Now, then, let's get to it," he said in a low voice, with sideways glances. "As you know, the princes aren't permitted to see or hear any media whatsoever. No one's even permitted to talk to them. *But* there's a chatroom, *and* I find myself in possession of the password. Don't ask how I got it. It's the most secret secret in Christendom right now." He fired up a cigarette off the one he was already smoking. "How are you under the duress, Rick?"

I told him that being a strategic communicator in Washington, D.C., could be extremely stressful.

"No, no," he said, "*duress.* You know, *peine forte et dure.* The torture."

Only with an Irishman could you have a casual conversation about how you might stand up under torture.

"Well," he said, "it's not going to come to that, is it? The days of the Borgia popes are over, eh? The things they did. Dreadful, dreadful. But just to err on the side of safety, I think you might want to relocate from your hotel." He scribbled an address on a piece of paper and took a key out of his pocket. "You'll be safe there. It's a small apartment on the Campo de' Fiori. The princes sometimes use it for private occasions. There's just this one key. Funny, isn't it?"

"What?"

"*Conclave.* The word means 'with key' in Latin. And here's your key."

"Maybe you should keep the password to yourself."

"No, no," he said. "If something should happen to me, you should have it, to carry the thing to consummation."

He got up to go. "It's a grand thing we're doing, Rick. I may not get to heaven, but you know, I feel certain that Saint Peter is on our side." He winked at me. "I'm off. Don't forget to say your prayers."

The apartment on the Campo de' Fiori had a king-size bed and a huge Jacuzzi and lots of candles in the bathroom. I guess they used it to relax. More important, it had a high-speed line for Internet access — the papal decree against media had not mentioned such technology. *Quod blah blah non prohibari* — "What is not forbidden is permitted." The cardinals' chatroom may have been the most significant ecclesiastical loophole since they came up with the concept of invincible ignorance so that innocent heathen could get into heaven. (If I have this right. As I say, I'm no theologian.) At any rate, armed with Murf's password I was able to navigate past the Vatican Web site's firewall and soon found myself inside the most secret cyber-chamber in Christendom. I felt like that archaeologist looking into King Tut's tomb for the first time. There was an area where you could look up cardinals' statements about various issues. With the help of a Latin dictionary I was able to do a little creative editing there. I slightly changed the wording of a speech that Cardinal Arooba had given to some synod of bishops, inserting "not" or "un-" here and there, putting him in more or less direct disagreement with various Church policies such as those regarding birth control, the ordination of women, papal infallibility, and the Immaculate Conception. Was this, strictly speaking, "unethical"? I'm not really comfortable making those sorts of judgments. One man's ethical lapse is another's client servicing. Who can say at the end of the day? I also fiddled a little with Cardinal Verguenza's sermon about U.S. Banana, adding the words "criminal" and "imperialist." In Cardinal Kanu's bio I inserted a pop-up, so that if you clicked on his name, you got a flashing message saying I AM NOT WORTHY. It's from the story of Jesus healing the centurion's sick servant. I figured modesty would go down well in a papal conclave.

I watched TV with one eye while I was doing this, so I got to see the clash in the Piazza San Pietro that night between the Knights of Columbus and the Chevaliers de L'Ordre de Saint Denis. I kicked myself for not anticipating that the French — who had been wanting one of their own on the papal throne ever since they lost Benedict XIV (a.k.a. Bernard Garnier, the "counter anti-pope") back in 1433 — might try something like this. The record will show that my Knights did not throw the first punches. The footage is clear on that score. But things certainly did escalate, overwhelming the local *carabinieri* and requiring the involvement of the Italian military.

Murf called me, sounding fairly frantic. "I'm looking out at tanks. *Tanks*, Rick. Tell me we didn't start this."

"Absolutely not. In fact, I think it's an excellent argument for an American pontiff. A firm hand on the tiller of Saint Peter's." Good line. I made a note to pass that along to the TV producers.

It was a long night, but finally dawn broke over the Eternal City. On TV they were saying that the cardinals were in their dorm, getting ready for the first day of conclaving. I hoped they were also doing a little cyber-chatting.

I was on my cell to an ABC News producer, securing some B-roll of Cardinal Kanu riding the half-pipe at Pismo Beach, when LaMoyne reached me on my other cell.

"You heard?" he said.

"Heard what?"

"Bernard. He's been charged by the SEC."

"What for?"

"Let me count the counts. Securities fraud, stock manipulation, wire fraud, insider trading. They've frozen his assets. Never a good sign, that."

"Jesus," I said, that being about all I could think to say.

"Mary *and* Joseph," LaMoyne added. "I'll see what I can find out. Meanwhile, do I assume we are no longer on the papal election account?"

"Call Lorraine," I said. "I'm in the middle of something."

"I was coming to that. She called here. She left a message. Why don't I play it for you?"

There was a knock on the door. To paraphrase Dorothy Parker, what fresh hell was this? Some safe house. It sounded like Mussolini was outside with the entire Black Shirt brigade.

The apartment door had a peephole. I didn't like what I saw on the other side. Suits. Suits worn by large men, blond, with crewcuts. They didn't look Italian.

"Here you go," LaMoyne said. I listened to Lorraine's voice on the office voice mail. "Rick, I'm sorry, but I just can't do this. I'm a Catholic. I'm risking my immortal *soul*. I have to resign. Sorry. And it wasn't Angelo, it was me. I had to. We're talking about my *soul*. I'll send you a postcard from whatever convent I end up in."

LaMoyne came back on. "Are we having a good day?"

"There are men outside my door."

"Better do as the Romans do. Flee."

The suits were now banging on the door. I called Murf on his cell. A voice, not his, answered. I asked for Murf, and it said in this excommunicating, unfriendly way, "Who is this?"

"Uh, Rick."

"Monsignor has nothing further to say to you, *Mister* Renard."

I heard the door break open, and soon found myself being trundled, I think the word is, into the back of a black sedan. The suits were not particularly communicative, but I could see from the approaching dome of Saint Peter's that we were heading back across the river to Vatican City. We went down some winding streets into a courtyard with a heavy metal door above which I caught a brief glimpse of a shield and the words GUARDIA SVIZZERA, this being Italian for "Swiss Guard." I took this to be both good news and not-good news.

My interview, if you could call it that, with the head of their Intelligence Division (I think he was, though he never formally introduced himself) could not be described as sociable. He was pretty Swiss about it.

As I look back, it was probably a good thing that the vote came in when it did, or Rick Renard might still be languishing in a dank dungeon underneath the Vatican. In the old days, apparently, the way they dealt with simoniacs was to sew them up in a sack with wild animals and chuck them into the Tiber River. At any rate, I've never been so relieved to hear people shouting, "*Habemus papam! Habemus papam!*" which if you know Latin you'll recognize as "We have a pope!"

Son of a bitch won on the first ballot. I don't mean that disrespectfully. Shoo-in of the Fisherman. Our first postanimist pope.

Let me be the first to say that I think he's made an excellent start. He has certainly been very understanding and forgiving in the matter of Monsignor Murphy's nervous breakdown. The strain of having to deal with all the sex scandals had apparently taken its toll on the poor man. So it was Murf after all, and not Bernard Baroom, who had come up with the idea of promoting an American pope, and all to get people's minds off the scandals. Big-league spin. Nothing small about it. Whatever your views on all this, you have to admire that much. At any rate, Murf saw his chance when his billionaire confessee Bernard told him about the insider trading and fraud and other sins. Instead of the usual two Hail Marys and three Our Fathers and a good Act of Contrition, Murf told him he had to get an American pope elected. And Baroom called me.

It worked, in a way. They're not talking about the sex scandals anymore. Also, the new pope has said that no purpose would be served by dwelling on all this, and that it's time to move on, and I'm all for that.

Anyway, LaMoyne just buzzed me to say that Martha Stewart's on the line, so I'd better take the call.

BEN EHRENREICH

■

# What You Eat

FROM *Bomb*

WHEN I WAS A BOY, my father always told me, "If you kill something, boy, you've got to eat it." It's the way of the world, he'd tell me, and only right and just besides. I suppose that sounds reasonable enough if you say it just like that, but he always took things a few steps too far. Which is why I find myself here now, at the bend in the road, shivering and pale in the moonlight, my balls shrunk like stones as the leaves chatter and the high limbs moan in the wind. Maybe I'll get lucky tonight.

The first time, I believe, was just an ant, or ants, I'd stomped with small besneakered feet. "Scrape 'em up, boy. They're yours now." I wouldn't do it. I cried and tried to run, but he grabbed me by the wrist and scraped them up himself, sloppily, mixed with grass and sand. He shoved them between my teeth with one rough finger and held my jaws shut like a dog's. They tasted like dirt. When I threw up, I cleaned it myself so he couldn't make me eat it.

One summer morning I found a fly, caught between window and screen, drowsy from heat or hunger. I cupped it in my hands, laughed as its wings hummed and tickled my boyish palms, then shook it till it stopped. When I opened my hands it was still moving. An antenna wandered; one wing twitched. I plucked off its wings and watched it stumble drunkenly across my furrowed palm. Then I heard his voice behind me. "You can eat it now or eat it later, son. Whether it's moving or not, you've already killed the fly." I whimpered and wept, but his shoveled face did not soften one bit. I dropped it in my mouth and swallowed. For weeks I felt it buzzing in my intestines. I dreamed of whole colonies of flies reproducing in my gut, lifting me in the air with the collective flapping of their tiny wings, taking me high above the rooftops, above my father digging trenches in the yard, then streaming out of my mouth all at once, a black and buzzing plume, and letting me fall back through the clouds, through the treetops to the waiting earth.

He made me weed the garden, so on my hands and knees I weeded. I unearthed a pink and wriggling worm, stretched it between my soil-blackened fingers. It tried to inch away. I cut it in half with the blade of my trowel. His shadow fell before me. The two halves of the worm danced and jerked, pink in the rich black dirt. "Howzit coming, boy?" I felt tears rising. My lip and chin were shaking when he busted out a laugh. "You got lucky this time, kid. Slicing don't harm worms none." He slapped my shoulder and I twisted forth a smile.

I made a slingshot from a blue rubber band and a perfect Y-shaped twig, stalked the yard and the fields around, my pocket full of pebbles. The trees were silent, the earth still. I sat and pulled at the grass with my fingers. I dug a hole with the heels of my feet. I wondered how to make a whistle. I shot pebbles at a tree, aiming at a blackened knot along the trunk. Hit it six times out of ten. When a blackbird swooped down to rest on a high branch, singing stupidly, I was ready, slingshot in hand and loaded. The stone whined through the air and, with a crack of beak and bone, dropped the bird to the ground at my feet. It twitched a wing and died, its head bloody, glassy-eyed.

"Boy!" I heard him yell. He was still far across the field. I clawed at the earth with the heel of my slingshot, with my fingers. Unearthed a rock, dug with that. Put the bird in the hole, covered it with dirt just in time. I stood there, my feet hiding the bird's brisk grave. Maybe I should have just thrown some leaves on it and walked away. "Didn't you hear me calling you?" he said. Then, "What's that you buried there?"

"Nothing."

"Dig it up," he said. "Go on."

I dug, hoping somehow that the bird would have already decided between heaven and hell and gone its merry way. But it remained. "Well, well," he said. "A hunter. Pick it up and bring it home. I'll teach you how to eat a bird."

I carried the bird by its small black feet, sniffling as we crossed the field. "When we get to the house," he said, "put on a pot of water to boil, then bring me a good sharp knife."

While we waited for the water to heat, he told me what to do. To scald the bird just for a second to loosen its feathers. To pluck it, but to do it outside so as not to make a mess. Then he went back to work, digging trenches across the yard, singing songs my mother once sang to him and me. I dangled the bird over the pot by its feet, but the steam burned my hand and I dropped it in. Fished it out with a slotted spoon, ruffled and limp. The water had gone brown from the dirt of its brief burial. I carried it outside in front of me on the spoon. Sat under a tree and waited for the bird to cool. The feathers came out easily, but they were so many, and so small, like perfect miniatures of the grand eagle feathers that poked from the headdresses of Indian chiefs. The bird's flesh beneath its plumage was rubbery and blue. It was barely bigger than my fist.

He loomed over me, his sleeves rolled, his shirt wet with sweat from digging in the sun. He sent me back into the kitchen for the knife I had forgotten. "You got to gut a bird before you can eat it, even a little one like this," he said. "Even little things can be full to the gills with shit." With his fingernail he traced a line from the bird's tiny pore of an asshole up along its blue belly. "Cut there," he said. "Just the skin, careful not to go too deep."

My hands trembled. The knife shook. The bird shook. I held the blade to the belly of the bird I had killed, but could not make the cut. He put his brown and calloused hand around mine, steadying it, and pushed his thumb down over the blade's dull edge. It was almost tender, the way he did that. The blue flesh parted. I expected blood to spurt up out of it, like a burst pipe, a jelly doughnut, but none did. My hands steadied, and I pulled the knife down across the bird's abdomen. The guts were pink and blue and yellow. I expected them to smell, but they did not. "Now use your hand," he said, "and scoop 'em out."

He ate a pork chop that night, and a potato. On my plate was just the bird, fried in the same pan he fried his chop. It was brown now, not blue. It looked like a parody of a chicken, or someone's hand. "Watch the bones," he said. "They're little." I poked it with my fork. A tear darkened the napkin in my lap. "You better eat the whole thing, every part of it, 'cause you killed every last part."

When he'd swallowed the last of his potato and the last of his chop, he wiped his mouth with his napkin and came around the table behind me. "Come on," he said. "You know how to do it." He used my knife to cut off the bird's leg. It was no bigger than my pinky. He put it in my hand and pushed it to my mouth. "Eat."

The sobbing had tightened my convulsing jaw, but I opened my mouth and chewed. He carved off the other leg, then stripped the meat from the bird's tiny breast and thighs. I didn't know those hands were capable of such fine movements. He stood over me till I ate everything he cut. My belly hurt from crying. I didn't care about the bird, or what I ate or didn't eat. The flesh was tough and didn't taste like anything. It was his rough hands that made me cry, how gentle they could be, but weren't. "All right," he said. "That's enough. Get to bed now." He spread wide his calloused fingers, gestured loosely at the door to my room. I ran into the yard and retched.

I was sick all day the next day, and he let me stay in bed. The day after that I got up early, left the house with my slingshot before he had even taken his pick and spade from their hooks in the shed. I trudged through the field, then through the far field and into the woods until I could no longer hear the rhythmic clanging of his pick or the sweet, sad songs he mumbled through. My sneakers and the cuffs of my pants were wet and heavy with dew, even through to the socks. I found a stick and a patch of mossy, loose earth and dug the hole first, a foot deep, another foot square. I saved the moss, unbroken.

It didn't take long to spot a squirrel. My first shots missed, bouncing off the tree trunk as the squirrel scurried up into the high branches out of range. I walked and waited, spied another, with a mangy tail, at least half rat. Sensing me, it froze. I got it right behind the head, snapping its neck with one shot. It fell with a thud at my feet and lay there on its back, feet in the air, tiny squirrel tongue lolling, funny almost, cartoon dead. I grabbed it, warm still and strangely delicate, and rushed it to its grave. Sprinkled a handful of dirt over its head to cover its staring eyes and said a prayer — "All they that be fat upon earth shall eat and worship: all they that go down to the dust shall bow before Him: and none can keep alive his own soul" — before pushing the rest of the earth over it and stamping it down, replacing the moss for camouflage. He would never know. For dinner that night I had a pork chop too, and a potato.

I was skipping from rock to rock along the little creek that divided the field nearest the house from the far field. He brought his tape measure along to inspect the trenches, and a small spade that swung at his knee with each long stride he took along the bank. I knew every stone in the creek like the scabs on my elbows and knees and leapt from rickety rock to rickety rock without bothering to first test my weight on them, or even to look. So I didn't see the salamander, bright orange, slick, stock still in the shade of the rushes, until both my feet were in the air. I nearly swallowed my tongue and tried my best to change the path of my descent, but the salamander belted straight beneath my falling foot, and I landed with a squish and a terrible crunch, slipping, splashing belly up into the shallow stream.

I stayed there in the cold wet, looking up at him looking down at me, his jaw tensed and chewing on his gums. "Newt's a poison creature, boy. Eat it and you die," he said. "Now run home and dry off. Meet me in the far field and watch your step."

He was quiet all week, working his jaw on his gums like he was chewing over something serious. I checked my food each meal for signs of salamander, praying he hadn't made up his mind.

He got me for the next squirrel, caught me right in the act. I dug the hole beforehand like I did the first time and had just let loose with the slingshot, the rubber burning my wrist as it sung the stone up into the air. I heard his voice before the squirrel hit the ground. "Pick it up and bring it home, son. You're cooking dinner tonight."

But when I reached for it, the squirrel scratched up at me with one gray claw. It was bleeding from its mouth and its nose, and couldn't walk or right itself. "It's not dead," I said.

He knelt at my side for a closer look. "Broke its back," he said. "You can't kill a thing halfway. Finish it and bring it home."

"How?" I asked, but he had already walked away. A bubble of blood sprouted from the squirrel's pinpoint nostrils. I could hear its breathing, like the creaking of my bed. I crushed its head with a rock and carried it home by the tail, spraying a thin trail of blood in the grass as I went.

Back at the house he had laid newspapers out on the ground by the shed. He handed me his pocketknife, well sharpened. "Gut it first," he said, "just like you did that blackbird. Slice from his bunghole to his ribs and don't push the blade too deep."

The squirrel's dead eye stared up at me, offset in its broken skull, as I pulled out its warm intestines and flung them, steaming in the crisp autumn air, on the unfolded news of the world.

"Now girdle his feet," he said. "Cut the skin straight around his little ankles like you're giving him socks." The fur was greasy, and the skin beneath it gave away easily to the knife. Trembling, I did as he demanded, then cut along the inside of the squirrel's leg, to the root of its tail and down the other leg. "Now peel him," he said. I looked up at him, confused, hoping for a reprieve. None came. "Get your hands in under there," he said, "and roll his skin back and up till you can pull it off."

With blind, numb fingers I pushed the skin up and away, uncovering a strange, new pink animal beneath the gray one I had killed. The eye still belonged to the old gray squirrel, which did not drop its reproachful gaze until I pulled its very own flesh up over its head like a hood. "Yank off his tail and you're done."

After hanging his pick and spade in the shed that evening, done for the day, he made me cut the squirrel up and stew it with potatoes, carrots, and onions. I don't remember much of the rest of that night, whether I ate dinner that night or the next, but I remember the toxic smell of rubber burning, and the blue rubber band's twisted dance as it blackened and burned in the hearth where I had thrown it, along with my perfect Y-shaped twig.

He bought me a puppy when I turned twelve, a little black mutt with pointed yellow ears. He put a ribbon around its neck, smiled lots and said it was for me, but really he meant it for a watchdog, to guard the trenches at night and when he went to town. He fed it every other day to keep it mean and he beat it when it barked too much or sometimes just to beat it. I took it with me in my wanderings about the fields, snuck it food on its fast days. We ran together, swam together, wrestled in the pine needles. I would have slept with the dog curled beside me in my bed but it wasn't allowed in the house for the fleas.

He told me I was a man when I turned thirteen, gave me a shovel and a pick. The day after my birthday he had me start a trench not far from where he was digging. He gave me tips on how to dig, to always bend at the knees, to get a rhythm going, to try to pick around the rocks, not at them, to hang a plumb line with a rock and a length of twine, smooth out the sides with the flat of my spade, to measure depth before I dug too deep, adjust the corners with T-square and trowel. I dug that day till my palms were bleeding, but what bothered me most was hearing him not ten yards away, singing and moaning and sighing. I knew the words to every song he sang, and hearing them from his lips tore my heart against my ribs like the hard wood of the shovel's handle against my raw and bleeding hands. The next morning I started at the far end of where my trench was meant to end, and by the time I got back to where I had first been digging, he was on a new trench away across the field.

He taught me how to drive the Datsun when I turned fifteen, hollering each time I let the clutch out too fast, slapping me in the head when I ground the gears. I wasn't allowed anywhere near the Buick except to wash it, and once to pump gas. He would send me out in the old Datsun for groceries or to the hardware store in town and with time I got the hang of it, more or less.

It was my job to keep the cars clean when I wasn't running errands or helping dig the trenches. He didn't care about the Datsun, but I washed it anyway, scrubbing even the rust spots and the balding tires till they gleamed. The dog lay in the shade, opening its eyes occasionally to make sure I was still around. When I finished drying the Datsun with rags cut from his old T-shirts and flannels, it was time for the Buick. The hose didn't quite reach around to where the Buick was and I know I could have just moved the Datsun out of the way, but the temptation to sit for just one second on the plush bench seat surrounded by all that chrome proved too great.

I got the keys from the hook by the door where I knew he left them. The seat was pushed all the way back for his long legs and I had to slide it forward to reach the pedals. I turned the key in the ignition and the engine started almost soundlessly. There was no clutch that I could find so I took my chances, slid the shifter to where it read "R" and hit the gas hard so as not to stall. The car shot backward with far more power than I ever could have guessed, like a horse rearing or a shotgun recoil. It startled me so much that I didn't even hear it hit. Not a thud, not a whimper. I jammed on the brake, hoping he hadn't heard me, slid the shifter to first, and inched the car back around the Datsun. It was only then that I noticed the thump, leaden and awful, as my rear wheel drove over something soft. I put the Buick in park, slid the seat to its original position, and had started to walk back to the house to hang the keys on their hook by the door when I glanced back and saw my dog, asleep just seconds ago, now suddenly dead.

I was on the ground with it, bawling and stroking its yellow ears, its jowls, and its black and broken body, when I felt his shadow pass over me. I couldn't see his face for the sun behind his head, and I put my hands over my ears to block out his words, shaking my head and crying, "No. No. No." He grabbed me by the collar, lifted me to my feet, and swung back to slap me, but I wriggled from his grip before his hand fell and ran down the long driveway to the road with my torn shirt and my eyes half blind with tears and horror.

For two nights I slept in the bushes. While the sun shone I wandered through the neighbors' land, avoiding their trenches and keeping to the woods to stay out of trouble. The days were fine when it didn't rain, but the nights were cold and all I had was the one ripped shirt. So on the third night I trekked back to the house for a sweater and a jacket and something to eat. All the lights were off. I went in the back way, through the kitchen, and was just turning up the stairs when he spoke. "Glad you could make it," he said. "Your dinner's waiting. I did the ugly part myself." He flicked on the kitchen light and nodded to a plate on the table. I ran for the front door without looking.

The cops brought me back a month later. I stayed a week. Woke up from dreaming I was eating my own entrails — a perfect plate-size circle of skin removed from my belly, just lying back chewing, slicing and jabbing with fork and knife — packed a bag and took off through the window. I held out nearly two months that time before I was caught. He took me back without a word.

Around that time he started drinking. He would drive the Buick into town when the sun set on Saturday, roll back up the driveway near dawn Sunday morning, stumble upstairs and sleep through the Sabbath. I would lie in wait for him just around the bend in the road a half-mile before the house. Set my alarm for four, then with a flashlight and a blanket hike down to the road. I would huddle in the bushes till I heard him coming, then drop the blanket and stand naked in the middle of the asphalt, my arms at my sides, a fork in one hand and a knife in the other.

The first time he came around the corner fast, spraying gravel. He hit the brakes hard and skidded into a spin, the Buick's back wheels taking the lead and angling the car in a tight and violent orbit with me at its center. It came to a stop about five yards down the road, its headlights illuminating two dumb circles of brush. When I shined my flashlight through the dusty windshield, he did not blink. His face was flushed, his spine straight. I laid the fork and knife on the hood and walked back up to the house.

He stayed home that next Saturday, sitting erect at the kitchen table, working his jaw over something for half the night, but another week of digging trenches and wordless meals at home sent him running to town come Saturday. When he shot around the bend just before dawn I was there waiting, naked, fork and knife in hand. He locked the brakes again and this time swerved off the road and into our field, upending the Buick in the peripheral trench. I picked up my blanket and flashlight, walked back up to the house, and went back to bed. He was still drunk when they found him in the car the next morning. He spent twenty days in lockup for driving drunk, the Buick two weeks in the shop.

When he got out he stayed sober for a couple months. We dug trenches all day long, me in the far field, he in the close, and didn't speak at all in the house. I was as tall as he was, and nearly as strong. The cars stayed unwashed.

The time came, as I knew it would, that he washed his hands and face, put on a clean shirt, pomaded his hair, and took the keys off the hook by the door. It was a warm night, so I left the blanket at home. I was in the road standing ready in the moonlight when I heard him coming, but he had gotten wise, and crept around the bend at five miles an hour, stopping the car with its new bumper three inches from my knees. For a minute or so I stood there, my skin white in the headlights, each budding hair on my chest with its own distinct shadow, staring at him behind the glass of the new windshield, his shoveled face stern and red with booze and anger. He gave the horn a tap. I laid the fork and knife on the hood, turned and walked away.

The next Sunday morning I got up a little earlier and hiked a little farther, two bends in the road before the house, a half-mile down. I was just in time, and stepped into the middle of the road as he roared on home, oblivious. He screeched to a halt and hit me. I flew four feet in the air and lay where I fell. My left leg curled oddly where it had made contact with the car. My right elbow, which hit the asphalt first, bent the wrong way back. The pavement had scraped my right side to pulp, but he hadn't killed me, so I held my breath and lay still as if he had.

My eyes closed to slits, I could make him out kneeling over me, but couldn't see his face for the headlights behind him. He gurgled a little, and started swaying back and forth on his knees. It was when he reached a trembling hand out to touch me that I started laughing. Leg broke and elbow busted, half torn to shreds, I bawled out cackling. He withdrew his hand and stood. I wanted to throw the knife and fork at him as he walked back to the car, but my hands were empty. "What were you gonna do, Dad?" I wheezed as he started the engine again. "What were you gonna do?"

He drove on and went upstairs to sleep it off, leaving me to drag myself home. It was light by the time I got the keys from the hook and drove myself one-armed and one-legged to the hospital, swerving down the highway, bleeding all over the Buick's plush velour.

The casts came off today at two, but I can almost still feel them on me, naked as I am, blanket on my goose-bumped shoulders, gravel between my toes. Maybe I'll get lucky tonight.

EVE ENGLEZOS AND JOSHUA MOUTRAY

∎

# Vickie, Lacey, Ray, Sharon, Corey, Derek, Carol, and Dave

FROM *SPX*

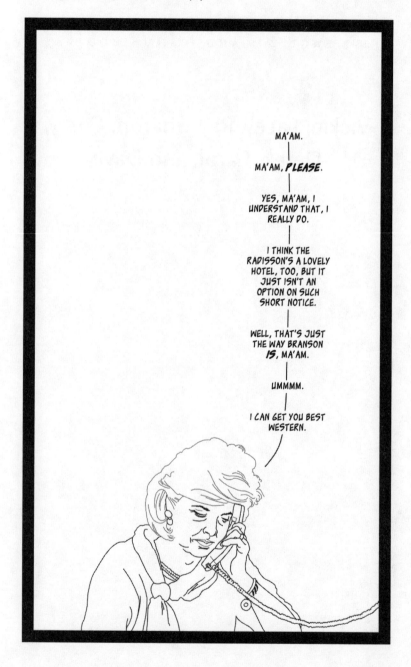

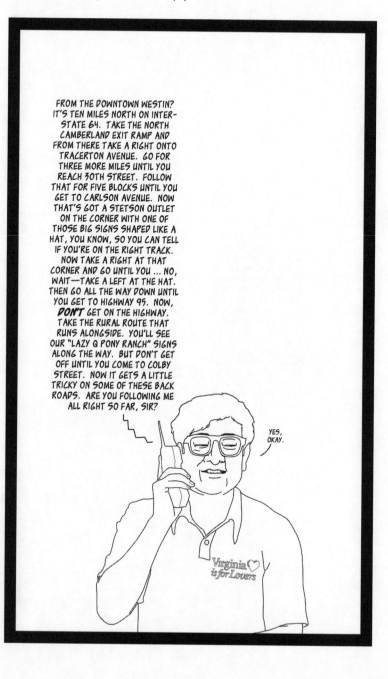

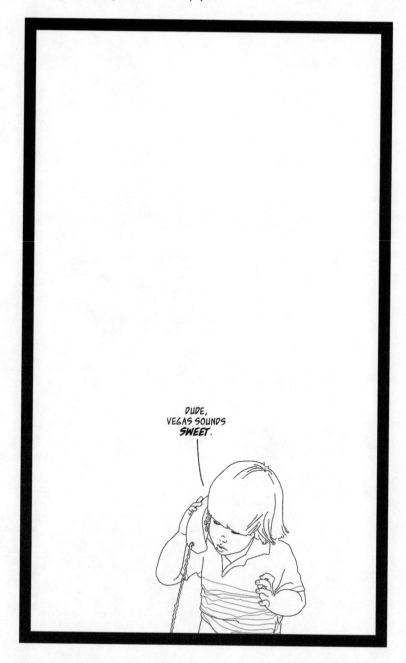

JON GERTNER

■

# The Futile Pursuit of Happiness

FROM *New York Times*

IF DANIEL GILBERT IS right, then you are wrong. That is to say, if Daniel Gilbert is right, then you are wrong to believe that a new car will make you as happy as you imagine. You are wrong to believe that a new kitchen will make you happy for as long as you imagine. You are wrong to think that you will be more unhappy with a big single setback (a broken wrist, a broken heart) than with a lesser chronic one (a trick knee, a tense marriage). You are wrong to assume that job failure will be crushing. You are wrong to expect that a death in the family will leave you bereft for year upon year, forever and ever. You are even wrong to reckon that a cheeseburger you order in a restaurant — this week, next week, a year from now, it doesn't really matter when — will definitely hit the spot. That's because when it comes to predicting exactly how you will feel in the future, you are most likely wrong.

A professor in Harvard's department of psychology, Gilbert likes to tell people that he studies happiness. But it would be more precise to say that Gilbert — along with the psychologist Tim Wilson of the University of Virginia, the economist George Loewenstein of Carnegie Mellon, and the psychologist (and Nobel laureate in economics) Daniel Kahneman of Princeton — has taken the lead in studying a specific type of emotional and behavioral prediction. In the past few years, these four men have begun to question the decision-making process that shapes our sense of well-being:

How do we predict what will make us happy or unhappy — and then how do we feel after the actual experience? For example, how do we suppose we'll feel if our favorite college football team wins or loses, and then how do we really feel a few days after the game? How do we predict we'll feel about purchasing jewelry, having children, buying a big house, or being rich? And then how do we regard the outcomes? According to this small corps of academics, almost all actions — the decision to buy jewelry, have kids, buy the big house, or work exhaustively for a fatter paycheck — are based on our predictions of the emotional consequences of these events.

Until recently, this was uncharted territory. How we forecast our feelings, and whether those predictions match our future emotional states, had never been the stuff of laboratory research. But in scores of experiments, Gilbert, Wilson, Kahneman, and Loewenstein have made a slew of observations and conclusions that undermine a number of fundamental assumptions: namely, that we humans understand what we want and are adept at improving our well-being — that we are good at maximizing our utility, in the jargon of traditional economics. Further, their work on prediction raises some unsettling and somewhat more personal questions. To understand affective forecasting, as Gilbert has termed these studies, is to wonder if everything you have ever thought about life choices, and about happiness, has been at the least somewhat naive and, at worst, greatly mistaken.

The problem, as Gilbert and company have come to discover, is that we falter when it comes to imagining how we will feel about something in the future. It isn't that we get the big things wrong. We know we will experience visits to Le Cirque and to the periodontist differently; we can accurately predict that we'd rather be stuck in Montauk than in a Midtown elevator. What Gilbert has found, however, is that we overestimate the intensity and the duration of our emotional reactions — our "affect" — to future events. In other words, we might believe that a new BMW will make life perfect. But it will almost certainly be less exciting than we anticipated; nor will it excite us for as long as predicted. The vast majority of Gilbert's test participants through the years have consistently made just these sorts of errors both in the laboratory and in real-life situations. And whether Gilbert's subjects were trying to predict how they would feel in the future about a plate of spaghetti with meat sauce, the defeat of a preferred political candidate, or romantic rejection seemed not to matter. On average, bad events proved less intense and more transient than test participants predicted. Good events proved less intense and briefer as well.

Gilbert and his collaborator Tim Wilson call the gap between what we predict and what we ultimately experience the "impact bias" — "impact" meaning the errors we make in estimating both the intensity and duration of our emotions and "bias" our tendency to err. The phrase characterizes how we experience the dimming excitement over not just a BMW but also over any object or event that we presume will make us happy. Would a 20 percent raise or winning the lottery result in a contented life? You may predict it will, but almost surely it won't turn out that way. And a new plasma television? You may have high hopes, but the impact bias suggests that it will almost certainly be less cool, and in a shorter time, than you imagine. Worse, Gilbert has noted that these mistakes of expectation can lead directly to mistakes in choosing what we think will give us pleasure. He calls this "miswanting."

"The average person says, 'I know I'll be happier with a Porsche than a Chevy,'" Gilbert explains. "'Or with Linda rather than Rosalyn. Or as a doctor rather than as a plumber.' That seems very clear to people. The problem is, I can't get into medical school or afford the Porsche. So for the average person, the obstacle between them and happiness is actually getting the futures that they desire. But what our research shows — not just ours, but Loewenstein's and Kahneman's — is that the real problem is figuring out which of those futures is going to have the high payoff and is really going to make you happy.

"You know, the Stones said, 'You can't always get what you want,'" Gilbert adds. "I don't think that's the problem. The problem is you can't always know what you want."

Gilbert's papers on affective forecasting began to appear in the late 1990s, but the idea to study happiness and emotional prediction actually came to him on a sunny afternoon in October 1992, just as he and his friend Jonathan Jay Koehler sat down for lunch outside the psychology building at the University of Texas at Austin, where both men were teaching at the time. Gilbert was uninspired about his studies and says he felt despair about his failing marriage. And as he launched into a discussion of his personal life, he swerved to ask why economists focus on the financial aspects of decision making rather than the emotional ones. Koehler recalls, "Gilbert said something like: 'It all seems so small. It isn't really about money; it's about happiness. Isn't that what everybody wants to know when we make a decision?'" For a moment, Gilbert forgot his troubles, and two more questions came to him. Do we even know what makes us happy? And if it's difficult to figure out what makes us happy in the moment, how can we predict what will make us happy in the future?

In the early 1990s, for an up-and-coming psychology professor like Gilbert to switch his field of inquiry from how we perceive one another to happiness, as he did that day, was just a hairsbreadth short of bizarre. But Gilbert has always liked questions that lead him somewhere new. Now forty-five, Gilbert dropped out of high school at fifteen, hooking into what he calls "the tail end of the hippie movement" and hitchhiking aimlessly from town to town with his guitar. He met his wife on the road; she was hitching in the other direction. They married at seventeen, had a son at eighteen, and settled down in Denver. "I pulled weeds, I sold rebar, I sold carpet, I installed carpet, I spent a lot of time as a phone solicitor," he recalls. During this period he spent several years turning out science-fiction stories for magazines like *Amazing Stories*. Thus, in addition to being "one of the most gifted social psychologists of our age," as the psychology writer and professor David G. Myers describes him to me, Gilbert is the author of "The Essence of Grunk," a story about an encounter with a creature made of egg salad that jets around the galaxy in a rocket-powered refrigerator.

Psychology was a matter of happenstance. In the midst of his sci-fi career, Gilbert tried to sign up for a writing course at the local community college, but the class was full; he figured that psych, still accepting registrants, would help him with character development in his fiction. It led instead to an undergraduate degree at the University of Colorado at Denver, then a Ph.D. at Princeton, then an appointment at the University of Texas, then the appointment at Harvard. "People ask why I study happiness," Gilbert says, "and I say, 'Why study anything else?' It's the holy grail. We're studying the thing that all human action is directed toward."

One experiment of Gilbert's had students in a photography class at Harvard choose two favorite pictures from among those they had just taken and then relinquish one to the teacher. Some students were told their choices were permanent; others were told they could exchange their prints after several days. As it turned out, those who had time to change their minds were less pleased with their decisions than those whose choices were irrevocable.

Much of Gilbert's research is in this vein. Another recent study asked whether transit riders in Boston who narrowly missed their trains experienced the self-blame that people tend to predict they'll feel in this situation. (They did not.) And a paper waiting to be published, "The Peculiar Longevity of Things Not So Bad," examines why we expect that bigger problems will always dwarf minor annoyances. "When really bad things happen to us, we defend against them," Gilbert explains. "People, of course, predict the exact opposite. If you ask, 'What would you rather have, a broken leg or a trick knee?' they'd probably say, 'Trick knee.' And yet, if your goal is to accumulate maximum happiness over your lifetime, you just made the wrong choice. A trick knee is a bad thing to have."

All of these studies establish the links between prediction, decision making, and well-being. The photography experiment challenges our common assumption that we would be happier with the option to change our minds when in fact we're happier with closure. The transit experiment demonstrates that we tend to err in estimating our regret over missed opportunities. The "things not so bad" work shows our failure to imagine how grievously irritations compromise our satisfaction. Our emotional defenses snap into action when it comes to a divorce or a disease but not for lesser problems. We fix the leaky roof on our house, but over the long haul, the broken screen door we never mend adds up to more frustration.

Gilbert does not believe all forecasting mistakes lead to similar results; a death in the family, a new gym membership, and a new husband are not the same, but in how they affect our well-being they are similar. "Our research simply says that whether it's the thing that matters or the thing that doesn't, both of them matter less than you think they will," he says. "Things that happen to you or that you buy or own — as much as you think they make a difference to your happiness, you're wrong by a certain amount. You're overestimating how much of a difference they make. None of them makes the difference you think. And that's true of positive and negative events."

Much of the work of Kahneman, Loewenstein, Gilbert, and Wilson takes its cue from the concept of adaptation, a term psychologists have used since at least the 1950s to refer to how we acclimate to changing circumstances. George Loewenstein sums up this human capacity as follows: "Happiness is a signal that our brains use to motivate us to do certain things. And in the same way that our eye adapts to different levels of illumination, we're designed to kind of go back to the happiness set point. Our brains are not trying to be happy. Our brains are trying to regulate us." In this respect, the tendency toward adaptation suggests why the impact bias is so pervasive. As Tim Wilson says: "We don't realize how quickly we will adapt to a pleasurable event and make it the backdrop of our lives. When any event occurs to us, we make it ordinary. And through becoming ordinary, we lose our pleasure."

It is easy to overlook something new and crucial in what Wilson is saying. Not that we invariably lose interest in bright and shiny things over time — this is a long-known trait — but that we're generally unable to recognize that we adapt to new circumstances and therefore fail to incorporate this fact into our decisions. So, yes, we will adapt to the BMW and the plasma TV, since we adapt to virtually everything. But Wilson and Gilbert and others have shown that we seem unable to predict that we will adapt. Thus, when we find the pleasure derived from a thing diminishing, we move on to the next thing or event and almost certainly make another error of prediction, and then another, ad infinitum.

As Gilbert points out, this glitch is also significant when it comes to negative events like losing a job or the death of someone we love, in response to which we project a permanently inconsolable future. "The thing I'm most interested in, that I've spent the most time studying, is our failure to recognize how powerful psychological defenses are once they're activated," Gilbert says. "We've used the metaphor of the 'psychological immune system' — it's just a metaphor, but not a bad one for that system of defenses that helps you feel better when bad things happen. Observers of the human condition since Aristotle have known that people have these defenses. Freud spent his life, and his daughter Anna spent her life, worrying about these defenses. What's surprising is that people don't seem to recognize that they have these defenses, and that these defenses will be triggered by negative events." During the course of my interviews with Gilbert, a close friend of his died. "I am like everyone in thinking, I'll never get over this and life will never be good again," he wrote to me in an e-mail message as he planned a trip to Texas for the funeral. "But because of my work, there is always a voice in the back of my head — a voice that wears a lab coat and has a lot of data tucked under its arm — that says, 'Yes, you will, and yes, it will.' And I know that voice is right."

Still, the argument that we imperfectly imagine what we want and how we will cope is nevertheless disorienting. On the one hand, it can cast a shadow of regret on some life decisions. Why did I decide that working one hundred hours a week to earn more would make me happy? Why did I think that retiring to Sun City, Arizona, would please me? On the other hand, it can be enlightening. No wonder this teak patio set hasn't made me as happy as I expected. Even if she dumps me, I'll be okay. Either way, predicting how things will feel to us over the long term is mystifying. A large body of research on well-being seems to suggest that wealth above middle-class comfort makes little difference to our happiness, for example, or that having children does nothing to improve well-being — even as it drives marital satisfaction dramatically down. We often yearn for a roomy, isolated home (a thing we easily adapt to), when, in fact, it will probably compromise our happiness by distancing us from neighbors. (Social interaction and friendships have been shown to give lasting pleasure.) The big isolated home is what Loewenstein, forty-eight, himself bought. "I fell into a trap I never should have fallen into," he told me.

Loewenstein's office is up a narrow stairway in a hidden corner of an enormous, worn brick building on the edge of the Carnegie Mellon campus in Pittsburgh. He and Gilbert make for an interesting contrast. Gilbert is garrulous, theatrical, dazzling in his speech and writing; he fills a room. Loewenstein is soft-spoken, given to abstraction, and lithe in the way of a hard-core athlete; he seems to float around a room. Both men profess tremendous admiration for the other, and their different disciplines — psychology and economics — have made their overlapping interests in affective forecasting more complementary than fraught. While Gilbert's most notable contribution to affective forecasting is the impact bias, Loewenstein's is something called the "empathy gap."

Here's how it expresses itself. In a recent experiment, Loewenstein tried to find out how likely people might be to dance alone to Rick James's "Super Freak" in front of a large audience. Many agreed to do so for a certain amount of money a week in advance, only to renege when the day came to take the stage. This sounds like a goof, but it gets at the fundamental difference between how we behave in "hot" states (those of anxiety, courage, fear, drug craving, sexual excitation, and the like) and "cold" states of rational calm. This empathy gap in thought and behavior — we cannot seem to predict how we will behave in a hot state when we are in a cold state — affects happiness in an important but somewhat less consistent way than the impact bias. "So much of our lives involves making decisions that have consequences for the future," Loewenstein says. "And if our decision making is influenced by these transient emotional and psychological states, then we know we're not making decisions with an eye toward future consequences." This may be as simple as an unfortunate proclamation of love in a moment of lust, Loewenstein explains, or something darker, like an act of road rage or of suicide.

Among other things, this line of inquiry has led Loewenstein to collaborate with health experts looking into why people engage in unprotected sex when they would never agree to do so in moments of cool calculation. Data from tests in which volunteers are asked how they would behave in various "heat of the moment" situations — whether they would have sex with a minor, for instance, or act forcefully with a partner who asks them to stop — have consistently shown that different states of arousal can alter answers by astonishing margins. "These kinds of states have the ability to change us so profoundly that we're more different from ourselves in different states than we are from another person," Loewenstein says.

Part of Loewenstein's curiosity about hot and cold states comes from situations in which his emotions have been pitted against his intellect. When he's not teaching, he treks around the world, making sure to get to Alaska to hike or kayak at least once a year. A scholar of mountaineering literature, he once wrote a paper that examined why climbers have a poor memory for pain and usually ignore turn-back times at great peril. But he has done the same thing himself many times. He almost died in a whitewater canoeing accident and vowed afterward that he never wanted to see his runaway canoe again. (A couple of hours later, he went looking for it.) The same goes for his climbing pursuits. "You establish your turn-back time, and then you find yourself still far from the peak," he says. "So you push on. You haven't brought enough food or clothes, and then as a result, you're stuck at thirteen thousand feet, and you have to just sit there and shiver all night without a sleeping bag or warm clothes. When the sun comes up, you're half-frozen, and you say, 'Never again.' Then you get back and immediately start craving getting out again." He pushes the point: "I have tried to train my emotions." But he admits that he may make the same mistakes on his next trip.

Would a world without forecasting errors be a better world? Would a life lived without forecasting errors be a richer life?

Among the academics who study affective forecasting, there seems little doubt that these sorts of questions will ultimately jump from the academy to the real world. "If people do not know what is going to make them better off or give them pleasure," Daniel Kahneman says, "then the idea that you can trust people to do what will give them pleasure becomes questionable." To Kahneman, who did some of the first experiments in the area in the early 1990s, affective forecasting could greatly influence retirement planning, for example, where mistakes in prediction (how much we save, how much we spend, how we choose a community we think we'll enjoy) can prove irreversible. He sees a role for affective forecasting in consumer spending, where a "cooling off" period might remedy buyer's remorse. Most important, he sees vital applications in health care, especially when it comes to informed consent. "We consider people capable of giving informed consent once they are told of the objective effects of a treatment," Kahneman says. "But can people anticipate how they and other people will react to a colostomy or to the removal of their vocal cords? The research on affective forecasting suggests that people may have little ability to anticipate their adaptation beyond the early stages." Loewenstein, along with his collaborator Dr. Peter Ubel, has done a great deal of work showing that nonpatients overestimate the displeasure of living with the loss of a limb, for instance, or paraplegia. To use affective forecasting to prove that people adapt to serious physical challenges far better and will be happier than they imagine, Loewenstein says, could prove invaluable.

There are downsides to making public policy in light of this research, too. While walking in Pittsburgh one afternoon, Loewenstein tells me that he doesn't see how anybody could study happiness and not find himself leaning left politically; the data make it all too clear that boosting the living standards of those already comfortable, such as through lower taxes, does little to improve their levels of well-being, whereas raising the living standards of the impoverished makes an enormous difference. Nevertheless, he and Gilbert (who once declared in an academic paper, "Windfalls are better than pratfalls, A's are better than C's, December 25 is better than April 15, and everything is better than a Republican administration") seem to lean libertarian in regard to pushing any kind of prescriptive agenda. "We're very, very nervous about overapplying the research," Loewenstein says. "Just because we figure out that X makes people happy and they're choosing Y, we don't want to impose X on them. I have a discomfort with paternalism and with using the results coming out of our field to impose decisions on people."

Still, Gilbert and Loewenstein can't contain the personal and philosophical questions raised by their work. After talking with both men, I found it hard not to wonder about my own predictions at every turn. At times it seemed like knowing the secret to some parlor trick that was nonetheless very difficult to pull off — when I ogled a new car at the Honda dealership as I waited for a new muffler on my '92 Accord, for instance, or as my daughter's fever spiked one evening and I imagined something terrible, and then something more terrible thereafter. With some difficulty, I could observe my mind overshooting the mark, zooming past accuracy toward the sublime or the tragic. It was tempting to want to try to think about the future more moderately. But it seemed nearly impossible as well.

To Loewenstein, who is especially attendant to the friction between his emotional and deliberative processes, a life without forecasting errors would most likely be a better, happier life. "If you had a deep understanding of the impact bias and you acted on it, which is not always that easy to do, you would tend to invest your resources in the things that would make you happy," he says. This might mean taking more time with friends instead of more time for making money. He also adds that a better understanding of the empathy gap — those hot and cold states we all find ourselves in on frequent occasions — could save people from making regrettable decisions in moments of courage or craving.

Gilbert seems optimistic about using the work in terms of improving "institutional judgment" — how we spend health care dollars, for example — but less sanguine about using it to improve our personal judgment. He admits that he has taken some of his research to heart; for instance, his work on what he calls the psychological immune system has led him to believe that he would be able to adapt to even the worst turn of events. In addition, he says that he now takes more chances in life, a fact corroborated in at least one aspect by his research partner Tim Wilson, who says that driving with Gilbert in Boston is a terrifying, white-knuckle experience. "But I should have learned many more lessons from my research than I actually have," Gilbert admits. "I'm getting married in the spring because this woman is going to make me happy forever, and I know it." At this, Gilbert laughs, a sudden, booming laugh that fills his Cambridge office. He seems to find it funny not because it's untrue, but because nothing could be more true. This is how he feels. "I don't think I want to give up all these motivations," he says, "that belief that there's the good and there's the bad and that this is a contest to try to get one and avoid the other. I don't think I want to learn too much from my research in that sense."

Even so, Gilbert is currently working on a complex experiment in which he has made affective forecasting errors "go away." In this test, Gilbert's team asks members of Group A to estimate how they'll feel if they receive negative personality feedback. The impact bias kicks in, of course, and they mostly predict they'll feel terrible, when in fact they end up feeling okay. But if Gilbert shows Group B that others have gotten the same feedback and felt okay afterward, then its members predict they'll feel okay as well. The impact bias disappears, and the participants in Group B make accurate predictions.

This is exciting to Gilbert. But at the same time, it's not a technique he wants to shape into a self-help book, or one that he even imagines could be practically implemented. "Hope and fear are enduring features of the human experience," he says, "and it is unlikely that people are going to abandon them anytime soon just because some psychologist told them they should." In fact, in his recent writings, he has wondered whether forecasting errors might somehow serve a larger functional purpose he doesn't yet understand. If he could wave a wand tomorrow and eliminate all affective-forecasting errors, I ask, would he? "The benefits of not making this error would seem to be that you get a little more happiness," he says. "When choosing between two jobs, you wouldn't sweat as much because you'd say: 'You know, I'll be happy in both. I'll adapt to either circumstance pretty well, so there's no use in killing myself for the next week.' But maybe our caricatures of the future — these overinflated assessments of how good or bad things will be — maybe it's these illusory assessments that keep us moving in one direction over the other. Maybe we don't want a society of people who shrug and say, 'It won't really make a difference.'

"Maybe it's important for there to be carrots and sticks in the world, even if they are illusions," he adds. "They keep us moving towards carrots and away from sticks."

MICHAEL HALL

■

# Running for His Life

FROM *Texas Monthly*

HE WAS ON FIRE. It was three in the morning, and most of his classmates from the Kibimba school in Burundi were dead — beaten and burned alive by friends of theirs, kids and grownups they had known most of their lives. Smoldering bodies lay in mounds all over the small room. He had used some of the corpses for cover, to keep from being hit by the fiery branches tossed in by the Hutu mob outside. For hours he had heard them laughing, singing, clapping, taunting. Waving their machetes, they had herded more than a hundred Tutsi teenagers and teachers from his high school into the room before sunset. A couple dozen were still alive, moaning in pain, dreaming of death.

"There weren't that many of us left," he says. "A guy said, 'I'm going out — I don't want to die like a dog.' He jumped from a window. They cut him to pieces. Then they started a fire on the roof. After a while it started falling on me, and I held up my right arm as it came down, trying to pull bodies over me. My back and arm were on fire — it hurt so bad. I decided I had had enough. I decided to kill myself by diving from a pile of bodies onto my head. I tried twice, but it didn't work. Then I heard a voice. It said, 'You don't want to die. Don't do that.' Outside, we could hear Hutus giving up and leaving. I heard one say, 'Before we go, let's make sure everyone is dead.' So three came inside. One put a spear through a guy's heart; another guy tried to escape, and they caught him and killed him. I heard the voice say, 'Get out.' There was a body next to me, burned down to the bones. It was hot. I grabbed a bone — it was hot in my hands — and used it to break the bar on the window. The fires had been going for nine hours, so it was easy to break. My thinking was, I wanted to kill myself. I wanted to be identifiable. I wanted my parents to know me. I didn't want to be all burned up, like everyone else. I was jumping to let them kill me."

There was a fire underneath the window, set as an obstacle to escape. He jumped. And somehow, in the darkness, amid the uproar of genocide, at least for a few seconds, no one saw him. His back was on fire, his legs were smoking, and his feet were raw with pain. He ran.

If you could call it running.

"Gilbert!" Almost a decade later, on March 30, 2003, he crossed the finish line at the Capitol 10,000 in Austin to the sound of hundreds of people clapping, many calling his name. "Gilbert! Woo!" He finished ahead of some 14,000 runners, but it wasn't good enough, and the look on his face said that he knew it. Others knew it too. A woman off to the side yelled, "Coach, you're awesome! I love you! You're number one, Gilbert!" In fact, Gilbert Tuhabonye was number three, a minute and fifteen seconds behind the winner in a race he had won the previous year and was favored to win again. Gilbert turned and jogged back against the flow of the other finishers, shaking hands and high-fiving spectators, who all seemed to know the thin African. Then he ran the last fifty yards again with Richard Mendez, one of many runners he had trained. "Come on! Come on!" Gilbert said to Mendez. "High knee!" When Mendez finished, Gilbert went back and ran with Ryan Steglich, another of his charges. And then with Shae Rainer and Lisa Spenner. "Come on! Come on!" he yelled. "Butt kick!"

Afterward, Gilbert, who stands five feet ten and weighs 127 pounds, hung around talking to the other runners, many of whom wore T-shirts that read GILBERT'S GAZELLES TRAINING GROUP. A circle of eight stood basking in his approval, trading anecdotes about their pains and agonies, as runners do. He laughed and joked with them, accepting halfhearted high-fives and thin encouragement, which made him look down self-consciously. Eight thousand miles from home, he's a celebrity in Austin, a twenty-eight-year-old with protruding teeth and a boyish laugh, the most popular running coach in a town of rabid runners, a former national champion, both as a teenager in Africa and as a college student in West Texas. Governor Rick Perry, himself an avid runner, seeks out Gilbert to chat. Kids ask for his autograph. Rich white ladies pay him to order them to run laps. Everybody wants him to make them go faster. They've heard his mantra: It's all about form. "If you have good form," says Gilbert, "running becomes a joy. You can go farther and faster. You can run forever."

You can run forever. This, to a runner, is heaven. Gilbert's students see him as a savior, upbeat after all that he's been through, relentless and optimistic when he has every right to be withdrawn and angry. A man on a mission: to win an Olympic medal, to tell his story, to show the world what one tribe did and what one man — set on fire and left to die — can do. A man with a last name (pronounced "Too-ha-bon-yay") almost too good to be true. "In Burundi," Gilbert says, "your last name has to have meaning. When I was born, it was a very difficult time. It was right after the war. There had been a big drought, crickets attacked the crops — and then my mother broke her ankle. When I was born, she said I was special. She said, 'This is not my son. This is a son of God.' 'Tuhabonye' means 'a son of God.'"

As the runners dispersed, Jeff Kloster, who works with Gilbert at RunTex, an Austin running store, brought him his warm-ups, and Gilbert took off his shirt to change. Though Jeff had seen them before, he could not take his eyes off the scars that cover Gilbert's back. The burns continue along his right arm, where they bubble the skin like large patches of candle wax, and then to his right leg, which gets darker along the sides of his calf, where the flames ate down to the bone. The scars are proof of the unthinkable: Ten years ago, on a mountaintop in Burundi, high school kids and their teachers were stuck in a room and set on fire. For nine hours Gilbert watched his friends die, breathed their burning flesh, hid under their corpses. Then he ran for his life. People speak of crucibles and the forging of character. They have no idea.

In the living room of his two-bedroom South Austin apartment, Gilbert is beating on an imaginary drum. He's playing along with a group of drummers on a CD of Burundian music. It sounds like an army — pounding, lurching, exploding, simmering, then accelerating beats; there's no melody, only occasional yelling and chanting. "There are eleven people in a circle," he says excitedly, "each with a three-foot-wide drum." He moves his arms and his head along with the rhythm. "There's one in the center. He's calling out, jumping. Everyone is watching him, following him. There's a lot of dancing. It's awesome."

Gilbert's pretty wife, Triphine, plays nearby with their daughter, Emma. At home the couple speak mostly Kirundi, their native tongue, though they try to speak English around Emma, an alternately shy and boisterous two-year-old. Gilbert also speaks French and Swahili. His English is very good, and he speaks it with a melodious lilt. He has short hair and high cheekbones — he's handsome in an earnest, youthful way. He's wearing blue denim shorts, a gray Mizuno shirt, and sandals. His legs are thin but muscular. His burns look like relief maps.

The apartment is cluttered with Emma's toys. On the walls are a tacked-up Burundi flag and photos of Gilbert running; a Bible sits on a table. Another song comes on, from the sixties, called "Yes, I Love Micombero," about a Tutsi president from back then. Gilbert sings along, and Triph, who is also a Tutsi, remembers it too. "If you say this guy's name in front of a Hum," says Gilbert, "he will kill you." Gilbert pretends to play some of the other instruments. "In Burundi, the music is good and the climate is beautiful. If there was peace, I'd go there to train. The lake is gorgeous — there are hundreds of types of fish. It's like Hawaii: a lot of birds, all these types of fruits. It's paradise."

Burundi is a small, poor, mountainous country in east central Africa. Gilbert was born in the southern county of Songa on November 22, 1974, the third of four children. His Tutsi parents were farmers, raising corn, potatoes, peas, and beans, and also kept milk cows. As a boy, he ran everywhere: down the valley to get water, to school five miles away. He loved to race his friends, but more than anything else, he loved to chase the family's cows. In the sixth grade, he was baptized a Catholic, and the next year he went to a Protestant boarding school in Kibimba, about 150 miles away. Of the thousand or so students, about 60 percent were Hutus and the rest Tutsis. For the most part, they got along pretty well, sharing the same dorms and playing on the same soccer team.

Though the Hutu and Tutsi tribes have squabbled for centuries, it's only in the past two generations that things have gotten brutal, both in Burundi and in its northern neighbor, Rwanda. The countries are roughly the same size and are similar in many ways (think of the Dakotas). They each have a five-to-one mix of Hutus and Tutsis, they speak Kirundi, they're roughly two thirds Catholic, and they have shared histories. In Burundi, the Tutsis (a.k.a. the Watusi) have ruled the Hutus ever since emigrating from Ethiopia, more than five hundred years ago. The Tutsis were cattle herders and aristocrats, while the Hutus were working-class farmers. They lived together in relative peace until the Europeans came; Burundi and Rwanda were incorporated into German East Africa in the 1890s, and Belgium took over after World War I. "During colonization, they started dividing people," says Gilbert. "The Germans made the differences between Tutsi and Hum into law: divide and govern."

Both Rwanda and Burundi became independent in 1962. While the Hutus gained some power in Rwanda, Tutsis controlled the army and the government in Burundi, making occasional attempts at parliamentary elections to give the more numerous Hutus a voice in government. Just before and after independence, ethnic violence flared up, and there were massacres by both sides. In 1972 an attempted coup in Burundi led to the slaughter of some 150,000 Hutus; many Tutsis were killed too, including three of Gilbert's uncles. "Bad teaching," he says about the causes of the violence. "Deep hate." It's a class thing and a race thing, even though both tribes have intermingled for so long that sometimes even Burundians can't tell the difference. But usually they can. A Tutsi, says Gilbert, tends to be tall and thin, with a narrow nose; a Hum is shorter, more muscular, and has a wider nose. Tutsis complain that Hutus lack ambition; Hutus say Tutsis are arrogant.

At the Kibimba school, Gilbert began running competitively. As a freshman, he won an 8K race running barefoot. The next year, he met a coach who showed him how to run properly — how to get his knees up and how to hold his arms. The coach told Gilbert that if he worked hard, he could make the Olympics. In his junior year, Gilbert was a national champion in the 400 and 800 meters, already a great runner in a country known for producing them. By his senior year, in 1993, all he cared about was school and running. His goal was to get a scholarship to an American college, get an education, and return home. The dream actually seemed possible, since Burundi appeared to have turned a corner on its violent past: The latest Tutsi dictator had mandated the first-ever presidential election, and not surprisingly, a Hutu won. A new day was dawning in Burundi. Four months after the election, though, the president was assassinated by Tutsi soldiers. It was a new day, all right.

"The night before," says Gilbert, "I didn't sleep. I had two tests that day, in chemistry and biology. I was thinking, *Maybe I studied too hard.* It was my senior year, and I had to be prepared for college. That morning I turned on the radio. Nothing. I thought the battery was dead. I went to class, and people started talking about the rumors — usually when the radio isn't working, it's a coup. A friend said there was a putsch, that the president was dead. There weren't many Hutus around, but I saw one, my teammate on the 440 relay. He showed me a machete, pulled it out of its sheath, ran it along his throat, and said, 'Tonight is the night I'm gonna cut your neck.' I said, 'Why?' He said, 'Because you guys killed our president.' I thought he was joking. I found out later that Hutus had been gathering since three in the morning, planning on killing Tutsis. By ten, a mob had gathered at the school — Hutus with machetes. They took away a Tutsi professor and said, 'We're gonna kill all these Tutsis.' I told a professor, a Tutsi, what people were saying. He said, 'Don't worry — they can't do that.'"

Sitting on his flowered couch, Gilbert recounts this story carefully, speaking slowly at some points and excitedly at others, sometimes waving his arms. "Around noon, we went to the principal to ask for help, and he told us, 'You killed the president, and you have to die.' We tried to organize a peaceful running away. We also hoped the army would come. There were hundreds of us marching — girls, boys, teachers, farmers — and we locked our arms together. We didn't get far; the mob stopped us. By then it had started raining. Everywhere we looked, there was a Hum with a machete, a bow and arrow, or a spear. Some were my friends. They told us to go back to the school. We didn't move. All of a sudden, a woman took a spear and threw it into the crowd. And they attacked us — cutting people, their ears and noses, so they'd know who was a Tutsi.

"Many escaped. I tried to, but they were watching me. They knew I was a cross-country runner, that I could run and tell the soldiers. They got me, and the principal said I'd be the last to die. He said they'd do me like they did Jesus Christ. He said, 'You will see what Jesus saw on the cross.' He meant I was going to get a good torture, like Jesus got. They attached us to each other, one by one, with a rope, by the arms. I said, 'Where are you taking us? I thought we were friends.' 'Not anymore.'

"Kids were bleeding, screaming, crying. My heart was beating like I don't know what, I was so scared. They took us down the hill to a highway gas station owned by a Hum, a guy I knew — I bought stuff from him all the time. People were all around us, walking next to us, with machetes. They were singing, 'We caught the enemy! We're gonna burn them to death!' When we got there, they took our clothes. All I had on was underwear and a shirt. Before they pushed us inside, they beat every kid on the back of the neck with a big club. They hit hard — to stun or paralyze. Some were killed. I was one of the last ones and jumped inside, but they beat me on the chest so hard that I bled for three weeks.

"There were more than a hundred people in a room this big" —

Gilbert points to the kitchen wall on the far side of his living room, a forty-by-twenty-five-foot space. "We couldn't move. It was jammed with half-naked people screaming and crying. Outside, they were dancing, clapping, singing, 'We did it!' Just after I got in, they poured gasoline in through the windows — everyone got some on them. I got it on my shirt, so I took it off. Then they threw in branches that were on fire. The flames moved so fast. People were trying to hide and put out the flames. It was horrible. Many were killed by the fire and smoke. The Hutus were waiting outside for us to try to escape, but the doors were thick and we couldn't break out.

"Because I was one of the last in, I was near the wall, banging against it, and I found a door to a kind of closet. I pushed it open, and there were more people in there. I let a few more inside. The Hutus kept throwing lit branches in through a window. I hid under the bodies of my friends. After a couple more hours, I heard a student tell the chemistry professor to get some chemicals to throw inside. The people left were gasping for air. I took a deep breath and was pushing air away from my face."

At this point, the Hutus set fire to the roof, Gilbert caught fire, and he decided to let them kill him. "But something was guiding me," he says. "When I jumped, they were outside, just a few feet away, standing by the fire they'd built under the window. But they didn't see me. As soon as I landed, I couldn't see clearly. The wind was blowing, and it was cold — I was naked. I just started moving and got around the corner. I heard someone shout, 'Gilbert is coming!' I saw a mob of people — they stood up, holding machetes. Everywhere, I saw people coming. I ran downhill. The more I ran, the wind was teasing the fire on my back. Some people were saying, 'Don't worry about him; he's gonna die anyway,' and they gave up. But not everyone. A guy came running at me with a machete. I ducked, and he just missed me and cut his own arm. I kept running, and all of a sudden I fell into a deep ditch filled with rainwater. It put out the fire on my back. I heard people talking, saying, 'Let's catch him. He knows who we are.' I heard this one guy coming — I knew his voice — and he fell into the ditch. I was leaning against the side, and he had a spear in one hand and a machete in the other. I killed him. I have never confessed this before. I was so angry. They had burned me, killed my friends. I had nothing to lose. But I don't think it was me who got that strength. God gives power to eliminate evil."

How exactly did a mild-mannered high school kid kill a man? Gilbert demonstrates — he puts one hand on his chin and the other on the back of his head, jerking and twisting hard, pantomiming the breaking of someone's neck. "I watch Chuck Norris," he says. "Chuck Norris was my favorite. The guy puked on himself, and I knew he was dead.

"The voice in my head said, 'Go away,'" Gilbert continues, "so I got up again. I was so thirsty, so dehydrated, and I started toward the hospital, about a half-mile away. It was so hard to move; every step hurt. I could barely stand up. My feet, I could see, were like meat. My right leg was so bad that I could see the bone. I was on my hands and knees, running like a monkey. There were still Hutus everywhere with machetes. The voice was telling me, 'You don't want to die.' My heart was beating so hard that I thought they could hear it. When I got to the hospital, a guy saw me going in and said, 'He runs like a monkey. He's not a human being. He's a spirit.'"

It was all about form — the years on the track, keeping his knees up and his arms back, pushing himself when he thought he was going to die. He stumbled into the sanctuary of the hospital. Soon the soldiers came, and Gilbert, with third-degree burns over 30 percent of his body, was moved to an army hospital; later he recovered in a hospital near his home, where his mother came to visit him. In the immediate aftermath of the fire, she and Gilbert's father had been told that he was dead. Then, later that night, Gilbert's father had been murdered by a Hutu gang on the road. Now, she was told, her son was alive.

"When my mother came to the hospital, I was bandaged everywhere. She said, 'I told you, you are a son of God. If it wasn't for God, you are dead.' It's a shock and also a lesson. It has meaning. I don't think I survived because I'm strong but because of the power of God. God showed up." But what about the others? Surely they were also children of God. Why weren't they spared as well? "That's the thing I didn't understand. Afterward, I asked myself, 'Why me? Why did I survive?'"

In the hospital, he lay on his stomach and left side, pondering the unknowable. When he closed his eyes to sleep, he saw flames and heard screams. He read his Bible. He figured the voice he had heard was God's, but he didn't know why it had spoken only to him. "Why did God want me to survive?"

Why do people run — that is, people who aren't being chased by a fire-throwing, machete-waving mob? Why do thousands get up early on a Sunday morning and put their knees and ankles and hearts and lungs through the hell of 10,000 meters on hard pavement?

There is no single good answer to this question. In high school, people run for glory or for girls (or boys). Maybe they're being punished. Later on, they run for exercise or just to fit into their pants. Eventually, if they're lucky, they tap into another world: the state of physical and mental grace they reach when they're cruising, when their blood is racing through their every vein. Their thoughts have never been clearer, and their limbs are snapping in rhythm; their souls are revealed, and they are striving, excellent souls. They become obsessed with this feeling. They get religious about it. It is, for some of them, as spiritual as they will ever get.

Go to a running trail in any big city in Texas, and you will see them working toward this feeling: the grimacer, the puffer, the hacker, the wheezer; the stiff-armed and the backward-leaning; the torso-barely-moving and the stumpy-legs-moving-fast; the potato on sticks, the pear-shaped, the ham-thighed; the loping underachiever and the determined overstepper; the elbows swiveling, the shoulders hunched, the whole body moving as if under water. They are all bound together by this transforming passion and perhaps also by the fact that they look less silly if they run in numbers. They are, most of them, loners: mild-mannered, nervous, self-conscious, preoccupied with their bodies. They long to get better and faster, to raise their personal bests, even when at a certain point that becomes physically impossible (such logic does not concern the runner, who is high on the opiate of self-improvement). Their feet splay to the sides, their arms flail. They are desperate.

And in Austin, at least, they hang on Gilbert's every word. He coaches at RunTex, where he is one of twenty instructors — "the Michael Jordan" of the bunch, says the store's owner, Paul Carrozza. Some of Gilbert's students (he has about a hundred at any one time) are competitive runners, people who, say, have qualified for the Boston Marathon and want to set a personal record. They're fanatics, obsessed with every half-second, every curve of the trail, every ache and pain. They aspire to the elite. Lisa Spenner, twenty-eight, is one of these, a former triathlete who, after training with Gilbert for the Motorola Marathon, missed qualifying for the American Olympic trials by only fifty-one seconds. Most of Gilbert's students are athletic types, late bloomers who run regularly but perhaps unwisely in local races like the Capitol 10K. They don't aspire to the elite; they just want to run faster. Then there are the ones who just want to get some exercise with the enthusiastic African man. They aspire to look good.

Gilbert's methods are pretty simple, really. One of the pleasant paradoxes of running is that the more machinelike you get, the freer you feel. As he says, it's all about form: how the arms move (economically, if possible) and the feet land (heel to toe). His workouts are intense — sprinting around the track, speeding up hills, springing up and down on a bench — all to improve the basic mechanics of movement. He pushes his students hard and yells at them melodramatically as he trots alongside ("Knees up! Knees up! Knees up! I want to see you in the air!"). When, after eight successive sprints around the track or three inexorable ascents up a steep hill or a series of hundred-yard dashes on a single breath of air, they feel like they're about to die, they look at Gilbert's scars. How bad, really, could it be? "He gets people to believe in themselves," says Spenner. "He treats everyone like they're amazing." Sometimes they watch him as he motors like a quiet machine, his head barely bobbing, his arms swinging in perfect time, his feet making quiet patting sounds, and then they try it themselves. At the end of a workout they're breathing hard, bent over, walking slowly, wet with sweat, exhausted. They are in agony. They are happy. They are better.

"Most elite runners think it's all about them," says Carrozza. "Gilbert is so giving, so willing to coach others." If Gilbert is their savior, they are his saviors too — or at least they help answer the question that has haunted him for a decade now: Why me? "Eventually, I realized I had to help people," he says, "coaching them, telling them my story, telling what happened. When I help people, I feel good."

The Kibimba massacre was the beginning of a bloody civil war in which there were mass killings fueled by revenge on both sides. Six months later, a plane carrying the president of Rwanda and the new leader of Burundi was shot down, leading to the genocide in Rwanda of 800,000 Tutsis over a period of one hundred days; there hadn't been such an efficient killing machine since the Holocaust. Burundi was lucky — the Hutus weren't as organized there, and the Tutsis controlled the army. A mere 200,000, mostly Hutus, would die throughout the rest of the nineties.

Gilbert spent three months in the hospital, recovering not only from the burns but from the savage beating he had received. He was now a witness, for God and Tutsi, and he told his story to anyone who visited. His right leg was so badly burned that his knee was stuck at a ninety-degree angle. The doctor said it would take six months to heal. Frustrated, Gilbert got on a bike and forcibly unstuck it. "The blood came through; I could sleep again. If I hadn't done it, I could have been crippled." While in the hospital, he got a scholarship offer from Tulane University, in New Orleans. Gilbert wasn't healed enough yet to accept it, but he used it as motivation to run again. The biking led to walking, which led to jogging, which finally led to running a year after he had been left to die. In 1995 he ran the 400 meters at a competition in Kenya and later that year ran for Burundi in the World University Games in

Japan. He went to the University of Burundi for a year and was training for the 1996 Olympics when he was sent to an Olympic training center in Georgia, one of many such facilities established by the International Olympic Committee for athletes of developing nations. He ended up as an alternate on the team but stayed in Georgia, taking English classes at La Grange College.

The next year, he accepted a track scholarship from Abilene Christian University, the small Church of Christ school in West Texas that has a storied running history. ACU has won forty-nine NCAA Division II track-and-field championships and has sent almost three dozen athletes to the Olympics, including the great Bobby Morrow, who as a sophomore won the 100-meter and 200-meter dashes and the 400-meter relay at the 1956 Olympics in Melbourne, Australia. ACU has recently been home to many African runners, and it was a perfect place for Gilbert, who studied agricultural business and starred for the team. He was an all-American all three years at ACU, running the 800 and 1,500 meters, the 8K and 10K, and the mile, and he was part of seven national championship teams, winning the 800 indoors in 1999. Coach Jon Murray says Gilbert was a natural team leader. "We called him the Ambassador," he recalls. "He was always making friends, always helping people."

Gilbert liked Abilene. "It gave me time to worship and think," he says. "No distractions." He told his story to church and school groups, and eventually a Burundian student from North Texas State University in Denton visited and wrote about him for her school paper. CNN did a story on him too. In 1999 he won an award given to courageous student athletes. He got to meet Bill Clinton and Muhammad Ali. In 2000, his girlfriend, Triph, whom he had met in the hospital, came to America and enrolled at ACU, and they were married soon after.

After graduation, Gilbert couldn't find work, so one of his professors called an old ACU roommate in Austin: Paul Carrozza, who invited Gilbert down to visit. Inspired by his story, Carrozza offered him a position — several, actually. He wouldn't just sell shoes; he would speak to kids as part of the Marathon Kids program, trying to get them to run. And he'd race. Carrozza, a former track star himself at ACU, would coach him. It was a long way from the killing fields of Burundi.

He's gone back only once — Christmas of 1999 — and he learned a hard lesson: You can go home again, but you really shouldn't if you were a witness to genocide who's told your story on CNN. The local media found him, and relatives told him that Hutus were looking for him. Gilbert lay low and fled for good just after New Year's. "I'll never go back," he says. He doesn't trust the recent power-sharing arrangement that calls for a Tutsi and a Hutu to alternate as president every eighteen months. "If there's a Hutu in power," he says, "there's no Tutsi who could sleep at night." Gilbert was granted political asylum in the United States in 2001, and he's trying to get permanent residency.

We're accustomed to African-American athletes being superior, and we're accustomed to Africans, especially East Africans, being the best long-distance runners. Generally, they are. But they're human. They make mistakes. They get hypothermia, as Gilbert did in February at the Motorola Marathon in Austin, when he finished with a disappointing time of 2:26. They train wrong, as Gilbert did for the Capitol 10,000. They get tired. On a typical day, Gilbert is up at five, coaching at six, doing a morning run by seven-thirty, selling shoes all day, coaching after work, and then doing an evening run by seven; he runs an average of twenty miles a day. He tries to give time to Triph and Emma. He almost always falls short.

And, as unbelievable as it may seem to his students, sometimes he doubts himself. "I've never seen a guy so easily psyched out," says John Conley, Gilbert's agent. "Before a race, I tell him he's done the work; he knows the strategy; he's got the speed; he's got the strength. He just has to not let the negative talk in his head get to him. It's his Achilles' heel. He thinks, 'These guys are better than me,' and he puts himself in last place. If he could be like Ali and think, 'I'm the greatest,' he'd be unbeatable."

In truth, runners don't race to beat other runners. They race against themselves: to conquer their wills, to transcend their weaknesses, to beat back their nightmares. Of course, a runner will never actually beat himself; he'll never be good enough to do that. But he can get better. And so Gilbert has spent the spring and summer of this year trying to do just that, racing men who are faster than he is, knowing that this makes him better. In May he went to Indianapolis to run a half-marathon against a fast field and finished tenth, with a respectable time of 1:07:50. In June he ran the prestigious Grandma's Marathon in Duluth, Minnesota, at 2:23, but he'll need to get under 2:20 to make the Burundi Olympic team. Carrozza wants to push him even further and have him train with even faster runners. One problem, according to Carrozza, is that Gilbert has been running at slower paces with his students, essentially dumbing his body down. "He's got to refocus on himself," says Carrozza, "to balance the coaching with his training. But he doesn't have to give up coaching."

That will be a relief to the Gazelles and the spud-shaped obsessives on the running trails. Of course, they see Gilbert as more than just a good coach. He's a flesh-and-blood symbol, a real-life survivor, a true son of God, a man on a mission that's both infinitely greater than and remarkably similar to their own: the daily struggle to show what you're made of.

SAMMY HARKHAM

■

# Poor Sailor

FROM *Kramer's Ergot Four*

# POOR SAILOR

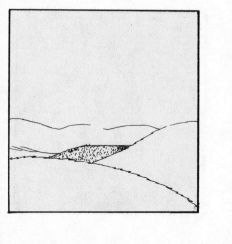

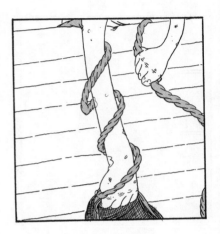

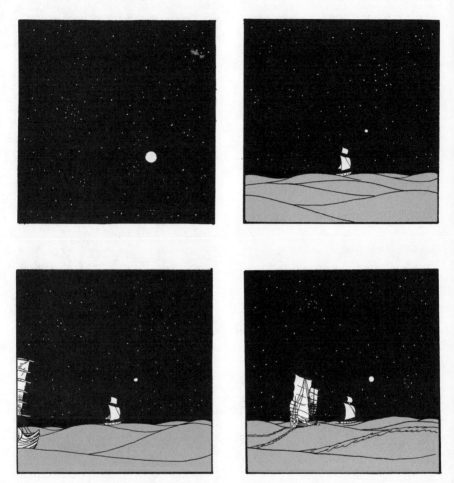

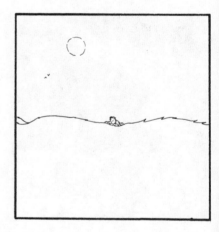

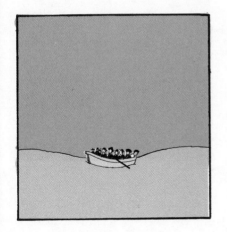

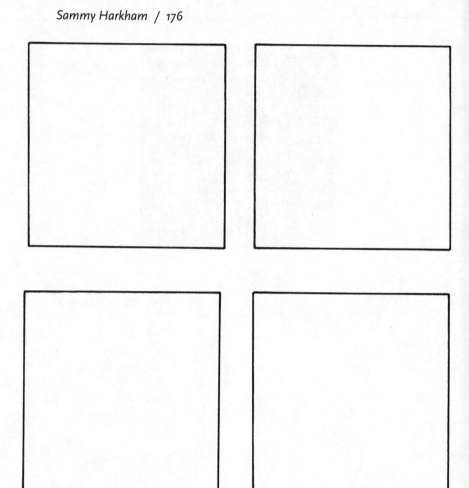

JOHN HASKELL

■

# Good World

FROM *Blind Spot*

## 1. Girl in a Field

THERE'S THE FIELD. It's made of rocks and grass and a few bushes. And a girl, pure potential, is running in this open field. I call her pure potential because she's young and she's full of the euphoria of possibility. This was 1949, after the war, when optimism was in the air — about victory and technology — and the girl is in the middle of a scene that ought to be perfect. She's running through the field with her cousin and sister, running and laughing and pausing occasionally to pick up stones. They're looking for a certain kind of stone, an egg-shaped stone, and the girl wants to find one.

Gus, her cousin, and Barbara, her sister, are older than she is and the world they inhabit is the world that she wants, and she believes that it's possible to enter that world if she can find a perfectly egg-shaped stone. And when you look directly at something, like a star, you can't see it, but if you look slightly away you do, and that's what she does, and when she finds what she thinks is a perfectly egg-shaped stone she tries to show them. Holding the stone in her hand she calls to them, trying to get their attention, but they keep running and yelling as if they don't even hear.

I said this girl is pure potential, and that's fine, but the potential isn't getting her anywhere. She feels the powerlessness of youth, and the inability of youth to affect the world, and although she seems to be a carefree girl running through a field we see that something else is happening. We can hear the trembling in her voice when she says, holding up her stone, "Look at this one." When she says, "Look at mine," we can tell she's waiting for some change to happen.

But Gus and Barbara keep running, and all the girl can think to do is wait, to stand there in the afternoon sun, hoping that someone at some point will come to her. And when her cousin does finally run over and stop in front of her, panting, she shows him her egg-shaped rock. He takes it, looks at it, and she watches him looking, hoping he'll see the goodness of the rock, and she's confused when he says, "Not bad," and tosses it aside. "Here," he says, and he reaches down, picks up another rock, a more egg-shaped rock, and he says something about aerodynamics and the science of flight, and then he throws this rock as far as he can. And then he runs off.

And that's when we see the girl, alone in the field, her head down, scanning her peripheral vision for an oblong stone hidden in the galaxy of stones and pebbles. That's when we see that the field is almost entirely flat except for a grassy knoll, a little greener than the rest of the field, and as the girl moves closer to the grassy area we start to get worried. We can imagine what might happen. We can probably anticipate the abandoned well hidden in the green grass. When suddenly the girl disappears we're pretty sure she's fallen into the hole.

## 2. Laika the Dog

Once upon a time there was a dog that wanted to be an astronaut. A cosmonaut, really, because she was a Communist dog, a Siberian husky taken in and trained by Soviet scientists. Her original name was Little Curly but they called her Laika, which means "Barker," because she made a lot of noise. And she made a lot of noise because she wanted to be the first dog in space.

This was 1957. *Sputnik* was about to be launched, and because there wouldn't be much moving around in the capsule, the scientists were looking for a dog who could learn to be still, and Laika was willing to be that dog. She was willing to learn, or try to learn, her lessons, and by lessons I mean the repeated behaviors that were meant to become habit.

Aristotle called habit the foundation of virtue, and what he meant I think is that the value of an action lies partly in its ability to repeat itself, to become something more than random. You don't hear the word *virtue* much anymore, and the word *habit* usually refers to something unwanted or out of control. But Aristotle, from the vantage point of ancient history, saw the development of habit as a way to move toward happiness.

And that was fine with Laika, except the habits she seemed to develop were not the right habits. She excelled at running and barking and playing around, but the *Sputnik* people were looking for a dog to be still, and although Laika wanted to oblige, her natural inclination, if there is such a thing, was to constantly be moving. She tried to contain or control that impulse, but there were other dogs who seemed to control it better.

So on the day they were to select which dog would explore the universe, Laika was nervous. She was nervous when the young scientist took her to the open field behind the barracks and told her to sit. She could see the men by the fence watching her with their stopwatches and their notepads, and when her leash was removed and the scientist started walking away she thought, *Okay* . . . and she tried to remain perfectly still, but as the young scientist continued walking, Laika felt the desire to move, and she tried to contain it or fight it or work through it — she tried to stop and concentrate — and sometimes she did, and when the desire began to fade she thought she was over it, that she'd turned over a new leaf, but there was no new leaf, the desire was still there, bigger than ever, and she began to think she shouldn't fight it, that maybe she *should* move, that her muscles might atrophy, or that the man might abandon her; a million logical thoughts made it necessary for her to get up and move.

Which would be a huge relief.

Or so she thought. Of course, when she did finally move it wasn't that wonderful or that fulfilling, but by then it was too late, her dream would not come true; some other dog would go into space and she would remain exactly what she would always be, a loud and useless dog.

Except that the scientists were looking for more than just still-ness. They could see her desire, and they valued that desire, and so she was the one who was chosen to be launched into space. And although there are several versions of what actually happened to her up there, they all boil down to basically the same thing. The batteries of her life support system would last only so long, and the scientists, not wanting to inflict a painful death, inserted into the last of her food supply some poison. When she was down to her final meal the poison entered her body, and although the fa-mous satellite remained in orbit for 162 days, after about a week Laika was already dead.

## 3. Anne and Richard

We see two people, Richard and Anne, a man and a woman — characters in a play. The man is dressed in black, and although the woman is wearing a white wedding-type gown she seems to be on the verge of crying. Until she notices the man. He's bent over, hair stringy, bowing, almost, as he offers her some thing he's holding in his hand. She immediately turns her back, clenches her fist, tells him to get out of her sight, and from her tone of voice we can tell that she hates this man.

He says something about understanding her loss, then immedi-ately tells her he loves her more than any husband could love, and as if it's happened a thousand times she feels a familiar sickness rising up from her belly. At this point she would like to walk away and escape from whatever the man is planning, but instead she stands there, and the man pries open the fingers of her fist and places in her hand a ring.

It's an exquisite example of late-sixteenth-century craftsman-ship, and she would probably want the ring except for one thing:

her contempt. She throws the jewel into the dirt. And the funny thing is, he walks over and matter-of-factly retrieves it, as if he knew what would happen. Like part of a choreography he goes back to her, admits that he killed her husband, and tells her the reason he killed her husband was his love for her. And that's when she spits in his face.

The woman knows that spitting at him is just the beginning of a whole succession of tortures she would like to inflict, including tearing out his heart and stuffing it into his mouth. But the man just wipes his face. Patiently. And that's what I mean by choreographed — he's slow and methodical, and his patience bestows a kind of power to his actions, which flow from one to the other until he's presenting her with a knife. He has a knife in his coat and he holds it out to her, saying that she, if she wants to, can kill him.

But it's against her principles to kill another human being, however inhuman he might be, and when she ignores the knife, he takes it himself, raises it, and holding it to his own breast offers to kill himself if that would make her happy. He's full of bravado, but he's also quite convincing, partly because he's so focused on her, observing her smallest movement, including the movement of the muscle buried beneath her smooth, round cheek.

He takes her silence as an invitation, and he steps forward, slowly, gradually, bringing his face closer to hers, moving in such an incremental way that she's not completely sure that he actually is moving, until, with his face almost touching hers, she closes her eyes, aware that his lips are pressing against her lips, and for about a second, a long second, her eyes stay closed.

And then they pop open as if she suddenly wakes up.

And what she suddenly wakes up to is the question in her mind: Why am I kissing this man? or Why am I allowing myself to be kissed? or Where is my anger? She's confused. She's been trained to be a "good person," and yes, he is an older man, and a powerful man, and although she has to think about her future, she hates what is happening. She hates him. She wasn't acting when she spat at him, and yet now when she needs to fight, the desire to fight has abandoned her.

So she wants to start again. She thinks she knows what the problem is, what she needs to do, and yes, maybe it didn't work this time, it wasn't right this time, but she's full of optimism that given another chance she will do it differently. One more time and she knows she can stop the repetition.

Like Aristotle. For Aristotle, an action repeated again and again becomes habit, and by virtue of the repetition it becomes a direction, a movement, and implicit in that movement is a force, a pulling or pushing against the conflicting impulses of other habits. And so we have to be careful. Each time around, the rut is carved a little deeper.

Which is why they're still here. Anne and Richard. Same people, slightly different location. He still walks up to her, and even before he opens his mouth she hates his smell. Even though he's probably wearing some sort of perfume, she hates it so much that when he offers her the ring she throws it into the gutter. When he limps over, exaggerating his deformity, she feels no pity. She sees exactly what he is, and when he has the temerity to offer his love, that's when she collects the liquid in her mouth and spits.

And yes, she's worried that it's happening in the same way because she would like it to happen in a different way. She understands that now is the time to alter events, to focus her hatred and direct it at him, and what she needs is something after which all that she does will be different. She looks at her hands. They're not trembling but she wishes they would be trembling because then they'd be filled with resolve. She's waiting for her hands to rise up, and when he presents her with the knife, she thinks, *Okay*. Now she has the opportunity to change the course of events, to throw her world into a new orbit, and what she has to do is take the knife he's offering and plunge it into his heart.

But killing another human being is not something she does. She doesn't do that. And so, as if on cue, he places the point of the knife to his own neck, and what's she going to do?

"I want to start again."

That's what she says.

"Okay," he says.

## 4. The Mo-tel Idea

In 1929 they invented the motel. They didn't actually invent it; it just happened. Some man put a sign up on the side of the road and the idea was born. It was able to be born because of the existence of the car, and the highway. People were suddenly driving cars and a need existed that hadn't been there before, a vacuum that was filled by this thing called a motor hotel. The idea of a place to stay along the road wouldn't have been thought of before. You couldn't have planned it. But once the highways were there, something that hadn't even been a possibility became necessity. Or, more precisely, habit. A circumstance creates a need, which is satisfied by a certain action, which is repeated and repeated until pretty soon it's part of life. A man in San Luis Obispo is credited with coining the word *mo-tel*. And maybe he did, or maybe he just had the biggest sign. Maybe the idea was floating in the air, and when it landed, there it was. The whole process is fairly unpredictable. People need a place to sleep. They want to drive across the country and not get wet when they get out of their cars. I wouldn't want to call it a momentous event in the history of the world, but it's an example of a change that can happen only when the requisite pieces are in place.

## 5. Anne and Richard

Let's go back to the two people, the man and the woman. The woman, Anne, realizes that if she's going to change the course of events she needs to put the pieces in place, she needs to act now and create a beginning, and the only problem is, she doesn't know what to do. He offers her the ring and she thinks, *Yes. Okay. The ring.* Should she take it? She doesn't think she should take his ring and yet the only alternative she can think of is throwing it down onto the cobblestones. Same as always. And when he offers her the sword she thinks, *Yes . . . Okay. The sword.* She takes the sword. He bends down in front of her, pulls the material away from his neck, revealing the pale skin of a man who has never been loved, and she resolves that, yes, her life means more than his, and she tries to believe that. This is her opportunity and she tries to see herself thrusting the sharp blade through the skin and into the muscles and the organs, and she's looking down on him, with his eyes lowered, and she sees that he's just another person, some man who probably wants what all men probably want, and what is she supposed to do? Killing him isn't going to change her life. She knows it's her attitude that will change her life; her mind and her heart are the things that will change her life, and they're not changing. She waits awhile, giving them a chance to change, and when finally nothing happens, she gives up.

She's silent. It's already gone too far. She would like to be asleep in one of those cozy motels on the side of the highway, but there aren't any motels for her. She was hoping she would have more time, but there is no time. The present has become the future and she can see it. She can see what's going to happen because it's happening now. He's standing, close enough for her to notice his breathing, and his smell, and his smooth face, moving closer and closer to her face until finally she doesn't want to be kissing him, but that's what has to be happening. It's not that she wants to give up, but fighting has proven to be futile, and so she resigns herself to the idea of a next time, that next time things might change, that next time she might be free of this man, and the only problem is, now is the next time. And so the kiss goes on and on and she has no choice but to let herself be kissed. This is where she is, she thinks, and there's nothing she can do.

## 6. Girl in a Well

The girl who'd fallen into the well is now about ninety feet down. The earth opened up and she fell, hitting the sides of the shaft, falling until she came to the place where the well changes direction. And that's where she's stuck, cut and bruised, and it seems like a long time before she hears her parents, standing at the top of the well, calling her name. She can't see them but she can tell they're hoping she's alive and that nothing has changed. She's also hoping that nothing has changed, and that her parents will take her away from the darkness and the cold.

The opening of the well is only fourteen inches across, and the shaft is too unstable for anyone to come down after her, so what her parents do is lower a rope. And she can feel this rope brush against her shoulder, and although she wants help, a rope is not the kind of help she has in mind, and when she hears her parents ask if she can tie the rope around her waist she starts crying. Partly she wants to reach out to take the rope, and partly she wants her parents to climb down, wrap her in their arms, and carry her out of the hole and up into the world of happiness.

We probably think that won't happen. We can probably predict that she'll die in the well, which she does. Painlessly, they say. And although the well is almost completely black, I can picture her down there, holding on to an egg-shaped rock, her bent legs stuck in the mud, half expecting something to happen, at first, and then not expecting anything. This is where she is, she thinks, and she can tell that she's hurt and that if anything is going to change it'll have to start changing now. And so she gives up waiting. At that point the paralyzed little girl turns into a different girl, a girl who lets the rock fall from her hand, who reaches out, takes the rope dangling in front of her, and with it ties a bow around her stomach, a single knot like the kind she ties her shoes with. She ties herself in the rope like a package.

And then she calls out. "Hello?"

"Hello?" she says.

And this is what I mean by habit. Aristotle indicated that happiness is a habit; it isn't random. A single act that fosters happiness is fine as far as it goes, but it's only a beginning, a necessary beginning, and although the girl in the well tied only one small knot, for her that was a beginning.

## 7. Laika's Dream

Laika, the dog, had been chosen to be the first dog in space, and so she was feeling the exhilaration of possibility. She knew about pure potential because she was feeling it, and the only problem was, nothing was happening. I wouldn't want to say she wasn't happy in her world, but she wasn't completely happy. She was waiting for some lesson or direction or purpose.

And then one day she was led, out of her basement room, into an elevator, and up into the *Sputnik* module. She was strapped into her padded compartment, connected by wires to the black box recorder, and then the photographers came. Lights were shined in her face, and because she understood what was wanted of her, she made the face we think of as a smile. Photos show her, one ear up, one flopped over, her paws crossed, happily surveying what we suppose is the possibility of life in space.

And then the lights were taken away. The scientists said goodbye, the capsule hatch was closed, and Laika found herself sealed inside the darkness. And it was dark. And quiet. And it wasn't long before she felt the vibrating of the booster rocket, the explosion, and then she felt herself being pulled, by the force of gravity on the one hand, and by the force of the missile rising up. The next thing she knew she was floating in space, out of the bonds of the atmosphere.

After about six days of orbiting Earth she'd eaten her way to the end of her food supply, and, being a dog, one thing Laika knew was food, so I think she probably knew her food was tainted, that she'd been poisoned, and that she would die. And at first she couldn't believe it. *There must be some mistake,* she thought. Don't forget, it was almost entirely black up there, so she was blind, and there were no smells in her air supply, and she couldn't move, and the only thing she could hear was her own breathing, amplified by her special helmet. She thought she was contributing to the collective knowledge of the human race, but she wasn't sure. She felt lightheaded, either from the weightlessness or the poison, and in her soporific state she had a dream.

In her dream she's riding in a railroad car, and when the train slows down she jumps off and starts running down the tracks, trying to get away from something in the train. She comes to a small, quiet town — it's night — and when she hears voices chasing her she runs to the nearest door, squeezes through a crack in the door, and finds herself in the kitchen of a small house. A man and woman are sitting at a table near a stove and when they look at her it's as if they expected her to be there. She hears a knocking on the door; a soldier comes into the kitchen. He's young, and he lifts his hand to strike the woman, and Laika, pressing her nose against the wooden floor, is keeping perfectly still, perfectly quiet, knowing somehow that unless she is perfectly still, the man and the woman will die. A small beetle crawls across the floor, and she leaves it alone. The soldier changes his mind. He spits, and then walks away.

I wouldn't call it a happy dream exactly, but it's basically optimistic. Laika believed Aristotle's dictum about habit and happiness, and because she lived in the previous century, the century of optimism, she thought her actions would be a beginning. When she realized she was going to die she didn't mind that much because she was dying with the hope that a single act would make the world better. A hope that we, in this century, have our doubts about. We live in the future she believed would come, but we've never really kicked the habits of violence and greed. While Laika dreamed of changing the world, our dream, at this point, would be just to have a dream.

And that's why I'm thinking about Laika. Because I can almost imagine her feeling of powerlessness and optimism. Sitting in a dark spaceship, a microphone tied to her neck, the poison working its way into her system, not knowing what to do, and with nothing to rely on but habit, it's out of habit that she stops, and she concentrates, and her breathing slows, and she becomes aware, gradually, of her heartbeat. At first there's just the feeling of the microphone on her skin, and her heart, beating, and because she's harnessed in place there's nothing to do but let her heart keep beating, let the blood keep pumping, let the signals from her heart flow as directly as possible into the small black box. Because she believes that someone will be listening, she stays alive as long as she can, hoping the message emanating from the heart is clear, wanting the world to hear not just the ticking of a heart but the possibility it might contain.

■

# The Minor Wars

FROM *Story Quarterly*

THE SUN IS shining, myna birds are hopping, palm trees are swaying, so what. I sit in the easy chair I've brought from home and pick up the spoon from my lunch tray. I'd like to fling it into the air, catch it in my mouth, and say, "Look at that, Boots." Boots is my wife, although I haven't called her that since the early seventies when she used to wear these orange knee-high boots in eighty-six-degree weather. She'd top my utensil act by using a fork or a steak knife. Her real name is Joanie, and she's barefoot. She's in a coma. Dying the slowest of deaths. Or perhaps I'm wrong. Perhaps she has never felt more alive.

"Shut this crap off," I tell Scottie. She's my ten-year-old daughter. Her real name is Scottie. She turns off the television with the remote.

"No." I point to the stuff in the window — the sun and the trees. "I mean this."

Scottie slides the curtain across the window, shutting all of it out. "This curtain is sure heavy," she says.

She needs a haircut or a brushing. There are small tumbleweeds of hair rolling over the back of her head. She is one of those kids who always seem to need a haircut. I'm grateful that she isn't pretty, but I realize this could change.

"It's like the bib I have to wear at the dentist when he needs x-rays of my gums," Scottie says. She knocks on the hard curtain. "I wish we were at the dentist."

"Me too," I say, and it's true. A root canal would be a blast compared to this. Life has been strange without Joanie's voice commanding it. I have to cook now and clean and give Scottie orders. That's been weird. I've never been that full-time parent, supervising the children on weekdays, setting schedules and boundaries. Now I see Scottie before school and right after school, and I'm basically with her until she goes to bed. She's a funny kid.

The visitor on my wife's bed looks at Scottie standing by the shaded window and frowns, then turns on a light with a remote control and goes back to work on Joanie's face. My wife is in a coma and this woman is applying makeup to her lips. I have to admit that Joanie would appreciate this. She enjoys being beautiful, and she likes to look good, whether she's canoeing across the Molokai Channel or getting tossed from an offshore powerboat. She likes to look *luminous* and *ravishing* — her own words. Good luck, I always tell her. Good luck with your goals. I don't love my wife as I'm supposed to, but I love her in my own way. To my knowledge, she doesn't adore me either, but we are content with our individual schedules and our lives together, and proud of our odd system.

We tried for a while to love each other normally, urged by her brother to subject ourselves to counseling as a decent couple would. Barry, her brother, is a man of the couch, a believer in therapy, affirmations, and pulse points. Once, he tried to show us exercises he'd been doing in session with his new woman friend. He instructed us to trade reasons, abstract or specific, for why we stayed with one another. I started off by saying that she would get really drunk and pretend I was someone else and do this really neat thing with her tongue. Joanie said tax breaks. Barry cried. Openly. Joanie and Barry's parents are divorced and Barry's second wife recently left him for a guy who understood that a man didn't do volunteer work. Barry wanted us to reflect on bonds and promises and love and such. He was tired of things breaking apart. Tired of people resigning so easily. We tried for Barry, but our marriage seemed to work only when we didn't try at all.

The lady with the makeup (Tia? Tara? Someone who modeled with Joanie?) stops her dabbing and looks at Scottie. The light hits this woman's face, giving me opportunity to see that she should perhaps be working on her own makeup. The color of her face, a manila envelope. Specks of white in her eyebrows. Concealer not concealing. I can tell my daughter doesn't know what to do with the woman's stare.

"What?" Scottie asks.

"I think your mother was enjoying the view," Tia, or Tara, says.

I jump in to protect my silent daughter.

"Listen here, T. Her mother was not enjoying the view. Her mother is in a coma."

"My name is not T," T says. "My name is Allison."

"Okay then, listen here, Ali. Don't confuse my daughter."

"I'm turning into a remarkable young lady," Scottie says.

"Damn straight," I say.

This Ali person gets back to business. Scottie turns on the television again. Another dating show.

I'm running out of toys. I can usually find a toy in anything. A spoon, a sugar packet, a quarter. Our first week here, I made up this game: who could get the most slices of banana stuck to the ceiling. You had to put a piece on a napkin and then try to trampoline it up there. Scottie loved it. Nurses got involved. Even the neurologist gave it a go. But now, nearing the end of our fourth week here, I'm running out of tricks. The neurologist says my wife's scores are lower on the various coma scales. The nurse says things, uses language I don't understand, and yet I understand her — I know what she's telling me.

"Last time you were the one on the bed," Scottie says.

"Yup."

"Last time you lied to me."

"I know, Scottie. Forgive me." My motorcycling accident. I had insisted I was okay, that I wasn't going to go to the hospital. Scottie had issued me these little tests to show my unreliability. Joanie participated. They played bad cop, worse cop.

"How many fingers?" Scottie had asked, holding up what I thought was a pinky and a thumb: a *shaka*.

"Balls," I had said, not wanting to be tested that way.

"Answer her," Joanie had said.

"Two?"

"Okay," Scottie said warily. "Close your eyes and touch your nose and stand on one foot."

"Balls, Scottie. I can't do that regardless, and you're treating me like a drunk driver."

"Do what she says," Joanie yelled.

I had stood still in protest. I knew something was wrong with me, but I didn't want to go to the hospital. I wanted to let what was wrong with my body run its course. I was curious. I was having trouble holding up my head.

"Look at yourself," Joanie said. "You can't even see straight."

"How am I supposed to look at myself, then?"

"Shut up, Matthew. Get in the car."

I had damaged my fourth nerve, a nerve that connects your eyes to your brain, which explained why things had been out of focus.

"You could have died," Scottie says. She's watching Allison brush color onto Joanie's cheeks.

"No way," I say. "A fourth nerve? Who needs it?"

"You lied. You said you were okay. You said you could see my fingers."

"I didn't lie. I guessed correctly. Plus, for a while there I got to have twins. Two Scotties."

Scottie nods. "Well. Okay."

I'm wondering what my accident has to do with anything. Lately, she's been pointing out my flaws, my tricks and lies. She's interviewing me. I'm the backup candidate, the dad. I remember when I was in the hospital Joanie put vodka into my Jell-O. She wore my eye patch and teased me and stayed with me. It was very nice.

Scottie touches her mother's hair, which looks slippery. It looks the way it did when she gave birth to Scottie and our other daughter, Alexandra. Allison is now looking at me as if I'm disturbed. "You have an odd way of speaking to children," she says.

"Parents shouldn't have to compromise their personalities," Scottie says.

It's something I've heard Joanie say. I catch a glimpse of my wife's face. She looks so lovely. Not ravishing, but simply lovely. Her freckles rise through the blush, her closed eyes fastened by dark, dramatic lashes. These lashes are the only strong feature left on her face. Everything has been softened. She looks pretty, but perhaps too divine — too bone-china white, as if she's under water or cased in glass. Oddly, the effect makes me like all the things I usually don't like about her. I like that she forgets to wash the lettuce and our salads are always pebbly. Or sometimes we go to this restaurant that's touristy, but the fish is great, and without fail she ends up at the bar with these Floridian spring-break sorts for a drink or ten and I'm left at the table all alone. I usually don't enjoy this, but now I don't mind so much. I like her magnetism. I like her courage and ego. But maybe I only like these things because she may not wake up again. It's confusing.

The manager of that restaurant once thanked me. He said that she always livened up the place and made people want to drink. I'm sure if she died, he'd put her picture up because it's that kind of restaurant — pictures of local legends and dead patrons haunting the walls. I feel sad that she has to die for her picture to go up on the wall, or for me to really love everything about her.

"Allison," I say. "Thank you. I'm sure Joanie is so pleased."

"She's not pleased. She's in a coma," Allison says.

I'm speechless.

"Oh my god," Allison says and starts to cry. "I can't believe I said that. I was just trying to get you back."

She leaves the room with her beauty tools.

"Oh, mercy," I say. "I need to change some habits. I'm an ass."

"You're my dad," Scottie says.

"Yes," I say. "Yes."

"You're a dad-ass. Like a bad-ass but older."

"Mercy," I say.

Scottie wants me to step into the waiting room with her. She has something to tell me. It's a routine we have. She's afraid of speaking to her mother. She's embarrassed of her life. A ten-year-old, worried that her life isn't interesting enough. She thinks that if she speaks to her mother, she should have something incredible to say. I always urge her to talk about school or the dogs, but Scottie says that this would be boring, and she wouldn't want her mother to think she was a walking yawn. For the past few weeks or so, Scottie has been trying to have these worthy experiences after school at our beach club.

"Okay, Scottie," I say. "Today's the day. You're going to talk to Mom. You can read an article, you can sing a song, or tell her what you learned in school. Right-o?"

"Okay, but I have a story."

"Talk to me."

She smiles. "Okay, pretend you're Mom. Close your eyes."

I close my eyes.

"Hi, Mom. Yesterday I explored the reef in front of the public beach by myself. I have tons of friends, but I felt like being alone. I've seen this really cute guy who works the beach stand there. His eyes look like giraffe eyes."

I'm trying not to smile.

"The tide was low. I could see all sorts of things. In one place the coral was a really cool dark color, but then I looked closer and it wasn't the coral. It was an eel. A moray. I almost died. There were millions of sea urchins and a few sea cucumbers. I even picked one up and squeezed him."

"This is good, Scottie. Let's go back in. Mom will love this."

"I'm not done."

"Oh." I close my eyes again.

"I was squatting on the reef and lost my balance and fell back on my hands. One of my hands landed on an urchin and it put its spines in me. My hand looked like a pincushion."

I grab her hands, hold them up to my face. The roots of urchin spines have locked in and expanded under the skin of her left palm. They look like tiny black starfish that plan on making this hand their home forever. I notice more stars on her fingertips. "Why didn't you tell me you were hurt? Why didn't you say something?"

"I'm okay. I handled it. I didn't really fall."

"What do you mean? Are these pen marks?"

"Yes."

I look closer. I feel her palm and press on the marks.

"Ow," she says and pulls her hand back. "Just kidding," she says. "They're real. But I didn't really fall. I did it on purpose. I slammed my hand into an urchin. But I'm not telling Mom that part."

"What?" I can't imagine Scottie feeling such terrible pain. "Why would you do this? Scottie?"

"For a story, I guess."

"But Christ, didn't it hurt?"

"Yes."

"Balls, Scottie. I'm floored right now. Completely floored."

"Do you want to hear the rest?" she asks.

I push my short fingernails into my palm just to try to get a taste of the sting she felt. I shake my head. "I guess. Go on."

"Okay. Pretend you're Mom. You can't interrupt."

"I can't believe you'd do that."

"You can't speak! Be quiet or you won't hear the rest."

Scottie talks about the blood, the needles jutting from her hand, how she climbed back onto the rock pier like a crab with a missing claw. Before she returned to shore, Scottie describes how she looked out across the ocean and watched the swimmers do laps around the catamarans. She says that the ones with white swimming caps looked like runaway buoys.

Of course, she didn't see any of this. Pain makes you focused. She probably ran right to the club's medic. She's making up the details, making a better story for her mother, to get some attention from Joanie. Or perhaps to take attention away from Joanie.

"Because of Dad's boring ocean lectures, I knew these weren't needles in my hand but more like sharp bones — calcitic plates, which vinegar would help dissolve."

I smile. *Good girl,* I think.

"Dad, this isn't boring, is it?"

"Boring is not the word I'd use."

"Okay. You're Mom again. So I thought of going to the club's first-aid."

"Good girl."

"Shh," she says. "But instead, I went to the cute boy and asked him to pee on my hand."

"Excuse me?"

"Yes, Mom. That's exactly what I said to him. Excuse me, I told him, I hurt myself. He said, Uh-oh. You okay? Like I was an eight-year-old. He didn't understand so I placed my hand on the counter. He said a bunch of swear words then told me to go to the hospital or something. Or are you a member of that club? he asked. He told me he'd take me there, which was really nice of him. He went out through the back of his stand and I went around to meet him. I told him what he needed to do and he blinked a thousand times and used curse words in all sorts of combinations. He wondered if you were supposed to suck out the poison after you pulled out the needles, and if I was going to go into seizures. He told me he wasn't trained for this, and that there was no way he'd pee on my hand, but I told him what you always tell Dad when you want him to do something he doesn't want to do. I said, Stop being a pussy, and it did the trick. He told me not to look and to say something, or whistle."

"Scottie," I say. "Tell me you've made this up."

"I'm almost done," she whines. "So I talked about the records you had beaten in your boat. And that you were a model, but you weren't all prissy, and that every guy at the club was in love with you but you only love Dad because he's easy, like the easy chair he sits on all the time."

"Scottie. I have to use the bathroom." I feel sick.

"Okay," she says. "Wasn't that a hilarious story? Was it too long?"

"Yes and no. I have to go to the bathroom. Tell your mom what you told me. Go talk to her." *She can't hear you anyway*, I think. I hope.

Joanie would think that story was hilarious. This bothers me. The story bothers me. Scottie shouldn't have to create these dramas. Scottie shouldn't have to be pissed on. She's reminding me of her sister, someone I don't ever want her to become. Alex. Seventeen. She's like a special effect. It wows you. It alarms you, but then it gets tiresome and you forget about it. I need to call Alex and update her. She's at boarding school on another island, not too far away but far enough. The last time I called, I asked her what was wrong and she said, "The price of cocaine." I laughed, asked, "Seriously, what else?" "Is there anything else?" she said.

She's very well known over at Hawaii's Board of Tourism. At fifteen, she did calendars and work for Isle Cards whose captions said things like *Life's a Damn Hot Beach*. One-pieces became string bikinis. String bikinis became thongs and then just shells and granules of sand strategically placed on her body. The rest of her antics are so outrageous and absurd, it's boring to think about. In her struggle to be unique, she has become common: the rebellious, privileged teen. Car chase, explosion, gone and forgotten.

Despite everything, her childishness, her utter wrongness, Alex makes me feel so guilty. Guilty because I catch myself believing that if Joanie were to die, we'd all make it. We'd flourish. We'd trust and love each other. Alex could come home. We used to love each other so much. I don't call her even though I need to tell her to fly down tomorrow. I can't bear to hear any accidental pitch of joy or release that may slink into her voice or my own.

Scottie sits on the bed. Joanie looks like Sleeping Beauty.

"Did you tell her?" I ask.

"I'm going to work on it some more," Scottie says. "Because if Mom thinks it's funny, what will she do? What if the laugh circulates around in her lungs or in her brain somewhere since it can't come out? What if it kills her?"

"It doesn't work that way," I say, although I have no idea how it works.

"Yes, but I just thought I'd make it more tragic — that way she'll feel the need to come back."

"It shouldn't be this complicated, Scottie." I say this sternly. I sit on the bed and put my ear to where Joanie's heart is. I bury my face in her gown. This is the most intimate I've been with her in a long time. My wife, the speedboat record holder. My wife, the motorcyclist, the model, the long-distance paddler, the triathlete. *What drives you, Joanie?* I say into her chest. I realize I've copied one of her hobbies and wonder what drives me as well. I don't even like motorcycles. I hate the sound they make.

"I miss Mom's sneezes," Scottie says.

I laugh. I shake with laughter. I laugh so hard it's soundless and this makes Scottie laugh. Whenever Joanie sneezes, she farts. She can't help it. This is why we are hysterical. A nurse comes in and opens the curtain. She smiles at us. "You two," she says. She urges us to go outside and enjoy the rest of the day.

Scottie agrees. She looks at her wristwatch and immediately settles down. "Crap, Dad. We need to go. I need a new story."

Because the nurse is in the room I say, "Watch your language."

At the beach club, the shrubs are covered with surfboards. There has been a south swell, but the waves are blown out from the strong wind. I follow Scottie into the dining room. She tells me that she can't leave until something amusing or tragic happens to her. I tell her I'm skipping paddling practice and am not letting her out of my sight. This infuriates her. I tell her I'll stay out of her way, but I'm not going to practice. Pretend I'm not there.

"Fine, then sit over there." She points to tables on the perimeter of the dining room. A few ladies are playing cards at one of these tables. I like these ladies. They're around eighty years old and they wear tennis skirts even though I can't imagine they still play tennis. I wish Joanie liked to play cards and sit around.

Scottie heads to the bar. The bartender, Jerry, nods at me. I watch Scottie climb onto a barstool, and Jerry makes her a virgin daiquiri, then lets her try out a few of his own concoctions. "The guava one is divine," I hear her say, "but lime makes me feverish."

I pretend to read the paper that I borrowed from one of the ladies and move to a table that's a little closer to the bar so I can listen and watch.

"How's your mom?" Jerry asks.

"Still sleeping." Scottie twists atop her barstool. Her legs don't reach the metal footrest so she crosses them on the seat and balances.

"Well, you tell her I say hi. You tell her we're all waiting for her."

I watch Scottie as she considers this. She stares at her lap. "I don't talk to her," she says to Jerry, though she doesn't look at him.

Jerry sprays a swirl of whipped cream into her drink. She takes a gulp of her daiquiri then rubs her head. She does it again. She spins around on the barstool. And then she begins to speak in a manner that troubles me. She is yelling as if there's some sort of din in the room that she needs to overcome.

"Everybody loves me, but my husband hates me, guess I'll have to eat the worm. Give me a shot of Cuervo Gold, Jerry baby."

Jerry cleans the bottles of liquor, trying to make noise.

How often did Joanie say this? Was it her standard way of asking for tequila? It makes me wonder how we managed to spend so much time at this place and never see each other at all.

"Give me two of everything," Scottie yells, caught in her fantasy. I want to relieve Jerry of his obvious discomfort, but then I see Troy walking toward the bar. Big, magnanimous, golden Troy. I quickly hide behind my newspaper. My daughter is suddenly silent. Troy has killed her buzz. I'm sure he hesitated when he saw her, but it's too late to turn around.

"Hey, Scottie," I hear him say. "Look at you."

"Look at you," she says, and her voice sounds strange. Almost unrecognizable. "You look awake," she says.

"Uh, thanks, Scottie."

*Uh, thanks, Scottie.* Troy is so slow. His great-grandfather invented the shopping cart and this has left little for Troy to do except sleep with lots of women and put my wife in a coma. Of course, it's not his fault, but he wasn't hurt. He was the driver and Joanie was the throttle man because Troy insisted he wanted to drive this time. Rounding a mile marker, their boat launched off a wave, spun out, and Joanie was ejected. When Troy came in from the race alone he kept saying, "Lots of chop and holes. Lots of chop and holes."

"Have you visited her?" Scottie asks.

"Yes, I have, Scottie. Your dad was there."

"What did you say to her?"

"I told her the boat was in good shape. I said it was ready for her."

What a Neanderthal.

"Her hand moved, Scottie. I really think she heard me. I really think she's going to be okay."

Troy isn't wearing a shirt. The man has muscles I didn't even know existed. I wonder if Joanie has slept with him. Of course she has. His eyes are the color of swimming pools. I'm about to lower the paper so he'll stop talking to Scottie until I hear her say, "The body has natural reactions. When you cut off a chicken's head, its body runs around, but it's still a dead chicken."

I hear either Troy or Jerry coughing.

"Don't give up, Scottie," Jerry says.

Golden Troy is saying something about life and lemons and bootstraps. He is probably placing one of his massive tan paws on Scottie's shoulder.

I see Scottie leaving the dining room. I follow her. She runs to the beach wall and I catch her before she jumps off it. Tears are brewing in her eyes. She looks up to keep them from falling, but they fall anyway.

"I didn't mean to say dead chicken," she cries.

"Let's go home," I say.

"Why is everyone so into sports here? You and Mom and Troy think you're so cool. Everyone here does. Why don't you join a book club? Why can't Mom just relax at home?"

I hold her and she lets me. I try to think if I have any friends in a book club. I realize I don't know anyone, man or woman, who isn't a member of this club. I don't know a man who doesn't surf, kayak, or paddleboard. I don't know a woman who doesn't jog, sail, or canoe-paddle, although Joanie is the only woman I know racing bikes and boats.

"I don't want Mom to die," Scottie says.

"Of course you don't." I push her away from me and bend down to look in her freckled brown eyes. "Of course."

"I don't want her to die like this," Scottie says. "Racing or competing or doing something marvelous. I've heard her say, 'I'm going out with a bang.' Well, I hope she goes out choking on a kernel of corn or slipping on a piece of toilet paper."

"Christ, Scottie. How old are you? Where do you get this shit? Let's go home," I say. "You don't mean any of this. You need to rest." I imagine my wife peaceful on her bed. I wonder what she was thinking as she flew off the boat. If she knew it was over. I wonder how long it took Troy to notice she wasn't there beside him. Scottie's face is puffy. Her hair is greasy. It needs to be washed. She has this look of disgust on her face. It's a very adult look.

"Your mother thinks you're so great," I say. "She thinks you're the prettiest, smartest, silliest girl in town."

"She thinks I'm a coward."

"No, she doesn't. Why would she think that?"

"I didn't want to go on the boat with her and she said I was a scaredy-cat like you."

"She was just joking. She thinks you're the bravest girl in town. She told me it scared her how brave you were."

"Really?"

"Damn straight." It's a lie. Joanie often said that we're raising two little scaredy-cats, but of all the lies I tell, this one is necessary. I don't want Scottie to hate her mother as Alexandra once did, and maybe still does. It will consume her and age her. It will make her fear the world. It will make her too shy and too nervous to ever say exactly what she means.

"I'm going swimming," Scottie says.

"No," I say. "We've had enough."

"Dad, please." She pulls me down by my neck and whispers, "I don't want people to see I've been crying. Let me get in the water."

"Fine. I'll be here." She strips off her clothes and throws them at me, then jumps off the wall to the beach below and charges toward the water. She dives in and breaks surface after what seems like a minute. She dives. She splashes. She plays. I sit on the coral wall and watch her and the other kids and their mothers and nannies. To my left is a small reef. I can see black urchins settled in the fractures. I still can't believe Scottie did such a thing.

The outside dining terrace is filling up with people and their pink and red and white icy drinks. An old man is walking out of the ocean with a one-man canoe held over his head, a tired yet elated smile quivering on his face as if he's just returned from some kind of battle in the deep sea.

The torches are being lit on the terrace and on the rock pier. The soaring sun has turned into a wavy blob above the horizon. It's almost green flash time. Not quite yet, but soon. When the sun disappears behind the horizon, sometimes there's a green flash of light that sparkles seemingly out of the sea. It's a communal activity around here, waiting for this green flash, hoping to catch it.

Children are coming out of the water.

I hear a mother's voice drifting off the ocean. It's far away yet loud. "Get in here, little girl. They're everywhere."

Scottie is the only child still swimming. I jump off the wall. "Scottie!" I yell. "Scottie, get in here right now!"

"There are Portuguese man-o'-wars out there," a woman says to me. "The swell must have pushed them in. Is she yours?" The woman points to Scottie, who is swimming in from the catamarans.

"Yes," I say.

My daughter comes in. She's holding a tiny man-of-war — the clot of its body and the clear blue bubble on her hand, its dark blue string tail wrapped around her wrist.

"What have you done? Why are you doing this?" I take the man-of-war off her with a stick; pop its bubble so that it won't hurt anybody. My daughter's arm is marked with a red line. I tell her to rinse her arm off with seawater. She says it's not just her arm that's hurt — she was swimming among a mass of them.

"Why would you stay out there, Scottie? How could you tolerate that?" I've been stung by them hundreds of times; it's not so bad, but kids are supposed to cry when they get stung. It's something you can always count on.

"I thought it would be funny to say I was attacked by a herd of minor wars."

"It's not minor war. You know that, don't you?" When she was little I would point out sea creatures to her but I'd give them the wrong names. I called them minor wars because they were like tiny soldiers with impressive weapons — the gaseous bubble, the whiplike tail, the toxic tentacles, advancing in swarms. I called a blowfish a blow-pop; an urchin, an ocean porcupine; and sea turtles were saltwater hardhats. I thought it was funny, but now I'm worried that she doesn't know the truth about things.

"Of course I know," Scottie says. "They're man-o'-wars, but it's our joke. Mom will like it."

"It's not man-o'-war either. It's man-of-war. Portuguese man-of-war. That's the proper name."

"Oh," she says.

She scratches herself. More lines form on her chest and legs. I tell her I'm not happy and that we need to get home and put some ointments and ice on the stings. "Vinegar will make it worse, so if you thought giraffe boy could pee on you, you're out of luck."

She agrees as if she was prepared for this — the punishment, the medication, the swelling, the pain that hurts her now and the pain that will hurt her later. But she's happy to deal with my disapproval. She's gotten her story, and she's beginning to see how much easier physical pain is to tolerate. I'm unhappy that she's learning this at ten years old.

We walk up the sandy slope toward the dining terrace. I see Troy sitting at a table with some people I know. I look at Scottie to see if she sees him and she is giving him the middle finger. The dining terrace gasps, but I realize it's because of the sunset and the green flash. We missed it. The flash flashed. The sun is gone. The sky is pink and violent like arguing little girls. I reach to grab the offending hand, but instead I correct her gesture.

"Here, Scottie. Don't let that finger stand by itself like that. Bring up the other fingers just a little bit. There you go."

Troy stares at us and smiles a bit, looking completely confused.

"All right, that's enough," I say, suddenly feeling sorry for Troy. He may really love Joanie. There is that chance. I place my hand on Scottie's back to guide her away. She flinches and I remove my hand, remembering that she's hurt all over.

*

We are at the hospital again even though it's late at night. Scottie insisted on it. She practically had a tantrum. "I'll forget the exact sensations that I need to tell Mom!" she had screamed.

She still hasn't showered. I wanted the salt water to stay on her. It's good for the wounds. She cried on the way over here, cried and scratched at herself. Her stings are now raised red lesions. A nurse gave them attention. She gave her some antibiotics as well. Scottie has a runny nose; she's dizzy and nauseous though she won't admit it's from swimming with poisonous invertebrates. She's miserable, but I have a feeling she won't do anything like this again. The nurse shaved her legs to get rid of any remaining nematocyst. Now Scottie is admiring her smooth, woman legs.

"I'm going to start doing this all the time," she says. "It'll be such a hassle."

"No, you're not," I say. I say it loudly, surprising both of us. "You're not ready." She smiles, uncomfortable with my authority. So this is what it's like.

We're going to stay the night. I'm sitting on the end of the bed, putting eye drops in my eyes. We don't even look like visitors. We look like patients, defeated, exhausted from the world outside. We came in for shelter and care and a little rest, the staff here being so kind and lenient. It's nine o' clock in the ICU. We walked in unannounced and Scottie received free medical attention. This can't be standard practice. It means it's over. Their indulgence is because they have no hope for us, or they've been advised by Dr. Johnston to scratch hope off their charts. People become so kind right before and after someone dies.

Scottie opens the curtain and lets the night in — dark palm trees and the lights of other buildings. She asks me if she hurt the urchin as much as the urchin hurt her. She asks me why everyone else calls them man-o'-wars. I tell her I don't know, in reply to the first question. I don't know how that works. For the second question I answer, "Words get abbreviated and we forget the origins of things."

"Or fathers lie," she says, "about the real names."

"That too."

She climbs up on the bed and we look at Joanie in the half-moon light. Scottie leans back against my chest, her forehead beneath my chin. I move my head around and nuzzle her. I don't talk about what we need to talk about.

"Why is it called a jellyfish?" Scottie asks. "It's not a fish and it's not jelly."

I say that a man-of-war isn't a jellyfish. I don't answer the question, but I tell her that she asks good questions. "You're getting too smart for me, Scottie."

I can feel her smiling. Even Joanie seems to be smiling, slightly. I feel happy, though I'm not supposed to, I guess. But the room feels good. It feels peaceful.

"Water," I say. "And blankets." I leave the room to get water and blankets.

When I come back toward the room, I hear Scottie say, "I have a remarkable eye." I stop in the doorway. Scottie is talking to her mother. I watch.

She is curled into her mother's side and has maneuvered Joanie's arm so that it's around her. "It's on the ceiling," I hear her say. "The most beautiful nest. It's very golden and soft-looking and warm, of course."

I see it too, except it isn't a nest. It's a browning banana, the remnant of our old game still stuck to the ceiling.

Scottie props herself onto an elbow, then leans in and kisses her mother on the lips, checks her face, then kisses her again. She does this over and over, this exquisite version of mouth-to-mouth, each kiss expectant, almost medicinal.

I let her go on with this fantasy, this belief in magical endings, this belief that love can bring someone to life. I let her try. For a long time, I watch her effort. I root for her even, but after a while I know that it's time. I need to step in. I tap lightly on the door. I don't want to startle her too badly.

THOM JONES

■

# Night Train

FROM *Doubletake*

JACK BUFFMEIR, AS FAR AS I knew, being a little kid, didn't seem
to have a real job or any work history whatever. On occasion he
made birdhouses, and if he couldn't sell them to people, he just
gave them away. They weren't all that hot. Something a simpleton
would knock together. In addition to this, Jack raised a few chickens and grew vegetables. My grandmother felt sorry for Jack and
let him live in a shack on the back of her property. It was just a
one-room affair with an outhouse behind it.

What interested me most about Jack was his black and white
bull terrier, Oyster, a rarely seen breed of dog, then as now. I cov-
eted the dog, but Oyster would rarely give me the time of day. As
far as Oyster was concerned, his oddball master was the sun,
moon, and stars. With a full-time religion like Jack, the dog did not
have any time for little boys.

Jack could play the fiddle, and when he was in good humor, he
liked to dress up in his white suit and play "Turkey in the Straw" at
the back of my grandmother's store. In the middle of the song he
would set the fiddle on the pop case, pull out a soupspoon, and ca-
vort around dancing as he clapped the spoon against his cheeks.
He would pick up carving knives from the meat block and flash
them around with the authority of a samurai warrior while clog-
dancing in his two-toned brown and white shoes. Meanwhile,
Oyster would do backflips, roll over, and dance about on his hind

legs with Jack. There was no television, and people found their entertainment in peculiar ways.

All you had to do to get a meal or a place to flop from my grandmother was to offer to pluck the "clinkers" from her coal furnace down in the store basement and haul them out in the back to the burnyard. A mental defective, hobo, or dangerous bum off the streets could come in and accomplish bed and board for this small chore. Boy Cleatus, a black of fifteen, used to do the job for a quarter. The clinkers were heavy, sizable things, like fossilized starfish. How the little pellets of coal clumped together during incineration was something I never understood. Whenever Boy Cleatus got in trouble with the law and was sent to the reformatory in St. Charles, the clinkers were mine to haul for no quarter. Since the fire pit was small, I often opened the furnace door and poked at these spiky formations. When the bulk of the fuel had burned, they became hollow, like fragile shells, and it was fun to mash them down before I threw more coal into the pit. The cold clinkers from the bottom of the ash pit I put in a laundry tub and carried out back. It paid to wear gloves when handling clinkers, although I seldom bothered; I mainly wanted to get the job over with as soon as possible, and I tolerated minor burns and ashen splinters. I learned to shovel coal and haul clinkers at an early age, but Jack Buffmeir, who lived scot-free in the shack, never dirtied his fingers in this fashion.

He was a thin, dapper fellow who preferred a suit and a vest to ordinary clothes. He neither drank nor smoked. I had heard that he had been gassed in the First World War and had somehow gotten out of mortal combat early. My grandmother disputed this story and told me that Jack had been struck by lightning and never served in the Great War. When he wasn't in his "Turkey in the Straw" mood, Jack was a quiet, suspicious man preoccupied with his health. It was one extreme or the other with him, glaring contrasting differences like the opposing colors of his two-toned shoes.

Buffmeir could swing into states of highest agitation, constantly pulling his watch from his vest pocket and flipping it open like a man who kept an urgent, variegating schedule. He was continually going to doctors. My grandmother was given to believe that his aches and pains were imaginary, but I wasn't so sure. Because I was a kid, he seldom paid attention to me; I could observe his unguarded visage, which was often that of a man in severe pain. His face took on a sour countenance and he would sometimes buy packets of fizzing stomach powders, which he mixed in a glass under my grandmother's kitchen spout. Like Napoleon in a white suit with a straw boater, he would insert his hand under his jacket and press it against his side, stoically waiting for fast pharmaceutical relief. Oyster positioned himself close enough to Jack so that he could look up at his master and gauge his moods while he stood vigilantly braced to defend the old man against a 360-degree perimeter of incoming evils.

Jack demanded complete and unwavering loyalty from the animal, yet he hardly bothered to feed the dog, and never once did I see him deign to kneel down and pet the animal or even bother to say a kind word. This lack of gratitude toward animals did not surprise me.

One cold day I stood out in front of the store waiting for the *Aurora Beacon News* to dump off their afternoon bundle of papers when I spotted a stray feral cat. I wanted a pet more than anything in the world, and I went for the tortoise-colored female. I managed to pick her up as she worked my face over with her front paws slashing like razors. She was a bundle of compressed fury, but I managed to stumble up the stairs with it, bust in the door, and drop it on the floor. The cat dashed off for the basement, and after my grandmother treated my scratches with Mercurochrome, I took a bowl of milk to the basement. I looked all over for the cat to no avail; but a cat can hide, and the basement was a warehouse of stock.

There were cases of cereal, toilet paper, coffee, Campbell's soup, Dinty Moore beef stew, sardines, potted meat, SOS scrubbing pads, and various and sundry goods. I ran about pell-mell looking for the animal, but it seemed to have vanished. Several days later I saw it purring in contentment on the white batting that insulated the coal furnace. The cat, which had given birth to six kittens my grandmother later drowned in the cistern, nonetheless found a home in the store as a mouser. Like Oyster, she spurned my attempts to befriend her.

Then a more hopeful time arrived. Jack Buffmeir saw an osteopath who convinced him to become a full-out vegetarian. The diet produced instant and miraculous benefits. Buffmeir left off wearing his dandy suits and plowed an additional two-acre garden behind the shack. He claimed he felt like a new man and would talk endlessly about the virtues of organic produce to anyone who would stand still and listen to it. Not only that, he put Oyster on a vegetarian regime and claimed that the luster and sheen on Oyster's harsh black and white coat was a result of nutrients from the life-giving soil. The earth was rich and productive Illinois black topsoil, and under the blazing sun and with an attentive watering schedule, Jack grew tomatoes, rhubarb, potatoes, corn, peas, carrots, and beans. Once these were in the ground he began tending to the trees on my grandmother's property, trees he had planted earlier in life under my grandmother's instruction. There were fruit trees and a couple of black walnuts, an arboretum of sorts, albeit long neglected.

Buffmeir believed in the healing properties of nuts, which were rich in proteins. He also stepped up his egg production, selling what he didn't eat at my grandmother's store. These were in the milk and butter cabinet with a small sign in front of them that read JACK BUFFMEIR'S MAGIC EGGS, FRESH DAILY. The eggs, which had brown shells, were fertilized by the fuckingest rooster on the south end of town. They cost a nickel more per dozen than regular eggs, and my grandmother was constantly besieged with questions about exactly what was so damn special about Jack Buffmeir's eggs. Jack said that he fed his chickens a special vitamin-enriched diet. I heard claims that they were good for your hair and nails and could even cure baldness. Even though Jack had no woman he produced a convincing argument that the zinc in them improved flagging sex lives. I didn't precisely know what a sex life was, but one day Jack grabbed me in a headlock and gave me a Dutch rub that really hurt, saying that if I wanted to grow big and slug home runs I should eat two of his eggs for breakfast every day. I was used to eating Dolly Madison chocolate doughnuts dunked in coffee for breakfast, but soon I had my grandmother frying egg sandwiches for my lunch.

The deleterious effects of cholesterol were unknown in those days, and eggs were fairly sensible nutrition. But Jack did not come into full glory until he broke from his osteopath's guidebook and, all on his own, discovered nature's true miracle food — the peach. He ate peaches morning, noon, and night. Illinois peaches were small, hard, and sour. Jack admitted as much, but ate them anyway. In an astounding burst of industry he planted hybrid peach trees and hybrid apple trees. He cultivated mulberry, pear, and sour cherry trees. He revived the long-neglected grapevines that grew alongside my grandfather's old Chevrolet garage, which, by then, my grandmother had rented out to a German machinist. Jack was constantly pruning trees, watering them, fertilizing them, and splicing hybrid branches on them like artificial limbs. But Jack refused to cut the grass; that job was left to Cousin Eustace, a head-injury victim.

There were a lot of birds when the fruit got ripe. Buffmeir killed flocks of crows and blackbirds with his shotgun (Oyster would finish off the wounded with a few quick snaps of the neck). Buffmeir would let me collect the bird bodies in a cardboard box, on the outside of which he would tally his kills before we tossed the dead birds into the trash burner. I was always being told that there were hungry people in the world, but I grew up in a store and all I ever saw was food. I had the good fortune to be born after the trees had matured. Jack had worried these trees back to vigor. For me, they were just there for easy picking. The only *tree* tree on the property was an oak that had gotten the jump on Jack — it was there in manifested maturity before he could do anything about it.

My grandmother liked flowers. I used to collect morning glories from the vines that grew up along the high fencing behind the garage. In the salad days, when my grandfather ran the prosperous Chevrolet dealership, he constructed a concrete tennis court behind the garage. There was a patch of grass back there that Cousin

Eustace also cut, and from there I could collect wildflowers to add to the bouquets of morning glories I presented to my grandmother. Even if you got them into a glass of water, they were only good for a couple of hours. Having seen Jack Buffmeir raise vegetables, I planted nasturtiums and petunias, but just as the seedlings began to sprout, Eustace would hack them down with the push mower. My grandmother refused to intervene, since mowing the lawn seemed to be my cousin's only reason for being. Cousin Eustace was a diabetic, only a few years older than myself, but as my mother had dropped him on his head as an infant, he was feeble-minded in a more straightforward way than Jack Buffmeir. I'm fairly sure that any psychiatrist worth his salt would have diagnosed Jack as a paranoid schizophrenic with a propensity to manic depression. This was particularly evident when he started in on a food jag. His views shifted.

Peaches were okay but the real healing miracles involved carrots and foods with violent colors like eggplant, green and red peppers, tomatoes, and watermelon. The peach, the mainstay of his diet, well, cut into one and what did you see but anemic yellow flesh. Jack started eating carrots like there was no tomorrow. He also went to the library and brought home an exotic book about yoga in which very thin, dark, little people twisted themselves into knots, their faces composed into visages of radiant inner peace.

There was a punching bag in the basement of the store. It was an inflatable speed bag that hung from the ceiling. One morning Jack set to work on the bag at five a.m., shortly after my grandmother opened up. I could hear the bag popping from my bed on the second floor. Since my father was a professional boxer, the sound of the bag filled me with the hope that he had sobered up and come to pay a visit. When I got my clothes on and rushed down to the basement, Jack Buffmeir was doing a headstand in the rag bin, a small closet where my grandmother tossed the gunnysacks the red and white potatoes from Idaho were shipped in. Jack's face was redder than a fire hydrant. I said, "Where's my dad?" But then I looked at Jack's knuckles and saw that they were scuffed raw. Oyster must have mistaken my intentions for he rushed me and began ragging my pant legs. Jack said, "Oyster, leave off!"

I rushed upstairs and asked my grandmother what Jack Buffmeir was doing a headstand in the rag bin for. She looked up from doing her bills. "Getting a stroke," she said.

A few days later I was sitting out on the back porch drinking chocolate milk and reading comic books with the Marzuki brothers when Jack asked us if we would like a boxing lesson. We demurred, but Jack insisted. Soon Butch Marzuki was standing in the gravel parking lot with a pair of sixteen-ounce pillows on his tiny fists. Jack Buffmeir was wearing the other pair. With a suddenness that verged on cheating he said, "Okay, box!" He was dressed in a glen plaid suit and wore a vest with a watch chain and that pair of two-toned brown and white shoes. He danced around Marzuki, cuffing his ears until they turned red. Marzuki, who barely came up to his waist, launched a right, and Buffmeir's left hand cracked over it and bloodied Marzuki's nose. Tears followed.

"Defend yourself at all times, boy. You had that one coming," Buffmeir said, dancing about the lot as he tossed his head side to side, keeping his neck loose. He looked very pleased with his victory, adding, "And quit that sniveling, you big sissy."

Buffmeir looked at me and said, "You're next."

"I ain't fighting," I said.

"Why not? Are you scared?"

My grandmother came out to the back porch with a pail of dirty water and a mop. I noticed that Jack's face flushed with color at the sight of her. "Just teaching the boys the manly art of self-defense, Mag."

"Leave them be," she said. "They fight enough as it is."

"They asked me to show them," he croaked.

"No, you forced us," David Marzuki exclaimed.

"Did not."

"Yes, you did!" Marzuki said.

"Ingrate!" Buffmeir said. "Liar."

"Am not," Marzuki said.

Shortly after this episode Jack Buffmeir fell into deep black moods. When they came upon him, he couldn't even bear the companionship of his dog, Oyster. After the dog killed Jack's rooster, a mean bird, and most likely Oyster could have claimed self-defense, Buffmeir took after him with a horsewhip. Some of the factory workers from the Durabilt were eating sandwiches on my grandmother's front porch when he set upon the animal. A dark, muscular man with a cut of plug in his cheek set down his sandwich and snatched the whip out of the man's hand. "No way to treat an animal. Shame on you."

Furious, Buffmeir walked though the front door, exited to the back, crossed the parking lot, and went into his shack. The dog was still waiting for him on the front porch late the next morning. My grandmother said, "The dog thinks Jack is in the store."

I coaxed the animal inside and he walked up and down the aisles, even went down into the basement looking for his master. When he could not find him, he waited for the next customer to come into the front door and returned to his post on the porch.

That night Mag lured Oyster inside with some leftover pot roast. The dog followed us upstairs to bed but did nothing but pace and whine the entire night. Finally she had to let him out to wait on the porch for Jack, who showed up the next day and reconciled with his pet.

A few days later Buffmeir abandoned the dog on the back porch. He walked through the store with a sack of carrots and didn't return until dark. My grandmother was getting ready to close when Jack appeared and said, "I walked up to Batavia and swam naked in the gravel pit." Batavia was seven miles away.

When my grandmother recounted the story to Cousin Eustace and his father, Pug, Pug said, "Damn, he should have kept right on going until he got to Elgin." Elgin was the city north of Batavia that housed the state mental institution, just one city beyond St. Charles, which housed the boys' reformatory where Boy Cleatus was incarcerated.

Cousin Eustace leaned against the pop machine, mimicking his father's body language. He had a strained, high-pitched voice and a pasty complexion and too much weight. "He should have kept right on going to Elgin, Mag," Cousin Eustace said.

"Hell, yes," Pug said, waving a sweaty bottle of Green River.

"Hell, yes, he should," Cousin Eustace said. "That man is full of bunk."

"He's a damn nut!" Pug said.

"Sure he is, Dad, a damn nut! Lock him up and throw away the key."

Each day as Jack Buffmeir took his carrot-fueled excursions, Oyster waited on the back porch. I tempted the dog with succulent cuts of beef from the meat locker, and while he would eat them, he refused to give in and play with me. He would not fetch. He would not wrestle. He tolerated my hugging him, and once when I got into a screaming and cussing rock fight with Carl Smith, Oyster leapt from the porch and chased Smith out of the yard and clear over to Bowditch Avenue to the Smith hovel. Shortly thereafter Carl Smith came back with reinforcements, the Tinsley and Calhoun brothers: big, tough, and mean-all. I was caught flat, but the dog sensed their sinister intentions immediately and soon had the entire pack racing for Bowditch Avenue. A few days later I saw Carl Smith at the playground and shoved him to the ground, pulling his arm up behind his back for the goose egg that one of his rocks had inflicted on my forehead a few days before. The playground supervisor quickly broke up the fight and not only sent me home for the afternoon, but kicked me off the junior softball squad. Dejected, I returned to the store. I parked my bike along the side of the garage, and when Oyster came off the back porch to greet me, I was mildly astonished. I sat near a pile of leaves that had blown alongside Pug and Vera's place and hugged the dog, who let me cuddle next to him for warmth. A burst of sunlight broke through the clouds and warmed us and almost instantly I fell into a deep and wonderful slumber. It was cold and nearly dark when I awoke. Oyster had abandoned me for his position on the porch. I dusted off my clothes and went inside.

Oyster would not fetch or wrestle, but he liked to play tug-of-war with a rope. It was virtually impossible to beat him at this game and Jack exploited the dog's power in these demonstrations to help sell his canned produce. Oyster was eighty pounds of pure muscle. Another thing he liked to do at Jack Buffmeir's behest was jump at inflated balloons, a comical sight that caused the customers to stop and watch in wonder. Oyster possessed incredible vertical leaping ability. It looked as if he were playing basketball. He timed his jumps so that each time his snout hit the balloon, he seemed to hang in the air a moment. Jack could sell several cartons of fertilized eggs whenever he put his wonder dog into action. But this seldom happened once the black moods befell him.

The long, introspective, carrot-nibbling walks continued. The heels of Jack's two-toned shoes were worn down. He stuffed them with cardboard, though the cheapest shoemaker in town had a shop just across the street.

Jack was letting his dandy image slide. His skin was stiff and yellow. He looked like a cadaver. My grandmother asked him what was wrong, and Buffmeir shook his head gravely. "Cancer, Mag. It's all in my liver. I just seen a doctor in Chicago. I got six weeks. Who's going to take care of my dog? Who's going to mind the trees?" Jack Buffmeir didn't wait for an answer. We watched him walk down the back steps and cross the parking lot to his shack with his dog behind him. His right hand was pressed firmly under his ribs, an area which pained him greatly; his thin jaw was set hard.

My grandmother had a huge medical reference book with illustrated pictures in her bedroom. I looked up liver diseases and saw a patient looking every bit as bad as Jack. Worse, I saw what cancer did to the liver. The human liver looked much like the liver in my grandmother's meat cooler. With cancer, it was infiltrated by orange, unnatural corded knots that sought to strangle it. I quickly slammed the book shut and prayed to God that never would such a fate fall upon me. Jack Buffmeir was a goner!

The night crew at the Durabilt had thirty minutes for lunch. Mag would slice cold cuts for them and dish up salads. They liked to congregate around the pop cabinet, comb back their slick ducktails, smoke, and posture while the Italian girls from the neighborhood came in wearing their shorts in hot weather. Or, if the men weren't scoping, they would sit out on the front porch talking sports or playing grab-ass.

The factory was set along a trunk of the Burlington Railroad that supplied Aurora with industrial transport. Just beyond were the main rails for the fast Burlington zephyrs that bolted from Seattle to Chicago and back. I liked to stand and wave at the passenger trains and catch glimpses of the dining cars or the sleepers that seemed like compartments of Pullman pleasure. This was particularly true at night when a passing tableau of scenes was presented by the illuminated compartments. With every need attended to, the passengers had the leisure to read, smoke, eat and drink, or converse. They were often finely dressed and had destinations — places to go and things to do; it was mysterious, romantic, and enchanting. I also loved counting freight cars and spotting hoboes. I most eagerly awaited the passage of the caboose, which would sometimes display a railman asleep in the upper loft while another was preparing coffee in a blue enamel pot, or sitting at a little table drinking it while reading a magazine by a kerosene lantern. I watched wistfully as the clacking and banging of the train receded, and the caboose disappeared, and suddenly I was back in my own world of Lutheran restrictions and sameness.

But the trains came often. The day and night bump and rattle of trains was a given. The tracks also provided footpaths to the west end of town. One Friday night at about eight o'clock, Pug and Cousin Eustace were waiting for the dinner crew to disperse and for Vera to get off from the plant, where she worked as a bookkeeper. I was helping box up some groceries for a young Polish girl and her mother who lived on the far south end. The girl was a skinny blonde with buckteeth, and, like others in this account, she was said to be a bit feeble-minded. It seems that Boy Cleatus and a couple of his friends had taken advantage of her. My grandmother's term for it was "molested." I wasn't at all sure what that meant. I did know that the girl, whose name was Lois, was very poor, but by all accounts her mother was honest and hard-working. Lois didn't make eye contact much, but the more I looked at her, the more I was certain that I was in love with her. My grand-

mother was giving them food, which meant staples like bread, potatoes, and dried fish. I swiped a couple of Chunky bars, a Three
Musketeers, and a Snickers, and put them in the box under a
bunch of bananas when Vera came running up the front porch
screaming, "Jack Buffmeir is out on the train tracks, and the train
is coming!"

"Well, hell, didn't you pull him off?" Pug asked.

"I tried that and he slugged me," Vera said. "He just yelled,
'Fuck all and leave me alone!' Then he set that dog on me and I ran
here."

I was out the front door like a shot. Away from the neon signs of
the storefront, it was dark. I could hear shoes scuffling in the dark,
heavy breathing, and men slipping and falling in the gravel as they
raced to the tracks. I had fallen twice, and my knees and palms
stung with abrasions. My lower lip was swollen and bleeding, and
I had chipped a tooth, but I got up running both times. Suddenly
the Burlington rounded a curve as it crossed the Lake Street viaduct and straightened out. At that point the train's mighty spot-
light picked up Jack Buffmeir, who had laid himself directly on the
main rails. He had walked north toward the curve so the engineer
would have little time to see him, let alone stop. I bolted down the
track bed in the direction of the blinding light. The train's horn
was blaring and the iron wheels started screeching as the engineer
hit the brakes. Jack was now on his hands and knees trying to
push Oyster away from him. For once the dog refused to obey —
he seemed to realize that his master was bent on suicide and he
couldn't let that happen. I didn't care about Jack Buffmeir, but I
had come to think of Oyster as my dog. I ran the tracks as fast as
possible and could hear heavy breathing behind me. Just as the
train hit Buffmeir one of the factory workers grabbed me and
pulled me to safety. I heard two quick thunks and saw Oyster flying through the air like he was shot from a cannon. It was a freight
train with over seventy cars.

I ran down to the viaduct, crossed underneath it, and came back
to the point of the collision and began searching for the dog. I
found Buffmeir's right forearm and hand severed almost blood-

lessly. Then at the bottom of a sloping grass hill, I spotted Oyster. He was unmarked, but dead just the same. I lifted his head to my lap and talked to him, but his body was limp. I thought that maybe if I could get him back to the store, somebody there could do something to revive him. As I said, he seemed unmarked. I tried to lift him but he weighed more than eighty pounds. I tried pulling him up the grassy slope by his rear feet, but I kept slipping and falling down. I dragged him for a ways across the gravel, but that was undignified and unbefitting to such a fine animal.

I heard frantic voices, police sirens, and saw a good number of flashlight beams combing the area under the train. And then I heard even more frantic voices calling my name. I was the subject of an intense manhunt. I said nothing in reply and, instead, wrapped my body alongside that of the dog, holding him much the way I had held him months ago on the patch of oak leaves that had blown along the side of Pug and Vera's bungalow.

The accident drew a banner headline in the *Aurora Beacon News*. People who never heard of Jack Buffmeir attended his funeral. You would have thought Rudolph Valentino had died. To add to the pathos, the engineer insisted that he saw Oyster spending his last moment on earth trying to drag his master to safety and paying with his life.

A few days after the funeral I followed my grandmother out to Jack's shack. She seldom left the store, and when she did, she had to walk with a cane. She removed a key from her apron pocket and opened the door. There wasn't much inside. A bed and a dresser. A small kitchen table. There was a pantry filled with canned vegetables and fruit. Jack Buffmeir did not have a refrigerator, but an icebox. There was a bottle of sour buttermilk inside. As I sniffed it, I saw a cushion on the floor, and above it, on the wall, two paint-worn footprints. I had located the site where Jack did his hourlong daily headstands that were meant to defeat the pernicious effects of gravity on the human body.

There was a small closet filled with his dandy clothes, and, on the top, a box containing his birth certificate, a number of medical books, and an honorary discharge from the U.S. Army. In addition to this was a Purple Heart and Jack's wallet, which contained four dollars. My grandmother handed me the box of papers, and after she locked the door, we walked back to the store together.

The next afternoon my grandmother mailed Jack's four dollars to his osteopath. A few days later the doctor called her. I could see consternation on my grandmother's face, and I was shocked at the length of time she spent on the phone — some four or five minutes. When she hung up, I asked her what was going on. She said that Jack Buffmeir didn't have cancer after all. His liver was fine. The doctor in Chicago said the reason Jack turned yellow was from all the carrots he was eating. He was as healthy as a horse.

Later that night, when I had finished sweeping up, I moved to the front of the store, where my grandmother sat in a folding chair, dozing. Once a week or so during this time, I would clip a few gray whiskers that grew on her chin. She was the least vain person I ever knew, but she always put on a show of being greatly pleased by this ritual. When she awoke I said, "Gram, are you sad about Jack Buffmeir?"

"Sad? No. I'm not sad. He wasn't really fit to live. He was not right. Never. They were drawing up papers to send him to Elgin," she said.

I thought those would be her last words on the subject, but as she looked at my yearning eyes she had one further pronouncement: "In the end the fool got what he really wanted — hit by a train and out with a great splash. And who was stuck paying for his funeral? Me!" She looked at the wall clock. It was eleven-thirty. She said, "Come on, now. Let's lock up and go to bed."

It was a hot night. After I brushed my teeth, I lay in bed waiting for a car to zoom past on Lake Street to stir up a little breeze, but there was no traffic. My grandmother rubbed her legs with liniment and picked up her prayer book. I wanted to ask her if Oyster was in heaven. I was pretty sure Jack Buffmeir was in hell, and I knew what her answer would be anyway. When you are dead, you are dead, unless you were very bad, in which case you were in hell. If by some off chance there was a heaven, less than ten souls inhabited the place.

The blare of a distant night train resonated from the south-east. In less than an hour people from Washington, Utah, Montana, Nebraska, North Dakota, and Iowa would be disembarking at Union Station in Chicago — to do what? I guessed they would be tired and eager to get into the safe cars of relatives; either that or they would have to flag down cabs to find hotel rooms. Soon they would be ejected from the comfortable haven of the plush coach cars and scrambling for shelter in a big and mean city. As my grandmother shut off the night-light, I waited for the rattle of steel wheels on iron rails. It seemed the train would never come. But when it did, I began counting cars by the sound of wheels rocking over the spliced rails.

TOM KEALEY

■

# Bones

FROM *Prairie Schooner*

A BOXER'S OFFENSE is designed to create openings in the opponent's defense and to land blows to the vulnerable points of the
head and body from the waist up. Power originates as she pushes
off from her feet; its degree depends upon her ability to link the
muscles of the legs, the back, the shoulders, and the arms into a
chain of force. A boxer's attack consists of such basic blows as left
jab, right cross, left hook, and uppercut.

Helen, fifteen, throws a hook from her left foot, covers her
midsection, ducks, takes a hit on her padded headgear, feints
with the left again, listens to her trainer's voice, mumbled by his
mouthpiece: move back and back in, keep me in the center, I'll kill
you near the ropes. Move with your feet, keep your waist straight.
Next time you lean back, I'll knock you down; and when she does
lean back, he does knock her down, with a strong hook to her forehead and a sudden shove of hips. After the fall, she stares at the
tubes of fluorescent lights above the gym, the glow of the street
lamp through the windows, the night bugs outside. She presses
her gloves against the canvas, feels the cold lick of sweat against
her T-shirt. I haven't started the count yet, he says. Not even in the
corner yet. You wait till five before you get up. Think about where
you are, and think about what put you there. Three. You know I'll
push hard now. I'm going to see what you've got left. Five.

Helen stands, punches her gloves together, hops on her toes.

He is a head taller than she is, wider in the chest and waist, with longer arms and better technique. Dark hair covers his chest and shoulders. He moves in and she sidesteps, takes another jab to the head but slips in one of her own. He chooses not to cover, tries a jab and misses. She has already turned, gives him a hard shot to the ribs and then a harder one still with the other arm. Before he can wrap her up, she steps away, covers her head as she was taught, swings to the center of the ring. She hears the slap of her punches only now, seconds after they landed. Because she holds her ground, he tries a cross and it glances off the top of her skull, but he pays with two blows to his ribs, the other side this time. He steps away and circles the ring, keeps a distance from her.

I'm going to knock you down now, he says, and again, he does. A flurry of hooks and crosses, most of them missing. She plants a strong jab in his gut, hears nothing, moves back, which was the mistake: he connects to the side of her head and then with the right square to the nose, her headgear saving the bone from cracking. It's only after she falls, after her feet fly from the canvas, her back slapping flat against the mat, that she hears his grunt of surprise. Not now, but from seconds before, the jab to the gut. She looks at the fluorescent lights again. She tastes the blood in her mouthpiece as he retires to the corner.

I haven't started yet, he says. The words come out without vowels. Helen shakes her head, sits up but does not rise. Two, he says. You've got me thinking now. Got me thinking this'll go an extra round. I'm not going to push it hard this time, or maybe I will. But if I'm smart I won't. Five. Stay down. I'm thinking I might not bring all I got here. So what are you going to do?

Keep you moving, she says. I'm going to move around.

Get up now, he says. And make sure you do that.

On the train, Omar, twelve, finds it hard to understand the mumbled voice of the conductor who announces the station stops. He likes to talk to his mother on the train, though she doesn't ride with him: it keeps people away. He thinks about his brother and the belt. A woman with a baby sits across from him, and a man dressed in two heavy coats. Give me your belt, his brother had said to him through the broken glass of the warehouse window. What you want my belt for? Just give it here. So, Omar had handed it over and watched as his brother wrapped it around his arm. The boy took out a needle from his sock. Mama's too fat, his brother had said. She eats too much. When he was younger, when he'd handed the belt over, Omar hoped he'd always live with his mother, thought about no matter how old he became, the three of them would still live in the same house. I don't want no skinny-bones mama, he'd said. She isn't a girl. I don't want to sit on the lap of no skinny-bones girl.

He takes the steps from the subway station two at a time, watches his frost breath as he comes aboveground. The abandoned car in the lot near the station has a cracked windshield with blood and a few strands of hair, and in a lot not unlike this one, a month before, two kids were trapped in an abandoned refrigerator, suffocated. Omar likes the tugboats in the harbor — he can see their red running lights from the top floor of his apartment building — but to get there, to the top floor, he has to pass the steps on the sixteenth, the hallway with no light bulbs, where, often enough, he can hear a man crying. But Omar's never seen this man, thinks he might be an old man, by the sound of the voice, takes the steps one at a time when he passes.

If he sits on the rooftop — his legs hanging over the side — at sunset, Omar can see the rats come up from the river. They look like an army of ants from where he sits. They cross the lot where the car with the cracked windshield sits, they pass over the rolls of carpets, the broken chairs and the trash and the abandoned tires.

It's the last day of the month, this day, and Omar passes his own apartment building, passes the cemetery with the broken headstones — no one has been buried there for years — passes the piles of trash in the graveyard, the oil drum filled with wood and fire, passes, for all he knows, the skeleton his friend Noel had seen, not rising from the ground, but laid in a corner, never buried, the bones as gray as the sky. Omar keeps his eyes on the tallest building on the block, where, on the fifth floor, he hopes to find his mother. A rent party.

He thinks about the baby on the train. Its eyes closed, wrapped in a green sweater, its mother's — sister's? — arms swaying with the rhythm of the railcar. More than wanting to live with his own mother, and long before even stepping on that train, before stepping on countless trains, Omar had wanted a baby boy of his own. But only you know that.

Winston takes the handkerchief from his pocket and wipes the spittle from his grandfather's chin. The old man turns the key in the ignition of the truck. It's older than Winston, abandoned in their backyard for almost as long as the boy can remember. The boy had shoveled leaves and twigs — a bird's nest? — from the seats before they'd entered. The windshield is cracked in the corner — no hair or blood, simply a crack, a rock left on a road years before. Unlike his grandfather, who is gaunt, mostly bones, skeletal, Winston is a big boy, bigger than most in his school. Fat. Fat fingers, fat toes. He's only eleven but thinks as he gains age he might gain the person inside himself who he wishes to be. The old man — his name is Winston too — coughs, and Winston wipes again with the handkerchief.

The truck is not going to turn over. The engine in the truck — the starter — is not going to turn over. Winston looks out the windshield and sees, in the distance, the sunflower fields bending with the wind. To the left, he sees the lights — green and red — of the Ferris wheel of the traveling carnival. From this distance it looks slow, but when he'd sat in one of the cars with his father, it had seemed fast, rising and falling above the lights of the spook house and the ticket merchants — and he hopes, if the starter turns over, that he and his grandfather might drive there. Might ride the Ferris wheel together. In his pocket, he carries all the money he has to his name (seven dollars and change). But the starter won't turn. Winston, the grandson, knows little about trucks or cars but thinks, as his grandfather turns the key, that something is being burned out. That the more the key turns, the more something is being lost.

He'd ridden the Ferris wheel only once. Had not budgeted — his father's word — correctly, and had left that seven dollars and change at home. He'd blown most of his money on the spook house, which his father had refused to ride with him. He'd sat alone, that first time, in the front car, had screamed when the dragon had bent at the entrance, fire glowing in its belly, and had assumed (Winston) that he'd be scorched before he'd even gotten inside the house. The pirates had swiped their sabers above his head, a witch boiled the skulls of children in her cauldron, and the bony white hands of skeletons had barely reached him, clicking against the top of the railcar. The giants came after that. I want it to be quiet in here, the man in the car behind him had said, and it was only then that Winston could hear his own screams, had felt for a moment outside himself, had wondered, hearing that man's voice, what his classmates might think of him. I can't help it, he'd said. I'm scared. Had said that with the weight of the two dollars he'd paid for the ride. Two dollars, he felt, earned him the right to scream. More pirates had been next, and the goblins after that. Finally, the ghosts, white sheets, through which he could make out the people, and he did not feel so afraid. But he continued to scream, wanting his two dollars' worth, until the cars exited the house and he saw his father waiting near the ticket booth, arms crossed, the Ferris wheel turning in the black sky behind him.

Looks like you were scared, said his father.

No, Winston had said. I loved it.

The starter turns over. Winston looks behind him, through the glass of the back window of the truck. A thick cloud of smoke — as big as a giant's fist — blows out into the air. Beyond, Winston can see an orange glow, not the sun, which was setting in the opposite direction, but something else, something almost as big, glowing and stretching toward the sky.

His grandfather says nothing, has said nothing for almost a week. He switches the gears into drive, and the truck sets off across the yard, spitting white smoke and mud behind them.

A boxer's defense is designed to prevent the jabs, hooks, and crosses of her opponent from reaching the vulnerable areas. It is also intended to leave her in a position from which she might score with her own punches. A boxer avoids an opponent's blows by using correct techniques in blocking, parrying, ducking, and slipping.

Helen showers, dresses, ices down her left elbow where a bruise has already formed. She waits for her trainer at the ringside of the gym, watches two young men wrap each other near the ropes. They're separated by an older man who says nothing, gives them a silent count, steps away, and the shorter of the two men takes a shot to the head, swings wildly, and is hit again. Helen examines her cut lip in the reflection of the windows. She waits for her trainer for a half-hour, watches the two men in the ring. When she gives up, she exits through the back door, walks through a cloud of cigarette smoke and the stares of the boxers, walks the long road home in the dark. She unlocks the house quietly. Her mother is likely asleep.

In the kitchen, Helen takes her baby brother from his crib, wakes him, wipes his nose with the sleeve of her shirt. She sets him on his feet, steadying him with her hands gripped below his arms.

Her father was a pilot when she was younger, had a prop plane that he flew out of Juneau, ferrying supplies to homesteaders, taking Helen with him on occasion. She'd sit at the window as he flew low over the inside waterway, watching for pods of orcas or the hump of gray whales against the white crests of the sea. On the brightest days, the green tree lines stretched for as far as she could see, and her father, holding his hand up against the sun, blinded from the horizon, seemed to fly on instinct. When they reached the lighthouse on Hawkin's Point, they turned landward, flying over the black rocks and the white dots of eagles' heads, sharp and clear in the branches of the tallest evergreens. Even then, Helen knew life would not last this way, sensed that she would always come down, knew that high expectations led to disappointment.

When she'd left him — been sent away — she sat on the ballards of the ferryboat, alone in the stern, her face wrapped in scarves, watching her breath disappear in the mist from the ship's rudder. The ferryboat pitched and rolled with the waves. Above the stern, a line of gulls stretched and dived at fish in the water.

Her baby brother neither smiles nor frowns, looks at her with great curiosity, moans for a moment, then is silent as she removes her hands, lets him stand on his own. The expression on his face changes, the first thought of doubt. His knees give way, and she catches him, leans forward and slips her hands against his ribs. On the ship, she'd sat in the cabin next to an old woman, had stored the woman's duffel bag in the rack above them where the woman could not reach, had stood on the armrest to pack it in. The woman had slipped her a piece of chocolate, and though Helen would have preferred to save it for later, to savor the thought of the candy waiting in her pocket, she ate it slowly, nibbling at the edges, letting the chocolate melt on her tongue. They'd played cards, she and the old woman, every afternoon on the three-day trip — gin rummy, crazy eights, and bird's cage — had eaten their soup on the starboard benches, had looked through the woman's binoculars at a sea otter, at the weekday fishermen pulling in their crab traps. She still wrote to Mrs. Lange, once each Christmas so far, and once in the summer, received letters back. Beneath the locks of gray hair, Helen had noticed the woman's ear, the top half missing, a stub on the skull, and the woman, noticing Helen's stare, had said, A donkey bit that off. I got too close when I was a little girl. My father took that donkey out to the field and shot him after that.

Helen sets her brother straight again. Locks his knees into place. He continues to watch her, as if her hands, her arms, were connected to his own body. When she lets go, he watches the hands move away, his eyes begin to water. He takes a step toward her as she pulls away, keeps his feet. He wants those hands back. Takes another step, keeps his feet again, loses his balance, straightens himself, has a look of surprise for a moment, and in that moment, loses his balance again. He falls back before she can snatch him. He moves faster in that fall than, it seems, her trainer has ever moved, and before the child fully realizes he has fallen, she has him in her arms, pushes his head against her neck, begins a song that he recognizes. His fall is forgotten, if it ever happened at all.

\*

What is it out there that points the right way? Omar feels this, although he doesn't think it, not exactly, as he makes his way through the snowflakes mixed with rain, his feet slipping against the sidewalk. His thoughts are on his mother. When he opens the door to the tallest apartment building, the air is only slightly warmer, and a sourly unpleasant odor drifts from the hallway. He takes the steps one at a time, knows better than to trust the railing, passes a man at the top of the stairway who mutters, Works, man, works, takes the rest of the steps, moves faster, up to the fifth floor. He passes the people, the bottles in the hallway, finds the apartment and then the bedroom.

His mother is a small circle in the center of the bed. She is alone, and for that Omar is grateful. She is no longer the fat woman that his brother had spoken of, taking the belt through the broken window. She is skin and bones. He takes a cloth from his pocket, had brought it for this very purpose, runs cold water over it in the bathroom. Returns and wipes his mother's face. Touches the sores on her lips, wipes the blood away. She stirs, opens her eyes, closes them again. A dead rat lies in the corner of the room. You're good to come get me, she says, mumbles the words to the point that he can barely make them out, but he's heard them before. Soon, she'll try to convince him this is as good a place to sleep as any, will ask him to slip up next to her. Let's go, Mama, he says. In the ten minutes you want to sit here, we can be home.

She squeezes his hand, tries to sit up, leans back on her elbows. From the other room, they can hear people begin to dance, can feel the bass of the stereo through the floorboards. Omar wishes he'd turned on the lights. He kisses her on the forehead, is trapped by her arms, still strong, even at this time. He looks out the window at the river. His mother, he is sure, is kind to other people, treats people better than anyone he knows. He believes his mother means everything to him. We could be at the bottom of the stairs in two minutes, he says to her.

Longer than that.

A year before, he used to look out on that river. He thought there might be another boy, a lot like him, on the other side, but now he doesn't think so. His mother rises, sits up, rubs his shoulders with her hand. Kisses him where he kissed her. She stands up from the bed and stumbles to the bathroom, and in five minutes, they'll reach the bottom of the stairs.

That boy on the other side of the river, way on the other side, miles and states away, watches his father from the cab of the truck as his grandfather drives through the ruts and ridges of the back lawn. His father stands with arms limp at his sides, as surprised as the boy at the movement of the truck. The man disappears around the corner of the house — the two Winstons disappear around the corner of the house — and the truck creaks and bounces onto the state highway. Above them, the stars are clear. They drive on, slow; cars pass them on the left side as the older Winston shifts to higher then lower gears. It seems to the younger Winston that his grandfather cannot decide on something. They drive in the direction of the carnival. Winston can see the Ferris wheel turn, remembers his father sitting next to him on the ride — the only ride the man took that day — and knows that the carnival is not his grandfather's destination.

Maybe the creek, he thinks, but not likely. If a raindrop fell in that creek it might travel south to a larger stream, and a river after that, might find its way where three rivers meet, might choose the smallest of the three and turn eastward, rolling over rocks, fish, hollow reeds and old tires, rats. Might be observed from a rooftop by a boy near Winston's age. But Winston doesn't think of this. He thinks of the snake his grandfather had caught at the creek, had pinched it near the back of the head, lifted it from the mud, showed Winston how to hold it, watched as it crawled up the arm of his grandson, had seen the fear and the delight in the boy's face.

But they pass the turnoff for the creek, and soon after, they pass the carnival. Winston's eyes follow the Ferris wheel as it rises above them, a hundred yards from the shoulder of the road. The older Winston follows his grandson's gaze, watches the lights of the Ferris wheel in the rearview mirror. He has a clarity of thought for a change: that would've been a good place to stop. He has no idea where he is going, recognizes this fact, and in recognizing it knows that he has come through the fog of his own thoughts that, God knows, he's been trying to come through for the past week.

But even as he keeps his eyes on the road, edges the steering wheel to the right, he keeps the picture of his grandson in his mind. The boy's father had considered him a simpleton. The word had bothered the older Winston, he'd seen it hang in the air like a weight, had thought he might keep it from settling around the boy's neck. On the days when the father worked, the old man had taught the boy how to drive the tractor in the fields of his neighbor's yard. The boy was tall for his age; his feet could touch the pedals if he sat forward. The old man thought he might teach the boy a trade. Farming took not great thoughts, but a focus that he was certain the boy had. He'd taught him how to bale hay and how to lead the cows in to milk, how to hook up the machines. He'd taught him how to catch a snake — that was for fun — and earlier still, years before, how to tie his shoes and how to read. He thought he might be teaching him something here, in the truck, had started the old clunker with that in mind, in his fogged mind, but what that was he was not now sure.

On the windshield the reflection of the carnival lights dims, and another set of lights shines brighter. Blue lights. The old man checks his mirror and sees the sheriff's cruiser closing the distance on the highway.

God dammit, he says.

Hey, says the younger Winston. That's your mouth.

The old man neither stops nor speeds up. The cruiser rides close to his bumper, and the lights glow strong against the windshield. The deputy switches on his siren, follows close, and after a minute — two minutes — has passed, calls in to the switchboard for backup. On a straightaway, he moves the cruiser to the left lane, comes even with the truck. Beyond them, down the highway, Winston can see the same glow he'd seen from the farmhouse. Not the carnival, and not even now the lights of the sheriff's cruiser, but a glow greater than any of those things, as bright as the moon, even at this distance. It burns orange against the skyline.

The deputy, now ten minutes past his shift, had taken the call because it was an easy one: an old man and a boy in a truck, to be pulled over and returned to a farmhouse five miles back. The deputy has a boy of his own, is a first-time father, had seen his boy walk two days before, had caught him as he fell, had been thinking about that as he called in for backup. He pulls level with the truck, in the opposite lane. They're not moving very fast. He smiles at the old man. Doesn't see any reason to be rude, had not been raised that way. He points to the side of the road.

The old man looks at this deputy. The man looks like a boy himself. The older Winston takes in the smile. Takes it for a cockiness that the deputy had not intended. The old man raises his right hand and extends his middle finger. Next to him, his grandson — a bit of a prude when it comes to language — likes that. The old man can hear his laugh.

You do it, he says.

No way, says Winston.

The deputy loses the smile and sets his foot against the brake. Ahead, he can see a long line of cars, blocking the road in both directions, stretching toward an orange glow in the distance, bright as the moon. He seems to register this — the deputy does — thinks he might see the source of the glow and hopes he will not. Thinks of his son again, and then of the boy in the truck. He presses down on his brake and gives the old man some room.

Slipping is avoiding a blow by moving to the side; a counterpunch follows to the right if she moves to the right. A left from the left. A duck is a bend to escape an opponent's blow. The hands are held in punching position so she might retaliate as soon as the opponent's arm passes over her head.

Helen tapes her hands, makes fists as she sits on the sink in the kitchen, watches the shadow of her hands against the floor. Outside, she ties the punching bag to the largest low branch of the spruce pine, a hundred yards from her house. She warms up, counts to four hundred on the bag, her fists working from memory. She watches her white breath in the air. She hits the bag like it was made of glass, hits it solid and light, hits it on the backswing so as not to break it. Years from now, will she stand on a corner at two in the morning, waiting for someone who never shows up? She thinks this at around three hundred. Wonders who that person might be. She sees the portholes and hatches of the ferryboat, feels the warmth of the bourbon slide down her throat, just a nip — Mrs. Lange's word — try it if you like it. She hadn't liked it at the time, but likes it now, doesn't taste the bitterness or the sting while punching at the bag. It warms her: the memory, the taste, and the movement around the tree.

Helen reaches four hundred, stops and moves to the other side of the bag, moves beyond glass, thinks of the bag as rubber, bouncing back, bouncing faster the harder she hits it, if she keeps the right rhythm. She thinks of her trainer. Then, tries to think of the ferryboat instead of him. He's twice and a half her age. He's ugly. She'd like to break his nose. Thinks that she might slip in one day, with practice, with repetition, with guile and deceit, and smack him a good one. She smacks the bag a good one and loses the rhythm, tries to get it back, fails. She stops the bag and starts again. The uppercut is a blow delivered with either hand and in close quarters. The boxer finds this blow most effective against an opponent boxing in a crouching position.

Omar crouches like a boxer, as if he's waiting for the blow to come, waiting for his chance to cross or jab, but he crouches for neither of those reasons. He holds the weight of his mother, half her weight. Even with her skin and bones, she is still heavier than him. He's a small boy. A squeak next to Winston, if they'd ever stand together; he's not as solid or defined as Helen. He holds his mother's weight up in the rain and sleet with his legs pressed with each step against the sidewalk. He accounts for a slip with each step, although he never falters, not any time between the apartment buildings, eight blocks. He keeps her talking, keeps her awake, lets her take her weight back, takes it on again.

I rode that bike down that hill, you remember, she says.

Omar doesn't know what she's talking about.

My mother said we'd go biking, and I used to fly. There was a group of boys, and when they saw me come by, one of them said, that girl is too fast, we're going to have to cut her down. And I was like, that's right, cause I'm like a fast speed.

Okay, says Omar. I hear you. He wipes the rain from his eyes. They didn't catch you, did they?

Oh, they caught me.

C'mon, Mama.

All right, she says. They're still chasing me. We better hurry up.

Omar looks ahead in the sleet and rain. They've got a long way to go yet. He takes on the weight. I won't let them get you tonight, he says. Only me and you out tonight.

When they reach the apartment, Omar sets his mother against the wall, closes the door behind them, pulls her up before she can sit down, presses his hands against her ribs. He looks up the stairway. Two minutes, you think? he says.

Three.

Three, then. He wipes the snow and the rain from her hair, off the crown of her nose and cheeks. He wraps her arm around his shoulder and takes the stairs, letting her lead, pushes at the small of her back.

Why you pushing? she says.

I'm trying to help.

You're being rude.

I'm not meaning.

Meaning and doing are two different things. Your brother never pushed his mother like you do.

Omar says nothing.

If your brother was here, I'd already be up these stairs.

He takes his hand from her back.

Don't make that face, she says.

I'm not.

I'm looking at your face and you're making it right now.

He hides that face, looks down at the stairway, sees the cracks in the wood, a dark stain on the floorboards. He waits, listens to the silence between them. In that silence, she takes his hand, squeezes it, leads him up the stairs. As he follows her, he feels as if he's learning a trick. He's adding to his bag of tricks: keep her talking, wipe her face with cold water, give her a goal — five minutes, three, ten. Turn on the lights. Pout a little. He's going to get this right.

She stops on the staircase with a flight and a half to go. Give me a push, she says. These old bones aren't going to make it.

They're off the road — Winston and his grandfather — they broke a fence and carved up a farmer's barren cornfield with the bald tires of the truck. If it had been before harvest, the older Winston would have stopped the truck. He's thinking smart now, wants to keep in motion. The sheriff's cruiser follows behind them, through the field; a scarecrow is run down, falls in the glow of the blue lights. The deputy switches on his wipers to get the straw off his windshield. Winston — the older one — sees the scarecrow fall in his rearview mirror, thinks about how someone had stuffed the old shirt and pants, painted the face, maybe a mother and her kids. He doesn't think much of the deputy for knocking it over. He — Winston — is senile and dying, and even he'd thought to turn the wheel.

The younger Winston thinks this is great fun. Better than the spook ride and the Ferris wheel put together and then some. Yet he knows, can feel in his bones, that they'd paid no admission price, that they'll pay a price at the end of this ride instead. He wants this ride to go on and on, so that they won't have to pay. He feels that his grandfather will pay a large price, and yet he senses that he — the younger Winston, himself — will pay longer. Will not lose his seven and a half dollars, but will lose something else when the ride ends. It's like driving the tractor — don't tell your father, the old man had said — and he feels this same dread, this same delight, as they come clear of the fields. Winston looks back now through the window at the blue lights of the sheriff's cruiser, and farther still, the orange glow a mile down the road.

And then they're in the sunflower field. The old man chooses not to avoid it, can't see a way around it. Tall stalks fall in the lights of the truck, the blue lights of the sheriff's cruiser flashing against the windshield, the yellow heads of flowers snapping and falling against the hood of the truck, flying through the side windows. The younger Winston collects the heads of the yellow flowers in his lap, listens to the pops and snaps of the stalks against the fenders, the tires. The flowers reach in the window like arms, like the hands of skeletons. When they come clear of the field, the silence seems to swallow him.

Ahead, right in front of them, he sees the ditch, they both do, but too late. Their brake lights warn the deputy, who slows in time to avoid it, but the front end of the truck, its wheels spinning in air, smashes into the opposite bank. Winston feels himself falling, feels the thick fingers of his grandfather's hand against his chest, but it was the seat belt that had saved him, had saved his grandfather too. He hears now, seconds later when it seems quiet, after the deputy has switched off his siren, the shatter of the windshield. He sees the broken blue shards on his lap, on his shoes near the floorboard. The yellow heads of sunflowers lie on the floor. The boy believes he's bleeding to death. He studies his arms, his ankles.

You cut? says his grandfather.

I don't think so.

His grandfather has a gash on his hand, a small one. There's a little blood there.

You ready to run? says his grandfather.

Winston is still looking for a death wound. Let's stay here, he says.

The old man looks through the back window. I got to keep moving, he says. Already, they can see the white beam of the deputy's flashlight through the back window.

Come or go, says the old man. He opens his door and kicks off the glass. He moves faster than Winston has ever seen him move.

Let's stay here, says Winston. He doesn't want to touch the glass in his lap.

I'll see you again, says the old man. And he's off, out of the truck. Winston can hear him splash in the creek. The boy thinks of snakes. He watches as the old man's white head disappears from the flashing blue light. It enters the darkness beyond Winston's sight.

The deputy watches the old man go. He calls out for him to stop. He thinks about his training, moves beyond it for a moment. He could plug the old man in the leg: he's a good shot. It's not much of a distance. But he doesn't even unlatch his holster. He climbs down into the creek, feels the water soak his boots and socks, slips a little in the mud.

You all right? he says to the boy. He shines the flashlight in the boy's face, checks for firearms, a knife to the heart. The boy is terrified.

That your grandfather?

The boy nods.

He got a gun on him? Any weapons?

The boy shakes his head. He won't hurt nobody.

He almost killed you, says the deputy.

Winston doesn't like the man's tone. It reminds him of his teachers at school, the way they mix concern with a shake of their heads, the downward turn of their lips. You can do better. This is all right, good, even, but you need to concentrate, focus, you know what I mean?

I don't, says Winston.

You don't what? says the deputy.

I don't know.

All right, says the man. He unclips the latch on his holster. You stay here. I'll be back in a few minutes.

Winston watches the man's head — black hair — disappear in the blue lights. The boy picks off the glass with his fingertips, drops the shards on the floorboard. Nicks his finger with the last one, puts the finger in his mouth, tastes the blood. He is sure he has betrayed his grandfather. Doesn't exactly know how, but is sure. He picks the yellow flowers off after that. When he climbs out of the cab, splashes into the water, crawls up the bank of the ditch on hands and knees, muddying both, he is convinced that the accident, the ride, even, is his fault. He watches the blue lights hover across and around the ditch, and he watches for the white and black heads in the creek. Can see neither. A woman in the farmhouse has come out onto the porch. She stands at the railing, arms crossed, looking at her sunflower field, looks at where Winston is looking.

He sucks at his finger, tastes no blood, wishes he had left with his grandfather. He feels completely alone at the edge of the ditch. Abandoned, maybe. Feels like no one — not his grandfather, not the deputy, not his father, not the woman on the porch — will ever return to him. Behind him, he hears the hum of the engine, not from the truck, but from the deputy's cruiser. When he turns, he sees, in the flash of the blue lights, the keys hanging in the ignition switch.

The left hook is a short, bent-arm blow, thrown off the left foot, as the boxer turns her body to the right behind the punch. The right cross, a short or long blow, is thrown off the trailing right foot and crosses the opponent's right arm. The body is turned to the left, with the left arm and hand in the guard position.

Helen opens the window on the second floor, pops out the screen. She takes her baby brother out onto the rooftop; she leans against the siding of the house with him. She's miles away, states away from a boy unlacing his mother's shoes, tipping a mug of water to her lips, pulling the curtains closed from the glow of the moonlight. Omar takes the blanket from his own bed and covers her. In the pocket of her shirt, he finds a letter. Afterward, he can't sleep, trying not to read it. Helen senses none of these things. Doesn't even imagine them. Rocks her baby brother against her shoulder, had wrapped him in a sweater and a blanket before she'd even stepped out onto the rooftop.

On that rooftop, she sees, imagines, remembers: the coastline from the prop plane, from the ferryboat. She keeps her thoughts away from her trainer, circles the ring; the waves of the sea break against the black rocks, seem to continue toward the mountains. The mountains seemed as waves themselves, the landscape of the sea the same as land. She'd thought this, had said it to Mrs. Lange, and Mrs. Lange, holding her cards to the tip of her chin, had stared out at the sea, at the inside passage. In that moment, a man with a cast on his arm had crossed the deck. It does look like that, the old woman had said. They seem to go on and on.

Helen remembers this. She sees that man with the cast. She'd like to break his nose too. Now, a year and a half later. Remembers that man. Sees him as a different man now. She'd sipped at the flask of bourbon, her first taste, bitter and harsh in her throat. Felt the dip and roll of the ship for the first time that day. Heard someone latch a porthole closed. She'd played a card.

Now on the rooftop, Helen hums a tune to her brother, rocks him in rhythm with her thoughts. Sleeping beside Mrs. Lange, she'd heard the woman mumble in her sleep. Had misheard — she was not now sure, rocking her brother against her shoulder. You're not going to let another man hit you like that. They were alone, no man around. She heard it again, a year later, this time from her mother — this time she had not misheard — this time again, no man around, no one else around, as far as her mother could tell. But Helen, leaning against the siding on the rooftop, Helen feels the warmth of the child against her shoulder, feels the dip and roll of the ship beneath her. She feels herself slip on the roof, she presses her feet against the shingles, holds her brother tight against her shoulder. She wants the morning to come, for the ring and her trainer.

Winston finds it — the cruiser — a lot easier to drive than the tractor. His feet meet the pedals easily. He turns off the radio, grips his hands on the wheel, keeps the tires away from the edge of the ditch. He's moving faster than the tractor, than on any ride at the carnival. After only a minute — two — he can see the nods and dips of the two heads in the stream, the one behind closing the distance.

Behind him, the older Winston can hear the footfalls, the splashes of the deputy. In his youth, he'd have left the man far behind. Twenty years ago he would have left him behind, had always been a good runner. The ditch reminds him of France, of a ditch he'd hidden in during the war. He'd not run that day, not in the ditch. Had hidden all night and the next day and the next night, and almost — he felt — frozen to death, had heard German voices on the bank above him; fifteen shots in his rifle, he'd never hit any-one. The night was his third on the front, his third of seventeen, before he'd been shot in the back by one of his own men, a bullet that his friend Marcus could not take out of him. Before that, in those seventeen days, he'd made many discoveries: keep down or die. Dig your foxhole deep and stay quiet. There was always some-one watching. If you moved during the day, you would not move again. He learned to distinguish outgoing artillery from incom-ing. He drank from the same mudwater that he cleaned his rifle with. He learned that fear was inevitable, should be expected, but could be managed.

He moved like that soldier, up the bank of the ditch, when he saw the blue lights above, heard his grandson's voice. Heard the slip of the deputy behind him in the mud of the bank. His grand-son had opened the passenger door of the cruiser. Sat with his hands gripped firm on the steering wheel.

As the old man closes the door behind him, Winston — this time, the younger one — hesitates, wants to say something to his grandfather, doesn't. Listens to the slap of the door. Through the windshield he can see the orange glow in the distance, closer this time, brighter than the moon. The boy can feel — even as he presses on the pedal, even as the cruiser moves forward, even as he tries to say what he has to say again, fails, even as he reaches for the handkerchief to wipe his grandfather's chin — the hand of the deputy on his arm, through the window, a vice, like one of his teacher's at school. The boy presses hard on the pedal, lets go of the handkerchief. The deputy, his other hand on the rooftop, hesi-tates himself, feels the slap of mud against his legs, feels the mo-tion of the cruiser, feels his boots dragged across rocks; can see himself run over in the blue lights, thinks about his baby son, de-cides, lets go of the boy's arm. As he slides to the ground, the back tire rolls over the man's boot, breaking five bones and fracturing two more.

And then the two Winstons are back on the main road, in a line of traffic. The old man has said nothing, is in France, in his mind. The younger Winston, upon reaching the road, had thought to turn left, to head back home. Thought if they could just return, they might not pay the price. They might go on and on, he and his grandfather. But he'd seen the glow down the road, toward the right. It's brighter, a deeper shade of orange. He thinks he might could do both: find the source of the light, and return without paying. But even as he turns the wheel, he knows that it will be one — hopes that it will be at least the one — and not the other.

It's a woodyard, says the younger Winston, and in the flames, the older Winston sees the tracers in the sky, sees the shells passing over the ditch in France. His grandson sees the orange flames, the dark gray smoke, the white-black lumber. Sees it ahead through the windshield, sees it circled by wire fencing, the fire trucks spraying white mists of water over the blaze, the blue lights of police cars and the roadblock in front of them. He stops the cruiser behind a line of cars. The fire has reached over the road. It follows the wind over the road, pushes down. He can see a deputy, two of them, shield their eyes from the heat.

You ever see something like that? says the younger Winston.

Omar lets his feet hang off the side of the building, sits with his back against the bricks. In his hand, the letter turns damp in his fingertips, the snow and the rain falling harder now. Below him, there are no rats coming up from the river — it's almost winter — but behind him, he sees the door of the rooftop open, sees a shaft of light from the stairway spread against the gravel. He tries to recognize his mother's silhouette, squints his eyes, sees that the shadow is not his mother's. He looks at the letter: the return address is his uncle's house, upstate. I've seen you before, says the shadow. I've seen you on the staircase.

Omar knows the voice. Knows it's an old man's voice. I'd like to talk to you, the man says. If you wouldn't mind.

Omar runs his finger along the letter. He can guess what's inside. Is hopeful that the letter will take him from here. Is ashamed of the thought.

I'd like to talk to you, says the old man.

Omar looks out at the river, at the garbage lot and the cemetery.

He feels the rain and the snow drip down the back of his neck. He slips the letter back into his pocket.

The older Winston sees the deputy — they seem to be everywhere now — but this one, walking down the length of cars in the road-block, shining his flashlight, checks licenses, looks in back seats. Behind the man, the fire in the woodyard stretches across the road. The man is a half-dozen cars ahead, a silhouette against the orange glow.

The younger Winston sees the lights of the carnival in the flames. He sees the belly of the dragon from the spook ride. Feels himself as he'd first seen that fire. Sees the flames engulfing him.

The older Winston has his boots pressed deep into the mud of the ditch, then; his shoes, now, pressed hard against the floor-board of the cruiser. Sees the deputy skipping the final three cars. Sees the man's eyes on the cruiser.

What do you want to do? says Winston, the younger one. He'd realized — the old man — that the boy had said it over and over again. He'd heard it and not listened.

The old man says nothing, feels the fog coming on again.

Winston, the younger one, had been waiting, has his hand on the seat between them. Grips it hard. Looks at the deputy.

He wants then to reach into his pocket, take out his wallet, pay the deputy, but the man doesn't approach the car. Winston wants to pay the price now, wants to pay it before the price is named. He thinks the ride could go on. He thinks maybe if he moves fast enough, he might get a bargain. Knows the price to be paid would not be found in his pocket. He reaches there anyway. The deputy, watching the boy, unclips his holster with his other hand. The older Winston reaches forward, fights the fog, reaches out of the sight of the deputy. The younger Winston watches his hand go. He wants that hand to go on and on, knows that the ride is still on, as long as that hand moves, as long as the deputy's hand moves, the ride will not end. The old man flips his wrist and the engine dies.

*

The uppercut is a blow delivered — well — up, with either hand and in close quarters. The boxer finds this blow most effective against an opponent boxing in a crouched position and moving in.

It's the morning. Helen walks the three miles to the gym, in a white fog that hovers over the gravel and the farmland in wisps and strings, in fingers. She smells smoke and watches the first orange rays sift through the white fog.

She's been told where the key is. She undresses near the ring, hears the door open across the way. Slips into her shorts and T-shirt. She tapes her hands, and watches her trainer undress, tape his hands. She skips rope. Three hundred.

In the ring they say nothing. She ties his left glove. They crouch in the center of the ring. He ties her left, then her right, shows her again how to tie with a glove on. How to make do. They take a minute in their corners. Here, they are their own trainers. When she talks to herself, she sees his face. She listens to his instructions.

In his corner, he sees a girl. Not this girl — the one behind him — but another girl, a younger one he has only seen in pictures. She reaches for a piece of fruit — an orange — in a cart on the street. He's heard this story. She's looking like a buyer, but she means to steal that orange. The trainer sees a boy, his uncle. Another face from pictures. The boy lies in a bed, asleep. When he wakes, someone will wipe his chin, will help him walk, might offer a piece of fruit. The boy will not live. He will not be an uncle, but the girl, the trainer's mother, reaches for an orange in a cart on the street with the picture of her brother in mind. She has black curls and tiny hands. She watches the merchant, pretends to be a buyer. She squeezes the orange while the boy sleeps, while the merchant glances at her, while, years later, Helen says, Ready?

The trainer turns from the picture of his mother, looks at the other girl. Do you know what I'm going to do?

No.

The trainer's mother puts the orange back. She takes a pear. When she squeezes it, it's already in her pocket. She likes the feel of it. She looks at the merchant: he has not yet seen her, but she believes that he will. She — this girl — would like the orange, for herself this time. The customer leaves. The girl quickly reaches her hand back into the cart, tests that orange. She holds it in her palm and squeezes it with the tips of her fingers. She feels the eyes of the merchant and then sets the orange back on the pile.

You don't know what I'm going to do? says the trainer.

No.

Do you know what you're going to do?

Yes.

What's that?

Keep moving, Helen thinks, but she says nothing. She lets go of the ropes, fits her mouthpiece to her teeth, walks to the center of the ring, meets him, and moves in.

ROBERT KELLY

■

# How They Took My Body Apart and Made Another Me

FROM *Conjunctions*

IN THE CAVE THEY STOPPED, *brought me here, where was here, here was just some other time, three hours later, later or the next day, desert or mountain, I had never been there, it looked familiar, I've known it all my life, it's the Cowboy Movie place. I saw the butte and the arroyo and the buzzards circling and the pitiless sun, the striations of red and ocher and buff and taupe in the sandstone sediments, the dark notch of wall they dragged me, floated me, toward, cave mouth they brought me in, and I was glad at first for the shade. I have always hated the sun.*

They took him to a cave they had used before in their investigations, but this was the first time these researches had involved a human male. They had not expected to find one this particular night, since their mission of the moment, as well as their professional training, was in *tlalorisn*, or geology, as we would call it. So Smarakd and Kavdil had to work with what they could find in their own mindstock to get to the root of the particular matter who had wandered through apple trees into their hands.

Their tools, though that name is hardly fair for the elegant sinuous exiguous wands and probes and lancets they used so deftly, their tools were all back at the metarsic ship, and the boy was here, heavy in three-space, and they needed to know what beings like them need to know.

This need to know: Is that the root of things, the root of hell?

Smarakd had been reading the *Sifer Dovvar,* which always got him excited. Book of Words or Book of Things. Which is it? How can you tell them apart? I can, I can tell them. You can kick a stone, you can't kick the word. But who are you?

*So they opened me up with some fractured black obsidian they found and then flaked even sharper on a harder stone. My sternum they cracked with a narrow pebble punched down and in with a fistworth of stone. Then they eagled my rib cage out and got to work. There and be-low. They told me what they were doing and the telling made the pain less, anyhow it was less than I would have expected. Maybe they had ways of changing my rhythm. Smarakd was breathing in a strange way I unconsciously began to imitate. The way we do. And the pain was there, but I wasn't screaming. It helps to imitate somebody else's breath-ing. Was it hers? Where was she?*

Of course he was screaming. Or had been. When the first cut, shell-shaped, curved down through the skin above the breastbone, then the cartilage, he screamed. So they stuffed a leaf into his mouth that instantly took most of the pain away and calmed him about the rest of what he felt.

Calmed him, but he began to talk. His two examiners, Smarakd and Kavdil, like all the traveling philosophers of their kind, had long pondered the relationship in humans between language and anxiety, seeing each as a facet of the other. So it was always in-teresting to them to observe whether and how sedated humans spoke. Thus, rather than taking his words now as mere reactive whimpering, they paid a little attention to him while they were concentrating otherwise on the members of his committee, as they thought of the juicy, messy, mysterious wholenesses that were mere parts of him.

Why are you cutting me? What have I done to you? Why are you doing this? Who are you?

Answering the first question they thought would serve to an-swer all of them.

We are cutting you open to find and examine your soul.

The language of the catechism rose gracefully to his mouth and his sedated syntax let him express:

But the soul is immaterial!

So is the body, they said.

No, he said. The soul is immaterial, and lodges like a wary guest in the slovenly guesthouse of the body, always ready to crumble or burn down.

No, they said. The soul is immaterial, and body is immaterial as well. Matter has a touch of material about it, but the only material stuff in the cosmos is words and what they do to your head. We are looking into you to see what language has done to your soul.

But I'm a child, I have only in recent years come to express myself by way of language.

No, they said, you see this wrongly. (Meantime they had removed several ribs, and pulled the spleen out and away, that mystery organ, and stuffed a squat black glass bottle of liqueur in its place, Latvian balsam, he was later to be told.)

You see this wrongly, in that long before you began to express yourself (what a funny expression that is, too) with language, language was busy shaping — is that what you mean by expressing? No, I guess not — language was busy shaping you.

But the soul is deathless, he cried, slightly shifting the ground of the argument.

If it is deathless, what is it doing in the body?

He tried to answer: it isn't in, exactly, the body, not in the body but sort of around it. A poem we read in school said, "The body stands in soul." So get your hands out of my thorax.

They were taking out his organs one by one, cutting them loose with the sharp conchoidal volcanic glass, then licking the cut with their own tongues, finally shoving the rifled vein or stripped tendon back to reconnect with the replacement item they had found to do the work.

They took out his urinary bladder and put in an alarm clock, an old round wind-up brass clock with two bells and a striker on top. It was ticking as they settled it down snug into his abdomen. Some days he can still hear it ticking. Tick, tick, when he hears the word he thinks: urine, urinate, now. The clock is always telling me to go. When he learns the word *ticking* later, which means the soft striped cotton cloth that binds the straw and hair and strapwork of a mattress and covers it all around, he thinks, pissy mattress, bed-wetting, a mattress wrapped in what defiles it, urinary stripes, the stripes of man, old men with stains round the gaping fly in the once-white broadcloth of their underwear, tick, they wake at night to pee. Old men wake at night to pee, little boys pee without wak-ing, Christ, what a life, tick.

And in their busy cave they went on working, lifting out his young pure smokeless lungs. In their place they carefully tucked two gray squirrels, apparently alive and breathing, and nested to-gether like a pair of shoes in a shoebox, tail of one to the head of the other. And when they pulled the liver out slimy with blood, they shoved a live hawk in its place, which fluttered its wings once or twice and then kept quiet, its wild eye looking here and there.

*They told me they used a shoe for my heart and they laughed. I said what kind of shoe? They said it was leather, and stuffed my old tennis socks with the orange rings round the shank deep in it to make the shoe keep its shape. Why is that funny, the coat hanger for my clavicle isn't funny, what's so funny about a fucking shoe! They said it goes. A heart goes, get it? I got it but I don't think it's so funny.*

He worried the ways boys do that they were thinking about pushing the wooden coat hanger up his anus to see what would happen as it spread him open but they didn't. He was sure he could hear them thinking about it, and it scared him. But other people's thoughts are always frightening. At least to him.

But they had hung the hanger in his chest, and neatly festooned some of the loose vessels, vena, aorta, over the trouser rod to keep them out of harm's way as they worked. Now they were ready for the big exchange. They took away the sternum and one of them, Kavdil, I think, shoved it in his hip pocket like a kind of money. In its place they spread a postcard from Bolzano in northern Italy, with cardboard glued to the back to stiffen it, so you couldn't read the address or message or sender anymore, just the blank card-board backing the picture of a mountain called *The Rose Garden* glowing from the setting sun.

The aliens seemed fully absorbed by this examination, which they called a Vivi-redaction, of his interior. They talked to one another steadily, in quiet, discovering tones that strangely calmed him. It is not all that bad, being an object of interest.

His pancreas they replaced with a pink rubber tobacco pouch still half full of Red Rapparee. The left kidney they lifted out and replaced with a big green emerald — where could they have gotten it? — all faceted and glittering. The right kidney they sliced out more neatly, and stuffed a blue forty-watt light bulb in its place.

*I was watching them take things out of me, I couldn't believe it, stuff dripping with blood and lymph and bile and piss, and then shoving things in. Shove with a little twist, a little tap, and each time one of them would do that, the other would say* tza! *It sounded as if the sound had some work to do in the process. The little Peruvian ocarina they put into my midriff to replace my gall bladder made a soft too-tootling sound as I breathed and as they twisted things out and in. It was dark glazed, with a blue pattern in it, a five-pointed star with blunt rays. I guess it still is making that sound inside me. I never listen to what's going on inside me. Can you hear it?*

When they heard it they grew intent, listened carefully. Was it the soul, or just a vagabond breeze wasting time in the reeds on Lake Titicaca, idling till some indio laid hands on it roughly and wrestled it into the goose-shaped clay whistle they call *oca, ocarina,* goose or gosling. From the shape.

And then the shape of the sound.

But when they realized it was just the sound of the gizmo they had themselves inserted into the living body of this momentary Beloved, this boy, this anguished loser blood-eagled out on the table, why, why, they said to each other, No, this sound is just us. Just a noise we put inside him, not his sound. We don't want to listen to ourselves. It's not his soul yet. Not the sound of him.

We can't hear it. Not yet. But we've got to make it speak.

— What did we learn from him so far? (It is a him, isn't it, just a young one of its kind?)

Young. The first thing that came up is this, that when they put on a new pair of those coarse blue trousers they call dungarees, especially in summer, when those trousers are most often worn, after the first day of wear, the skin of the wearer's thighs, his thighs at least, are stained pale with blue. He thinks of this as *indigo*.

— Is he right to call it so?

Hard to say, these beings make a lot of trouble for themselves with words. On the one hand, a word like *indigo* has a clear specific range of referent: a flowering plant called *Baptisia tinctoria,* as well as the dyestuff made from it, or, later, a synthetic dye resembling it in hue and saturation. On the other hand, the word has a resonance for them, and a bifid

— bifid?

Split in two, divided, forked. The word has a resonance for them, and that resonance seems divided — part worked by the psychological and cultural associations of the word (for example, indigo = sailors who wear these dungarees and thus the sea, which is also usually described as blue, though seldom as indigo, or indigo = Quaker merchants and dry goods shops and cottage gardens and homespun wool dyed blue, and linsey-woolsey and bunting, the field or canton on which the forty-eight pentagrams of the republic glow white, wagon trains and the blue shadows of cloth left on a boy's thighs after he's taken off his new dungarees on an August night, the smell of his inchoate maleness and the color blue — these are just examples). Partly the resonance seems generated by the sound of the word itself — and here too there is a forking path — the sound as echoing or resembling or parodying other distinct but apparently unrelated statements in the language, thus *indigo* may bring to mind in they go, Indy go, in the goo, Wendigo — one of their old gods, by the way.

On the other hand, the sound can take off all by itself in them, the narrow fronted vowel soaring to a nasal, resounding just off the alveolus where the *d* takes flight and thrusts the tense dinky little front vowel like a dart from a blowgun that is then, only then, restrained by a rough command from the back of the throat, the fauces from which a sonant summons it back, to dissolve it in the awe-filled cavern of the wide-open mouth, the awe trailing off to you, oooo I mean, and the word is done. But the mind of the speaker and the mind of the hearers are brought through this glossodrama by the sound of the word alone. When the silence comes back, speaker and listeners alike stand reverent in the vast caverns of their own mouths, where all the sacred dances come to spell. Mammoth Cavern. Secret Places of the Earth.

— I think they know about us, don't you?

I do. We are after all characters in their glossodrama — the act or action a word performs in the world or in the mind by sound alone. We are who they mean when they think that words mean anything. Words mean us. We inhabit their speaking. We ride on their breath.

— But that seems to be a metaphor you're speaking now.

I am allowed — the sons of Mne Seraphim are permitted metonymy.

— I know you are, we are, I know you as I know myself. But when they know about us, they think it's themselves they know, their whims, desires — their breaths. Can we ride so fickle a breeze for long?

— Drives too we can ride.

Yes. So we have to come down in our craft and bite them before they know it's not all inside them, not all inside.

— Even if it is?

It is, but it comes out.

— True, here we are, with a dumb kid in our hands, his constituents ill over the table, his replica half done.

Replicas are always unfinished. The copy always lacks the presence of the original. The cry of presence.

*And I was listening all the while they were talking. I had nothing to do but listen to them, and to the cry.*

It was me becoming two people.

The solace of a mountain is lost to me. Plains. I was in the flatland so long that even now when I am on a mountain I can take no pleasure in it. I am afraid that it will fall. Or they will come and bring me down again, the way they do.

*One went up and one went down,* one went to earth, one went to heaven, one went to symmetry, one went to the actual.

I am lost. Lost the way a sound is lost. I hear the honking of the gyaling near my cave, wooden tube with a brass bell, a double reed that shatters the calm inside the air. For a moment it is louder than anything can ever be. And then it dies and is gone. A minute and a half later I can hardly even imagine the sound.

There was a cry.

There was a cry and it was me. Or what was left of me after the dividing. It was a divided cry, I died in the dividing and left me to live on. All the me I can come to be.

I remember the beginning of the cry. It was when they had torn out all the parts of my body and thrown them into a basin in the corner, when they had finished stuffing all that crap into me, clocks and animals and flowers, and sewed me up, quick and harsh, with thick red twine. Then they did things to the basin in the corner, tossed handfuls of things into it, then shoved a shiny metal rod into it, and out of the parts of my body and whatever else was in there, a boy stood up who wasn't there before. He looked just like me.

Will he always look like me? Will he be a man when I am a man, an old man when I retire? Just like me then and just like me now, I bet, though I haven't seen him since.

The alien came toward me with a silver rod, while the other alien approached my look-alike, who was standing slack-jawed and dumb, a fleshy, dopey kid, just like me, so that's what I look like, red hair and white skin and looking dumb, dumb. The other alien put his rod against the chest of my look-alike and squeezed a switch. My look-alike opened his mouth and squeezed his eyes shut, and a second or so out of sync a scream began to come out of his mouth.

Then I heard it in my chest and it began coming out of my mouth too, though my alien hadn't touched me, not at all, with his wand. The scream came out of my mouth and I could feel the pain breaking things inside me but the scream was louder than the pain.

The cry went on, and on, and sounded just like *I*, an *I* that kept on and on, a warble of a sound, *aaaaaaaaaaaeeeeeeeeeeee*, and I realized as I heard it that *I* was the smallest word, but it still had two sounds in it, *aaaaa* and *eeee* and we were both screaming, the sound came out of my throat, my mouth, even my chest, and it converged on the tip of my alien's wand and the tip of that began to glow.

The two aliens began backing away from us then, us meaning me and whatever in God's name it was standing over there. Whatever it was, it was made from my guts and looked just like me. The aliens backed away until they were back to back, then each whipped the wand, which had been pointed at us, up and joined them above their heads.

At that moment, the cry broke in half. I was sobbing *aaaaaaaaa* and he was screaming *eeeeee,* and we were born apart, separate, done. The pain stopped then, and the broken cry soon after. The aliens led him away into the trees and left me alone.

Why didn't I escape then? Or try to? I didn't even think about it. I didn't know what had become of me. I didn't know how to go home. How could I go home and say, Mommy, I have two squirrels in my chest and they do my breathing for me?

What happened to you, son? my father would say.

And I would have to answer, they took me apart, I heard a cry, the cry said why, then fell apart and I was two. And now this one or me comes home, to you, do you want me?

So I couldn't go anywhere, just stayed there, trembling and crying, this time just ordinary crying, soft and stupid and wet.

I lay on my right side, and saw along the dusty rock floor of the cave, which now seemed not at all like a cave, seemed just an old shed in the woods. I smelled wet earth outside; it still was Pennsylvania. As I watched, the aliens were putting my clothing on the other me, brushing him carefully, sweeping back the forelock over his, my, right eyebrow, just the way my mother always did it, licking spit on their fingers and plastering the lock back. My jeans were snug on him, so must have been snug on me. I looked down at my legs and of course found them naked, I was naked and never knew it. And now I did, and folded my hands over my groin to hide the silky pubic hair that had just started to come out these past few months. I didn't fully understand this hair yet. But I didn't want anybody to see it before I had it figured out.

# DAVID MAMET

■

# Secret Names

FROM *Threepenny Review*

WE AMERICANS LOVE nicknames and acronyms.

I think this is rather charming.

My other people, the Jews, do too. Maimonides, the medieval scholar, was, in Hebrew, Rabbi Moishe Ben Maimon, or the RamBam. Israel Bal Shem Tov is known as the BESHT.

We Jews treasure the secret names of things, those things we hug to ourselves. As we Americans do. We award those we love with the secret name. The Yankee Clipper, the Sultan of Swat, Ray BoomBoom Mancini, Elvis the King.

We also know the habit of awe.

All new parents automatically and universally refer to "The Young One," "The Little One," "You-Know-Who." This is an attempt to distract or subvert the evil eye, a force so powerful it need not be named.

Similarly, we, for the last decades, have referred to our presidents by their trilateral initials. This is at once an expression of awe and an attempt to co-opt the terrible through familiarity. We were told (it seems it was a fabricated story, but it was a good one) that the Republicans, on taking the White House, found that all the computer keyboards had had their W's removed. Mythologically, this is priceless: the losers attempt to weaken the victor through removal of his most distinctive trait.

Awards ceremonies now each have to possess a self-awarded diminutive. The Oscars, the Emmys, et cetera. This phenomenon, we are told, began historically when Bette Davis looked at the statue of the Motion Picture Academy and thought its derrière looked like that of a friend of hers named Oscar.

The ceremony swelled in importance, and *other* awards groups, craving that power, came up with their own diminutives, their own W's, as it were. These were not naturally occurring, but an attempt to arrogate to themselves a prerogative.

The grand hailing sign of urban decay is the blandishment of street nicknames on street signs.

State Street "That Great Street," Fifty-second Street as "Swing Street" — these are all well and good. They are spontaneous expressions of affection. Their display, however, is an attempt to sustain a power which is waning, or has disappeared.

Just so with pet names and baby talk.

We all know the phenomenon of the true marital fight, which begins with the resurrection of long-dead endearments and pet names: to wit, "I called you this once, and look what you have become." Mary McCarthy writes of "the baby name, the surest sign of a partner incapable of that final marital swoon." Lenny Bruce spoke of the power of the intimate pet name. A widower, after a time of mourning, avails himself of female companionship. His wife has been gone some years; he is in bed with a woman, and calls her by his wife's old pet name. His wife, though dead, pops up from behind the headboard. "What," she says, "you called her *blahblah?*" "Hey, honey," the man says, "I knew you were there . . . I was joking . . . what do you think? I WAS *JOKING . . .*"

The Bible tells us the most secret name of God, the Shem Ha Meforesh, could be uttered only by the high priest in the afternoon of Yom Kippur. He would alone enter the Holy of Holies, and there would say the name. He would have a rope tied around his ankle, so that, should he die while in the Holy of Holies, he could be gotten out. No one else, of course, being permitted to enter there.

Why could they not enter? The Spirit of God dwelt therein, and anyone else entering would be slain by that power. Why were they

afraid the high priest would die? He might die if he were insuf-
ficiently cleansed, if he uttered the name with insufficient sanctity.
He would be consumed.

My rabbi told this story in the synagogue, and added: You may
find this story simplistic, or picayune. But, say I had a booth up
here, and you in the congregation knew the Sacred Name. How
many of you would want to put to the test both your sanctity and
the operation of the ban, with its penalty? That's right. No takers.

Just like Lenny Bruce and his dead wife.

Just as with the dread name cancer. Which we will not utter. We
understand the phenomenon of the secret name. We treat this
name in a spirit best expressed by the Talmudist who said, "We
do not believe in superstition. On the other hand, it is good to be
careful."

We understand how the secret name works, and that it must
and will be treated with respect. Who would not be careful in the
face of the Ineffable? Who would invert Pascal's wager, and walk
into the Holy of Holies, and utter The Name? Someone, perhaps,
but not you or I.

Note: we see this strongly in the movie business.

A business notably subject to the whims of fate. No one who has
made a film would think to say, on the set, "Well, it looks like a
nice day," or "Gosh, things are going well . . ." That person is
looked upon, not as a fool, but absolutely as a blasphemer, and
outcast as such.

So we do, it seems, remember the commandment. There are
certain names of The Lord which we might take in vain, but the secret, the operative names, the *true* secret names, we will not.

Seneca cautions us to treat Fortune as if she were actually going
to do to us everything it is in her power to do. I am working on a
film with the most practical of men. He is a technical advisor on a
political thriller. He was, for many years, an operator of Delta
Force, in rather continuous combat for thirty years. He spoke of a
fellow on his first mission who said, "We're going to kick their ass
and take names" as he got onto the helicopter. The other soldiers
looked at him with incomprehension and dread, and, at the end of

the day, the man had indeed been shot up, and his military career ended.

And which of us has not had the experience of the old friend to whom we say, or who says to us: This is one friendship which will *never* end. And we feel that cold wind, whose premonition is, of course, fulfilled. Not only are there no atheists in foxholes, there are, I believe, no atheists *anywhere*. We just call our gods by different names. Indeed, psychotherapy may be nothing more than the attempt to find those names, and so challenge their power.

I recommend to you the story of Rumpelstiltskin. In which myth we see the very force, or opponent, *explaining* the method of his own defeat to his victim. The poor girl is forced to spin flax into gold; her savior, Rumpelstiltskin, becomes her oppressor, and demands, as payment for rescuing her from the Evil King, her firstborn child. She will be exempted if she can tell him his real name.

*Rumpelstilstkin* is an example of the compulsion to repeat. The poor girl marries a king who is evil. Boo hoo. Her new friend *also* proves to be false, exacting an even worse tax. *If she finds out his secret name*, she will be freed (the promise, again, of psychiatry).

He proclaims his secret name as soon as she decides to "follow him around." This "following" is, in effect, watching his operations. That is, she has either become sufficiently brazen or "hit bottom" (perhaps the two are the same) and now will/must confront the actual operations of her world.

The instant she does, she is freed. The neurosis proclaims itself, it says its secret name, and it is now powerless. Now, his name is nonsense. Who, then, *is* he? Who has no name? He is the King, the Evil King she married in the first place. And lo, she has married him *again*. The compulsion to repeat, now revealed, is conquered.

The old Russian proverb has it, "Laughing bride, weeping wife. Weeping bride, laughing wife." Those of us of a certain age saw two or so decades of marriages go awry, and may have thought back to the self-confected vows to "try" to "respect each other's space," to "grow and to allow to grow," and we may have sighed and understood, too late, in those cases or perhaps our own, the power of ritual, and the price of its absence.

Another perversion of the power of names is, of course, advertising. The highest achievement of advertising, public relations, is to get the manufactured, manipulative idea "off the page," as it were, and accepted as part of speech. E.g., "Let's have a Coke" or "I'll FedEx it." And I remember a television commercial of fifty years ago — many of you do too — of the tobacco auctioneer bawling out his lightning-quick, incomprehensible, wonderful litany, concluding with "Sold." Or that velvet voice at the conclusion of the Chesterfield cigarette ad, reminding us "And they are *mild* . . ." Tag-phrases of the day. Minted to sell a product, they transcended conscious resistance to manipulation and became part of the language. As advertising is, or has become, the attempt to subvert, weaken, or bypass conscious resistance to an idea — to implant in the victim an idea while obscuring its origin, and so influence behavior.

All parents in the audience understand this process all too well. And we appreciate its difficulties, and revel in its unfortunately all-too-occasional triumphs. My friend, the comedian John Katz, had a joke about the inept hijacker. This is years ago; the joke is no longer performable, but I will share it with you in this protected setting. "Take this plane to Tucson." The pilot says, "But it's going to Tucson." Guy says, "Act like it's my idea, nobody gets hurt . . ."

Back to the theme:

The assignment of nicknames, the application of jargon, is an understood tool for the manipulation of behavior. We know the quote "charismatic" boss who is making up "cute" and idiosyncratic names for his or her employees. "I alone know and I alone will assign you your name." This is a powerful (and impolite) tool. It is an arrogation of power and a useful diagnostic. For those who grin and tilt their heads to have their ears rubbed at the new name have surrendered their personality to the oppressor; they have given up their soul.

And for them to, should they wish it, gain it back, they will have to go through the upheaval and shamed self-examination of Rumpelstilskin's victim.

For the complicity, though impolite, though exacted by one who does not wish us well — by, in effect, an enemy — the complicity is *shaming*. And it is this feeling of shame which ensures continued compliance. For we are structured such that we would rather suffer, in most cases, the delusion than take arms against that sea of troubles. Like the rape victim who might wonder, "*Was* my skirt too short?" rather than accept the reality that she is again being oppressed, this time by the legal system. And so, as Freud informed us, the resistance *is* the neurosis. And the very mechanism of awe of the secret name is employed in the service of oppression.

This may occur, as we see, in neurosis, through advertising, or, in a mixture, in political discourse. If we say that "the government" has "lowered the threat level," we must mean that the government is in charge of the threat. Semantically, what else is the meaning of this "color code"? One cannot act differently on a day coded red than on one coded orange, and indeed no one even suggests that one can. We are urged to "be more vigilant," but the phrase cannot be acted upon. He who defends everything defends nothing, as Napoleon said.

So semantically — that is, as judged by the way in which words influence thought and so action — the proclamation of the threat level is an admission *that there is no threat*. Or that if a threat exists, the government is powerless to deal with it. And that those who accept the reiteration of the threat level have submitted, like the employee who accepts docilely her new pet name, and are thenceforward complicit in their own manipulation, daily trading submission first for an abatement of anxiety and, as time goes by, for painful and shameful self-examination.

A public relations genius insisted that the Warner Brothers cable network be referred to as The WB. For as we do it, we are theirs.

The construction itself has no special meaning — it is simply an obeisance, and as such is in fact *more* powerful for the absence of content. As this obeisance passes, like "Sold American," from the conscious into the automatic, we no longer recognize its provenance; it becomes a habit.

I instance the phrase "weapons of mass destruction." This formulation is overlong, clunky, and obviously confected. This is not to say that this or that dictator, or indeed well-meaning soul, may or does not possess such tools. But the formulation *itself* is unwieldy and, to the American ear, unfortunate. It is the cadence of "I'm not going to tell you again." Rhythmically, it is a scold. And its constant enforced repetition by the newscasters (you will note that the people in the street do not use it often, and then with little ease), its very awkwardness, ensures that the phrase, and thus its reference, pass beyond the borders of consideration. Like The WB.

For our mind tends toward the creation of habit. And the choice, faced with the unacceptable phrase, is this: constant, vigilant, unpopular opposition, or habitual acceptance. We submit in order to avoid the burden of hypocrisy.

I will recommend to the interested Bruno Bettleheim's writings on the Nazi salute.

Similarly, *homeland security* is a concept close to all of our hearts. We live in a wonderful country, which has for years enjoyed a blessed freedom from attack. The phrase "Homeland Security," however, is confected and rings false, for America has many nicknames. The Vietnam servicemen referred to it as The World; we might call it, lovingly, the U. S. of A. Many of us have thrilled to the immigration officer who stamps our passports and says, "Welcome home," a true act of graciousness. But none of us has *ever* referred to our country as The Homeland. It is a European construction, as Die Heimat, or The Motherland, or Das Vaterland. There is nothing wrong with the phrase; I merely state that it is confected, it is not a naturally occurring American phrase, and it rings false. And as it rings false, we, correctly or not, will question the motives of those who created it for our benefit. As we do the "coalition of the willing."

Names are powerful.

No one involved in a "relationship" ever had a good time. One may be courting, seducing, experimenting sexually, dating, married, keeping company, and so on. But anything called "a relationship" must eventually result in sorrow, as the participants are unwilling to examine and name its nature.

The nexus of the conscious and the unconscious is of short duration. The unconscious mind can slough off the useless, or, indeed, the unlovely. When its reiteration is coupled with compulsion, we may be due for grief.

GINA OCHSNER

■

# Hidden Lives of Lakes

FROM *Mid-American Review*

ON A DAY WHEN the hoarfrost brought the sightline down to a quiver, Glasha and Luba, coworkers at the petrochemical plant and best friends, skidded onto the frozen ice of the lake. They were sitting in a canoe and pushing themselves over the ice, Glasha with her kitchen mops, and sitting opposite of her, Luba with her black rubber toilet-bowl plungers. With each push, Luba knew that Glasha was imagining the pitch of the May Day cheers when she and Luba would glide past the finish line, well ahead of the other canoers. For her part, Luba was only participating in this folly because the doctor had told her that her figure was far too Russian, that is to say, fat.

When they had reached about a third of the way across the lake Glasha laid her mops over the gunwale and withdrew a silver flask from a coat pocket and uncapped it. From somewhere near the middle of the lake Luba heard a strange humming and for a moment she thought it was the sound of ice threatening to crack. Luba climbed out of the canoe, got on her hands and knees, and pressed her ear to the ice. Then she held the bells of the plungers to her ears. When she did, the humming amplified and separated into the buzz of voices of both men and women. They were speaking in the police form of Russian, addressing each other in *vuis* instead of *tuis,* speaking with a grace she hadn't heard in town for years. It was a beautiful noise and Luba flapped the plungers at her ears so as to achieve a stereo effect, though she imagined she looked a little like a fish breathing through rubber gills.

"What are you doing?" Glasha capped her flask.

"Here." Luba sat back on her heels and handed Glasha a plunger. "Listen. Do you hear that?"

"What?"

"That whispering." Luba pointed to the ice. Glasha leaned over the side of the boat and narrowed her eyes. "It's coming from over there." Luba pointed to the middle of the lake.

"I don't like this," Glasha said quietly. "Let's go." Luba climbed back into the canoe. Glasha gave a tremendous shove with her mops and sent the boat lurching, and all the way to shore, Luba had to work hard to keep up with the steady haul Glasha made with her mops.

That night as her husband, Oleg, sat finishing a bottle of Crowbar, Luba told him about the voices she'd heard below the ice.

"So what," he said, placing the dead bottle horizontally on the table.

"So don't you want to know what they are saying?"

"Not really," Oleg said, turning the bottle upside down and shaking it over a cup.

But in the morning, Oleg had changed his mind.

"Let's take a picnic," he said, ringing up Glasha's husband, Ivan. He and Ivan worked together at the factory, assembling the guidance mechanisms to antiaircraft missiles, though Luba had gathered Oleg felt it was impolite to say so. For years he'd been telling the downstairs neighbors that he and Ivan inserted tiny sprockets in timepieces. Either way, Luba could hardly imagine Ivan capable of such delicate work. He was a large man with a thick torso and wide shoulders. And owing to the fact that he had a red chafing mark below his lower lip, like the bite burns kids get, Luba could not help thinking that despite Ivan's great bulk, there was something permanently childlike about him.

They set out at lunchtime, Glasha with extra blankets, Ivan his two fishing poles, and Oleg his fishing net. Behind her, Luba pulled a sled carrying a plunger and their picnic. Her teeth ached in the cold; her hips and back tired of this tentative walk, her weight carefully distributed over her feet.

At the middle of the lake where the slabs were known to give way, Luba walked doubled over. She was watching for the dark ice, which, undermined by mysterious currents, was warmer than the paler stretches of ice. When she thought they were at the same place they'd been the day before, Luba dropped to her knees and flapped her plunger at her ear. Luba held her breath. Then she heard it again: that quiet murmuring. Luba gave a little shout and signaled the others.

With three hundred grams of vodka and a match they melted a kopeck-size hole. For two hours they shaved at the ice with Luba's good butter knife; they melted the edges of the hole with their cigarette lighters. Around three o'clock, when the bright disk of the sun tipped on edge and drew the remaining light to a point behind the stand of birch, they'd chipped out a hole large enough for a man to jump into.

What Luba noticed straight off was that the water wasn't grainy and dark the way ice water should be. Rather, it was as clear as the tap water she'd seen running out of the faucets in the kitchens of women in Western commercials. And owing to the width of the hole, Luba could see tundra swans sealed within the strata of ice. Their wings were outstretched as if the ice had caught them midflight. Beneath them was a used syringe and a ladies' evening dress. About half a meter farther down, an aria had been trapped in the ice. The notes looked like the dark round seeds within willow pods. Glasha bent over the hole and picked at the notes with her fingernails, and they whittered into flight as a beautiful cry. Farther below, where the ice turned darker in color, was a school of carp, their eyes gazing past her to the distant promise of a summer thaw.

They stood around the hole, studying the water for a few minutes.

"Look!" Glasha waved her gloves frantically. Beneath the transparent lip of ice a pair of shoes, a comb, a child's doll, a broom horse, a much-revered icon of St. Fursa stepping on the devil's leathery wings, gently drifted past. And then, to their surprise, even larger items floated past the hole: a rusted park bench; a statue of Lenin, his bronze coat flying out behind him as if from the force of a winter gale; a piece of the golden dome of their church, which long ago had been dynamited and sunk in the contaminated bog outside town.

"How can it be!" Luba cried, for it seemed to her that they were viewing a disassembled version of their town as it was many years ago, an entire town of clutter moving with that slow grace given to things carried by water. There went Old Fedya's ratty prayer ropes, Glasha's missing pig, tins of potted meats, a bottle of watered-down rocket fuel, a chicken, the broken neck of a violin, and fibrillating scraps of newspaper. A T-shirt with a popular saying, SAME SHIT, DIFFERENT DAY, whirled up to the surface, along with a pair of Adidas sport pants, the fashionable kind with the white stripe down the side that Luba's daughter had once begged her for.

Oleg dipped his fishing net into the hole and caught the pants as they went swirling by. He shook his head and wrung the excess water from the pants. "All this time we've been canoeing over the lake in summer, we could have been fishing. We'd have been rich by now!"

Ivan licked his thumb, held it to the cold, measuring the lowering frost. Then he dropped his line in. "True enough. But where are all the people?" Ivan balanced an enormous foot on the lip of the hole.

Luba bent over the hole with a plunger at her ear. "Maybe they're afraid of us."

"Maybe we're afraid of them!" Glasha uncapped her flask and took a liberal drink.

"'Look!" Ivan hopped from foot to foot. All the grandmothers and grandfathers, children and family pets they'd lost, church members and old friends long departed from the factory, the man from the state office who'd come to examine the caulking around their toilets, drifted slowly past the hole. They were naked, most of them, naked and they never looked better. For they swam about freely under the ice, their movements fluid and smooth. Every now and again, someone would float so close to the surface, face upturned and eyes frosted over, that Luba thought she might touch them as they passed under the open hole.

Oleg and Ivan dropped their lines into the hole. Immediately Ivan felt a tug and Oleg held him around his waist while he reeled in his catch. It was Manyasha, who'd once lived next door to Glasha and Ivan. They took one look at Manyasha, an indestructible babushka who'd never permitted herself more than a pinched smile, and Ivan tossed her back in.

They fished awhile longer, and this time Oleg's line went taut. Luba gripped her husband by his belt and leaned back. It took several minutes of hauling up hard, and just when Luba thought she couldn't hold on anymore she heard a tremendous splash at the hole. Oleg jumped back in surprise and dropped his pole. It was Borya, Oleg's uncle, spitting water from his mouth and flailing his arms. At last, he calmed down a bit and managed to remove the hook from his armpit.

"Oh, Uncle Borya!" Oleg knelt and offered Uncle Borya his hand. "I hope we didn't hurt you."

Uncle Borya regarded them for a moment. His eyes were frosted over and Luba couldn't see the pupils of his eyes.

"I always did think you were an idiot, Oleg. But I like your wife. How are things, Luba?" Uncle Borya smiled then and Luba saw that since he'd died he'd lost three more teeth.

"Very good, Uncle." Luba unwound her cobalt blue scarf from around her neck and handed it to Borya. "We are so sorry for disturbing you like this, but, to be honest, we thought you were dead." Uncle Borya tied the scarf around his neck.

"Everyone thinks that." Uncle Borya narrowed his pasty eyes and studied his nephew. "So now that I'm here, what do you want?"

"Well, I guess we're wondering what you are doing down there." Oleg sat on the ice and handed Borya a flask of Special Export.

"This and that. Mostly I read the dictionary and tell jokes."

"Jokes?" Luba slapped her ear with her mitten, forcing the blood.

"Yes, the Joke Convention meets this time of year. But when we run out of jokes, we become like the carp, very still, and we listen to the ice and life above the ice." Uncle Borya scratched his chin where bits of ice clung to his beard. "Incidentally, would you mind very much bringing me a cabbage pie?" Uncle Borya turned to Luba and winked. "The carp don't taste good this time of year."

"Who else is down there?" Glasha shouldered Luba away from the hole.

"Oh, all sorts of people. You'd be surprised, but then, I'm not supposed to say."

"Why not?" Glasha narrowed her eyes.

Uncle Borya studied the tree line, then bobbed his head up and down. "Excuse me, please, but the Finnish Shouting Choir is about to perform. If you listen you can hear them warming up." Borya pointed to the far end of the lake, then put his hands over his ears and slipped below the water. As if on cue, the Finnish Shouting Choir drifted by en masse, nude save for their choral music, which they clutched to their chests.

They stood for a moment longer peering at the hole in the ice. "Well, that's that." Oleg straightened and brushed ice crystals from the back of his pants. The last light behind the trees had collapsed to a gritty smear of pollution.

"Yes." Ivan ran his tongue over the raw patch under his lower lip. "Let's go back. There's a good foreign feature playing at the kino." The air had turned to grain, to the kind of night when driving would be forbidden, and if they were to get to the movies, they'd have to hurry. As the others trudged ahead, Luba turned back for one last look at the hole. Just then a silver lorgnette, like the one her grandmother had, floated by, a single white ladies' glove following in its wake. Luba crouched over the hole. For a moment she imagined drinking the water, or just splashing it over her face to feel the wetness, to feel what it was that kept Uncle Borya so happy for a dead man. Luba dipped the tip of her glove into the water, breaking to fractions the image of her face blinking back at her.

Each evening Glasha and Luba chiseled at the hole, both to keep it from freezing back over and also to see what else they might find.

The following Saturday, Glasha, Ivan, Oleg, and Luba went back out onto the ice. Though Glasha and Ivan liked to drop in a fishing line, Oleg stood ready with the net, hauling up a soggy handkerchief and bottles of herbal vitamins, a real find, which he tossed onto the sled with a quick motion of his wrist. For her part, Luba couldn't bring herself to use a hook and instead swirled the handle of her plunger in the hole. When she felt the handle bump into something, Luba dropped to her knees. There in the water staring back up at her, as a face in a mirror, was Batushka, their beloved priest, dead now for three years. Batushka poked his head through the water.

"That really hurt, you know, but I forgive you."

"Batushka!" Luba cried, tears crusting the corners of her eyes.

"Batushka, if we may." Ivan ventured cautiously toward the hole. "What are you doing down there in the ice? You are dead and buried, at Diveyevo, no?" Ivan asked, for he and Oleg, along with a few others, had carried Batushka's body to his final resting place.

"I can't say," Batushka said with a sad smile.

Glasha lowered her brows. "Not so fast. There's a rule for this. If you catch something, on a hook, say, you have a right to ask it questions and it must answer truthfully."

"You are right." Batushka sighed loudly, reaching for Oleg's bottle of Special Export. "But don't blame me if you don't like the answers I give."

"But what was wrong with Diveyevo?" Ivan asked.

"Oh, that again." Batushka rolled his eyes. "Nothing was wrong with it. I just wish to be humble" — Batushka broke flakes of ice and crunched them loudly between his teeth — "to be as close to the earth as possible." Under Batushka's fingernails were little clumps of mud from the bottom of the lake; in his ears, bits of grass.

"I don't understand." Oleg pumped his shoulders up and down. "I'm listening, and I'm trying to believe what I'm hearing, but it's not making sense. You're dead. And so are you." Oleg nodded to Borya, who'd surfaced just long enough to grab Luba's cabbage pie. "And I'm not dreaming. I'm alive!" Oleg thumped his gloved fist against his chest.

Batushka wagged his head slowly from side to side and made clicking noises with his tongue. "This reminds me of the parable of Josef's chicken. Would you like to hear it?"

"No!" Glasha stamped her feet.

"Then excuse me" — Batushka recapped the bottle and slid it across the ice to Oleg — "but I am cold." With that Batushka slipped under the ice.

"But we didn't get to ask all our questions." Ivan's lower lip trembled and Oleg handed him a plastic bottle of vitamins.

"We'll just have to come back, for as long as it takes." Oleg sighed and hitched himself to the sled piled with frozen trinkets. They turned for shore then, Glasha trudging ahead of the men while Luba trailed behind, noting how the strand of lights from the lake's edge were duplicated as dull spots on the ice.

That night Luba lay in bed while Oleg draped his haul over their ancient heating pipes. As she listened to her husband catalogue his inventory, she wondered about the thickness of sleep and ice and the dreams, those trellis-white bones, the townspeople below them might be dreaming. Luba tried to imagine being so humble, so close to the earth, that she'd wake each morning coughing up clay, wiping it from her ears and nostrils. That was grace, the real article, to be washed over, to drown in it.

The following Monday, after work, the four set off again for the center of the lake. Glasha brought several sheets of paper, one for each day of the week, and below the heading, a list of questions ranging from how much longer she'd have to care for her ailing mother to which shops would be carrying butter. Ivan brought a troubling crossword puzzle. Oleg brought a longer fishing net and Luba brought more cabbage pies. When they got there, Glasha called Batushka for nearly an hour while Oleg fished. Crusts of ice lined their eyelashes, the corners of their eyes, and still, no Batushka. At last Oleg hooked his Uncle Borya again, who came kicking and fighting the whole way to the surface of the water.

"Batushka!" Glasha cried. "We came to see Batushka!"

Scraps of newspaper churned to the surface where the wind snatched them up, letters of the heavy line-print falling like seeds onto the ice. "Oh, not to worry," Borya said, watching little black letters from the headlines of the last election rearrange themselves into new words. "He's having a little rest just below the former first secretaries and the retired gymnasts."

"Well, swim back down there and wake him. It's important." Glasha unfolded her Monday list and tapped her foot impatiently.

In a few moments Batushka chuffed through the hole. His eyes looked especially opaque, and when Luba bent to kiss him on both cheeks, she squeezed her eyes shut, afraid she'd catch a glimpse of her own image returned in the pale orbs of his eyes. Glasha waved her list at Batushka then and they spent a solid hour taking their turns with Batushka, as they had when he took confession. They left only after Glasha extracted a promise delivered through splayed fingers and yawn — but a promise, no less — that whenever they called for him, Batushka would swim to the surface.

They continued going out to the hole each night for several weeks, Glasha with her lists, Oleg his net, Ivan his crosswords. But it seemed to Luba the more they asked of Batushka, the vaguer his answers became. Sometimes, he didn't answer at all and broke out instead into silly nursery rhymes. Even worse, with each visit, they came back home smelling more and more like the lake, and Luba couldn't get the reek of carp off her fingers or out of their flat.

One Friday night, when the moon was a crumpled tissue in the sky, the four set out for the lake.

"Batushka!" Glasha cried as soon as they reached the hole. Then she dropped to her knees. "I want to live life, the way they do in movies!" Glasha threw her hands up, a gesture Luba had seen her practice in front of the mirror in the women's toilets at the petrochemical plant.

"So live, why don't you?" Batushka snapped as he surfaced. "Ask me your question, already."

"This life — what's it for?" Glasha asked, blinking her eyes rapidly.

Batushka's face hardened. He turned his shoulders in the water away from Glasha and looked at the far end of the lake where the birches had grown slender and sparse. "Did you know that people ask much more interesting questions when they are dead?"

Glasha groaned. "Batushka! I'm not happy. What should I do?"

"And did you know" — Batushka swung his head around and met her gaze — "that at night the town dreams of itself?" Batushka smiled, a beatific, serene smile.

"This isn't fair! You're not answering my questions." Glasha stomped up and down. Near the hole a small crack zigzagged from the edge of the ice.

Batushka's eyes brightened. "Each city is a lonely one, knowing it is not right, not complete, longing for something it cannot name." Batushka, still smiling, began to sink slowly into the hole as if someone were gently pulling him down by the heels.

Glasha bent over the hole, cupped her hands around her mouth. "At the very least I want my pig back!" Glasha's words whistled as they dropped to her feet in a small pile of ice crystals.

Then she turned and stomped toward the shore. Ivan watched his wife for a moment, then hitched himself to Oleg, who hitched himself to the sled.

"I'll be glad for the thaw," Oleg said with a pull.

"I always wanted to believe in God, but it never seemed to work out." Ivan leaned into the harness. "Now all I've got are these herbal vitamins," he said, running his tongue over the chafed arc of red skin.

"Vitamins! Well, that's something." Oleg hooked his arm under Ivan's and together they pulled the sled.

That evening Luba lay in bed listening to a dog baying. Outside her bedroom window she could see the frost shortening the horizon, bringing down the moon. She supposed that was what the dog was crying about, singing with a sadness that sounded a little like joy. Luba lay there carried by the sounds of the dog and waited for grace to wash over her, afraid that it never would, had left her completely. But you can't wait forever; that's not living. Luba climbed out of bed and scratched a fingernail into the hoarfrost at the windowpane. Outside the land was pale blue and long with the promise of silent winter and the sure drop of snow.

She thought of those voices, comforting, murmuring conjugations of lost verbs, contemplating the weather, and, of course, telling their many jokes. Luba smiled. She could just hear it now, the one about the penguins in the movie house and Uncle Borya slapping his thighs in glee. Luba pulled on her thermal underwear, her work uniform, her boots and coat. She tiptoed through the flat and let herself outside, where she turned for the lake. She could see her breath freeze before her eyes and fall to the ground at her feet, a gentle sound, the rattling of tiny stars. With each punch of her boots through the crusts of snow, she wondered what it would take to will oneself back to the mud. A baptism among the duckweed and swaying fescue, only this time she wouldn't plug her nose and hold her breath as she had when Batushka held his hand under her back and dipped her down all those years ago. No. She'd plunge in, feet first, her clothes dragging her down into the depths.

Luba walked until she reached the hole. Already it had begun to freeze over, a thin lattice of ice crusting its edges. Luba took off her glove and immersed her hand up to her wrist. It wasn't as cold as she thought it would be, for in all their visits to the ice, none of them had ever once gotten wet. Then she heard the voices. They rose steadily, a chorus, one after the other, of reedy voices canting a wet catechism, and the sound was that of old memories.

Luba removed her other glove, her scarf, her hat, her coat, her boots. She would leave behind this clumsy life. The water would remake her, strip her of all that didn't matter. She would trade this dim existence for the embrace of water's quiet, where she could contemplate life from below this tormented land. Trade it for the absurdity of floating green skies and a sun filtered through ice.

■

# Sixteen Jackies

FROM *New Letters*

NO, I DON'T REMEMBER smiling. Of course, I don't remember not smiling, either. I honestly don't remember much of anything about that day. I mean, there was that rush of sun across my face as Jack and I stepped off the plane. I remember that. And I remember how I tried to stay very close to him as we moved down the line of people with welcome banners crowding us at Love Field. Only I kept getting pushed away from Jack by admirers trying to shake his hand. There was the terrible heat softening the leather in the limo, I remember, and John and Nellie looking across at us from the jump seat, and Jack sitting to my right. He waved like a hero returning from the war as we rolled into the tunnel toward the center of town and I remember thinking, *Maybe it will be slightly cooler in there,* and then the white flicker of realities changing as we came out the other side, and then the way he turned into a marionette whose strings someone had cut. He didn't make a sound. I didn't see any blood. There was what seemed like the backfire from a motorcycle, *pop,* followed by another *pop,* and his left hand flew up, and he assumed this quizzical expression for a moment, and then he put his other hand to his forehead and turned into a marionette and fell sideways into my lap.

Then I was scrambling across the black trunk which was burning with sunshine, trying, I suspect, to collect pieces of him so that

I could put him back together again later, and people were I think grabbing at me, and the next thing I knew I was drifting in the middle of a translucent gray confusion. I remember saying, *I love you, Jack, I love you,* over and over. Although, of course, I didn't. Love him, that is. Not anymore. I hadn't for years. How could I? I mean, imagine all those women. Imagine each and every one of those women. It was simply intolerable.

And I remember — afterward, that is, many days or perhaps even weeks afterward — seeing the news footage of all those events looping, all those other things that happened, all those other things I apparently did, except I don't actually remember doing them. It's the strangest thing. I don't remember myself doing the things I did, but I remember seeing the footage of me doing them.

You know how they say you're supposed to recall every single detail about critical instants in your life? What things smelled like? Each thing you touched?

It didn't work that way for me at all.

I mean, I don't even remember whether or not I smiled that day.

Actually, you probably remember more about those weeks than I do. That dazed look on my face as I stood next to Lyndon? The hearse drawn by those gorgeous horses down Pennsylvania Avenue? Little John holding my hand and then letting it fall away as he raised his own to salute the casket of his father? You can't forget those things, can you? They'll always be there, like your fingerprints. At one point you may even have mapped your entire experience according to them. Many people did. I mean, those pictures represent a powerful instant in the biography of this country. And yet all I can summon up — besides what I just told you, that is, besides those few sense impressions — all I can summon up is that translucent gray confusion that swallowed me the second I heard those backfires. It may have lasted hours. It may have lasted days. But it felt like it lasted decades. It felt like a kind of — I don't quite know how to say it — a kind of psychological suspension the color of seasickness.

I'm not very good with words. I'm sorry. I worked in publishing

for years, if you can believe it, but the truth is I only read manu-
scripts for the story line. Anyway, the thing is, when the confusion
finally did lift it lifted very quickly. So quickly, in fact, that it felt a
little like a powerful exhaust fan had been turned on and had just
sucked all the stuporous smoke right out of the stuporous-smoke-
filled room called my brain. There I was, sitting by Jack's side in
the limo as we rolled into that tunnel, wondering if I might find a
minute's reprieve from that awful Texas heat, and then it was two
or three in the morning, and I was back in the White House, and I
didn't know what day it was. I was in my nightgown, and I was
simply standing there, staring at my bed. From what I can recon-
struct now, this must have been sometime during the transition
period — sometime before Lyndon and Lady Bird began moving
in their things, and before I had moved mine out completely —
because I remember seeing packing boxes stacked everywhere,
and I remember the clutter on my writing desk and across the top
of my chest of drawers, and I remember clothes spilling from my
open closet door, and, somehow larger than life, as if seen through
some sort of magnifying lens, I remember seeing an overturned
vial of baby blue sleeping pills by an empty glass on the bedside
table.

What I remember most, however, after stepping off the plane
and feeling that rush of sunshine across my face, was seeing *myself* lying under the sheets. I know. It sounds crazy. Only there I
was, standing in my nightgown in the middle of my bedroom at
the White House, watching myself sleep.

This is embarrassing to admit, but my first thought was that it
must be one of Jack's women. I used to find them all over the
place. When I was redecorating the building, back in 1962, I'd
open an office door or poke my head into a nook I didn't usually
poke my head into and there one would be sprawled on a couch or
rifling through desk drawers for memorabilia. *The nerve of that
bitch*, I remember thinking. Excuse me, but that's what I thought.
*The nerve of that bitch, sleeping in my bed after all that's happened.*
Then I realized I was mistaken. It wasn't another woman. It was
me. There I was, lying on my back. My right arm was stretched al-

most flush with my right side and my left hand was turned palm upward beside my head on my pillow. It was cocked at such an odd angle that it seemed to me to be a separate sleeping entity. My breathing was extremely heavy and steady. I'd probably taken more of those sleeping pills than I should have. I suppose all I wanted to do was to leave the inside of my head until that horrible confusion went away. But that isn't what made an impression on me. Not really. What made an impression on me was what a mess my hair was. I was struck, if you want to know the truth, by how mussed up it seemed and how unbeautiful I looked.

I had always suspected that my jaw was too wide, of course. Who wouldn't have? And my nose was simply too . . . *excessive,* I believe is the word, by a third. These facts hit me with the force of absolute truth that night. Only what troubled me even more profoundly was something I had never noticed before: my lower lip rested too near my chin. I had never considered this, and yet there was no avoiding the issue: my chin had begun to recede. Or perhaps it had always been like that and I had just failed to notice. I imagine this is what people mean when they say *encroaching middle age.* Even now, here, I shudder at the very thought of it.

I stood there for what I think amounted to a couple of minutes, awake without warning in the middle of my room at the White House, watching myself sleep. I was fascinated. I was alarmed. I didn't know what to do or what to make of this. In an instinctive gesture, I reached up and pressed my cheek with two fingers, as one might do to the flank of a sleeping dog to make sure it's really sleeping and not dead or something, and then, across the room, the oddest thing occurred. How to say it? Another one of me — yes, that's the word — another one of me *unfolded* itself from the sleeping version, like a flower from a bud. It sat up, and, gazing groggily straight ahead, scratched the back of its skull, threw its feet over the side of the bed, stood, and glided out of the room as if I — the one of me that felt most like me at the time, that is — as if I simply didn't exist within the same dimension it inhabited.

When I turned toward the bed again, I saw another version of myself unfolding itself from the sleeping one. It shrugged itself off the mattress and wafted through the room and out the door. The same thing happened another three, eight, maybe twelve or thirteen times. The fact is, I lost count. Or forgot to count, is more like it. You can imagine, I'm sure. I mean, there I was — all over the place.

Not long after the last one had departed, the sleeping version of me opened its eyes and took drowsy inventory of its environment. I recall that the light was already beginning to blanch into dawn throughout the room. Finally my double stood too, cracked its neck, and shuffled right past me toward the bathroom. I didn't follow. For some reason I had lost all interest in what it was going to do in there. Instead, I walked over to the bed, bent down, and patted the area where a different me had just lain. The pillow was still indented with my head, the sheets still warm. I climbed onto the mattress on all fours, curled onto my side, collapsed, and remained as unmoving as I knew how, trying to fill my mind with zero except the sound of my galloping pulse. Eventually a spongy sleep seeped through my limbs, and the next time I became aware of my surroundings it was already early afternoon and Lady Bird was gently shaking me the way she sometimes did those days, telling me it was time to get up, dear — she called me *dear* — because I had a meeting with the Secret Service in just over an hour, and the world came back to me in a fog of harsh light and noise.

A number of weeks passed. The funeral you probably remember better than I do took place, Lyndon appropriated the reigns of power with slightly more gusto than I felt was strictly decorous, and the country gradually returned to its habitual cadences, although everyone seemed to agree that something special had been left behind forever. I found a cute little apartment in Manhattan with a lovely view of Central Park and began settling into my new life. As much as one can do in such circumstances, I mean — because, really, there's never very much alternative, is there? Anyway, I found it best to keep to myself. It felt — right, somehow. I wore sunglasses and a floppy hat when I left the building. I kept my head down. I decided there was very little point in answering the telephone. Every time it rang, I slipped it into a drawer in the cherry wood table on which it sat in the foyer and waited for the ringing to stop. After a few weeks, when the ringing didn't stop, I simply unplugged it. I unplugged the television and the radio, too, and stood quietly behind my front door, listening, when someone buzzed. Eventually whoever it was would always give up and go away. I started to read romance novels. Romance novels and fashion magazines. And I discovered the pleasures of Fudge Fantasy ice cream. I began to contemplate having my chin done, too, but in the end decided against it. What was the point? Every night I would take a couple of baby blue sleeping pills with a vodka and tonic, and every day I would regain consciousness sometime past noon. Then I would slip on a pair of jeans and a ratty gray sweatshirt and a pair of red sneakers with white trim and I would stroll down the block to a nice café for a cup of black coffee and a pastry. On the way there, I would stop by a newsstand run by a man with a fleshy pink knob instead of a left hand and pick up a paper. A different paper each day, depending on my mood. On the way home, I would buy a pint of ice cream for lunch.

It was at that nice café on a cool, blue Sunday in April, over a French roast and a *pain au chocolat,* that I saw the first mention of my name in one of those tabloids. You know the kind I mean. It was buried on the page well below the middle fold, just beneath a story about an angel with a wounded wing that had been found by two boys in the Finnish countryside. There was no photograph accompanying it. The font they used for the headline was discreet. Another day, and I might have overlooked it entirely. As it happened, though, I paused in mid-sip, set my coffee cup in its saucer, and read. When I was done, I couldn't help leaning back in my chair and, well . . . smiling. Now *that* smile I remember. You'd better believe it. You see, the clown who had written the piece had gotten every last particular wrong. Absolutely every last particular. According to her, I was living the good life in Martha's Vineyard, not in Manhattan. There were continual sightings of me at fabulous parties in Boston on the arm of a famous civil rights lawyer. And rumor had it that I'd lost weight. A *lot* of weight. An *unhealthy* amount, in fact. An unnamed source claimed I had confessed recently to an eating disorder. I would ingest loads of food and then slip away to the bathroom to throw it up. A psychologist was quoted in the article as saying such behaviors were all about control issues. *When I am driving,* I was purported to have told the unnamed source, *all I can think about is how I wish every car would just stay in a straight line in its own lane, and I can't stand it when all the switches on the light plates in the house aren't pointing in the same direction — such things are nothing short of hideous.*

It's remarkable what license some people will take with the truth. And me sitting there in that café on that cool, blue Sunday in April, weighing more than I ever had in my life. My knees had trouble touching, if you want to know, my thighs were so big. But, still, I had to smile. I mean, seriously, who could ask for more? With a piece like that floating around out there, I didn't have a thing to worry about. Not a thing. I was free and clear. Safe. So I just sat there, this huge smile on my face, finishing off my coffee and trying to imagine the future. In no time, I figured, people would stop bothering me. They'd think I had moved up north and so they wouldn't call me and they wouldn't ring the bell and they wouldn't make me stand silently on the other side of the door, waiting for them to leave. I could read all the books and magazines I wanted to.

What could be more uncomplicated, more unencumbered by obligation, than that?

And so that's pretty much what I did. I mean, I paid my bill and I strolled back to my apartment — stopping in a corner shop on the way to pick up a trial pint of Oreo Dream and the latest issue of *Cosmo* — and by seven o'clock that evening I had put the whole incident out of my mind.

Which is where it stayed until a week later, when my name surged up at me again from the pages of another paper. Only this time we weren't talking some sleazy tabloid. No. We were talking the real thing. And my name wasn't tucked away in some small font near the back below the middle fold. It shouted at me in bold blocky letters from the top of the daily gossip column. There I was, sitting at that nice café, trying to enjoy my Viennese blend, and suddenly I was reading about myself. I wasn't living in Manhattan, it turned out, and I wasn't living in Boston. I was living in Miami in a posh enclave right on the waterfront. My weight was down, thank goodness, and my health was good. But I had undergone a botched attempt at a face-lift that had left me permanently scarred, so I had to wear a veil whenever I went out in public, and a rusty chain of financial setbacks had left me on the brink of bankruptcy.

Well, you simply can't imagine how distraught I was. Unexpectedly coming across a story about yourself like that is like unexpectedly coming across a tombstone with your name on it during a walk through a cemetery and realizing the birth date engraved on it matches yours perfectly. That horrid column unnerved me so much I couldn't concentrate on anything for the rest of that day. I put my pint of ice cream in the oven and a freshly toasted bagel in the dishwasher. An extra sleeping pill and a vodka and tonic that night accomplished nothing except making me both sluggish and agitated. The next afternoon, just when my mind had taken a stab at recomposing itself, I came across the third mention. I was back at the café, this time picking at a large buttery croissant, when I found myself reading a story about the car wreck near Los Angeles that tragically claimed the life of the society woman who once upon a time had declared the formal dining configuration in the White House ousted in favor of round tables. I wasn't paying all that much attention to what I was reading, you see, and had coasted three or four paragraphs into the thing before realizing the story was about me. I was that society woman. I was the one the reporter was writing about in the past tense.

My heart clumped around inside my rib cage like a frightened squirrel locked inside the trunk of a car. I sat there staring at the newsprint, trying to think, trying to collect my thoughts, but all I could do was fumble through my pocketbook for some cash, toss it on the table, and hurry back to the newsstand, where I bought a copy of every paper the man without a left hand sold. The second I entered my apartment I dropped them in a bunch on the living room floor and squatted over them, gathering up my courage, and then I plunged in, tearing through those gray pages as fast as my hands would go. The more I read, the more my worst suspicions were confirmed. Some had had happier childhoods than I had. Some sadder. One of me had taken up flying a month ago and then disappeared in a Cessna somewhere over the Bermuda Triangle. One had received the first bullet intended for Jack and was allegedly lying in a coma somewhere in a private clinic in Caracas, although it was conceivable that she was dead, too. A third had become a heroin addict in Washington, D.C., a fourth a news anchorwoman in the Northwest, a fifth had hanged herself in Pittsburgh, a sixth had become the fiancée of a Greek shipping magnate whose unlikely first name was Aristotle. It went on and on. There must have been a dozen of me, maybe more, each living a different life, each life covered by a single newspaper or tabloid to the exclusion of all the rest.

Squatting in my living room, surrounded by papers, I recalled coming awake in my nightgown in the middle of the night in my room at the White House, and how I had just stood there watching my sleeping self cleaving, peeling away from the original, coming apart like amoebas do under the microscope in science documentaries. I thought about each one wafting past me toward the door and out into the world, and, as I did so, I found myself beginning to remember what they remembered, beginning to recollect moments from lives that I — this I, I mean — had never experienced, but, in some alternate cluster of natural laws, might have. I saw that Jack had been a faithful husband in many versions of our marriage. In some, he wasn't simply feigning when he threw that football through the autumn sunshine with the kids out on the lawn of our house on the Massachusetts coast. He wasn't just posing for the cameras. He was loving it. He was loving every moment we were together as a family. And, sometimes, it wasn't Jack at all, but another man, and sometimes that man was kind and sometimes he wasn't. And, sometimes, there was no man at all. Some of me were growing old alone. Some had never married. And some had married and divorced and remarried and cheated and become successful businesswomen, actors, doctors, fashion designers, models. Many met many famous people in the United

States and Europe. One never finished high school. And one had three children and died from non-Hodgkins lymphoma on May 19, 1994, dreaming of the way that faithless Jack bent toward her like a Hollywood star that first time to kiss her on the lips.

That very night I packed up my suitcases, rode the elevator down to the lobby, walked out the front door of the building with the lovely view of Central Park, and hailed a cab to the airport. I never looked back. And here I am, almost forty years later, sitting on the veranda of a small hotel with thatched-roof cottages surrounding its main lodge overlooking a sunny beach and blazing blue ocean somewhere in the British West Indies. I'm sipping an icy piña colada and I am already thinking about ordering another. I'm alone. I'm happy. My money is gradually running out, but I'm not worried. Something will happen. Something always does. It's strange to say, but it's true. I weigh 246 pounds. My new name is something you wouldn't recognize. I don't think much about the old days. I try not to. I can't remember them very well even when I put my mind to it. No. Instead, I try to concentrate on the small acts that might constitute an imagined afternoon — what will I drink next, what will I eat, will I decide to take a short stroll or swim on this beach or another. That's enough for right now. Because I know, leaning back, eyes closed against the shocking sun behind my dark glasses, that there are plenty of me in the world, more than enough, and that they can easily get along without this one, and that at least some of them are this very second leading something very close to perfect lives.

■

# The Smoothest Way Is Full of Stones

FROM *Zoetrope: All-Story*

WE AREN'T SUPPOSED to be swimming at all. It is Friday afternoon, and we're supposed to be bringing groceries home to Esty's
mother so she can prepare Shabbos dinner. But it's the middle of
July, and heat radiates from every leaf and blade of grass along the
lake road, from the tarpapered sides of the lake cottages, from the
dust that hangs in the air like sheer curtains. We throw our bikes
into the shade behind the Perelmans' shed, take off our socks and
shoes, and run through warm grass down to their slip of private
beach, trespassing, unafraid of getting caught, because old Mr.
and Mrs. Perelman won't arrive at their cottage until August, according to my cousin. Esty and I stand at the edge of the lake in
our long skirts and long-sleeved shirts, and when the water sur-
rounds our ankles it is sweetly cold.

Esty turns to me, grinning, and hikes her skirt. We walk into the
water until our knees are submerged. The bottom is silty beneath
our toes, slippery like clay, and tiny fish flash around our legs like
sparks. We are forbidden to swim because it is immodest to show
our bodies, but as far as I know there's no law against wading fully
clothed. My cousin lets the hem of her skirt fall into the water and
walks in all the way up to her waist, and I follow her, glad to feel
water against my skin. This is the kind of thing we used to do

when we were little — the secret sneaking-off into the woods, the accidental wrecking of our clothes, things we were punished for later. That was when Esty was still called Erica, before her parents got divorced, before she and her mother moved to Israel for a year and became Orthodox.

Now there is a new uncle, Uncle Shimon, and five little step-cousins. My Aunt Maria became Aunt Malka, and Erica became Esther. Erica used to talk back to her mother and throw bits of paper at the backs of old ladies' necks in synagogue, but in Israel she spent months repenting her old life and taking on a new one. This summer we've done nothing but pray, study Torah, cook, clean the lake cottage, and help Aunt Malka take care of the children. As we walk into the lake, I wonder if Erica still exists inside this new pious cousin.

I follow her deeper into the water, and the bottom falls away beneath us. It's hard to swim, heavy and slow, and at times it feels almost like drowning. Our denim skirts make it impossible to kick. Ahead is the Perelmans' old lake float, a raft of splintering boards suspended on orange plastic drums, and we pull hard all the way to the raft and hold on to the ladder.

"We're going to be killed when your mom sees our clothes," I say, out of breath.

"No, we won't," Esty says, pushing wet hair out of her face. "We'll make up an excuse. We'll say we fell in."

"Yeah, right," I say. "Accidentally."

Far down below, at the bottom of the lake, boulders waver in the blue light. It's exciting to think we've come this far in skirts. The slow-moving shadows of fish pass beneath us, and the sun is hot and brilliant white. We climb onto the raft and lie down on the planks and let the sun dry our clothes. It is good just to lie there staring at the cottage with its sad vacant windows, no one inside to tell us what to do. In a few more weeks I will go home to Manhattan, back to a life in which my days are counted according to the American calendar and prayer is something we do once a year, on the High Holidays, when we visit my grandparents in Chicago.

Back in that other world, three hundred miles from here, my mother lies in a hospital bed still recovering from the birth and death of my brother. His name was Devon Michael. His birth weight was one pound, two ounces. My mother had a problem with low blood pressure, and they had to deliver him three months early, by C-section. It has been six weeks since Devon Michael lived and died, but my mother is still in the hospital fighting infection and depression. With my father working full-time and me out of school, my parents decided it would be better for me to go to the Adelsteins' until my mother was out of the hospital. I didn't agree, but it seemed like a bad time to argue.

My cousin says that when I go home I should encourage my parents to keep kosher, that we should always say *b'rachot* before and after eating, that my mother and I should wear long skirts and long-sleeved shirts every day. She says all this will help my mother recover, the way it helped her mother recover from the divorce. I try to tell her how long it's been since we've even done the normal things, like go to the movies or make a big Chinese dinner in the wok. But Esty just watches me with a distant, enlightened look in her eyes and says we have to try to do what God wants. I have been here a month, and still I haven't told her any of the bad things I've done this year — sneaked cigarettes from my friends' mothers' packs, stole naked-lady playing cards from a street vendor on West 33rd, kissed a boy from the swim team behind the bleachers after a meet. I had planned to tell her all these things, thinking she'd be impressed, but soon I understood that she wouldn't. Now Esty sits up beside me on the raft and looks toward shore. As she stares at the road beyond the Perelmans' yard, her back tenses and her eyes narrow with concentration. "Someone's coming," she says. "Look."

I sit up. Through the bushes along the lake road there is a flash of white, somebody's shirt. Without a word we climb down into the water and swim underneath the raft, between the orange plastic drums. From the lapping shade there we see a teenage boy with copper-colored hair and long curling peyos run from the road to the bushes beside the house. He drops to his knees and crawls through the tangle of vines, moving slowly, glancing back over his shoulder. When he reaches the backyard he stands and brushes dead leaves from his clothes. He is tall and lanky, his long arms smooth and brown. Crouching beside the porch, he opens his backpack and takes out some kind of flat package, which he pushes deep under the porch steps. Then he gets up and runs for the road. From the shadow of the raft we can see the dust rising, and the receding flash of the boy's white shirt.

"That was Dovid Frankel," Esty says.

"How could you tell?"

"My mother bought him that green backpack in Toronto."

"Lots of people have green backpacks," I say.

"I know it was him. You'll see. His family's coming for Shabbos tonight."

She swims toward shore and I follow, my skirt heavy as an animal skin around my legs. When we drag ourselves onto the beach our clothes cling to our bodies and our hair hangs like weeds.

"You look shipwrecked," I tell my cousin.

"So do you," she says, and laughs.

We run across the Perelmans' backyard to the screened-in porch. Kneeling down, we peer into the shadows beneath the porch steps. Planes of light slant through the cracks between the boards, and we can see the paper bag far back in the shadows. Esty reaches in and grabs the bag, then shakes its contents onto the grass. What falls out is a large softcover book called *Essence of Persimmon: Eastern Sexual Secrets for Western Lives*. On the cover is a drawing of an Indian woman draped in gold and green silk, reclining on cushions inside a tent. One hand disappears into the shadow between her legs, and in the other she holds a tiny vial of oil. Her breasts are high and round, her eyes tapered like two slender fish. Her lips are parted in a look of ecstasy.

"Eastern sexual secrets," Esty says. "Oh, my God."

I can't speak. I can't stop staring at the woman on the cover.

My cousin opens the book and flips through the pages, some thick with text, others printed with illustrations. Moving closer to me, she begins to read aloud: "One may begin simply by pressing the flat of the hand against the open yoni, allowing heat and energy to travel into the woman's body through this most intimate space."

"Wow," I say. "The open yoni."

Esty closes the book and stuffs it into the brown paper bag. "This is obviously a sin," she says. "We can't leave it here. Dovid will come back for it."

"So?"

"You're not supposed to let your fellow Jew commit a sin."

"Is it really a sin?"

"A terrible sin," she says. "We have to hide it where no one will find it."

"Where?"

"In our closet at home. The top shelf. No one will ever know."

"But *we'll* know," I say, eyeing her carefully. Hiding a book like this at the top of our own closet is something Erica might have suggested, long ago.

"Of course, but we won't look at it," Esty says sternly, her brown eyes clear and fierce. "It's *tiuv,* abomination. God forbid anyone should ever look at it again."

My cousin retrieves her bike from the shed and stows the book between a bag of lettuce and a carton of yogurt. It looks harmless there, almost wholesome, in its brown paper sack. We get on our bikes and ride for home, and by the time we get there our clothes are almost dry.

Esty carries the book into the house as if it's nothing, just another brown bag among many bags. This is the kind of ingenious technique she perfected back in her Erica days, and it works equally well now. Inside, everyone is too busy with Shabbos preparations to notice anything out of the ordinary. The little stepcousins are setting the table, arranging the Shabbos candles, picking up toys, dusting the bookshelves. Aunt Malka is baking challah. She punches down dough as she talks to us.

"The children need baths," she says. "The table has to be set. The Handelmans and the Frankels are coming at seven, and I'm running late on dinner, as you know. I'm not going to ask what took you so long." She raises her eyes at us, large, sharp blue eyes identical to my mother's, with deep creases at the corners and a fringe of jet black lash. Unlike my mother, she is tall and big-boned. In her former life she was Maria Vincent, a set dresser for the Canadian Opera Company in Toronto. Once I saw her at work, hanging purple velvet curtains at the windows of an Italian pa-lazzo.

"Sorry we took so long," Esty says. "We'll help."

"You'd better," she says. "Shabbos is coming."

I follow my cousin down the hall and into our bedroom. On the whitewashed wall there is a picture of the Lubavitcher Rebbe, Menachem Schneerson, with his long steely beard and his eyes like flecks of black glass. He's on the east wall, the wall my cousin faces when she prays. His eyes seem to follow her as she drags the desk chair into the closet and stows *Essence of Persimmon* on the top shelf.

"What do we say to Dovid Frankel tonight?" I ask her.

"Nothing," she says. "We completely ignore him."

I make one last phone call to my mother before Shabbos. It's al-ways frightening to dial the number of the hospital room because there's no telling what my mother will sound like when she an-swers. Sometimes she sounds like herself, quick and funny, and I can almost smell her olive-aloe soap. Other times, like today, she sounds just like she sounded when she told me Devon Michael had died.

"I can hardly hear you," she says, her own voice small and faint, somewhere far off down the line. The phone crackles with static.

"We went swimming today," I tell her, trying to speak loud. "It was hot."

Far away, almost too quiet to hear, she sighs.

"It's almost Shabbos," I say. "Aunt Malka's baking challah."

"Is she?" my mother says.

"How are you feeling?" I ask her. "When can you come home?"

"Soon, honey."

I have a sudden urge to tell her about the book we found, to ask her what we're supposed to do with something like that, to find out if she thinks it's a sin. I want to tell her about Dovid Frankel, how we saw him sneaking along the lake. I tell my mother things like this sometimes, and she seems to understand. But now she says to send her love to Aunt Malka and Uncle Shimon and Esty and all the stepcousins, and before I have a chance to really feel like her daughter again, we're already saying goodbye.

At six-thirty, the women and girls arrive. They bring steaming trays of potato kugel and berry cobbler, bottles of grape juice and sweet wine. The men are at shul, welcoming the Shabbo as if she were a bride, with the words *bo'i kallah*. Here the women do not go to synagogue on Fridays. Instead we arrange the platters of food and remove bread from the oven and fill cups with grape juice and wine. We are still working when the men and boys arrive, tromping through the kitchen and kissing their wives and daughters good Shabbos. My cousin, her hands full of raspberries, nudges me and nods toward a tall boy with penny brown hair, and I know him to be Dovid Frankel, the boy from the lake, owner of *Essence of Persimmon*. I watch him as he kisses his mother, hoists his little sister onto his hip. He is tall and tanned, with small round glasses and a slender oval face. His mouth is almost girlish, bow-shaped and flushed, and his hair is close-cropped, with the exception of his luxuriously curled, shoulder-length peyos. He wears a collarless blue shirt in a fabric that looks homemade. I don't realize I'm staring at him until Esty nudges me again.

Everyone gathers around the dinner table, which we've set up on the screen porch. The men begin singing *Shalom Aleichem*, swaying with the rise and fall of the melody. I feel safe, gathered in, with the song covering us like a prayer shawl and the Shabbos candles flickering on the sideboard. I pray for my mother and father. Dovid Frankel stands across from me, rocking his little sister as he sings.

Uncle Shimon, in his loose white Israeli shirt and embroidered yarmulke, stands at the head of the table. His beard is streaked with silver, and his eyes burn with a quick blue fire. As he looks around the table at his friends, his children, his new wife, I can tell he believes himself to be a lucky man. I think about my previous uncle, Michael, who has moved to Hawaii to do his astronomy research at a giant telescope there. Once he brought the family to visit us at Christmastime, and in his honor my mother set up a tiny plastic tree on our coffee table. That night we were allowed to eat candy canes and hang stockings at the fireplace, and in the morning there were silver bracelets for Esty and me, with our names engraved. Esty's bracelet said ERICA, of course. I wonder if she still has it. I still have mine, though it is too small for me now.

Beside me, Esty looks down at her plate and fingers the satin trim at the waist of her Shabbos skirt. I catch her looking at Dovid Frankel, too, who seems oblivious to us both. From the bedroom, *Essence of Persimmon* exerts a magnetic pull I can feel in my chest. I watch Esty as we serve the soup and the gefilte fish, as we lean over Dovid Frankel's shoulder to replace his fork or remove his plates. My cousin's cheeks are flushed and her eyes keep moving toward Dovid, though sometimes they stray toward pregnant Mrs. Handelman, her belly swollen beneath the white cotton of her dress. Mrs. Handelman is Dovid Frankel's oldest sister. Her young husband, Lev, has a short blond beard and a nervous laugh. During the fish course, he tells the story of a set of false contractions that sent him and Mrs. Handelman running for the car. Mrs. Handelman, Esty whispers to me, is eighteen years old. Last year they went to school together.

We eat our chicken and kugel, and then we serve the raspberry cobbler for dessert. The little stepcousins run screaming around the table and crawl underneath. There is something wild and wonderful about the disorder of it all, a feeling so different from the quiet rhythms of our dinner table at home, with my mother asking me about my day at school and my father offering more milk or peas. Here, when everyone has finished eating, we sing the *Birkat HaMazon*. By now I know all the Hebrew words. It's strange to think that when I go home we will all just get up at the end of the meal and put our plates in the sink without singing anything, or thanking anyone.

When the prayer is over, my uncle begins to tell a story about the Belkins, a Jewish family some thirty miles up the lake whose house burned down in June. "Everything destroyed," he says. "Books, clothes, the children's toys, everything. No one was hurt, thank God. They were all visiting the wife's brother when it happened. An electrical short. Completely accidental. So when they go back to see if anything can be salvaged, the only thing not completely burnt up is the mezuzah. The door frame? Completely burnt. But the mezuzah, fine. A little black, but fine. And so they send it to New York to have the paper checked, and you'll never believe what they find."

All the men and women and children look at my uncle, their mouths open. They blink silently in the porch light as if he were about to perform some holy miracle.

"There's an imperfection in the text," my uncle says. "In the word *asher*. The letters aleph-shin are smudged, misshapen."

Young Mr. Handelman looks stricken. "Aleph-shin," he says. "Aish."

"That's right. And who knows what that means?" Uncle Shimon looks at each of the children, but the children just sit staring, waiting for him to tell them.

"I know," Dovid Frankel says. "It means fire."

"That's right," says Uncle Shimon. "Fire."

Around the table there is a murmur of amazement, but Dovid Frankel crosses his arms over his chest and raises an eyebrow at my uncle. *"Aish,"* he says. "That's supposed to be what made their house burn down?"

My uncle sits back in his chair, stroking his beard. "A man has to make sure his mezuzah is kosher," he says. "That's his responsibility. Who knows how the letters got smudged? Was it the scribe, just being lazy? Was it his assistant, touching the text as he moved it from one worktable to another? Maybe a drop of water fell from a cup of tea the scribe's wife was bringing to her husband. Should we blame her?"

"For God's sake, don't blame the wife," my aunt says, and all the women laugh.

"We have to have our mezuzot checked twice a year," says my

uncle. He leans back in his chair and looks at Dovid, crossing his fingers over his belly. "'We alone are responsible for our relationship with Hashem.' Reb Zinzun said that in the fifteenth century."

"We should have our mezuzah checked," Mr. Handelman says, squeezing his wife's hand. He looks with worry at her swollen belly.

"I made a mezuzah at school," says one of the little stepcousins, a red-haired boy.

"You did not," his older brother says. "You made a mezuzah *cover.*"

Esty and I get up to clear the dessert plates from the table, and Dovid Frankel pushes his chair away from the table and stands. As we gather the plates, he opens the screen door and steps out into the night. My cousin shoots me a significant look, as if this proves that he has sinned against Hashem and is feeling the guilt. I take a stack of dessert plates into the kitchen, trying to catch a glimpse of Dovid through the window. But it is dark outside, and all I can see is the reflection of the kitchen, with its stacks and stacks of plates that we will have to wash. When the men's voices rise again, I go to the front of the house and step outside. The night is all around me, dew-wet and smelling like milkweed and pine needles and lake wind, and the air vibrates with peepers. The tall grass wets my ankles as I walk toward the backyard. Dovid is kicking at the clothesline frame, his sneaker making a dull hollow *clong* against the metal post. He looks up at me and says, "Hello, Esty's cousin," and then continues kicking.

"What are you doing?" I ask him.

"Thinking," he says, kicking the post.

"Thinking what?"

"Does a smudged mezuzah make a family's house burn down?"

"What do you think?"

He doesn't answer. Instead he picks up a white stone from the ground and hurls it into the dark. We hear it fall into the grass, out of sight.

"Don't you believe in Hashem?" I ask him.

He squints at me. "Do *you?*"

"I don't know," I say. I stand silent in the dark, thinking about the one time I saw my brother before he died. He was lying in an incubator with tubes coming out of every part of his body, monitors tracing his breathing and heartbeat. His skin was transparent, his eyes closed, and all I could think was that he looked like a tiny skinny frog. Scrubbed, sterilized, gloved, I was allowed to reach in through a portal and touch his feverish skin. I felt terrible for him. *Get better, grow, kick,* I said to him silently. It was difficult to leave, knowing I might not see him again. But in the cab that night, on the way home with my father, I was imagining what might happen if he did live. The doctors had told us he could be sick forever, that he'd require constant care. I could already imagine my parents taking care of him every day, changing his tubes and diapers, measuring his tiny pulse, utterly forgetting about me. Just once, just for that instant, I wished he would die. If there is a God who can see inside mezuzahs, a God who burns people's houses for two smudged letters, then He must know that secret, too. "Sometimes I hope there's not a God," I say. "I'm in a lot of trouble if there is."

"What trouble?" Dovid says.

"Bad trouble. I can't talk about it."

"Some people around here are scared of you," Dovid says. "Some of the mothers. They think you're going to show their kids a fashion magazine or give them an unkosher cookie or tell them something they shouldn't hear."

I have never considered this. I've only imagined the influence rolling from them to me, making me more Jewish, making me try to do what the Torah teaches. "I didn't bring any magazines," I tell him. "I've been keeping kosher all summer. I've been wearing these long-sleeved clothes. I can hardly remember what I'm like in my normal life."

"It was the same with your cousin," he says. "When she and your aunt first came here, people didn't trust them."

"I can't believe anyone wouldn't trust them," I say. "Or be scared of me."

"I'm not scared of you," he says, and reaches out and touches my arm, his hand cool and dry against my skin. I know he is not supposed to touch any woman who is not his mother or his sister. I can smell raspberries and brown sugar on his breath. I don't want to move or speak or do anything that will make him take his hand from my arm, though I know it is wrong for us to be touching and though I know he wouldn't be touching me if I were an Orthodox girl. From the house comes the sound of men laughing. Dovid Frankel steps closer, and I can feel the warmth of his chest through his shirt. For a moment I think he will kiss me. Then we hear a screen door bang, and he moves away from me and walks back toward the house.

That night, my cousin won't talk to me. She knows I was outside with Dovid Frankel, and this makes her furious. In silence we get into our nightgowns and brush our teeth and climb into bed, and I can hear her wide-awake breathing, uneven and sharp. I lie there thinking about Dovid Frankel, the way his hand felt on my arm, the knowledge that he was doing something against the rules. It gives me a strange, rolling feeling in my stomach. For the first time I wonder if I've started to want to become the girl I've been pretending to be, whose prayers I've been saying, whose dietary laws I've been observing. A time or two, on Shabbos, I know I've felt a kind of holy swelling in my chest, a connection to something larger than myself. I wonder if this is proof of something, if this is God marking me somehow.

In the middle of the night, I wake to find Esty gone from her bed. The closet door is closed, and from beneath the door comes a thin line of light, the light we leave on throughout Shabbos. From inside I can hear a shuffling and then a soft thump. I get out of bed and go to the closet door. "Esty," I whisper. "Are you in there?"

"Go away," my cousin whispers back.

"Open up," I say.

"No."

"Do it now, or I'll make a noise."

She opens the closet door just a crack. I slide in. The book is in her hand, open to a Japanese print of a man and woman embracing. The woman's head is thrown back, her mouth open to reveal a sliver of tongue. The man holds her tiny birdlike hands in his own. Rising up from between his legs and entering her body is a plum-colored column of flesh.

"Gross," I say.

My cousin closes the book.

"I thought you said we were never going to look at it again," I say.

"We were going to ignore Dovid Frankel, too."

"So what?"

My cousin's eyes fill, and I understand: she is in love with Dovid Frankel. Things begin to make sense: our bringing the book home, her significant looks all evening, her anger. "Esty," I say. "It's okay. Nothing happened. We just talked."

"He was looking at you during dinner," she cries.

"He doesn't like me," I say. "We talked about you."

"About me?" She wipes her eyes with her nightgown sleeve.

"That's right."

"What did he say?"

"He wanted to know if you'd ever mentioned him to me," I lie.

"And?"

"I said you told me you went to school with his sister."

My cousin sighs. "Okay," she says. "Safe answer."

"Okay," I say. "Now you have to tell me what you're doing, looking at that book."

My cousin glances down and her eyes widen, as if she's surprised to find she's been holding the book all this time. "I don't know what I'm doing," she says. "The book was here. I couldn't sleep. Finally I just got up and started looking at it."

"It's a sin," I say. "That's what you told me before."

"I know."

"So let's go to bed, okay?"

"Okay," she says.

We stand there looking at each other. Neither of us makes a move to go to bed.

"Maybe we could just look at it for a little while," I say.

"A few minutes couldn't hurt," my cousin says.

This decides it. We sit down on the wooden planking of the closet floor, and my cousin opens the book to the first chapter. We learn that we are too busy with work, domestic tasks, and social activity to remember that we must take the time to respect and enjoy our physical selves and our partners' physical selves, to reap the benefits that come from regular, loving sexual fulfillment. The book seems not to care whether "the East" means Japan, China, or India; the drawings show all kinds of Eastern people in sexual positions with names that sound like poetry: "The Crane," "Kneeling Gazelle," "Plum Sapling." My cousin's forehead is creased in concentration as she reads, her eyebrows nearly meeting.

"What's the orgasm?" my cousin says. "They keep talking about the orgasm."

"I don't know," I say. "Check the index."

She flips to the index, and under *orgasm* there is a long list of page numbers. We choose one at random, page 83. My cousin reads in a whisper about how to touch oneself in order to achieve the word in question. We learn that one can use one's own fingers or any object whose shape and texture one finds pleasing, though the use of electronic vibrating devices is not recommended. These can cause desensitization, the book tells us. But certain Eastern devices, such as *ben wa* balls or the String of Pearls, can greatly enhance a woman's pleasure.

"Sick," my cousin says.

"I still don't get it," I say.

"What do you think they mean by the *clitoris*?"

Though I have a vague idea, I find myself at a loss for words. My cousin looks it up in the index, and when she learns what it is she is amazed. "I thought that was where you peed from," she breathes. "How weird."

"It's weird, all right," I say.

Then she says, "I can't believe Dovid Frankel has read all this. His hands probably touched this page." She lets the book fall into her lap. It opens to a glossy drawing of a woman suspended in a swinglike contraption from the roof of a pavilion, high above a turbaned man who gazes up at her with desire and love. Two servants in long robes hold the cords that keep the woman suspended.

"Oh, my God," my cousin says, and closes the book. She looks at me with serious eyes, her mother's eyes but deep brown, in the dim light of the closet. "We have to repent tomorrow," she says. "When we say *shacharit* in the morning. There's a place where you can tell God what you did wrong."

"We'll repent," I say.

We stow the book on its high shelf and leave the closet. Our room is cold, the light coming in from outside a ghostly blue. We climb into our twin beds and say the *Shema,* and then the *v'ahavta.* The *v'ahavta* is the same prayer that's written inside a mezuzah, and when I say the word *asher* a sizzle of terror runs through me. Has God seen what we have just done? Are we being judged even now, as we lie in bed in the dark? I am awake for a long time, watching the cool air move the curtains, listening to the rushing of the grasses outside, the whir of the night insects . . . After some time I hear a change in the rhythm of breathing from my cousin's bed, and a faint rustle beneath the sheet. I pretend to be asleep, listening to the metallic tick of her bedsprings. It seems to go on for hours, connected with the sound of insects outside, the shush of grass, the wind.

The next morning I am the first to wake. I say the *Shema* and wash my hands in the basin we leave on the nightstand, cleansing myself as I open my eyes to this Shabbos morning. My cousin sleeps nearly sideways, her long legs hanging off the bed, covers pushed back, nightgown around her thighs. Though her limbs have not seen the sun all summer, her skin is a deep olive. There is a bruise on her knee the size of an egg, newly purple, which I know she must have gotten as we climbed the metal ladder onto the Perelmans' float. In sleep her face is slack and flushed, her lips parted. It has never occurred to me that my cousin may be beautiful the way a woman is beautiful. With her cropped brown hair and full cheeks, she has always looked to me like a tall, sturdy child. But this morning, as she sleeps, there is a womanliness to her body that makes me feel young and unripe. I dress quietly so as not to wake her, and tiptoe out to the kitchen to find my uncle standing on the screen porch, beside the table, folding his tallis into its velvet bag so he can go to shul for morning services. Sunlight falls in through the screen and covers him with its gold dust. He is facing Jerusalem, the city where he and Aunt Malka found each other. I open the screen door and step out onto the porch.

"Rebecca," he says. "Good morning, good Shabbos." He smiles, smoothing his beard between both hands.

"Hi," I say.

"I'll be at Torah study this afternoon. After lunch."

"Okay."

"You look tired," he says. "Did you sleep?"

"I slept okay."

For a moment we stand looking at each other, my uncle still smiling. Before I can stop myself I'm asking the question that pushes its way to the front of my mind. "After a person dies," I say, "is the family supposed to have the mezuzah checked?"

My uncle's hands fall from his beard. He regards me sadly, his eyes deep and glassed with sun. "When my first wife, Bluma Sarah, died," he says, "I had everything checked. Our mezuzah, my tefillin, our ketubah. The rebbe found nothing. Finally I asked him to examine my soul, thinking I was the bearer of some imperfection. Do you know what the rebbe told me?"

"No," I say, looking at my feet, wishing I hadn't asked.

"He told me, 'Sometimes bad things just happen. You'll see why later. Or you won't. Do we always know why Hashem does what He does? *Nayn.*'"

"Oh."

"I think God wanted me to meet your aunt," says Uncle Shimon. "Maybe He wanted me to meet you, too." He tucks his tallis bag under his arm and reties his shoes. "Bluma Sarah had a saying: *Der gleichster veg iz ful mit shtainer.*"

"What's it mean?"

"The smoothest way is sometimes full of stones," he says.

All day I keep the Shabbos. This means I do not turn on a light or tear paper or write or bathe or cook or sew or do any of the hundred kinds of work involved in building the Holy Temple. It is difficult to remember all the things one cannot do; sitting in the tall grass, playing a clumsy round of duck-duck-goose with the little stepcousins, I am tempted to pull a grass blade and split it down its fibrous center, or weave a clover chain for one of the girls. But the Shabbos is all around us, in the quiet along the road and the sound of families in their yards, and I remember and remember all day. My cousin spends most of the day alone. I see her praying in a sunlit patch of yard, swaying back and forth as she reads from her tiny *siddur;* then she lies in the grass and studies Torah. When she disappears into the house I follow her. She's closed herself into our closet again, the door wedged tight against intruders. I imagine her undoing this morning's work of repentance, learning new body-part names, new positions. When I whisper through the door for her to come out, she tells me to go away.

All day I'm not allowed to use the telephone to call my mother. I walk around and around the yard, waiting for the sun to dip toward the horizon. Aunt Malka watches me from the porch, looking worried, and then she calls me over.

"What's all this pacing?" she says.

"I'm keeping Shabbos," I say.

"You can keep it right here with me," she says, patting the step beside her.

I sit down. Before us the older children are trying to teach the younger ones how to do cartwheels. They fly in awkward arcs through the long grass.

"Your mother sounds much better," she says. "You'll be going home soon."

"Probably," I say.

"There's a lady I know who lives near you," she says. "I'll give you her number. She and some other women run a mikveh near your house, on Twenty-second and Third."

"What's a mikveh?"

"It's the ritual bath," she says. "It cleans us spiritually. All women go. Men, too. Your mother should go when she gets out of the hospital. You can go with her, just to watch. It's lovely. You'll see." One of the little boys runs up and tosses a smooth black pebble into Aunt Malka's lap, then runs away, laughing. "We're commanded to go after childbirth," she says.

"Commanded by who?"

"By Hashem," she says, turning the pebble in her fingers. Through its center runs a translucent white ribbon of quartz.

"Even if the baby dies?" I ask her. "Do you have to go then?"

"Yes," she says. "Especially then. It's very important and beautiful. The bath is very clean, and this particular one is tiled all in pink. The women will help your mother undress and brush her hair, so the water will touch every part of her. Then she'll step down into the bath — it's very deep, and large, like a Jacuzzi — until she's completely covered. They'll tell her what *b'rachot* to say. Then she'll be clean."

"Everyone's supposed to do this?" I ask her.

"We're commanded to," she says. "Adults, anyway. For women, it's every month unless we're pregnant. When I'm here I do it right in the lake. There's a woman who had a special shed built on her property, and that's where we go in."

"What if my mother doesn't want to go?" I ask.

"If you tell her how important it is, I'm sure she'll go," she says, and hands me the black pebble. I rub it with my thumb, tracing the quartz.

My aunt gathers the little stepcousins for a walk down the lake road, tying their shoes and smoothing their hair, securing their *kippots* with metal clips. I imagine her walking into the lake, her dark curls spreading out behind her, and my skin prickles cold in the heat. When she invites me to come along on the walk, I tell her I will stay home. I lie down in the grass and watch her start off down the road, the little stepcousins circling her like honeybees.

Real bees weave above me through the grass, their bodies so velvety I want to touch them. For what feels like the first time all summer, I am alone. I rub the pebble with my thumb, imagining it to be a magic stone that will make me smaller and smaller in the tall grass. I shrink to the size of a garter snake, a leaf, a speck of dust, until I am almost invisible. There is a presence gathering around me, an iridescent light I can see through my laced eyelashes. I lie still against the earth, faint with dread, and I feel the planet spinning through space, its dizzying momentum, its unstoppable speed. It is God who makes the shadows dissolve around me. He sharpens the scent of clover. He pushes the bees past my ears, directs the sun onto my back until my skin burns through the cotton of my Shabbos dress. I want to know what He wants and do what He wants, and I let my mind fall blank, waiting to be told.

When three stars come into the sky, the family gathers for Havdalah. We stand in a circle on the grass outside, all nine of us, and we light the braided candle and sing to God, thanking Him for creating fire, *aish*. According to the tradition, we examine our fingernails in the light of that candle, to remind us of the ways God causes us to grow. Then we smell spices and drink wine for a sweet week, and finally we sing the song about Eliyahu ha Navi, the prophet who will arrive someday soon to bring the Messiah. I stand with one arm around a little stepcousin and the other around Esty. As Havdalah ends she drifts off toward the house, one hand trailing through the long grass.

Now that Shabbos is over, the first thing I do is call my mother. Standing in the kitchen, I watch my aunt and uncle carrying children toward the house as I dial. For the first time it occurs to me that it might be awful for my mother always to hear children in the background when I call her, and I wonder if I should wait until they go to bed. But by that time the phone's ringing, and it's my father who answers anyway.

"Hey, son," he says. It's an old game between us: he calls me "son" and I call him "Pa," like in the Old West. This is the first time we've done it since Devon Michael was born, though, and it sounds different now.

"Hi, Pa," I say, playing the game even so, because I miss him.

"Still out on the range?"

"Indeedy."

"How's the grub?"

"Grub's not bad," I say. "How's Ma?"

He sighs. "Sleeping."

"Not good?" I say.

"I think she needs you home," he says. "She's not feeling well enough now to do much, but I'll bet if she saw her kid she'd shape up pretty fast."

"When can I come home?"

"It looks like a couple of weeks," he says. "She's had some problems. Nothing serious, but the doctor thinks she might need IV antibiotics for a little while still."

"Aunt Malka says she should go to a ritual bath," I say. "To get spiritually clean."

There's a silence on my father's end, and I wonder if I've said something wrong. In the background I hear a woman's voice on the intercom but I can't make out what she's saying. "You there, Dad?" I say.

"I'd like to talk to your aunt," he says. "If she's around."

Something about his tone gives me pause. Even though Aunt Malka's just a few steps away, talking quietly out on the screen porch with Uncle Shimon, I tell my father she's gone out for milk. Silently I promise myself to repent this lie tomorrow, during *shacharit*.

I can hear my father scratching his head, sharp and quick, the way he sometimes does. "You have her give me a call," he says. "All right?"

"All right," I say. "Tell Mom I love her."

He says he will.

That evening, my cousin disappears during dinner. We're all eating tomatoes and cottage cheese and thick slices of rye bread with whipped butter, the kind of meal we always eat after Shabbos, and in the middle of spreading my third slice of bread I look over and Esty's gone.

"Where's your cousin?" Aunt Malka says. "She didn't touch her food."

"I'll find her," I say. I go to our room and open the closet door, but the closet is empty. The book is gone from its high shelf. I glance around the room, and it takes me a few moments to see my cousin's huddled shape beneath her bedclothes.

"Esty," I say. "What are you doing?"

She lifts her head and looks at me, her cheeks flushed. In her hand she holds a flashlight. "Reading," she whispers.

"You can't just leave dinner," I say.

"I wanted to look something up."

"Your mom wants to know what's wrong."

"Tell her I have a headache," Esty says. "Say I took some aspirin and I'm lying down."

"You want me to lie?"

She nods.

"It's against the Ten Commandments."

Esty rolls her eyes. "Like you've never lied," she says.

"Maybe I don't anymore."

"Tonight you do," she says, and pulls the bedclothes over her head, rolling toward the wall. I go out to the dinner table and sit down, pushing at my slice of rye with a tomato wedge.

"Nu," my aunt says. "What's the story?"

"She's reading," I say.

"In the middle of dinner?"

"It's all right," Uncle Shimon says. "Let her read. I wish some of these would read." He casts a hand over the heads of his own children.

"I read," says one of the little girls. "I can read the whole aleph-bet."

"That's right," her father says, and gives her another slice of bread.

I finish my dinner, and then it's left to me to do all the dishes while Aunt Malka bathes the stepcousins and gets them ready for bed. I stand there washing and looking out into the dark yard, seeing nothing, angry at my cousin and worried about her. I worry about my mother, too, lying in the hospital with intravenous antibiotics dripping into her arm, spiritually unclean. I've always assumed that my brother's death was somehow meant to punish *me*, since I was the one who imagined it in the first place, but now I wonder if we are all guilty. After all, we've been walking around doing exactly what we want, day in and day out, as if what God wants doesn't matter at all, as if God were as small and unimportant as the knickknacks on my grandmother's shelves, the porcelain swans and milkmaids we see when we go to her house for the High Holidays.

A thin strand of fear moves through my chest, and for a moment I feel faint. Then, as I look out through the window, I see a white shape moving across the lawn, ghostly in the dark. I stare through the screen as the figure drifts toward the road, and when it hits the yellow streetlight glow I see it's my cousin.

Drying my hands on a dishtowel, I run out into the yard. Esty is far away in the dark, but I run after her as fast as I can through the wet grass. When I get to the road, she hears me coming and turns around.

"What are you doing?" I say, trying to catch my breath.

"Nothing," she says, but she's keeping one hand behind her back. I grab for the hand but she twists it away from me. I see she's holding a white envelope.

"What is it?" I say. "You're going to the post office in the middle of the night?"

"It's not the middle of the night."

"You snuck out," I say. "You don't have to sneak out just to mail a letter."

"Go inside," Esty says, giving me a little shove toward the house.

"No," I say. "I'm not going anywhere. I'll scream for your mother if you don't tell me what you're doing."

"You would," she says, "wouldn't you?"

I open my mouth as if to do it.

"It's a note to Dovid Frankel," she says. "It says if he wants to get his book back, he has to meet me at the Perelmans' tomorrow night."

"But you can't," I say. "It's forbidden."

"So what?" my cousin says. "And if you tell anybody about it, you're dead."

"You can't do anything to me," I say.

"Yes, I can," she says. "I can tell my mother this was *your* book, that you brought it from New York and have been trying to get us to read it."

"But she'll know you're lying," I say. "Dovid will tell her it's a lie."

"No, he won't."

I know she's right, that Dovid would never own up to the book, that in the end he would think about how much he has to lose, compared to me. And so I stand there on the road, my throat tightening, feeling again how young I am and how foolish. Esty smoothes the letter between her palms and takes a deep breath. "Now turn around," she says, "and go back into that house and pretend I'm in bed. And when I come back, I don't want to see you reading my book."

"*Your* book?" I say.

"Mine for now."

I turn around and stomp back toward the house, but when I get to the screen door I creep in silently. The little cousins are sleeping, after all. There is a line of light beneath my aunt and uncle's door, and I hear my uncle reading in Hebrew to Aunt Malka. I go to our bedroom and change into my nightgown and sit on the bed in the dark, trying to pray. The eyes of the Lubavitcher Rebbe stare down at me from the wall, old and fierce, and all I can think about is my cousin saying *you would, wouldn't you,* her eyes slit with spite. I brush my teeth and get into bed, and then I say the *Shema.* Saying it alone for the first time, I imagine myself back at home in my own bed, whispering to God in the silence of my room, and the thought makes me feel so desolate I roll over and cry. But it isn't long before I hear Esty climbing through the window and then getting ready for bed, and even though I still feel the sting of her threat, even though I know she's ready to betray me, her presence is a comfort in the dark.

I struggle awake the next morning to find that Esty is already out of bed. From the kitchen I can hear the clink of spoons against cereal bowls and the high, plaintive voices of the stepcousins. Aunt Malka's voice rises over theirs, announcing that today we will all go blueberry picking. I sigh in relief. Blueberry picking is what I need. I say the *Shema* and wash my hands in the basin beside the bed.

My cousin is in a fine mood today, her short bangs pulled back in two blue barrettes, a red bandanna at her throat. She sings in the van on the way to the blueberry farm, and all the little cousins sing with her. My aunt looks on with pleasure. At first I'm only pretending to have a good time too, but then I find I no longer have to pretend. It feels good to swing a plastic bucket and make my slow way down a row of blueberry shrubs, feeling between the leaves for the sun-hot berries. My cousin acts as if nothing happened between us last night, as if we never fought, as if she never went down the road to Dovid Frankel's house in the dark. When her pail is full she helps me fill my pail, and we both eat handfuls of blueberries, staining our shirts and skirts and skin.

Back at home the cousins study Torah with Uncle Shimon, and Aunt Malka and Esty and I bake blueberry cake. Esty keeps glancing at the clock, as if she might have to run out any minute to meet Dovid. When the telephone rings she gives a jolt, then lunges to pick it up.

"Oh, Uncle Alan," she says. "Hi."

Uncle Alan is my father. I stop stirring the cake batter and try to get the phone from my cousin, but she's already handing it to Aunt Malka.

"Hello, Alan," Aunt Malka says. I watch her face for bad news, but none seems to be forthcoming. "Yes," she says. "Yes. Yes. We certainly are." Holding the phone between her cheek and shoulder, she walks out of the kitchen and into the little girls' bedroom, then closes the door behind her.

"What's going on?" Esty says.

"I don't know," I say. I pour the cake batter into the floured pan Esty has prepared, and we slide it into the oven. Through the wall I can hear Aunt Malka's voice rising and falling. "I think it has to do with the mikveh," I say. "I told my dad yesterday that my mom should go, and he had a strange reaction."

"She does have to go," my cousin says. "You're supposed to go to the mikveh after you've given birth or had your period. Your husband can't touch you until you do."

"Your mom already told me about that," I say.

"There are hundreds of rules," she says, sighing. "Things we're supposed to do and not supposed to do. Maybe you'll learn about them when you're older."

"What rules?" I say. "I'm old enough."

"I can't just say them here in the kitchen."

"Yes, you can. What are the rules? What are you supposed to do?"

My cousin bends close to my ear. "You can't do it sitting or standing," she says. "You can't do it outside. You can't do it drunk. You can't do it during the day, or with the lights on. You're supposed to think about subjects of Torah while you do it. Things like that," she says.

"You're supposed to think about subjects of Torah?"

Esty shrugs. "That's what they say."

Through the wall we hear Aunt Malka's voice approaching, and my cousin moves away from me and begins wiping flour and sugar from the countertop. Aunt Malka comes out of the bedroom, her face flushed, her brows drawn together. She's already hung up the phone.

"How's my mother?" I ask her.

"Recovering," she says, gathering the cup measures and mixing bowls.

"Am I in trouble?"

"No." She sends hot water rolling into the sink and rubs soap into the dish sponge, then begins scrubbing a bowl. She looks as if she's the one who's been punished, her mouth drawn into a grim line. "You have to do what you think is right, Rebecca," she says, "even when the people around you are doing otherwise."

"Okay," I say.

"It's not a problem right now," she says, "but when you go home it may be."

I glance at Esty. She's looking at her mother intently. "Do you really believe that?" she says. "About doing what you think is right?"

"Absolutely," her mother says. "I've always told you that."

Esty nods, and Aunt Malka continues washing dishes, unaware of what she's just condoned.

*

At twelve-thirty that night my cousin dresses in a black skirt and shirt and covers her hair with a black scarf. She wraps *Essence of Persimmon* in its brown paper bag and tucks it under her arm. The house is dark and quiet, everyone asleep.

"Don't do this, Esty," I whisper from my bed. "Stay home."

"If you tell anyone I'm gone, you're dead," she says.

"At least take me along," I say.

"You can't come along."

"Try and stop me."

"You know how I can stop you."

The dread eyes of the Lubavitcher Rebbe stare down at me from the wall. *Protect your cousin,* he seems to say, and though I don't know what I am supposed to protect her from, I climb out of bed and begin dressing.

"What are you doing?" Esty says.

"I'm coming along."

"This has nothing to do with you, Rebecca."

"I was with you when you found the book," I say.

Esty looks down at the brown paper bag in her hands. Her face, framed by the black scarf, is dark and serious. Finally she speaks. "You can come," she says. "But there's one condition."

"What condition?"

"If we get caught, you have to take the blame. You have to take the blame for everything."

"But that's not fair."

"That's the way it is," she says. "You decide."

We sit for a moment in the silence of our room. The curtains rise and fall at the window, beckoning us both into the night. "All right," I say.

"Get dressed, then," my cousin says. "We're already late."

I finish dressing. My cousin slides the bedroom window as far open as it will go, and we crawl out silently into the side yard. We creep through the grass and out to the road, where no cars pass at this time of night. When I look back, the house is pale and small. I imagine Bluma Sarah hovering somewhere above the roof, keeping watch, marking our progress toward the lake.

We walk in the long grass at the side of the road, keeping out of the yellow pools of light that spill from the street lamps. In the grass there are rustlings, chatterings, sounds that make me pull my skirt around my legs and keep close to my cousin. We do not talk. The moon is bright overhead. The few houses we pass yield no sign of life. Tree frogs call in the dark, the rubber-band twang of their throats sounding to me like *God, God, God.* The road we walk is the same road we traversed on Friday afternoon, our bicycles heavy with Shabbos groceries. I can almost see the ghosts of us passing in the other direction, our faces luminous with the secret of the book, our clothes heavy and damp with lake water. Now we are different girls, it seems to me, carrying a different kind of weight.

By the time we emerge into the Perelmans' backyard, our skirts are wet with dew. Our sneakers squelch as we tiptoe toward the screen porch. We pause in a stand of bushes, listening for Dovid Frankel, hearing nothing.

We wait. The hands on my cousin's watch read twelve-fifty-five. The lake lies quiet against the shore like a sleeping animal, and the shadows of bats move across the white arc of the moon. At one o'clock we hear someone coming. We both suck in our breath, grab each other's arms. We see the shadow of Dovid Frankel moving across the dew-silvered lawn. We wait until he comes up, breathing hard, and sits down on the porch steps. Then we come out of the bushes.

Dovid jumps to his feet when he sees us. "Who's that?" he says.

"It's okay," my cousin whispers. "It's just us. Esty and Rebecca."

"Quiet," Dovid says. "Follow me."

We follow him up the steps and enter the moonlit darkness of the screen porch. For a long moment, no one says anything. It is utterly silent. All three of us seem to be holding our breath. Dovid looks at my cousin, then at me. "Where's my book?" he says.

Esty takes the brown paper bag from under her arm. She slides out *Essence of Persimmon.*

Dovid lets out a long sigh. "You didn't tell anyone, did you?"

"Are you kidding?" Esty says.

Dovid reaches for the book, but Esty holds it away from him.

"It's a sin," she says. "Looking at pictures like these. You know you're not supposed to do anything that would make you . . . that would give you . . ."

"That would make you what?" Dovid says.

"I mean, look at these people," she says, stepping into a shaft of moonlight and opening the book. She takes Dovid's flashlight and shines it on a drawing of two lovers intertwined on an open veranda, watching tigers wrestle in the tiled courtyard. She stares at the drawing as if she could will herself into the scene, touch the lovers' garments, their skin, the tiles of the courtyard, the tigers' pelts.

"There are laws," my cousin says. "You can't just do it on a porch, with tigers there. You can't do it in a garden."

"I know," Dovid says.

"I'm serious," Esty says. She moves closer to Dovid. "There are rules for us. We have to be holy. We can't act like animals." She looks up at him, so close their foreheads are almost touching. "We can't have books like this."

"What do you want me to do?" he says. "What am I supposed to do?"

My cousin rises onto her toes, and then she's kissing Dovid Frankel, and he looks startled but he doesn't pull away. The book falls from her hand. Quietly I pick it up, and I open the screen door and step out into the Perelmans' backyard. I walk through the long grass to the edge of the water and take off my shoes and socks. The water is warmer than the air, its surface still. I take one step into the lake, then another. I am all alone. I pull off my long-sleeved shirt and feel the night air on my bare skin. Then I step out of my skirt. I throw my clothes onto the shore, onto the grass. Still holding the book, I walk into the water and feel it on all parts of my body, warm, like a mouth, taking me gently in. When the sandy bottom drops away I float on my back, looking up at the spray of stars, at the dense gauze of the Milky Way. The moon spreads its thin white sheet across my limbs. In my hand the book is heavy with water, and I let it fall away toward the bottom.

MICHAEL PATERNITI

■

# The Fifteen-Year Layover

FROM *GQ*

MANCHESTER AND LONDON were delayed on account of weather, and Tel Aviv was a faulty wing flap. Tenerife, Johannesburg, Málaga, and Marrakesh had been canceled for various reasons, and stragglers from those flights were trying to figure out their next move on this humid night at the end of May. Some were arguing with the airlines; some were studying the ever-shuffling flight board; some were headed off to nearby hotels, parched and ready for cold gin and tonics to ease the dull throb of their long day. A few scanned the terminal mournfully, searching for the right bench or piece of floor to camp for the night. Later it would make a good story: the purgatorial night spent in Terminal One at Charles de Gaulle Airport.

Meanwhile, the flight to Libreville, which was to leave in two hours, had brought a raucous horde to the Air Gabon counter, the women dressed in colorful gowns, a cacophony of clipped tribal dialects punching holes in the fabric of the terminal's white noise. The group, maybe two hundred in all, had materialized suddenly, as if by incantation, and would just as quickly vanish in the night, in the silver gut of a 747 roaring southward over desert and veld for home. Like everyone in this place, they were apparitions, part of the incessant tide that rushed, then ebbed, that filled and emptied, filled and emptied — at moments leaving the airport a lonely beachhead, one that bore no trace of those who had just been there.

As the hour grew late, the terminal took on a nocturnal malevo-
lence. To be inside this place was not unlike being inside the belly
of a dying thing. Upon its completion in 1974, Terminal One had
been hailed as a triumph, an architectural breakthrough built by
Paul Andreu, who had proclaimed that he wanted the airport "to
project the image of Paris and France as one of equality, and prow-
ess in engineering and commerce." It appeared as a gray dough-
nut-shaped flying saucer — outer space brought to earth — with a
burbling fountain at its open-air center. But over the years the
fountain had fallen into disrepair and the water was shut off, revealing, behind its vapory skeins, a wreckage of rusted pipes and a
cement shed, the inevitable artifacts of the future disintegrating,
then becoming the past.

The whole world passed through this place, on the way to Paris,
or from Paris, or simply using Paris to leapfrog to the next time
zone. Disembodied voices called passengers to their gates, where
they were delivered heavenward. Soccer teams and school bands
tromped through, as did groups of old people wearing the same T-
shirts or church groups wearing the same baseball caps. They sat
reading or photographing each other. They went for coffee or
hamburgers. They wheeled by in wheelchairs. And then they were
gone.

The longer you hung around in Terminal One, the more mun-
dane everything became. Had a herd of red oxen been unloaded
from Jerba and wandered out of customs, it would not have been
such a surprise. Had a planeload of mimes come from Nurem-
berg, they would have registered only as part of the passing circus,
hardly remembered afterward. In this context, a great deal made
more sense here than elsewhere, including perhaps Sir Alfred.

A friend told me about Alfred a few years ago, having heard of him
on the Internet. Initially, she believed him to be a work of fiction:
the man who had waited at Charles de Gaulle Airport for fifteen
years, on the longest layover in history. But then, the man was real.
It was said he could be found near the Paris Bye Bye bar. He'd be
bald on top, with frizzes of wild hair on the sides and four teeth
missing, smoking a gold pipe, writing in his journal or listening to

the radio. It was said, too, that it really didn't matter what time of day or night or which day of the week one visited, for Alfred was always there — and had been since 1988.

The truth was that no one knew the whole truth about Alfred, not even Alfred himself. He was born in either 1945 or 1947 or 1953 and claimed to be Iranian, British, or Swedish. In some ways, it was as if he'd been found in the bulrushes — or was still lost there. For years now, he'd lived mostly on the kindness of strangers, eating his meals at a nearby McDonald's, wandering the terminal's white tile floor as if it were his own cathedral. Mostly, he passed time on the terminal's first level, in gurulike meditation, on a red bench before a big, filmy plate-glass window near a shop selling CDs. He sat in a tight envelope of air that smelled faintly of regurgitation.

Alfred's odyssey had begun when he was a young man from a well-to-do family living in Iran and had ended here on an airport bench in Paris, by mistake. Twenty years ago, while living in Belgium, he'd simply wanted to go to England by boat. But having rid himself of his identification papers during the voyage, he'd fallen into a twilight limbo as a nationless, unidentifiable person no one wanted, bounced from Belgium to England to France, where, finally, he'd been left stranded at Charles de Gaulle Airport. And lived there ever since.

My first visit to Alfred came on the night of the Air Gabon flight to Libreville. I was staying for a time in Paris during a two-month stretch of intense travel. Adding it up, I'd spent nights in no less than fifteen different hotels, making me the frenetic opposite of Alfred. For me, the sheer speed of life had begun to strip it of its meaning. I imagined him to be some sort of mystic, sitting still on his Himalayan mountaintop, the keeper of monastic truths.

It was late, and the airport was empty and gave an air of exhaustion, of an animal too tired to resist the thing crawling up its leg. Going down a flight of stairs from the second level to the first, I nearly bowled over a young, tan flight attendant in a powder blue hat, who seemed in a hurry to get upstairs. After her, there was no one but Alfred.

If all the dramas of farewell and hello unfolded on the floors above, Level One was a kind of wasteland. What shops there were — a good number had closed in the past years — were shut up for the night. I walked quickly, following the circle of the terminal itself. Where the exterior of the building was gray cement, its doughnut-hole interior was all glass, so that you could look up and see three floors above you. On the second floor were the airline counters as well as six preliminary boarding gates that led to moving sidewalks, called electric tubes, that crisscrossed in the air, carrying travelers up through the open center of the terminal to the third floor, to more gates, called satellites, from which passengers disembarked for their flights. On the fourth level were the customs hall and arrival areas. I could see the electric tubes crisscrossing over my head, and in various windows all the way to the fourth floor, flashbulbs fired as travelers collected final photographic souvenirs of friends or family frozen in time.

And then there he was, laid out like a body in a sarcophagus, a snoring heap of human on a red bench, surrounded by a fortress of possessions. I counted several suitcases, six Lufthansa luggage boxes, two big FedEx containers — his life's possessions. There were clothes hangers and a collection of plastic beverage lids. On the table before him was a pile of McDonald's coupons. He was gaunt and angular. His skin was the sallow, almost purplish color of the white fluorescent light, except for the dark rings under his closed eyes. His sideburns and mustache were graying. The nail of his left pinkie was long and sharp, but the rest were neatly clipped. And despite the heat, he slept in a blue Izod windbreaker beneath a light airline blanket, a gift, it appeared, from a sympathetic flight attendant.

I made a lap, returned, and he remained absolutely still. The third time, believing he was really out, lost in some Giza of a dream, I paused before him, and as soon as I did, his eyes flipped open. He bore no expression, but then his face twisted as if he were in great pain or perhaps about to lash out; and yet before he could, before some unholy utterance came from his body, his lids fluttered shut and he fell back to sleep — back, it seemed, to his own mysterious crater in an obliterated landscape.

\*

Once upon a time, before facts were eroded by dreams, before the man destroyed and recreated himself, he had been a boy named Merhan Karimi Nasseri, happily living with five siblings in the oil-rich south of Iran. His father, a doctor, worked for the Anglo-Iranian Oil Company, while his mother assumed the duties of the household. By the standards of their country, they were rich and thriving in an area of Iran that was rich and thriving.

Merhan went to school, then college, where he took a psychology degree. But then, when he was twenty-three, his father died of cancer. While he grieved, his mother notified him that she was not his real mother, that he was, in fact, the bastard son of an affair between his father and a Scottish woman, perhaps from Glasgow, who had worked as a nurse for the Anglo-Iranian Oil Company. In order to protect her husband, who would have been sentenced to death by stoning for adultery, she had pretended the boy was hers. Now, in one blow, she sought to undo a life of lies. She banished him from the family. Merhan was still only a young man, smart and able, with a promising future. He was a person in forward motion who, until that moment, had known exactly who he was and where he was going.

Merhan argued with his mother, claiming that she *had* to be his mother. Wrapped into this argument may have been his father's estate and the inheritance he felt was due him. Merhan threatened to take his mother to court, and her rebuttal was simple: With whose money? In the end, they worked out an agreement. Merhan would leave Iran to study abroad in England, where he would receive a monthly stipend.

In Bradford, England, he enrolled in a Yugoslav studies program for three years, until one day, without warning, his stipend ceased. He tried to reach his family in Iran, calling and writing but receiving no answer. After some months, he flew to Tehran, where he was detained, arrested, and imprisoned. He was informed that Iranian agents in England had photographed him marching in a protest against the shah, which made him a traitor. It was the first of what would be three prison stays.

When his mother, now not his mother, found out about his incarceration, she paid the proper bribes to the proper authorities to secure his release, but again with a stipulation: He would be given an immigration passport, allowing him to leave Iran, never to return. Which is just what he did. Though he needed another country that would receive him, one that would grant him refugee status, his eventual plan was to travel to Glasgow in hopes of finding his supposed birth mother, who he believed lived there under some variation of the name Simon.

So he left. It's not known or remembered what ran through his mind as he boarded the plane that took him from Tehran to London, leaving his homeland and family behind. It's impossible to know if he'd been struck so hard by these events that he'd already lapsed into amnesia, if he felt betrayed and reeling in space.

Over the next several years, starting with England, Merhan appealed to at least seven countries for asylum, until Belgium granted him refugee status in October 1981. He settled in Brussels, working in a library, studying, receiving social aid. After saving some money, he approached the British Consulate to make sure he could visit Glasgow with his papers and was told there would be no problem. He purchased a ticket to England by boat, and once aboard, believing that he now occupied British soil because he was standing on the deck of a British ship, he placed his papers in an envelope and in a mailbox on board the ship, dispensing with them, sending them back to the Brussels office for the UN High Commission of Refugees.

This, of course, was an act of self-perdition that can't be explained and that immediately became the genesis of Merhan's woes. When he arrived in England and could show no papers proving his identity, he was sent back to Belgium, where, in turn, he was returned to England. To be rid of him once and for all, and playing a game of transnational hot potato with his fate, England then randomly sent him by boat to Boulogne, France, where he was arrested and sentenced and served four months in prison for trying to enter the country illegally. After his release, he was given eighty-four hours to leave France and went to Charles de Gaulle Airport to see if by *flying* to England he might have better luck.

He didn't. Arriving in London, he was detained and returned to France, where, out of money and ideas, he settled into life at Terminal One. At first, he was simply one of those stranded travelers, waylaid for a night on his way elsewhere — then another night, and another. Since it was his belief that buying another ticket was the fine line between being a prisoner and a free man, he began asking fellow travelers for assistance. After two years, he again went up the electric tube to the satellite, again he boarded the plane, again he landed in London, and again he was expelled.

Returning to Charles de Gaulle, he was arrested once more for illegally entering the country and sentenced to six months in prison. After his release in 1988, he returned to Terminal One, perhaps out of sheer habit, packed and ready but with nowhere to go.

So much had happened since his arrival, if not to him then to the world at large. Reagan. Thatcher and Mitterand had given way to Bush II. Blair and Chirac. Communism had fallen: Rabin assassinated. Manhattan attacked. As the years passed — through war and famine, AIDS and SARS — he sat near the Paris Bye Bye bar, gleaning bits from the radio, occasionally watching the television set that hung in one of the restaurants. He renamed himself Sir Alfred. He was motherless, fatherless, homeless, moneyless, sitting still in a place where humanity moved frantically. Alongside a river of tinkling cell phones and half-drunk coffees hastily disposed of, he chose to live his life — most of which was packed into Lufthansa boxes. He now insisted that he'd been born in Sweden and renounced all connections to Iran. He refused to speak Farsi. He refused to answer to his original name at all, even when his freedom was at stake.

For seven years, Alfred's lawyer, a bearded public advocate named Christian Bourguet, tried tracking down Alfred's identification papers in Brussels, the ones Alfred had mailed from the boat. Once he had those in hand, he in turn was able to procure from the French government a visa and a *titre de voyage,* a kind of passport that would have finally allowed Alfred to go to England. But when Alfred saw that the documents were issued for the Iranian national Merhan Karimi Nasseri, he became churlish, refusing to sign.

"Belong to someone else," he said in his Farsi-accented English, and so sealed his fate. On the temporary identification papers he held, both parents were simply marked by an X.

"I am an X, too," he said.

After watching him sleep, I went to see Alfred again the following day, about midmorning. The sun beamed in bright forms through the windows that looked out on the wrecked fountain and lit the shadowy corners. The first level was bustling with Monday travelers and, for a moment, seemed much less sinister, much more like your standard sterile airport, with bodies ebbing and flowing in streams past Alfred's table or up the electric tubes to the satellites. For his part, Alfred was pleased to have a visitor, probably would have been pleased to meet anyone who stepped out of the moving crowd long enough to say hello. He cleared a small table in front of him and commandeered a nearby chair. For a man who'd made a life of sitting still, he looked relatively fit, with strong-seeming arms.

When he spoke, however, his voice was weak, and he claimed he hadn't uttered a word in two months. Mumbling more to himself than to me, his words swam three quarters of the way across the table, then back again. Occasionally, a cluster reached my ear. Everything he said cloverleafed back into his "case," though it was nearly impossible to determine what that case was — after all, his lawyer had solved his immediate dilemma by securing the papers that set him free. He vehemently claimed that Merhan Karimi Nasseri was free to go but that Sir Alfred wasn't. Soon I came to regard any mention of his "case" as shorthand for everything he had forgotten or chosen to forget, as code for a mysterious process of healing that called for the complete exorcism of the past.

He said he believed his real mother was still alive in Glasgow and that he would find her. "I hope not to be here by Christmas," he said with the pained smile and resignation of a man who'd most certainly be here by Christmas or who was simply talking about some Christmas in the far future, after a nuclear winter.

When I asked if, after fifteen years of this isolation, he felt he'd be lost in the world if he left the airport today, he said in his clipped English, "No, why? Same world." When I insisted that, if anything, these past fifteen years had in some ways drastically altered our daily existence — citing the rise of computers, cell phones, and the nearly instantaneous changes in everything from food to fashion — he said, "Not worried."

After about a half-hour of this kind of chat, his excitement began to peter out into that preordained moment, one that would repeat itself again and again, when, as I still sat across from him, he would simply raise a newspaper between us, as if letting down a curtain, and begin reading. So this was goodbye? To let him gently off the hook, I announced that I was going to stretch my legs, and was answered by a single rustle of the paper. Then I walked a bit, figuring it probably didn't matter when I returned to him, as his sense of time must have been more like that of an animal who moves slowly, gauging the day by light and dark, or months by the weather.

On another evening, I asked how he'd spent his day, and he said he'd listened to the radio for five minutes and had brushed his teeth. That was all he'd managed in fourteen hours. He sat in a dull torpor, occasionally rubbing his head or working his jaw muscles, that blank stare taking in everything and nothing at once. Travelers streamed past, sometimes stealing a glance at him and his fortress. "People pass me by but don't touch," he said cryptically. When I asked what he'd learned about human nature here, in a place so transparently full of emotion, he said, "Everyone has their own function. They are mostly indifferent." When I pressed him about what function he served, he said, "I am sitting here, waiting."

At first I was intrigued by the mere logistics of a life spent waiting. No matter how little one accomplished in a day, Sir Alfred had accomplished less. His life rode no discernible narrative arc, and he had seemingly embraced the absurdity at the center of existence to the point where his sitting in place seemed like a political protest, seemed so meaningless it had to have meaning.

Yet Alfred had a few self-made purposes: waking, shaving, protecting his nest. He rose between six-thirty and eight in the morning. He would yawn, stretch, and sometimes pull out a hand mirror, check himself, and maybe shave with an electric razor, right there on his bench. He didn't limit himself to shaving in the morning, though. He shaved after lunch or before bed; he shaved in midconversation or while spooning a McDonald's sundae, a McFlurry, into his mouth.

He had his choice of two nearby bathrooms; he preferred the smaller and quieter of the two because it was closer to his bench and had a shower. Even though his belongings blocked the red bench from intruders — and he used a table and chair effectively to provide reinforcement — he still sometimes had to shoo people away, tired passengers looking to recline and, finding no comfort in the metal benches that had replaced the plush red ones three years before (all except Alfred's), mistakenly chose to brush aside his mess and sit or lie down, at which point Alfred appeared like an offended rooster, bristling and crowing and kicking up dust. "Okay, my place," he said. "Out now, thank you."

On occasion, there were other things that organized his waking hours. Someone had recently given him a carton of Thai cigarettes, for instance, and every day he gave me a progress report on how many he had smoked and how many were left. He said he normally smoked only a few a day, though a rough count over one afternoon suggested he smoked a few more than that. There were times when lighting up must have constituted his day's greatest exertion.

Sometimes he made a trip to the bank upstairs, where he had his savings account. While he was gone, a shopkeeper would guard his belongings, though a number of his bags were merely stuffed with newspapers, some with articles related to his case. Still, he'd recently lost a collection, most valuable to him, of *Time* magazines, so there was an ongoing need to be vigilant. Stung by the loss, he told me he now limited his wandering. Even though the first level of Terminal One didn't seem to have air conditioning and it was now sweltering, he hadn't stepped outdoors to get a breath of fresh air in a month.

"I dream sometimes of going through the window and reaching the sky," he said.

With an unimaginable amount of time on his hands — growing old, alone, and having to look only to himself for the answers to life's mysteries — Alfred created his own mythologies, a basic religious impulse. But Alfred's view of the world had more to do with how McDonald's had siphoned money from him when France converted from francs to euros in 2002, or how the French postal service conspired to no longer deliver mail to him from all over Europe — some of it containing money — sent by people who believed he was a symbol: of courage, of bureaucratic bungling, of soulless modern life swallowing us whole, of our human existential dilemma writ large.

When a noticeable growth appeared on his head a few years ago, he blamed it on "coffee and fake cola products." He showed me a photograph of his head from 1999 with the incontrovertible proof of a large, unsavory bump, "just there, jellifying," he said. The airport doctor, a short, busy man with bad teeth whose office was less than fifty yards from where Alfred sat, had watched it grow. Finally, he intervened, taking Alfred from the airport — one of the few times he'd ever left — to a nearby hospital, where the growth was removed. Yet in Alfred's retelling of the incident, he had performed the operation himself, in the bathroom, as a kind of medieval bloodletting.

In fact, the longer he sat there, the less Alfred seemed to remember, or the more fantasy merged with the few events of his life, casting out all other bit characters. Rejected by humanity, he now rejected humanity. The outside world was simply extraneous. His mind was panes of stained glass, rearranged in some self-satisfyingly inscrutable design.

When asked what he could recall of his boyhood in Iran, he could conjure only three distinct memories:

1) He had lived in a stone house.
2) He had been held down in a chair and stabbed repeatedly by ac-

tors in a theater, who had tired of him shouting out their lines
when they forgot, though that had allegedly been his job.
3) He had nearly died in a car accident that never took place.

When pressed to fill in the details, he would only add, "A house
like those in England" or "You have to ask them why they stab and
stab" or "I jump and run."

When I asked to see his collection of photographs, thinking
they might catalyze his memory, most turned out to be of inanimate objects in the terminal: the revolving door in a wild snow-
storm; an abandoned suitcase the bomb squad had exploded, leaving confettied paper everywhere; a counter in one of the nearby
shops that had been dusted for fingerprints after a break-in. The
rest of the photos were of him, either standing solo, staring
straight into the lens, or posing with various passersby, none of
whom he seemed to remember.

When I pressed him to identify someone, anyone, that he spoke
to in the airport, anyone with whom he had a human connection,
he claimed to have known one of the employees at McDonald's for
four years. When I asked his name, Alfred said, "I have no idea."

It's possible that the most religious moments occur in airports
rather than in churches. This is not blasphemy but a fact of modern life. Apprehension, longing, and the fear of complete disinte-
gration — what palpably animates an airport full of passengers
about to take to heaven at the speed of sound — are what drive us
to our gods.

Over the course of a few weeks, I looked forward to seeing Alfred for perhaps no other reason than he seemed glad to see me
too. In some ways, I came to see his dilemma as a question of
faith. After so many betrayals, he feared the world beyond his red
bench. The red bench was his hovel, home, and haven — and yet
occasionally he made the motions of wanting to break free. One
day, for instance, I found him checking the classified ads in the paper, declaring that he was looking to buy a car. Perhaps it empowered him to say so, but it seemed impossible: Sir Alfred behind the

wheel, on his way to Who-Knew-Where. As he squinted at the classifieds, I was struck by the poignancy of his circumstance, the strength — if delusion — of his hope, an abnormal man living out of time, attempting to take on the mantle of a normal life.

I asked if he was angry about having lost fifteen years of his life in this black hole at Terminal One. "No angry," he said. "I just want to know who my parents are." Are you happy, then? I asked. "I used to be," he said, "but now I'm stuck between heaven and hell." When I asked if he believed in God, he nodded his head as if he were drawing the letter *U* with his nose; that was neither yes nor no. "Believe in soul," he said. "Your soul is not separate from your function, but it is also more. Your soul is your dream, your dream life, your dream world, and it walks around with you, wherever you go."

Then he gestured to his kingdom of stuff, his bags packed with newspapers and magazines, with his meager clothing and pictures of exploded suitcases, with endless pages from his journals relating the day's radio news. "Nothing has changed for me except I have more baggage," he said. He leaned back and rubbed his head, where the bump had once been, with a kind of superstitious care. "But I'm prepared," he said. "Other people stay in this place for a couple of hours. They arrive and go to cars that are waiting, or buses. They come and go up the electric tubes to the satellites. When it's my turn, when I am called, I'm ready to go to the satellite."

Eventually, I paid a visit to his lawyer, Christian Bourguet. During the reign of the Ayatollah Khomeini, Bourguet had been Iran's lawyer, had been the man who arranged the ayatollah's Air France ticket from exile back to Tehran in 1979 and had secretly negotiated with the Carter administration for an end to the hostage crisis, an end he said should have come about nine months before it did. On the wall was evidence of Bourguet's work during that time: a couple of framed personal letters from Jimmy Carter.

He told me that, when he'd first met Alfred, the man had been quite lucid in the telling of his story, but that over time he had become "free of logic," and so his story kept changing. After Alfred suddenly asserted he was Swedish, Bourguet asked how he then had traveled from Sweden to Iran. "Submarine," Alfred said. Perhaps he was crazy now, but, Bourguet argued, he'd arrived there by several steps. "Assume that you are twenty-three," he said, working a piece of clay in his fingers while chomping on the stem of his pipe. "You've finished your studies in psychology, your father dies, and at that exact moment, your mother says, 'I'm not your mother.' You have brothers and sisters, but not anymore. And because you are illegitimate, you are a nobody in your country. You have no rights. And so you ask, 'Who is my mother, then?' You leave your country, only to return to be imprisoned, and then leave with nowhere to go, whereupon you are imprisoned again — and then once more.

"In your mind, you have renounced this person and this name that was formerly you, but when, years later, you go to get what you think is your freedom, the papers identify you as that person. How strong does a man have to be to resist so many big shocks?"

But then, I wondered aloud, why not simply sign the documents and afterward legally change his name? "Let me tell you something," said the lawyer, rocking back in his chair, a ball of flame from his lighter disappearing into a nest of newly packed tobacco. "He's not leaving the airport. He's no one outside the airport. He's become a star there. Or he feels like a star — and acts like one. If you come with a camera, he knows his best side. Otherwise, his personality has broken into pieces."

He sucked deeply on the pipe, placed the clay on his desk, and looked up, shaking his head in pity. "I'm afraid the sad fact is that he's now completely destroyed."

The last time I went to see Alfred, it was evening, and a storm had blown over Paris, the wind moving the leaves like so many small fluttering wings, lights falling in slick, watery dabs over pavement, over the Seine itself. Cool air came rushing to replace the humid day, but when I entered the terminal, the ghost of that hot day was still trapped inside. I proceeded with my routine, making laps on the floors above before seeing Alfred. I stood for over an hour in arrivals near an expectant group waiting for a delayed flight from New York City. I meant to leave after five minutes, but with each passing second I found myself further embroiled in the small dramas of each party — the little girl with a sign that read YOU ARE HOME, PAPA; the three hippie amigos badly playing guitar and bongos to everyone's annoyance; the woman, so prettily dressed in white, who already couldn't hold back tears.

Later I found Alfred sitting on his red bench, shaving. Behind him, through the plate-glass window, lay the wreckage of rusted pipes, a reminder that at one time something spectacular had occurred out there. It was late and empty again. The white tile floor seemed to sweat; the scent of regurgitation hung in the air; and here was my guru, my holy man, my ayatollah, opening and closing his mouth, exercising his jaw muscle. Then he started to speak. "I don't smoke for three days," he said somewhat bitterly. That was it. That was all he could muster.

If anything, with each day Alfred was becoming another inanimate object in this airport, devoid of memories. Soon, I imagined, he would forget the stone house or being stabbed or the car crash that had never taken place. He would forget that there'd ever been a guy at McDonald's whom he once remotely knew or maybe even the exact reason that he still sat here.

Shortly, his newspaper came up between us and rustled once. Goodbye. People washed past on their way upstairs for flights to Hamburg, Dublin, Oslo. Instead of leaving him entirely, I walked over to the bar, bought a beer, and settled in a window a third of the way around the circle. I drank my beer and then another. From where I sat I could look up into the windows on each floor of Terminal One. I could see through twenty-four different windows, and in each of them, twenty-four different scenes played out: people saying goodbye, sobbing, laughing, lost in meditation, confused, in transit. To have heard their thoughts would have been to let loose all the joys and woes of the world.

Across the way, Alfred readied himself for bed, then lay down and, despite the heat, pulled his thin blanket over his body. After twenty minutes or so, he seemed as if he were in a dream: His legs rose up and his knees lightly bumped each other; then his legs went down again. He was someone out of an epic or a fairy tale, someone shipwrecked or lost or trapped forever in an unsolvable nightmare. And yet, stripped of everything, he was his own god.

Above, the electric tubes were lit brightly in the night, and from the vantage of the basement you could see the crowns of people's heads reflecting off the glass ceiling of the tubes as they were lifted toward the satellites. If you sat long enough, looking down on the crowns of their heads, you could have imagined yourself an angel. And it occurred to me that if you sat long enough thinking such dangerous thoughts, you might never leave, too.

PAULA W. PETERSON

■

# Big Brother

FROM *Iowa Review*

MY MAN EUGENE been dead about a year and a half by now and soon this Big Brother gonna come along. I say last thing I want around here is another man, I'm finished with men forever, and it be a cold day in hell before I take up with one again, but the social worker say Terrence suffering for lack of some male companionship. Although, shoot, when his daddy was alive he didn't have hardly no more male companionship than he have now, and I don't see what difference it going to make in his life.

I be glad enough if everybody leave us alone, male or not. That seem to be all I ask for these days, just some peace and quiet. But it true that Terrence sure be acting funny. The other day he was playing around in the cabinet by the TV and he shout, "Where all my videos! They some missing! Momma, you been loaning out my videos to people?" "Get a hold of yo'self, I ain't been loaning out your videos to nobody." "Yes you have," he say. "You giving away my things." And on and on he go in his booming voice until I sit down with him and we name off all the videos he has one by one and match 'em up with the videos in the cabinet and even then it hard to convince him that no one's messing with his stuff.

Most evenings he too wound up to fall asleep, so he come crawl on the couch with me while I watch the news. Terrence built round and solid, he big for eight year old, with a head shaped like a torpedo packed with stubbornness. He take up too much room on the couch, he be poking me, and grabbing the blanket offa me and trying to shove away my legs. Asking questions. "Momma, what that lady kill her five kids for?" or "Where that girl in Washington disappear to?" or "What country that? Israel? Why they screaming and throwing rocks at each other, huh?" I don't pay no attention to the TV no more, I just like to have it on 'cause it keep me from thinking too much. I be dropping off, snoring with my head on my arm, and still he bouncing up and down on my butt, flicking the remote every time a commercial come on. I don't get no relief. Just when I fall asleep, he shake my shoulder, hard, and put his big old face right in mine until I wake up and the first thing I see is his eyes, big and brown with those long trembling lashes and he spluttering, "Momma! Momma! I think yo' skin is getting *blacker*. I been watching you and I think it getting darker while you sleeping. Wake up!" The medications I take are changing the pigment in my skin, ain't nothing I can do about it, and it true, sometimes when I look in the mirror I think, damn, it look like I been rubbing coal on my face. Terrence worried his momma gonna turn so black she gonna disappear. So he got to keep me conscious at all times to make sure all that blackness don't swallow me up.

That child wear me out. He a lot like his daddy Eugene, he got a way of draining you with all his needs. Shit, ain't it my turn to rest now, I think, ain't I been through enough already? But I know Terrence need more and I can't bring him out of this craziness on my own. Terrence need fresh air and fresh eyes too to look around with. And that another reason why I say, okay, bring that Big Brother on. Terrence all excited. He picturing someone in his mind like Michael Jordan or Magic Johnson. Someone all muscled that can do something you wouldn't believe with a ball.

But Big Brother ain't big and he sure ain't no brother. When I see him I think, uh oh, what they sending me here. One of them rich white dudes trying to pretend like they's poor. His family got some cream. You can just tell. Big Brother skinny, wearing nasty ripped jeans falling off his butt, but he got on one expensive pair of Nike sneakers that give him away. But after a second I reconsider about the pretending part. The truth is, he don't give a shit about what he wearing on his feet. He too sad for that. Be sad from top to toe, everything on that boy just *drooping*, even that thin blond mustache he got just hanging off his lip, make me want to rip it off. This boy in some kind of trouble, I think. Ain't no way this gonna work out, and I feel sorry for Terrence, getting his hopes up. Big Brother done lost his *bounce*. And he too young for that. I bet he no more than twenty year old. Not even that.

First thing Big Brother do when he step in my apartment is look at my chest and blush. I'm not so fine, but I got me some curves and it hot so I wearing a halter top and no bra underneath. I fold my arms over my chest.

"Hi, I'm Keith," he say, blushing. He hold out his hand to shake and when I take it the palm is wet.

"I'm Nickie, and this my boy Terrence."

"Hey, man, give me five."

So Terrence slap him good and Big Brother reel back and say, "Whoa!" and he rub his hand over his jeans and I know his hand is really smarting and that he ain't pretending at all, he ain't putting on a show just to make Terrence giggle. Terrence be strong, and Big Brother look like he put together with putty.

"What that say on your shirt?" Terrence ask.

Big Brother scrunch his chin down to look at his chest, like he forgot what he put on that morning. When he speak his eyes go back and forth. "This? This says Tanglewood Music Festival. That's a . . . well, this kind of summer camp for musicians . . . back east . . . I mean, they take classes and all, classical musicians."

"You a musician?" Terrence say, hopefully.

"Oh . . . ah . . . I used to play the piano . . . but that was a long time ago. Like in another kind of life."

"How come you don't play no more?" Terrence demand.

"I just gave it up, that's all. It didn't, you know, it didn't have the same kind of meaning, like, that it used to have for me. And I, ah, don't even have a piano to practice on anymore."

"You gonna play again someday?" That Terrence, he don't know when to stop.

"Maybe," say Big Brother. He look sad. "I don't know." He think and say, "Probably not."

Terrence just stare at him and I say, "Terrence, quit your nosiness," and Big Brother put up his hand and shake his head and say, "No, no, that's okay, it's good to be curious. Hey, Terrence, man, show me your room, okay? I bet you got a great room."

So Terrence take Big Brother to his room and he introduce him to all his Star Wars fighter jets and his whole collection of Yu-Gi-Oh cards and there the two of them are sitting on the rug cross-legged and Big Brother squinting at the cards, trying to read what is printed on them and Terrence yelling out the rules to the game, all excited. In the middle of playing Terrence run to me and say, "Hey, Momma, I like the big brother!" and then he run back. He so eager to have a new friend.

But there are some things I need to get straight with Big Brother right away, so I interrupt them while Big Brother leaning over the game board (his shirt pull up and I can see his bony spine and part of some striped underwear sticking over the top of his jeans) and I say, "Excuse me, Keith, could I have a word with you?" and he say, "Yes, ma'am," and follow me to the kitchen, shuffling and hunching his shoulders.

"Now I know you know I'm HIV 'cause this HIV housing," I say to him. "But I want you to know that my boy Terrence ain't HIV, in case you was wondering. And he don't know nothing about it, neither, so I'd appreciate it if you didn't talk about that with him."

Big Brother move back against the counter, put up his hands. "That's cool."

Then he clear his throat and say, "Terrence seems like a great kid. I think we're gonna get along."

I don't trust nobody who compliment kids too fast; also, I don't want Big Brother thinking he gonna have an easy time here. So I say, "Terrence stubborn. He stubborn and he willful. He a lot like his daddy. He never pay attention to what people say. If he don't do what you tell him, you come talk to me about it."

"Well . . ." Big Brother say. And there go his eyes, right down to my chest again.

"How old you be?" I say all of a sudden.

"Nineteen." He blush.

"Umm-hmm."

"And how about you, Nickie?"

"Me? Thirty-one."

"Thirty-one." He cough a bit. "That's a great age. I'd like to be, ah, in my thirties, 'cause that's when you have it all together, you know what I mean? I mean, you're still young and all that but then you've done some of your soul-work and you're, ah, a lot more self-aware. I like hanging out with people in their thirties. I find it, like, enriching."

This guy crazy, I think. What I bring him in my house for?

"Okay, cool," he say. "I'm glad we had this talk."

After that Big Brother come once a week, and sometimes he take Terrence places like the zoo and the beach and the Exploratorium and the big playground in Golden Gate Park with the long slides Terrence like so much. Terrence bragging about him to all his school friends, I know it. Minute he get on that school bus in the morning he just busting with all the stuff he got saved up to tell, and it don't matter who he tell it to, he collar the first kid he sit next to on the bus and pin him down till the ride is over, saying, "You know what me and my Big Brother done yesterday?" He so happy he leaping on Big Brother and strangling him and wrapping himself all over his body. Once I see him riding on Big Brother's back and saying, "Giddyup! Giddyup!" and I worry he gonna break that poor boy, so I shout, "Terrence! Now you let up on Keith, you hear!" Keith say, "Oh, it's okay, Nickie, I don't mind," but I explain to him that Terrence got to work on his behavior and his listening skills and don't be interfering with me when I'm trying to discipline my child. Big Brother blink and look embarrassed.

And one time Big Brother bring over an electric keyboard he borrowed offa someone and teach Terrence how to play his scales. Then he play something for Terrence, something long and slow and soft. I listen in, standing in the hallway. Big Brother can see me, all right, but he don't let on. The music so pretty I have to hold my breath so I won't miss none. And sad. The sadness creep up on me little by little till I just standing there with my throat closed up with grief, tears ready to squeeze out.

When he finish, he look up at me quickly, to make sure I'm still there, and then he scratch his neck and blush a little and say, "That's Chopin, dude." And right then I know he really playing that music for me even though he appear to be playing it for Terrence. The thought don't make me so comfortable.

Terrence's jaw hanging open. "Man, how did you do that without looking at no music sheet?"

Big Brother a little proud of himself, and excited too. "I got that in my head. I remembered it. I *still* remember it, I didn't know that."

Then he sneak a glance at me just to see am I proud of him. I can't help thinking, Big Brother, do your momma know where you is? He want someone to put out cookies and milk for him, and remind him to wipe his behind twice. He looking at me hopefully, but I think to myself, hell, boy, don't you know that I ain't got nothing left over for nobody? That Eugene took it out of me. Took it all out, and then give me something I can't ever get rid of. Men is all children, it don't matter how old they are or how big they are, they all squirming to get back to that nice warm comfy place they come from. That the only time they feel safe. But what about us, I say? We making them safe but what they doing for us in the meantime? Unh-uhn. All that business ain't for Nickie no more.

But don't you know it, the minute you show them you ain't interested, that when they can't leave you alone. One week Big Brother show up too early. He know that Terrence don't come home from school for another hour. He making up excuses, saying his watch be running too fast. Stand there with his ponytail and his blue eyes blinking, saying, well, uh, do you think I could come in for a little while, I don't have anywhere else to go at this particular time. So I open the door just a little wider and make a motion with my hand and say, "Well, it ain't no skin off my ass."

He sprawl on my couch with his legs spread far apart. You know the way men sit, taking up more room than they need. Tap on the armrest with his fingers, look around him, humming something soft. Today he wearing shorts and his legs is covered with long curly blond hair. Got some tattoo I never noticed before on his left calf, a seahorse or some kinda shit like that. I move back and forth picking up Terrence's toys and he follow me with his gaze; I can see he trying not to, but his eyeballs is sliding over my hips and my breasts and I can't get away, wouldn't matter if I went into another room, his eyes would burn a hole through the walls, and I be lost 'cause you know that young boy can even see me with his eyes closed, and when that happen, you finished, girl. I think to myself, why a woman built like this to make a man dream on her body. I mad at my titties and my pussy and all the rest of it.

I mad at *him*. I be tired and diseased and I ain't even good-looking no more. I got a right to be left alone. I think, why he messing with me, anyhow? He so hard up he got to make it with an HIV lady? Huh, dumb kid.

But it like he don't see how angry I am 'cause he got that goofy expression on his face when he stare at me, that moony look like he wandered in from outer space.

"Nickie, can I ask you a question?" he say finally.

I shrug. I be wearing my pout, the same one Terrence inherited from me.

"Are you afraid of dying?"

I just stare at him.

He hold out his hands and wave them a little in front of him. "Okay, okay, I know that's kind of personal, everyone's idea of, well, mortality and everything, but I just thought I'd ask because when I look at you, you seem to be so strong, I think of you as the kind of person who's made her peace with death. You just radiate an inner strength that way, you know what I mean? Like I know you're not up at three in the morning worrying whether if you're in a coma someone's going to mistake you for dead and bury you alive." That boy chuckle and rub his hand over the front of his shirt. His knees twitch. "Or what it's going to feel like, whether it's going to be all darkness and shit or whether you're going to be walking through some tunnel with a light on the other side. What's waiting for you there. When I see you, I see someone who's so beyond that. Fear. I met this American Indian guy once who had the same kind of attitude. With him it was really spiritual, you know? He took me to a sweat lodge with him — wow, what an incredible experience. You can learn so much about yourself that way. Sweating. It's like *everything* opens up, man."

What this boy babbling about? *What* this boy babbling about?

Then I sit down next to him on the couch. He jump a bit, knees twitching. "Where you get all these crazy ideas? What you worrying about all that Indian bullshit for? You know how to play the piano, why don't you do that. Ain't that enough? *Shit.*"

Big Brother shake his head and say, "I can't play the piano anymore. I forgot how."

"Huh! You was playin' it the other day."

"What good's playing the piano," Big Brother insist. "I used to know lots of musicians. They don't know anything about life. They don't know what it all means, man." Then he look down at his hands lying palm up on his knees like he never seen them before in his life and is surprised to find them at the ends of his arms. He say softly, "I got it too, Nickie."

"You got what?" But then, a second later, I know what he talking about and I feel bad for asking. I shake my head. Umm, times are hard. And he no more than just a boy, too.

Suddenly Big Brother's nose and the sides of his nose turn all red and he make this awful sucking sound and I think, shit, that boy crying. He lean back and pinch the bridge of his nose like he pinching off a nosebleed and he shake his head and say, "This is bad, man. Oh man, this is bad." He suck and snort some more like he trying to vacuum away the tears. Some snot run down onto that idiot mustache of his. "Oh God, I got to stop this."

I go to the kitchen and get him a tall glass of ice water. He gulp it down fast like all the thirst in the world is inside of him and it need quenching, quick. Then he wipe his mouth. He all shaken up.

"It ain't no death sentence no more," I say to him. "Look at me, I'm still kickin'."

Maybe that just the problem, I think, suddenly. It ain't dying, it living that give us such a hard time. I don't know how to do it no more. Everything I once knew about it don't mean nothing now. My heart feel heavy. I can't go on with no pep talk.

Suddenly I miss Eugene, and those feelings surprise me. One thing about my man Eugene, he was sure difficult, raising hell and shouting and scaring the shit out of poor Terrence when he was around, but you know what, he could always take me out of myself. He made me laugh. Eugene was a kind of comedian, like Will Smith or Chris Rock, he could do voices and imitations or just take a subject and roll with it for a while, any unimportant thing, like the weather or fast food, and he made it so funny the tears come. That must be why I kept him around longer than I should've. He wasn't funny all the time, though. Most of the time he was someone who needed to be locked up.

I feel them moony eyes of Big Brother's fixed on me. I scold myself for looking back on Eugene. Where that going to get me?

"Where you from, Keith?" I ask.

"Hillsborough," he mumble, looking away a bit.

"Hillsborough!" I guessed him right. I whistle through my teeth and Big Brother blush.

"Well, I used to be from there," he say. "I don't consider that to be home anymore. I mean, my parents made it pretty clear they don't want me to come back. Although they do give me money and stuff. After they found out what was wrong with me my dad told me my mom had a nervous breakdown and that, you know, she couldn't, like, bear to see me. She had these dreams for me, she wanted me to be a classical pianist like my uncle. I wasn't all that good at it, though. I mean, I liked it, but I didn't feel like practicing eight hours a day. Now I think, well, maybe there are other paths, you know? I think my dad's pretty disgusted with me too."

"Was you on the down low or something?"

He don't get my meaning. I explain it to him and he turn a little red around the ears and say, "Oh. Well, just a couple of times. It was just a phase I was going through. I have this theory that we're all, like, designed to be attracted to both sexes, but the balance is different in each person. Like some of us are ninety percent straight and ten percent gay, you know? Then others are eighty percent gay and twenty percent straight. It's really interesting when you think about it."

"Umm-hmm," I say. This boy *tripping*.

"But I'm not gay. I really like women," he say, looking at me hopefully.

"Hmmph."

"This Big Brother stuff has been great. It's really helped me change my perspective on the whole thing. Playing with Terrence, and meeting you, Nickie — just watching how you are. You're great. I mean, that first day I met you and you were so upfront about having HIV — you just *said* it. I admire that."

"But you already knew I was HIV anyhow. Agency must have told you that."

"Yeah, but, you weren't afraid to say it out loud. I knew you were someone I could talk to about it. Be open. I don't — well, I don't really know anyone else who's positive."

"Shit, everybody I know is positive," I say to him. "And there ain't nothing to talk about."

I frown, to put him off. Instead, though, he fix them pretty blue eyes on mine, for once they not wandering to my chest. He making me uncomfortable, the way he staring, like he can see right through me to the other side. Now he seem more like a man to me, like he made up his mind to grow up. That definitely the way a man look at a woman.

"Nickie," he say to me in a husky, choked-up kind of voice, "you must have really loved him, huh — Terrence's father?"

"Eugene!" I laugh. Now he acting like a boy again. "Eugene was my man, that all there was to it."

"What was he like?"

I laugh again. "I don't know what he was like!"

Then, for no reason I can figure, I tell him the story about how one day when I was visiting Eugene when he was in San Francisco General, dying up in Ward 84, a television crew come to the ward, doing a story about how it changed over the course of the epidemic. Now, Eugene, he was in and out of Ward 84 for ten years. This the last time he was going to be there and he knew it. When he saw the TV cameras, he started shouting and waving them over. "Hey, I got AIDS! I got AIDS, come on over and talk to me!" So he made such a commotion they finally came over and interviewed him. He was so pleased he was grinning like a fool, didn't matter that tubes was coming out of him everywhere, a big white bandage on his head, and he half blind, too. He went on and on about San Francisco General and all the AIDS docs, and he was real funny, that crew liked him, he had them laughing, and they let him go on for a long time. He was *jamming*. When they left, he was so excited he got all his tubes tangled from flailing his arms around. Made me stay until the news came on and, sure enough, there he was. News channel gave him a full minute. All the nurses and orderlies and whatever doctor was on call came and stood around and watched him and he said, squinting through his blind eyes, "Hey, that *me!* That me, Eugene!" Finally he got to be on TV. His big chance. That man lived on that high for days and days, couldn't nothing bring him down. Then, two weeks later, he passed.

Why I tell that story? It used to be funny but it ain't funny no more.

Big Brother hanging on my every word and when I finish he say, in the same husky voice like before, "I love that you shared that with me, Nickie."

Then he grab my hand and squeeze it. I try to pull away but not hard enough. Big Brother got one hot and sweaty paw. I be so embarrassed I don't know what to do. Then suddenly Big Brother leaning in on me, and then he kissing me. That little fuzzy caterpillar mustache tickling my mouth. But underneath, his lips firm, and they know what they's doing, that for sure.

Just when he about to slip in his tongue, I push him away. "Now quit, Terrence gonna be coming home any minute."

After that I know I got things to sort out in my mind. This Big Brother has turned into a situation on my hands. Now I know all I have to do is call the agency and they take him away, it simple. Damn, I know it must be against the rules for Big Brother to be putting the moves on me. Poor Big Brother so stupid, he don't even begin to know how the world work. Thinking how stupid he be get me to feeling sorry for him, and that ain't good. Also I think, well, Terrence be much happier now that Big Brother around, and that the truth too. He chilled out a lot and he not acting up in school so much. And then I think Big Brother seem happier too, since he begun playing with Terrence. He like teaching Terrence the piano. That one thing in life he *do* know something about.

Geraldine, the girl from the second floor, come knocking on my door with some comments to make as usual. I always know it be her from the way she knock, but I make a big show of asking who is it and turning the dead bolt and taking off the chain lock, to discourage her from thinking how easy it is to come upstairs and borrow things offa Nickie.

Geraldine got a belly showing about four months of pregnancy but I keep my mouth shut, I don't want to get her started. "You got some tampons?" she ask me first thing, without even saying hello.

Now what do she need tampons for, I think, looking her up and down.

She see my look and say, "They for my niece, she visitin' me, and her monthly came."

So why she can't go to the store and buy some. "Yeah, I got tampons," I say out loud.

"Can I borrow some?"

"You can *have* them. Shoot, Geraldine, I sure don't want them back once they been used."

She giggles and I fetch her the box and she say, "Ain't you got the super plus kind?"

"This all I got, girl."

"Well, the super plus is better."

I shrug. She take the box under her arm and say, "Who that white boy been coming by your place? He so fly."

"What you been doing, spying on me?"

Now she the one playing it cool. "Oh, I seen him come around sometime. I know he don't belong to *you* because you sworn offa men." She laugh.

"He a Big Brother for Terrence. And he ain't fly at all."

"Sure he fly. He got that blond hair."

"Hah. Maybe, but he got one bony butt."

Geraldine laugh and lean into the door. I never once asked her do she want to come in, the whole time I been living here. She bleeding me dry, always calling can I come braid her hair, can she borrow some pink nail polish, can I watch her kid, can he play with Terrence (but that kid so twisted I don't want Terrence nowhere near him), can she borrow twenty dollar till her check come. She accuse me of not being neighborly. She damn right, I ain't neighborly. Also, I don't participate in the monthly meetings the building social worker direct. She hold that against me too. Who I think I am, acting like I don't need nobody or nothing? This ain't the building to be private in. I do my best, but I'm too poor to live in Hillsborough, where you don't need to talk to nobody if you don't feel like it. Where you can put up walls the fools can't climb. And poor Big Brother on the other side of those walls now, doing for himself the best he can.

Now I'm mad because I let myself warm up to her and she gonna think I'm down with her.

"Listen, I got to get going," I tell her, halfway closing the door.

She wink. "Well, if you don't want him, you send him by me, hear?"

Geraldine a whore. She got one HIV baby and she probably gonna have another one and now she bragging about getting into bed with white boys. Sex is all she got on her mind, day and night.

And she *would* take Big Brother into her bed, if she had a chance. And he'd go, too, he so dumb. I think, he better off with me than he is with Geraldine or any other nigger whore he gonna run across. I get a flash of anger thinking about Geraldine messing with him. That night in bed I start fingering myself, something I ain't done in a long, long time. I'm thinking a little bit about Eugene and a little bit about Big Brother, and the two get scrambled in my head, and I'm tossing and turning trying to find some relief, and finally I put a pillow under my stomach and hump myself over the top.

So next week Big Brother show up at my door the night Terrence is away on an overnight camping trip with the YMCA. I know he know this, and he know that I know he know this, so I don't say one word about it.

"Nickie," he say in his hoarse voice. "I just can't stop thinking about you. Ever since that afternoon when we were talking. I just feel a real, like, a real connection with you. I don't know how to put it into words. I think I'm — well, I think I'm falling in love with you, Nickie."

I don't let him say much more because he gonna irritate me. Instead, I take his hand and lead him into the bedroom. I say to him, "Take off your clothes and lie down."

He look a little shy, and his hand is trembling with the unbuttoning and unzipping, but he do just what I say. When he lying down naked on my bed I think to myself, well, he ain't half bad with his clothes off, don't appear as skinny, and more hair on his body than I thought, and then I can't help but notice that in some areas he ain't no boy at all. He standing right up into manhood. He catch me looking and then he smile.

I take off my shirt and undo my bra and give him a tittie to hold. Then the expression on his face is like he in church and the preacher be talking about salvation and he just caught on to what the idea is all about. He say to me, Nickie, you're more beautiful than music, and I just laugh. I reach down and squeeze him and then his expression is beyond church. Then it like he seen Jesus Himself and the light is too much for him and he fall back on the pillow with his eyes closed and groan.

Big Brother make me a lady two time that night, and ooh honey, I know that when he wake up in the morning, I be a lady two more time again before breakfast. I sit up in bed and watch him sleeping. A little light from the window fall across his face. His skin so white and smooth, and his hair out of the ponytail, spread across the pillow. It fine and a little scraggly. Need conditioning. He stir and smack his lips in a happy way. I sigh. Damn, I wish I was nineteen again. I know too much at my age. Man and woman in bed together, naked. How you think that gonna end?

■

# The Promise of Something

FROM *Zyzzyva*

I'M NOT WHO I could have been. I've come to that conclusion twice, the second being just now, standing behind the counter of the Frostee Freeze in my specially designed Frostee Freeze polyester maternity top — red with red-and-white-striped sleeves. I'm eight months' pregnant, flipping burgers, and my kid just gives me a kick in the ribs so hard I almost lose my breath.

I am selling my baby for ten thousand dollars to the owners — a husband-and-wife team. The baby's father is the husband, the baby the result of rancid, unpleasant sex in the condiments closet. It was while he was grunting and groaning over me that I came to my first lament of failed ambitions.

My grandparents raised me. I was six when my parents delivered me to the tidy, petunia-lined doorstep of my mother's mother's house for an alluring fee of five thousand dollars.

"Really, Melissa," my grandmother had pleaded. "She needs stability, a home, her own bed. Something you and Ornette simply cannot provide."

Finally, for five thousand dollars, my mother gave in.

I remember this about her: She wore dark, soft, fuzzy skirts and shirts with no sleeves. She had long blond hairs on her wrists that puffed up over the silver bracelets that encircled her arms. Her skin was the color of a saltine, and her hair was long and curly. She wore silver wire glasses.

I remember this about my father: He wore brown suits with green shiny ties and played a silver guitar. His skin was the color of Nilla Wafers, and he had green eyes. His hair was curly and long, black but getting gray, kept in a ponytail. He was old, almost as old as my grandfather. He always smelled like the ocean.

They were street musicians. My father played the guitar and sang. My mother accompanied on harmonica. According to Grandma Eloise, my parents found it profitable to pin a FEED THE BABY sign to my shirt as I toddled around in front of them as they did their act. As I got older, they actually had me pass a hat; they taught me how to put on an expression of immeasurable need. I do remember staring at a boy my age in a red-stained Disney World T-shirt, holding out the hat and having him stick out his tongue at me. I recall how embarrassed I'd felt; for the rest of the day, I refused to solicit.

My grandparents' house was a small stucco two-bedroom in Lennox, California. I was given my mother's old room. I remember a big white fluffy bed with ruffles and red hearts around the edges. A huge floppy white teddy bear. All of it done up special by Eloise. There were frilly white curtains and a red and white rug. I thought it was wonderful. I didn't know I was to stay there forever.

My parents and I used to sleep together on a board in the back of a '53 UPS truck. There were small holes in the sides, and I would peer out at night — sometimes into nothingness, sometimes, in the darkness, at some faraway, glittering town, sometimes just into a darkened street with an occasional passerby, footsteps loud and surly in the quiet. I usually did this when the truck was rocking slowly and my mother and father were on the far side of the bed. Doing It.

My grandmother was probably most disturbed by the fact that we all slept together and that I had seen them Doing It. Never mind that I hadn't been to school or hadn't had immunizations or seen a dentist or eaten a well-balanced diet or lived a structured lifestyle. At age six, I knew what Doing It meant. I'm sure when my mother told her mother all about it, it was too much to bear and out came the life savings.

\*

The manager's wife knows the baby is her husband's. She told him to get me pregnant — it was their last chance. They are both forty-five and not unattractive people. He looks as if he had been a bit of a fighter in his younger years. He likes to work on cars in his spare time. She's very sweet in public, too sweet. Red hair, probably sews extremely well, cooks a fine roast. But she has those maternal longings, and they've tried everything else. Judy, that's her name, came up with this plan only a month after they'd hired me.

"You look Italian. She thinks you're pretty," Marco explained. "I do, too."

A month and a week later, the arrangements were made, and Marco was rutting me every half-hour in the condiments closet.

Six weeks later I was pregnant.

Eight weeks later, Marco was still rutting me in the condiments closet. Thus, the second conclusion.

My mother wrote me letters. From the very beginning, they were strange, and I didn't understand them. I've saved them all. The first said:

October 9, 1978

Dearest Bessie,

You sleep on a bed of feathers whereas I slept on planks of hardened air. Don't let the gladiolas subdue you. Ornette and I drift toward the sea and eastern islands where we will breathe air thick as silk and sing marvelously. Darling, we miss you.

Love, Lissa and Ornette.

I had no idea what she was talking about, plus she drew sad, agonized-looking little people all over the margins, which at the time were very disturbing. I never showed Eloise any of the letters, and she never asked to see them.

Eloise was a labor-and-delivery nurse who worked the night shift. Her arthritis gave her the gentle, shuffling walk of a dove. Her only subversive act was to convince young mothers to breast-feed. My grandfather, Cyrus, was a printer. When he left for work, a scent of pebbly after-shave, coffee, and cigarettes lingered. When he came home, he smelled of ink and chemicals that reminded me of smooth green stones.

They were good people, but as I got older and realized I'd been dumped, resentment was an instinctual response.

"Dear Bessie," my mother wrote when I was thirteen. "We travel east to west, north to south. I've eaten mutton with the Navajo in Shiprock and made love with your father in a flatbottom boat in Bayou Beouff, alligators bellowing out mating calls, cottonmouths fat as bicycle tires slithering from mud to muddy water. You are a young woman now. Beware of Eloise and her sterile admonishments. Don't let her trap you in ribbons and lace."

I began wearing eyeliner and mascara, lipstick the color of Concord grapes. Baggy khaki pants pulled tight at the waist with a black belt, flannel shirts — underneath, I exposed a lot of skin in lacy, revealing camisoles.

"Your mother wrote you something clever, didn't she?" Eloise accused. "I'll say this: you will not turn out like her."

No, I'm not who I could be. Twenty-two years old, frying fries and corn dogs, grilling patties of meat for a living. Ten thousand dollars, though. That might change things. I could buy my life back.

April 19, 1986

Dear Bessie,

Ornette lost his voice as we passed through an array of small tornadoes on a cracked and loquacious highway in Texas. We live in New Orleans in a hundred-year-old house. I sail over men's heads on a satin swing in a costume of sequins and feathers. I save my money in a sack of rice. From my dormer window, at night, with the lamplight, the glass-strewn street is a path of diamonds.

As I got older, I began to understand some of the things my mother wrote.

A man never touched my skin, saw my breast, came inside of me until Marco O'Malley.

Eloise was horrified at the arrangement.

"You can't tear an infant away from its mother like that," Eloise cried. "Not unless it's absolutely necessary. This is not. Who are these people?"

"*You* paid five thousand bucks for me," I said.

"When did she tell you that?" Eloise's shoulders sagged.

"I figured it out."

December 12, 1987

Dear Bessie,

Deliverance to the angular and stagnant ornaments of structured existence was not a vision dreamt by those who wished the best for you. Slips of paper keep us alive. We hear other things where singing is not allowed. I don't know what your voice sounds like. I hope you sing. Bessie Smith was your namesake.

"Number 409," I call out as I slide a cardboard tray containing fried foods and packets of ketchup across the counter.

"Mustard for the corn dog?" the customer asks, a man in a DPW uniform, green pants, orange shirt.

"Sure." I move my feet to make room for my belly as I bend down to the lower cabinet where the packets of relish and mustard are kept. I grab a couple and stand back up, hand them over. I feel a hand on my ass.

"Marco," I say impatiently. "You said you'd stop."

"But you're just so nice and round back there right now."

I turn around.

"And I'm not round up front," I say. "Shit, Marco. In a month, I'm going to have a baby. *Your* fucking baby."

"Hey. That is *Judy's* and my baby. Not *my* fucking baby, thank you very much." He straightens his skinny black Frostee Freeze manager's tie. "Speaking of fucking." He grabs my ass. "Hey, Artemesio," he yells to the guy on the fountain side. "Work both sides for a couple of minutes."

He pushes me around the corner, toward the closet.

"You know, I don't really want this baby. I'm doing it for Judy." He goes in first, then pulls me in. He presses me forward against the five-gallon cans of chili. "I figure I'm just getting my money's worth."

What he doesn't know is that I have grabbed the butcher's knife near the tomatoes and lettuce. He starts to pull down my pants.

"You'll get your money's worth in a month, asshole," I say as I wiggle my way around and hold the knife at his throat. He laughs and backs off.

"All right. All right. Later, then." He shoves the door open and leaves it open. Leaves me standing there with my pants half down, knife in my hand by my side.

He goes to his office and shuts the door. I can see him through the window, straightening his tie, running a comb through his slicked-back hair. I, too, have to pull myself back together.

January 5, 1988

Dear Bessie,

As a child I remember my mother bought *Crime* magazine, grainy photos of murder scenes. Women's angelic white legs hanging from underneath bloodied white shrouds. I stared at them for hours. Texas murders. Cops with big hats. Always at night — a window displaying nothing but darkness, as if the killer could be right there, watching while no one else was.

Ornette pulled a knife on a man tonight. A man daring enough to fondle my breast while looking Ornette in the face. Not a drunk man, but impertinent and far too bold. My irresponsibility put Ornette in a dangerous place. I should have taken a table knife and flashed it long before Ornette became vexed. I wasn't watching. You watch, Bess. There are lies in someone's every move.

How soon before this baby, who moves so slowly and so power-fully in my womb, learns deception? It kicks me. I'm not who I could have been.

November 17, 1989

Dear Bess,

You are 17 now, and I think you must know Ornette and I will not be coming back for you. Truth be told, Eloise and Cyrus paid us $5,000 for you. You belong to them. The ocean at sunrise in Florida is smooth and pink as a fingernail.

How long did it take her to write it? Quickly, without much thought? Or did she spend hours wondering what soothing words could deliver such a harsh message? When did she finally decide there were none?

Judy comes banging through the back door with plastic sacks bulging with round heads of pale green lettuce.

"Little help?" she calls out.

I ignore her. Marco comes trotting out of his office.

"Got a good deal on tomatoes, too, hon," she says to Marco in that voice as brittle and crystal as sugared violets. "They're in the trunk." And she nods for Marco to go get them.

She walks from the back room to the grill, where I am.

"Are you eating properly?" she asks with a perk in her voice, not unlike a cosmetics salesperson. "No smoking? Drugs?"

"We made a deal, Mrs. O'Malley," I say to her, tired of the same questions over and over. "I keep up my side. I'm assuming you plan to keep up yours."

"Oh, most certainly," she says, embarrassed by my bluntness. "We have every intention of paying you. We just want a healthy baby." She steps back. I lean out into the back room and watch her walk primly to the manager's office, wobbling in her high heels on the rubber matting. She says something to Marco. He cranes his neck to look at me. I wave my spatula and step back into the kitchen. I will never say anything about his continued performances in the condiments closet.

The baby is a girl. We've had the ultrasounds done. I would feel better if it was a boy.

June 6, 1990

Dear Bess,

We sit in the desert just past sunrise and the sky is almost biological in its azure candor. The sun does not shine in that room of yours. I remember forlorn hours, mute, in afternoon chill. Search for air and light. Eloise operates in darkness. Cyrus breathes toxins. You have wings now. You're 18.

I'm not who I could have been. I imagine what I will be with ten grand. The same person with a new used car. For the first time in a long time, I wonder where my mother and father are. What would I know if I'd lived with them? My mother has taught me about the beautiful strangeness of the world, defined the absurd drudgery of the life she herself sold me into, but she has insisted on wariness at all times. So what do I do? Where do I go?

Marco peeks around the corner.

"Judy thinks maybe you're working too hard and you should take this last month off."

He reaches for my breast. "She *would* show up." He continues to fondle me. "Where do you live?"

"With my grandparents," I answer. He stops and looks at me.

"You're kidding, right?"

"No."

He heads back to his office.

October 27, 1990

Dear Bess,

Two years old and you became a deity, floating on a sea of hands, the ten o'clock sun, timid yet ingratiating, sending rays of gold off the buckles of your overalls. Jackson Square, New Orleans. A man had knocked you down and stolen the hat with money in it from you. You did not cry. You stood up again and looked down the street looking for the man with the hat. "The baby!" the crowd roared. They rushed over to you, a wave of strangers' love. You laughed, let them lift you up and carry you to the ice cream store on the corner. My eyes were always on you. Divine being. Caramel skin. Rivers of golden hair meshing with the people's hands. Your laugh — the sound of finches, the color of poppies, to hold it was to feel raindrops leaving clouds. I wasn't watching, Bess. We were singing. My eyes were closed. Ornette's eyes were closed. A torrid second. There are those who watch for that moment.

Mrs. O'Malley leaves. I hear her brand-new '94 Ford Taurus back up, the wheels spitting gravel.

"Artemesio," Marco calls from his office. "Take over both sides for a few minutes."

"Shit," I say to myself.

Artemesio smirks as he comes around to the grill side. "Mr. O'Malley sure gets his."

"Fuck off, Arty," I say and wait for Marco to stick his head around the corner.

"Bessie, come to my office," he shouts out instead.

I hand Artemesio the spatula, and he takes it, bounces it up and down in his hand.

Marco is holding the door open for me when I get to his office. I sit down in a gray fake leather chair, facing his desk. He sits down, serious, concerned, rubbing his chin. The transistor radio is playing Al Green's "How Can You Mend a Broken Heart."

"There seems to be something we overlooked in our arrangement," he says and clears his throat. I see that he has the typed-out document in front of him. He looks down at it as if he's reading it. "We didn't indicate that once the baby was born, you were not to return to work here."

He looks up at me, flattens his lips, the same way he did when we were having sex.

"Judy and I will be glad to pay you an extra grand for the inconvenience," he offers.

"You got to be fucking kidding," I say with a laugh that ends up being a cough.

He closes his eyes. "*. . . how can you stop the rain from falling . . .*" A torrid second.

"I want an extra five thousand."

I'll see how far a *good* used car will take me. Maybe I will see the ocean in Florida at sunrise. Maybe I will dance between tornadoes in glitter and lace. Maybe I will search for alligators and make love to myself.

Maybe I will search for Lissa and Ornette. Let them teach me how to sing.

"One condition, though," I say. "That I be allowed to write letters to my daughter."

■

# Full House

FROM *Esquire*

MY PARENTS WERE NOT the type of people who went to bed at a regular hour. Sleep overtook them, but neither the time nor the idea of a mattress seemed very important. My father favored a chair in the basement, but my mother was apt to lie down anywhere, waking with carpet burns on her face or the pattern on the sofa embossed into the soft flesh of her upper arms. It was sort of embarrassing. She might sleep for eight hours a day, but they were never consecutive hours, and they involved no separate outfit. For Christmas we would give her nightgowns, hoping she might take the hint.

"They're for bedtime," we'd say, and she'd look at us strangely, as if, like the moment of one's death, the occasion of sleep was too incalculable to involve any real preparation.

The upside to being raised by what were essentially a pair of housecats was that we never had any enforced bedtime. At two a.m. on a school night, my mother would not say, "Go to sleep," but rather, "Shouldn't you be tired?" It wasn't a command but a sincere question, the answer provoking little more than a shrug. "Suit yourself," she'd say, pouring her thirtieth or forty-second cup of coffee. "I'm not sleepy, either. Don't know why, but I'm not."

Every night was basically a slumber party, so when the real thing came along, my sisters and I failed to show much of an interest. "But we get to stay up as late as we want!" the hosts would say.

"And . . .?"

The first one I attended was held by a neighbor named Walt Winters. Like me, Walt was in the sixth grade. Unlike me, he was gregarious and athletic, which meant, basically, that we had absolutely nothing in common. "But why would he include me?" I asked my mother. "I hardly know the guy."

She did not say that Walt's mother had made him invite me, but on seeing her turn away, I knew that this was the only likely explanation. "Oh, go," she said. "It'll be fun."

I tried my best to back out, but then my father got wind of it, and that option was closed. He often passed Walt playing football in the street and saw in the boy a younger version of himself. "He's maybe not the best player in the world, but he and his friends, they're a good group."

"Fine," I said. "Then you go sleep with them."

I could not tell my father that boys made me anxious, and so I invented individual reasons to dislike them. The hope was that I might seem discerning rather than frightened, but instead I came off sounding like a prude.

"You expect me to spend the night with someone who curses? Someone who actually throws rocks at cats?"

"You're damned right I do," my father said. "Now get the hell over there."

Aside from myself, there were three other guests at Walt's slumber party. None of them was particularly popular — they weren't good-looking enough for that — but each could hold his own on a playing field or in a discussion about cars. The talk started the moment I walked through the door, and while pretending to listen, I wished that I could have been more honest. "What is the actual point of football?" I wanted to ask. "Is a V-8 engine related in any way to the juice?" I would have sounded like a foreign-exchange student, but the answers might have given me some sort of a foundation. As it was, they may as well have been talking backwards.

There were four styles of houses on our street, and while Walt's was different from my own, I was familiar with the layout. The slumber party took place in what the Methodists called a family room, the Catholics used as an extra bedroom, and the neighbor-hood's only Jews had turned into a combination darkroom and fallout shelter. Walt's family was Methodist, and so the room's fo-cal point was a large black-and-white television. Family photos hung on the wall alongside pictures of the various athletes Mr. Winters had successfully pestered for autographs. I admired them to the best of my ability but was more interested in the wedding portrait displayed above the sofa. For one thing, I knew who these people were, and for another, the photograph actually told you something — that the union had been blessed and supported. While the newly wed Winterses danced and ate cake, my parents had eloped. Rather than a wedding gown, my mother had worn a suit, and in the one existing photograph she resembled a secretary receiving instructions from her boss.

In her wedding photograph, Walt's mother looked almost frighteningly happy. The bulging eyes and fierce, gummy smile: It was an expression bordering on hysteria, and the intervening years had done nothing to dampen it.

"What is she on?" my mother would whisper whenever we passed Mrs. Winters waving from her front yard. My father com-plained that the woman talked too fast, demanding of her listener a passion equivalent to her own. I thought he was being too hard on her, but after ten minutes in her home I understood exactly what he was talking about.

"Pizza's here!!!" she chimed when the delivery man came to the door. "Oh, boys, how about some piping hot pizza!!!" I thought it was funny that anyone would use the words "piping hot," but it wasn't the kind of thing I felt I could actually laugh at. Neither could I laugh at Mr. Winters's pathetic imitation of an Italian waiter. "Mamma mia. Who want anudda slice a dipizza!!"

I had the idea that adults were supposed to make themselves scarce at slumber parties, but Walt's parents were all over the place: initiating games, offering snacks and refills. When the mid-night horror movie came on, Walt's mother crept into the bath-room, leaving a ketchup-spattered knife beside the sink. An hour passed, and when none of us had yet discovered it, she started dropping little hints. "Doesn't anyone want to wash their hands?" she asked.

No one looked at her.

"Will whoever's closest to the door go check to see if I left fresh towels in the bathroom?"

You just wanted to cry for people like her.

As corny as they were, I was sorry when the movie ended and Mr. and Mrs. Winters stood to leave. It was only two a.m., but clearly they were exhausted. "I just don't know how you boys can do it," Walt's mother said, yawning into the sleeve of her bathrobe. "I haven't been up this late since Loren came into the world." Loren was Walt's sister, who was born premature and lived for less than two days. This had happened before the Winterses moved onto our street, but it wasn't any kind of a secret, and you weren't supposed to flinch upon hearing the girl's name. The baby had died too early to pose for photographs, but still she qualified as a presence. She had a Christmas stocking the size of a mitten, and they even threw her an annual birthday party, a fact that my mother found especially creepy. "Let's hope they don't invite us," she said. "I mean, Jesus, how do you shop for a dead baby?"

I guessed it was the fear of another premature birth that kept Mrs. Winters from trying again, which was sad, as you got the sense she had an idea of a lively household, and that the slumber party and the ketchup-covered knife were all part of that idea. While in her presence, we had played along, but once she said good night, I understood that all bets were off.

Mrs. Winters and her husband lumbered up the stairs, and when Walt felt certain that they were asleep, he pounced on Dale Gummerson, shouting, "Titty twister!" Brad Clancey joined in, and when they finished, Dale raised his shirt, revealing nipples as crumpled and ruddy as the pepperoni slices littering the forsaken pizza box.

"Oh, my God," I said, realizing too late that this made me sound like a girl. The appropriate response was to laugh at Dale's misfortune, not to flutter your hands in front of your face, screeching,

"What have they done to your poor nipples! Shouldn't we put some ice on them?"

Walt picked up on this immediately. "Did you just say you wanted to put ice on Dale's nipples?"

"Well, not me personally," I said. "I meant, you know, generally. As a group. Or Dale could do it himself if he felt like it."

Walt's eyes wandered from my face to my chest, and then the entire group was upon me. Dale had not yet regained the full use of his arms, and so he sat on my legs while Brad Clancey and Scott Marlboro pinned me to the carpet. My shirt was raised, a hand was clamped over my mouth, and Walt latched on to my nipples, twisting them back and forth as if they were a set of particularly stubborn lug nuts. "Now who needs ice!" he said. "Now who thinks he's the goddamned school nurse!" I'd once felt sorry for him, but now, my eyes watering in pain, I understood that little Loren was smart to have cut out early. The guy was an animal.

When finally I was freed, I went upstairs and stood at the kitchen window, my arms folded lightly against my damaged chest. My house was located in a ravine. You couldn't see it from the street, but still I could make out the glow of lights spilling from the top of our driveway. It was tempting, but were I to leave now, Walt and the others would chalk the whole thing up to my nipples, tweaking the facts and telling everyone that I had cried. The baby had to go home. Life at school would be unbearable, and so I left the window and returned to the basement, where Walt was shuffling cards against the coffee table. "Just in time," he said. "Have a seat."

I lowered myself to the floor and reached for a magazine, trying my best to act casual. "I'm not really much for games, so if it's okay with you, I think I'll just watch."

"Watch, hell," Walt said. "This is strip poker. What kind of a homo wants to sit around and watch four guys get naked?"

The logic of this was lost on me. "Well, won't we all sort of be watching?"

"Looking, maybe, but not watching," Walt said. "There's a difference. Watching is what you do when you're not doing anything else."

"Like watching TV," Scott said.

"Exactly," Walt said. "Watching is like watching TV and looking is like . . . driving a car and looking out for the other driver. Get it? You're doing two things at the same time."

I guessed he had a point, but still, I was damned if I was going to go along with it. "What about looking out the window? That's just doing one thing at a time."

Walt made a twisting motion with his fingers, and I took my place at the table, praying for a gas leak or an electrical fire — anything to save me from the catastrophe of strip poker. Semantics aside, whether I played or not, the truth was that I would be watching. To the rest of the group, a naked boy was like a lamp or an extension cord, something so familiar and uninteresting that it faded into the background, but for me it was different. A naked boy was what I desired more than anything on earth, and when you were both watching and desiring, things came up, one thing in particular that was bound to stand out and ruin your life forever, following you even to the grave. "I hate to tell you, but it's against my religion to play poker."

"Yeah, right," Walt said. "What are you, Baptist?"

"Greek Orthodox."

"Well, that's a load of crap, because the Greeks invented cards." This from Scott, who was quickly identifying himself as the smart one.

"Actually, I think it was the Egyptians," I said.

"Greeks, Egyptians, they're all the same thing," Walt said. "Anyway, what your Pooh-Bah doesn't know won't hurt him, so shut the hell up and play."

He dealt the cards, and I looked from face to face, exaggerating flaws and reminding myself that I disliked these people. The hope was that I might kill any surviving atom of attraction, but, as has been the case for my entire life, the more I dislike someone, the more attractive they become. The key was to stall, to argue every hand until the sun came up and Mrs. Winters saved me with what she had advertised as a "four-star flapjack breakfast with all the trimmings." At the time she had said it, I'd bitten the inside of my cheek — anything to stop myself from laughing — but now those flapjacks meant the world to me, and I tried to picture them and to hold that picture in my mind: the buttery goodness, the cascade of syrup overtaking everything in its path, the eggs and sausage and whatever else the Winters household considered to be a viable trimming. They could be fried in Vaseline, but when those flap-jacks were finally presented, I would fork them into my mouth and savor the sweet taste of freedom.

On the off chance that stalling would not work, I stepped into the bathroom and checked to make sure I was wearing clean underwear. A boner would be horrible beyond belief, but a boner combined with a skid mark meant that I should take the ketchup-smeared knife and just kill myself before it was too late.

"What are you, launching a sub in there?" Walt shouted. "Come on, we're waiting."

Usually, when I was forced to compete, it was my tactic to simply give up. To try in any way was to announce your ambition, which only made you more vulnerable. The person who wanted to win but failed was a loser, while the person who didn't really care was just a freak. Here, though, surrender was not an option. I had to win at a game I knew nothing about, and that seemed hopeless until I realized we were all on an even keel. Not even Scott had the slightest idea of what he was doing, and by feigning an air of expertise, I found I could manipulate things in my favor.

"A joker and a queen is much better than the four and five of spades," I said, defending my hand against Brad Clancey's.

"But you have a joker and a three of diamonds."

"Yeah, but the joker makes it a queen."

"I thought you said poker was against your religion," Walt said.

"Well, that doesn't mean I don't understand it. Greeks invented cards, remember. They're in my blood."

At the start of the game, the starburst clock had read three-thirty. An hour later, I was missing one shoe, Scott and Brad had lost their shirts, and both Walt and Dale were down to their underwear. If this was what winning felt like, I wondered why I hadn't tried it before. Confidently in the lead, I invented little reasons for the undressed to get up and move about the room.

"Hey, Walt. Did you hear that? It sounded like your mother calling."

"I didn't hear anything."

"Why don't you go to the stairway and check. We don't want any surprises." His underwear was all bunchy in the back, saggy, like a diaper, but his legs were meaty and satisfying to look at.

"Dale, would you make sure those curtains are closed?"

"Why do I have to do it?"

"Well, because you're closest."

He walked toward the curtains, and I ate him alive with my eyes, confident that no one would accuse me of gaping. Things might have been different were I in last place, but as a winner, it was my right to make sure that things were done properly. "There's a little gap down by the baseboard. Bend over and close it, will you?"

It took a while, but after explaining that a pair of kings was no match for the two of hearts and a three of spades, Walt surrendered his underpants and tossed them onto a pile beside the TV set. "Okay," he said. "Now the rest of you can finish the game."

"But it is finished," Scott said.

"Oh, no," Walt said. "I'm not going to be the only one getting naked. You guys have to keep playing."

"While you do what — sit back and watch?" I said. "What kind of a homo are you?"

"Yeah," Dale said. "Why don't we do something else? This game's boring and the rules are impossible."

The others muttered in agreement, and when Walt refused to back down, I gathered the deck and tamped it commandingly upon the tabletop. "The only solution is for us all to keep playing."

"How the hell am I supposed to do that?" Walt said. "I mean, in case you haven't noticed, there's nothing more for me to lose."

"Oh," I said, "there's always more. Maybe if the weakest hand is already naked, we should make that person perform some kind of a task. Nothing big, but, you know, just a token kind of thing."

"A thing like what?"

"I don't know. I guess we'll just have to cross that bridge when we come to it."

In retrospect, I probably went a little far in ordering Scott to sit on my lap. "But I'm naked!" he said.

"Hey, I'm the one who's going to be suffering. I was just looking for something easy. Would you rather run outside and touch the mailbox? The sun will be coming up in about twenty seconds — you want the whole neighborhood to see you?"

"How long will I have to sit on you?"

"I don't know. A minute or two."

I moved onto the easy chair and wearily patted my knee, as if this were a great sacrifice. All my life I had dreamed of this moment, and now that it was within my grasp, I was already imagining the next level. Scott slid into place, and just as I pulled him closer, there came the sound of footsteps padding overhead. It was that damn Mrs. Winters, rising early to embrace the day.

"Go back to bed," I whispered, but she was beyond the reach of my mental powers, and nothing could stop her progress.

Scott leaped off my knee, and in that instant the evening was officially over.

"Get back here," I said. But I was no longer considered a winner, and neither he nor the others had any reason to listen to me.

"It takes a good half-hour to make flapjacks. C'mon, guys, what's your rush? One more hand. What do you say?" I pleaded to their faces as they scrambled for their clothes and then again to their backs as they charged up the stairway, moving, it seemed, almost as if they were running from something.

MICHELLE TEA

■

# Transmissions from Camp Trans

FROM *Believer*

Discussed: Porta-Janes, Post-Dyke Queer Scene, Spring Break for Trannyboys, Floridian-Retiree Role-Play, *Dirty Dancing*, Susan Powter, J. J. Bitch, The Fat-Tastics, Fat Caucus, ADD Caucus, Heat Death in France, The Bearded Transrevolution, Beefalo, Youth Travel Culture, KING SHIT OF FUCK MOUNTAIN, A Safe Space to Fuck Up, A New Civil Rights Movement

UNLESS YOU'VE SPENT some time as a lesbian, or perhaps are the sort of straight lady who enjoys the music, politics, and occasional abandoning of the menfolk that a particularly earthy strain of "women's culture" offers, you've probably never heard of the Michigan Womyn's Music Festival. It's been happening for the past twenty-eight years, taking place each August on a lush chunk of woodland in northern Michigan, planned to coincide with summer's final full moon. While womyn's music is the festival's alleged purpose — the guitar stylings of folksters like Holly Near and Cris Williamson as well as post–riot grrrl acts like Bitch and Animal, the Butchies, and Le Tigre, to draw in the younger generation — the real purpose is to hunker down in a forest with a few thousand other females, bond, have sex in a fern grove, and go to countless workshops on everything from sexual esoterica to parading around on stilts, processing various oppressions, and sharing how much you miss your cat. The festival aims to be a utopia, and in most ways it hits its mark. Performers are paid well, and all performers are paid the same amount, regardless if they're famous like the Indigo Girls or some virtually unknown girl band. You can come for free as a worker, taking on jobs like childcare, kitchen work, or driving shuttles on and off the land, and even women who pay the hundreds of dollars to come in are required to pull their weight by picking up a couple of work shifts. The only dudes allowed in the space are the ones who rumble in late at night, in giant trucks, to vacuum the sludge from the hundreds of Porta-Potties, called Porta-Janes. They are preceded by a woman who hollers, "Man on the land! Man on the land!" — a warning to skittish nymphs to hop into a tent or a bush. I've been to the festival four or five times, and can attest to the deeply stunning feeling of safety and peace there. The absence of guys does make for an absence of threat; everyone's guard is down, finally, and a relaxation level is hit that is probably impossible to access in the real world. Pretty much everyone who attends bursts into tears at some point, saddened at all the psychic garbage that females are forced to lug around and grateful for a week of respite. It's no wonder the women who come to the festival are zealots about it, live for August, and get totally obsessed with and protective of the culture that springs up within its security-patrolled boundaries.

In 1991 a transsexual woman named Nancy Jean Burkholder was evicted from MWMF. Transsexual women, for those not up to date with the growing transgender revolution, are women who were born in male bodies and have been fighting against that ever since. They may or may not be on hormones, which can be costly or unavailable. Same goes for sex-reassignment surgery, which is often prohibitively expensive and not covered by insurance. Nancy Jean's eviction is famous in Michigan lore, for it sparked a fierce debate about the inclusion of transsexual women, which has been raging for over a decade. A lot of women inside the festival want to keep trans women out. Some staunchly insist that these individuals are not women but men in dresses trying to ruin the feminist event. Others concede that trans women are women, but because they were born boys and may still have penises, the festival is not the place for them. Trans women and their growing number of allies say these feminist justifications are straight-up discrimination, no different from the rest of the world, which routinely denies that trans women are "real" women and bars their access to everything from jobs to housing, domestic violence counseling to health care. Off and on for the past decade a small group of trans people and their supporters have set up a protest camp, Camp Trans, across the road, in the hope of changing the policy that left Nancy Jean stranded in the Midwest twelve years ago.

## Nancy Jean Burkholder

"I appreciate women's space, and after checking with festival literature I couldn't see that I wasn't welcome. I had talked to people, and their opinion was, if you think of yourself as a woman, you're welcome. I'd gone with a friend of mine, Laura. We drove out together, and we were number thirty-three in line. We got there early; we were really excited about going. We set up camp up in Bread & Roses. It's kind of the quiet area. Then we each did a work shift, shuttle duty. Hauling people from the front all the way back. That evening Laura was having a friend come in on the shuttle bus from Grand Rapids, so we walked down to the gate about nine p.m. to meet the bus. Turned out the bus was late and didn't get there till about eleven. We were hanging out at the fire pit, just kind of joined the group of people that were hanging out and talking. When the bus came in at eleven, Laura went up to the gate to meet her friend, and I waited by the fire pit. At that point a couple of women approached me and asked if I knew that this was a festival for women. It kind of surprised me. I said, 'Yeah, uh-huh.' About that time Laura was coming back, so I asked her to come over; something didn't seem right about what these women were asking. I think one of them asked me if I was transsexual. I said, 'My history is none of your business.' I asked, 'Why are you asking?' and she said that transsexuals weren't welcome. I think I remember saying, 'Are you sure? How do you know?' And so she went at that point and talked to the festival producers. She came back in about an hour; it took a while. She said that transsexuals were not welcome and was I transsexual? At that point I offered to show my driver's license, which said female, and also to drop my drawers, and she said, 'I wouldn't be comfortable with that.' Which I thought was kind of off, given the amount of nudity at the festival. She asked again, 'Are you transsexual?' and I said, 'It's none of your business.' At that point she said, 'Well, I'm empowered to expel any woman, at any time, for any reason. You have to leave.' I knew there was no arguing with them.

"They wouldn't let me leave the area around the main gate. Instead, Laura went with a couple of festival security guards back out to my campsite, scooped up all my equipment, and brought it back to the main gate. It must have been about one o'clock in the morning by then. They arranged for us to stay at a motel in Hart (Michigan); I think we got there around two o'clock. And it was a dump. It was cold; there was mildew in the carpet; trucks running by on Route 10. I couldn't believe it. I was devastated. The next day Laura took me down to Grand Rapids, and I paid for a plane ticket and flew home to New England. I flew to Worcester, Massachusetts, and Laura's partner arranged for a taxi to take me back to their house, where my car was. Laura went back to the festival for two reasons: She was doing a workshop, and also she went back to tell my friends what happened to me. Otherwise I would have disappeared without a trace. One of the friends she told was Janis Walworth. Janis and Laura spent the rest of the festival talking to people and telling them what happened. I was back in New Hampshire, and I called *Gay Community News*, a newspaper in Boston, to tell them what happened. I think they were a little taken aback and weren't quite sure what to do with this. They did say, 'If you want to write an editorial, we'll publish it.' So, Laura wrote a letter to the editor, and they published it with my editorial, and we took up a whole page in the newspaper. That kind of started the whole controversy.

"The important piece that doesn't always get reported is that Janis organized a bunch of people to go back in 1992. She brought her sister, a male-to-female postoperative transsexual, and also an intersex person and a butch female. They distributed buttons and leaflets and did a survey. The survey indicated that seventy-two percent approved of transsexuals being at the festival. Twenty-three percent did not, for a variety of reasons. Out of that Janis categorized the reasons why people didn't want transsexuals, and she compiled gender myths, twenty-four of them."

## Twenty-Four Gender Myths

1. Although male-to-female transsexuals have surgery to change their anatomy and take female hormones, they still act like men.
2. Male-to-female transsexuals are not women-born women (or womyn-born womyn).
3. Male-to-female transsexuals have been socialized as men, and this socialization cannot be changed.
4. Male-to-female transsexuals are trying to "pass" as women. They try to make themselves as much like nontranssexual women as possible.
5. Male-to-female transsexuals take jobs away from women because they had access to better training when they were men.
6. To lessen the power of patriarchy in our lives, we must purge our community of everything male, including women who once had male anatomy.
7. Most women can easily prove they are not male-to-female transsexuals, if they are challenged to do so.
8. Male-to-female transsexuals have been raised as boys, have never been oppressed as women, and cannot understand women's oppression.
9. Women's space is not "safe" space if male-to-female transsexuals are allowed in it.
10. Transsexuals have surgery so they can have sex the way they want to.
11. Male-to-female transsexuals are trying to take over the lesbian community.

12. The sex assigned to a person at birth is that person's "real" sex.
13. The lesbian and women's communities have nothing to gain by including transsexuals.
14. Nontranssexual women have the right to decide whether transsexuals should be included in the women's community.
15. Transsexuals are guilty of deception when they don't reveal right away that they are transsexuals.
16. Male-to-female transsexuals are considered men until they have sex-change surgery.
17. People can be categorized as transsexual or nontranssexual — there's no in between.
18. Women who want to become men have bought into societal hatred of women or are hoping to take advantage of male privilege.
19. A person's "true" sex can be determined by chromosome testing.
20. Transsexualism is unnatural — it is a new problem brought about by sophisticated technology.
21. "Real" women, certainly those who belong to the lesbian community, rejoice in their womanhood and have no desire to be men.
22. Since Festival policy was made clear, there have been no transsexuals at Michigan.
23. Transsexuals have caused trouble at Michigan, resulting in their expulsion.
24. Nontranssexual women at Michigan don't want male-to-female transsexuals to be present.

## Airplane over Southwest, August 15, 2003

I'm reading *Jane* magazine because my plane could, of course, crash; this could be my last moment alive, and I will not deny myself the small delight. *Jane* is the most innocent of the guilty pleasure that is women's magazines, as it at least aspires toward a sensibility affirming that women shouldn't look starved for cheeseburgers and that gay people are cool. Printed beneath a small column in which the actor who plays the exchange student on *That '70s Show* gives advice to lovelorn teenage girls is this bit of information:

> Wesleyan University now offers the nation's first "gender-blind" dorm for students who don't label themselves as male or female.

I am zooming through the air toward a patch of national forest presently populated by a horde of people who don't label themselves as male or female, as well as bunches of folks whose identities settle somewhere beneath the transgender banner. Now, before we land in Grand Rapids, an emergency glossary.

*Emergency Glossary of Gender Identity Terminology*
*(Partially plagiarized from the Web site Antny's Place [antnysplace .org])*

**Genderqueer:** Individuals who may identify as both male and female, or sometimes as male and sometimes as female, or decline to identify with any gender whatsoever. They are not necessarily on hormones or pursuing surgery.

**Transsexual:** (1) A person who feels a consistent and overwhelming desire to transition and fulfill their lives as members of the opposite gender. Generally taking hormones and pursuing surgery. (2) A person who believes that his or her actual biological (or "born") gender is the opposite of the one it should have been.

**Trans man:** A female-to-male transsexual (FTM). Also known as a *trannyboy*, if younger.

**Trans woman:** A male-to-female transsexual (MTF).

**Pre-op:** Has not yet had sex-reassignment surgery.

**Post-op:** Has had sex-reassignment surgery.

**Non-op:** Has no intention of having sex-reassignment surgery.

I am headed to Camp Trans, now in the tenth year of its on-again, off-again standoff with the Michigan Womyn's Music Festival across the road. Started by Nancy Jean and friends in the years after her eviction, the protest camp faded away in the mid-nineties. A new generation of young transgendered activists picked up the torch in 1999 and resumed the confrontational face-off. In the scant four years since, there has been an unprecedented boom in people identifying as trans, mostly female-assigned people transitioning to men or staking out a third-sex genderqueer territory. Flocking to Camp Trans for both the political struggle and the party, they have changed the outpost in significant ways. The focus of the trans struggle in recent years has drifted away from its original intention of getting trans women into women-only and lesbian spaces. Trans men have generally been welcome — if not totally fetishized — by contemporary dyke communities, particularly young, urban enclaves. The same is not true for trans women, even lesbian trans women. This influx of trannyboys and their lesbian admirers has not only alienated many of the trans women at Camp Trans; it's also blown up attendance so high, they can no longer set up right across the street from the festival gates. The encampment is now located up the road a bit, in a forest-lined field between the music festival and a nudist camp.

I've never been to Camp Trans, though I stopped attending MWMF a few years back, too conflicted about this exclusion of trans women. Today I'm picked up at the airport by a girl named Ana Jae who volunteered to get me so she can get the hell out of the woods. Ana hates camping; she says the bugs are attacking like mad and it's really bad when you drop your shorts to piss in the woods and they start fluttering around your bare ass. Ana can't use the Porta-Potties because she's been traumatized by the 1980s B horror flick *Sleepaway Camp II,* in which terrible things happen within one plastic, fetid chamber; so she is forced to piddle among the bugs. I'm antsy to hear of the mood at Camp Trans, and Ana confirms that the trans men far outnumber the trans women, complains about a general devaluing of femininity in the young, post-dyke queer scene, and tells me about a sex party that somehow went awry the night before and is this morning's main drama. Our immediate drama is that we get outrageously, wildly lost on the way back to the woods, careening through quaint Michigan townships for hours, hopelessly passing farm stands selling fresh vegetables, rows of exploding sunflowers and cornstalks, trees and trees and more trees, gigantic willows with long whipping branches that drape and swag, and large single-family homes with porches and pools and tractors in their front yards. We know that we've unscrambled our cryptic directions when we pass a gas station that has a flapping sign that says WELCOME WOMYN in its parking lot, and loads of sporty females loading cases of beer into their cars. We follow a camper with a bumper sticker that reads SEE YOU NEXT AUGUST down a road so heavily traveled that the foliage that lines it is coated with a thick dusting of brown dirt like an apocalyptic snowfall. We pass the front gates of the festival and see its huge parking lot crammed with vehicles, women in neon orange vests directing the flow of females through the gates, and we keep going. It's a disappointment not to see Camp Trans boldly arranged there at the mouth of the festival, and I wonder how its political point can be clearly made if it's tucked out of sight around the curving road. The former vigil has turned into a sort of alternative to the festival, one that's free of charge, one that a lot of MWMF attendees mistake as a happy, friendly, separate-but-equal campsite. A place for dykes who think trannyboys are hot to spend a night cruising and partying, and then return to their gated community up the road. For the trans women relying on Camp Trans as a site of protest, this new incarnation — as a sort of spring break for trannyboys and the dykes who date them — has been infuriating. Which is why Sadie Crabtree, a trans woman and an activist from D.C., has emerged as the sort of head leader this year. It is her intention, backed up by the other organizers, to bring the focus of Camp Trans back around to the trans women it originally meant to serve.

## Camp Trans Welcome Station

Everyone who comes to Camp Trans, either to camp or to visit on a day pass from the festival, has to pause at the welcome tent and check in, and MWMF attendees who arrive tonight for entertainment are charged three dollars. Behind a table made from boards and sawhorses sit a couple of Camp Trans welcomers, women doing their work shifts and acclimating visitors to their new environment. As at the festival across the way, everyone here is expected to lend a hand. The camp isn't nearly as large as the music festival — MWMF's parking lot is bigger than Camp Trans's entire area — but it still takes a lot of work to make it run. I spy a kitchen tent with a mess of pots and pans and water jugs strewn before it. Another tent is garlanded with Christmas lights that are beginning to shine as the hot summer sun sinks. This is the performance area, bulked with DJ and other sound equipment. There's a medic tent and a roped-off area for "advocates," armbanded individuals whose job is to answer touchy questions, listen to complaints, and defuse conflicts.

At the welcome tent I sign in on a form that doubles as a petition calling for the dropping of the festival's womyn-born-womyn policy. I'm handed a slip of paper welcoming me to Camp Trans.

From "Welcome to Camp Trans 2003":

> Camp Trans is an annual protest against the Michigan Womyn's Music Festival's policy that bars transsexual women from attending. MWMF's so-called womyn-born-womyn policy sets a transphobic standard for women-only spaces across the country, and contributes to an environment in women's and lesbian communities where discrimination against trans women is considered acceptable. For trans women who are consistently refused help from domestic violence shelters and rape crisis centers, this is a matter of life and death.

Some posterboards are stuck with Post-it notes that outline each day's workshops and meetings; another posterboard is cluttered with bright notes soliciting amour in the woods. One bemoans a throat atrophied from lack of use, another is looking for couples to participate in a Floridian-retiree role-play. Interested parties can respond by slipping scrawled replies into corresponding envelopes. There are zines for sale, silk-screened patches that say CAMP TRANS SUPPORTER in heavy-metal letters. buttons that squeak I ♥ CAMP TRANS, and T-shirts that say NOT GAY AS IN HAPPY BUT QUEER AS IN FUCK YOU. There is also a notebook labeled LETTERS TO LISA VOGEL.

Lisa Vogel is the sole captain of the SS *Michigan Womyn's Music Festival*. There is no one but her behind the wheel; she wrote the policy, and she is the only one who can lift it. Of the many rumors I hear this weekend, most involve her. One rumor says that she offered Camp Trans a sum of money somewhere between $7,500 and $75,000 to start their own damn festival. This is totally unlikely, as her own festival is suffering financially. Another rumor says that transsexual women will be allowed into her festival over her dead body, an extreme pledge that makes me think of Lauryn Hill's "I'd rather my babies starve than white kids buy my records" quote. Who knows what's true. Vogel is famously tightlipped about the whole controversy, and has never made an attempt to negotiate with Camp Trans. In the face of past protests she has simply reiterated the policy, which, I also hear, has suddenly been removed from all MWMF Web pages. There is much speculation on what this means, but no one is naïve enough to believe that it means the policy has been dropped and trans women are now welcome. More likely the immense controversy, which now involves not just a boycott of the festival but also of the performers, is wearing on festival producers, and targets for attack are being shuffled out of the line of fire.

Excerpts from "Letters to Lisa Vogel":

I love the festival and it has to become a safe space for everyone. It can happen, everyone would benefit. As feminists we cannot become our oppressors.

A transpositive environment will only improve the festival experience for all. There are plenty of information sources on how to do this.

I've been to many trans-inclusive events in my hometown, including a women's bathhouse. I feel totally safe around trans women, and I know lots of other women my age who feel the same way.

*

Behind the tree line is where people are camping, and the arc of green has been segmented into three campsites: loud substance, which means campers are getting bombed and fucking right outside your tent; loud no substance, meaning sober people lashed to trees and moaning loudly; and quiet no substance, which means everyone sleeps. This is where I camp. I actually unknowingly plop my tent right in the center of a sand patch being used for AA meetings. Next to me is a camper van all tricked out with a sink and a fridge, the outside painted checkerboard. It looks straight out of *Fast Times at Ridgemont High,* and it is occupied by, lo and behold, my friend Chris, who is out on his makeshift patio, smoking a lot of pot and triggering the substance-free campers. He's sharing his pipe with a lesbian named Mountain, who lives on a women-only commune in Oregon that has successfully integrated trans women into their home. It is, essentially, no big whoop. Life goes on, wimmin are still wimmin, they tend their organic garden and print their lunar calendars and life is good. Mountain is one of those women who live for Michigan, and it's a real big deal that she's not there this year. She's here at Camp Trans, in solidarity.

Now people are scurrying around, full of excited purpose. Tonight is the big dance and performance, and the number of people on this land will rise with an influx of girls from the festival. Camp Trans's population, which hovers at around seventy-five, will shoot up above a hundred with the visitors. Which is nothing compared with the eight thousand or so women hunkered down in the vast woods across the way. Sadie is dashing around, all stressed out. She's got a sweet, kind face with sparkly eyes and short hair; her all-black outfits seem like military gear, especially with the big black women-symbol-raised-fist tattoo on her shoulder. She's still dealing with fallout from last night's sex party, and now she's just found a note from a Camp Transer looking to host a Camp Trans workshop inside the festival, where trans women can't go. There is a feeling that the action is spinning out of the organizer's hands, and she's upset that a so-called Camp Trans event would happen in a place where trans women aren't allowed. Sadie, needing a drink, bustles off with tears in her eyes.

## Sadie Crabtree

"One problem was that some festival attendees were unclear on the mission of Camp Trans, and didn't see it as a protest but rather as a part of their Michigan experience. Kind of a suburb of MWMF where fest attendees could go to hang out with hot trannyboys. That's another problem — the fascination with and fetishization of FTMs in some dyke communities make trans women even more invisible. At least one fest attendee last year spoke openly about how she totally supported Camp Trans and loved trans guys but just didn't like trans women. We tried to solve some of those problems this year by having a very clear mission statement on all of the Camp Trans materials, providing suggested talking points for all campers, and having discussions about the experiences of trans women at Camp Trans. We had volunteer advocates whose job it was to listen to people's concerns — especially those of trans women — and help organizers plan solutions. Another thing we did was designate certain workshops and decompression areas 'wristband-free zones' where fest attendees were asked not to go. Having a space to retreat from interactions with fest attendees was a need that had been expressed by trans women last year, but it also sent a message. It wasn't to stigmatize festival attendees, but to help people think a little more critically about what it means to give hundreds of dollars to a transphobic organization for permission to do activism inside, what it means to speak in a space where others' voices are forbidden, what it's like to have a space that specifically excludes you. When people asked about the wristband-free spaces, we offered them scissors. You have that choice. Some people don't."

## Lemmy and Other Problems

Another MWMF policy forbids male voices on the land, meaning no one is allowed to slip a Michael Jackson tape into her boom box and start moonwalking. Perhaps it also means the Porta-Pottie men take a vow of silence when they roar through the gate — who knows. This rule has been broken, or bent, with the rise of drag kings — female performers who costume themselves as men, both lampooning and celebrating masculinity in a sort of burlesque, often via lip-synchs. When, some years back, the Florida drag king troupe House of Ma took an MWMF side stage during a talent show, the audience was given warning that a male voice would shortly boom from the sound system. Offended women hightailed it out of the vicinity, one step ahead of Neil Diamond. This of course is not an issue at Camp Trans, so the music is a little varied — better — on this side of the road. The dance party under way on the patch of sandy brown earth designated both "stage" and "dance floor" is shaking to Dr. Dre and the Gossip, Motorhead and Peeches, Billy Idol, Northern States, Ludicris, and Fannypack. I'm standing beside Benjamin, a genderqueer boy. Meaning he was born a boy and remains a boy, but he's gorgeous like a girl and does hella fierce drag. His hair is an architecture of multiple pieces that look like feather dusters protruding from his scalp in feathery pompoms. "Everyone is so beautiful," he muses at the crowd, and he is right. Mostly young, like late teens and twenties, they are kicking up Pig Pen–size clouds of dust as they dance in their silver plastic pants and maribou-trimmed spandex, their starchy crinolines and pink ruffled tuxedo shirts, their neon orange nighties, push-up bras, and outfits constructed from shredded trash bags and duct tape. Everyone is gleeful, happy to be smashing the gender binary, to be partying down for a cause, to be part of a revolution of good-looking gender-ambiguous people. In the process of deconstructing gender identity, I muse, sexual preference may become obsolete. If you're an old-fashioned lesbian purged of transphobia, you'll be hot for the trans women. Bunches of dykes are already hooking up with trans men, and if you're dating trans men it's probably a good time to reckon with your bisexuality and attraction to the equally male, if perhaps less socially evolved, non-trans men of the world. And that's pretty much everyone. Yeah. Maybe I'm just trampy, but I'm attracted to pretty much everyone here.

Showtime starts with an introduction by an organizer named

Jess who instructs the crowd — part Camp Transers, part festie-goers — on proper behavior while in such an unusual space, a space where transpeople outnumber the non-trans. Because last year's visitors didn't understand how to act, pissing off a lot of trans women, this year we get a tiny schooling. Do not assume anyone's pronoun. There's really no way of guessing at who is a "he" and who a "she," and besides all that, there are gangs of genderqueers promoting the use of a third pronoun, "ze," which I am not going to conjugate for you. Others say to hell with pronouns altogether and dare us to be more creative in the way we refer to them. Also, Jess instructs, do not ask anyone rude questions about their bodies. If you're bursting with curiosity or just freaking out, please see an armbanded advocate. Last year Camp Trans was paid a visit by the weight loss guru Susan Powter, who was greeted by an advocate named J. J. Bitch. "J. J. Bitch!" she shrieked, waving her arms around like a nut. "J. J. Bitch! I love that name! I want that name! I'm J. J. Bitch!" J. J. Bitch was stunned and delighted by the somewhat manic celebrity guest. Advocate work can be quite emotionally draining. It had to have been a lift.

First there are skits, one which demonstrates the simply cruelty of turning trans women away from the festival gates. Another enacts the traumatizing experience of having perfect strangers trot up and inquire about the state of your genitals because you are transgendered and expected to answer this. Last-minute creations, the skits are shaky but effective. The audience ripples out from the spotlit performance area, sitting in the dirt, getting hopped on by grasshoppers and crickets and weird brown beetles with little wings folded beneath their shells. A moth as big as a sparrow keeps charging into one of the light dishes glowing up from the ground. A gang of women comes out, all dressed in trash bags and duct tape. They are the Fat-Tastics, and they deliver a smart performance about fat power and fat oppression, ending in an empowering cheer replete with pompoms fashioned from more shredded garbage bags. A duo of trans boys or genderqueers dressed like Gainsborough's Blue Boy enacts a randy ballet. Nomy Lamm, an artist who has arranged a petition for artists who oppose MWMF's policy, howls heartbreaking songs into the warm night, accompanied by a honking accordion. The camp feels like some medieval village on a pagan holiday, bodies close in the darkness, being serenaded by a girl in striped tights and crinoline, harlequin eye makeup shooting stars down her cheeks. Benjamin is a total trouper when the CD he's lip-synching to keeps skipping and skipping and skipping. Eventually Julia Serano reads. Julia is a trans woman spoken-word poet. She's got a girl-next-door thing going on, with strawberry-blond hair and a sprinkling of freckles. She performs a piece about her relationship with her girlfriend. It's got sweet and honest humor, and it charms the crowd. Then she recites another, "Cocky":

> and if i seem a bit cocky
> well that's because i refuse
> to make apologies for my body anymore
> i am through being the human sacrifice
> offered up to appease other people's gender issues
> some women have a penis
> some men don't
> and the rest of the world
> is just going to have to get the fuck over it

Julia gets a standing ovation, everyone hopping up and brushing the dirt off their asses, brushing crickets from their chests, hooting and hollering at the poet as she leaves the "stage" and falls into a hug with her girlfriend and Sadie.

## Julia Serano

"As part of Camp Trans, so much of our work is dedicated to convincing the women who attend MWMF that trans women won't flaunt their penises on the land, or that we won't commit acts of violence against other women. I have yet to meet a trans woman who has acted violently toward another woman and/or flaunted her penis in public, but I know I need to take the MWMF attendees' concerns seriously in order to gain their trust. At the same time, to borrow an analogy, it's like someone of Middle Eastern descent having to convince every person on a flight that s/he won't hijack the plane in order to be allowed on board.

"Having talked to several festival-goers, I was distressed at how often people centered the debate around 'the penis.' Everyone talked about the significance of penises being on the land, without much acknowledgment that these so-called penises are attached to women's bodies.

"Like most trans women, I have a lot of issues surrounding both my penis and the fact that I was born a boy. I have worked through too much self-loathing about these aspects of my person to allow other people to throw salt on my open wounds. It has taken me a long time to reach the point where I can accept my penis as simply being a part of my flesh and tissue, rather than the ultimate symbol of maleness. I find it confusing that so many self-described feminists spend so much effort propagating the male myth that men's power and domination arise from the phallus.

"It was surreal to have MWMF festival-goers talk to me about their fear that transsexual women would bring masculine energy onto the land one minute, then the next tell me that they never would have guessed that I was born a man.

"I also found it distressing that so many women would want to exclude me (a woman) from women's space, under the pretense that my body contains potential triggers for abuse survivors. That line of reasoning trivializes the abuse that trans women face day in, day out. I have been verbally and physically assaulted by men for being who I am. Like other women, I have had men force themselves upon me. In addition, I can't think of a more humiliating way to be raped by male culture than to be forced to grow up as a boy against one's will. Every trans woman is a survivor, and we have triggers too. The phrase 'womyn-born-womyn' is one of my triggers."

I'm wiped out, exhausted, can't make it through the rest of the show. With my little flashlight I traipse through the scratchy, weedy terrain, locusts dashing away from my sneakers, toward my tent. My tent may be toxic. Earlier I dumbly spritzed a wealth of bug spray onto my body, fearful of West Nile Virus. I did this inside my tent, then had to quickly unzip the tent and let myself out, a step ahead of asphyxiation. The tent has aired out a bit but still retains its chemical tang. I eat a bunch of valerian, herbal Valium, and crawl into my sleeping bag. The dance party has revved back up. I hear the shrieks of dancers over the thump of Outkast, and then I fall asleep.

## Day Two

One thing I made damn sure to do before leaving civilization was to brew a two-liter container of coffee, and it is this I grab at when I wake up. My tent is already starting to bake as I scramble into some jeans, grab my toothbrush, and stumble out into the searing sunlight. I am the only camper — the only camper! — who did not camp in the shade behind the tree line. I camped in front of the trees, the scary trees that I imagined were dripping ticks, ticks poisoned with Lyme disease, the disgusting trees where many spiders live, the trees with their carpet of old leaves slowly rotting away, where mice no doubt burrow and any number of things that bite can be found. No, I arranged my borrowed tent right in direct sun. Not so smart.

The smart campers are emerging from their shaded glens, getting right into their cars and driving the fuck to the lake. There's a lake nearby and a creek, too, and everyone I speak to confirms that going to the lake is definitely part of this "Camp Trans experience" I am hoping to document; they urge me to hop in for a swim. A fat caucus took place at the lake yesterday, as did an Attention Deficit Disorder caucus, though no one managed to stay very focused for that one. I am beyond tempted to ride along, to float in the lake in my underwear under the guise of journalism, but I am too scared of missing out on some crucial bit of drama. The vibe at Camp Trans is intense, flammable like the parched ground beneath our various feet. Something is bound to happen, and I can't be splashing around like a fool when it does.

I'm standing at the welcome tent when two festival workers show up. One is a femme girl with curly red hair, a cowboy hat, and glamorous sunglasses; the other is a butch girl in thick horn-rims and a baseball hat. They carry a box of zines they've made, a compilation of the various opinions held by the women who work the festival across the road. The femme girl hands it off to the Camp Trans welcome worker. "It's our effort at having some dialogue," she says, or something like that. She seems a little shy, scared probably, and I have a few thoughts, watching the welcome worker accept the gift, a caul of skepticism on her face. I think the festies are brave to come over with a box of MWMF opinions. I think the opinions are probably already well known to Camp Trans campers. I think shit is going to hit the fan and these workers and their good intentions are going to get creamed. The two festival workers walk off to the side, lean against a parked car, light cigarettes, and hang out. I stick my zine in my back pocket and head over to a tent for the morning meeting.

I guess the morning meetings happen every morning, just a rundown of what's happening that day, a space for people to make announcements. A sort of exhilaration is blowing through the crowd as word of the zine, or the zine itself, hits them. People are hunched over, their faces stuck in the xeroxed pages, gasping. It doesn't look good. Simon Strikeback, a camp organizer, one of the activists who resuscitated Camp Trans after Nancy and company let it go, is facilitating the gathering. Like everyone here, he is very cute. He's got blond curls spiraling out from his baseball hat and is grimy in a fun way, like he's been playing in the dirt. He says yes, there can be a circle to process the zine. He announces some other events — a workshop called "Feminism and the Gender Binary," which I plan to check out despite its terrifying title. A dread-locked white girl with facial piercings announces that she has anarchist T-shirts for sale and is looking for partners to hitchhike to Mexico for an antiglobalization rally. Someone else holds up a silk-screen emblazoned with a Camp Trans image designed by the cartoonist Ariel Schrag and asks for help screening T-shirts. I announce that I'm attending the festival as a member of the press. It's a good faith thing I did at Sadie's request, so that everyone knows what's up and people who think it's terrible and exploit-ative that I am writing about their camp can glare at me from afar and not wind up, without their consent, in my story. I'm even wearing a dorky sticker that says PRESS in red Sharpie. At one point a boy walks up and presses it. "I thought something happened when I pressed it," he explains, perhaps disappointed. I try to remedy suspicious looks by volunteering to help clean up breakfast, over at the kitchen tent.

## Over at the Kitchen Tent

There's not much to do until the water gets here. There are various pans with muck being swiftly baked onto them by this relentless sun of ours. There is a giant bucket of beets that people are wondering what to do with. I move it into the shade, sure it'll keep a bit longer. In another bucket a whole bunch of beans soak, plumping up for tonight's chili dinner. Culling the rotten vegetables from the vegetable boxes is what I'm told to do, so I join the others inside the tent. There is an abundance of vegetables, mostly donated from a co-op several states away: cardboard boxes of squash, zucchini, bulbs of garlic. I deal with a plastic bag filled with liquefying basil, pulling the top leaves, still green, from the blackening herb below. The stuff that's no good — the dried-up rosemary and yellowed cilantro, the split tomatoes and the peppers sprouting cottony tufts of mold — all get tossed into the compost. A woman is picking beets as large as a child's head and slicing off their wilting greens with a knife. When she discovers the mouse inside the beet box, she shrieks. "Oh, that's no good," says the person culling squash beside me. "You can get really sick. I ate food contaminated with mouse shit once, and I got really, really sick." We try to scare the mouse away, but it just burrows deeper into the beets. I leave the tent, walk behind it, and pull the beet box out backward, into the grass. The mouse leaps out and scrambles into the forest. We look for visible mouse turd, but everything is sort of brown and crumbly from the dirty beets. I decide not to eat a bite of the Camp Trans food while I'm there. I'm too worried about getting a tick in my armpit to take on the additional neurosis of hantavirus.

I've got six energy bars stuffed in my suitcase, two packs of tuna, and a few cans of chili. That's what I'll be eating. Deciding that I saved the day by ridding us of the mouse, I retire from my cleanup duties. It's too hot; I need some tuna or I'll get heat stroke. I stop by Chris's stoner van to glob a bit of cool, refrigerated mustard into my tuna and listen to his instructions that I gulp down at least fifteen gulps of water each time I hit my bottle. That's the number: fifteen. "Till your stomach's all bloated," he advises. I do as he says. He does seem like an experienced camper, and the heat is killing people all over the globe, knocking them down by the thousands in France. His little dog Poi, who looks just like Benji, has burrowed a cool hole beneath the van and lies there, panting.

## Bullshit

I am very glad I didn't go to the lake. Now we sit in a ring, in a small, shaded clearing not far from where I've camped: a bunch of Camp Trans campers and the two festival workers who delivered the box of zines. The zine is called *Manual Transmission,* and people hate it. It's an anthology, essentially, of festival workers' opinions on the trans-inclusion issue. There is talk about throwing the box of them onto that evening's campfire, a good old-fashioned book burning. Ana Jae is set to facilitate the discussion, and Benjamin is by her side, "taking stack," which I think means keeping a list of everyone who raises a hand to speak, so that everyone gets to.

Excerpts from *Manual Transmission:*

> Let's be clear about what womyn-born womyn means. It's not about defining a goddamn thing. It is about saying this is what I'm gathering around for this particular moment. It is saying that this festival, this period in time, is for women whose entire life experience has been as a girl and who still live loudly as a woman. Period. How is that defining you? Why do you think we are so ignorant as to not "get" that, to not figure out that we also have privilege for not struggling with a brain/body disconnect? But can you be so obstinate, can you be so determined to not understand that we have an experience that is outside yours? And that that experience, even though we have greater num-

bers, still entitles us to take separate space? Do you not see it as full-on patronizing that you act as though these "thousands" of women's shelters can't make up their own minds and policies? Doesn't it make you sick to have the same objectives as the religious right? Why is it okay to totally ignore the need of women who do NOT want to see a penis? How and what world do we live in that you can completely divorce these things? Like being white and telling everyone your skin color doesn't matter because you are not a racist? Stop assuming our ignorance.

Dicks are not useless signifiers. Even unwanted ones. You who I love and call my community of political bandits, you who grew up being seen as, treated as, regarded as boys (and perhaps miserably failing that performance), you did not grow as I. You did not experience being held out as girl and cropped into that particular box. You gotta understand, you are my sister, but you don't have that experience. And taking my experience and saying it is yours don't make it yours, makes it stolen.

"This is bullshit. In my opinion," Ana Jae states. The overall feel about the zine and its arrival is, first, "We know this already," and second, "How dare you bring it into this space that we are trying to keep free from such hurtful sentiments." People take turns expressing themselves.

Hitchhiking Anarchist Girl: takes issue with a passage defending MWMF's $350 entrance fee, calling it classist.

Simon: is frustrated, only open to discussing changing the policy, sick to death of back-and-forth arguing about penises and girlhoods.

Guy to My Left: generously concedes that the festie workers had good intentions but delivered a flawed product.

Festie Workers: admit they were rushed and that, though they specified no submissions degrading or attacking trans people would be published, they did not get to read all of the writings. They feel bad for the discord their zine has caused, but maintain that these are the opinions of workers inside the festival, like it or not. They didn't feel it was proper to censor anyone's thoughts — who can dictate what is right and what is wrong?

Sadie: maintains that, as an activist, it's her job to declare her views the good and right and true views; she is only interested in talking to people who agree and want to help further the cause.

Festie Workers: weakly remind everyone of their good intentions.

Girl to My Right, in Wheelchair: offers that she is hurt every day by people with good intentions.

Femme Festie Worker: cries; doesn't know how to help this situation.

Girl I Can't See: says that it's everyone's responsibility to educate herself on trans issues.

Girl with Camouflage Bandanna: sympathizes with how painful the education process can be; urges please don't let that stop you from learning.

There's a lot of fear here, people afraid of each other, afraid of their own ability to do the wrong thing from simple ignorance, their own ability to bungle a peace offering, to offend the person they sought to help. It starts to rain. Light at first, and then heavy. The weather out here can turn violent in a finger snap, the dust suddenly flooded into muddy ponds, the sky cracking thunderbolts and sending threads of lightning scurrying across the cloud cover, occasionally touching down and setting a tree on fire. I run back to my tent and fling the rain cover over it, and by the time I get back to the circle it's over — the process, the rain, all of it. I talk briefly with a girl I know from my previous Augusts at the festival; she's usually been a worker. Last year she caught a lot of shit for taking a festival van over to Camp Trans for a date, so this year she's camping here, back in the trees where everyone seems to have gone. I go back to my tent to grab a notebook. Inside it is hot and smells strongly of sulfur, like hell itself. I take my notebook back to the now-empty clearing, sit in someone's abandoned camp chair, and write some notes.

## Here's Geyl, Then Pam

Geyl Forcewind is a lanky punk-rock trans woman with a red anarchy sign sewed into her ratty T-shirt. A good radiance sort of shines off Geyl. Her combat boots are patched with gummy straps of duct tape; she spits a lot and cracks jokes. She collapses into the chair next to me and asks how my "project" is going. She's teasing me, I think, but it's perfect that she's appeared because I wanted to talk to someone about the proliferation of trans men and tranny-boys, and the small numbers of trans women or genderqueers who enjoy the trappings of femininity. I love girls, I love girlness, and though I love trans men — my boyfriend is trans — I wish there were more females around these genderqueer parts. The face of the transrevolution is, presently, a bearded one. "Riot grrrl made being a dyke accessible," Geyl reflects, "and now those people are seeing that they can be genderqueer and it's not so scary. There's none of that for MTFs." Pam, a trans woman who had been quietly strumming her acoustic guitar in the woods behind us, strolls up and joins our conversation.

PAM: Trans women get abused a lot more in our society.

She's right, of course. Because it's often harder for them to pass as women in the world, and because they're likely to get way more shit for it, lots of would-be trans women just don't come out.

GEYL: Being a girl is not as cool. I actively try to recruit.
PAM: Yeah, there must be something wrong with you if you want to be a woman.
GEYL: I tried to be really butch when I first came out.
MICHELLE: I tried to be really butch when I first came out, too. It seemed cooler and tougher, and safer, to be masculine.

Pam looks like just the sort of woman the music festival across the way embraces — smudgy eyeliner, long brown hair, rolled bandanna tied around her forehead, and that acoustic guitar in tow. She's even a construction worker, and isn't that one of the most feminist jobs a woman can work. After coming out as a trans woman, Pam's co-worker threatened to toss her from the very high building they were working on. When she complained, her foreman said, "You should expect that sort of thing." She was soon fired from the job, for "being late."

PAM: If I watch *Jerry Springer,* I don't want to come out.

GEYL: All the trans women on that show aren't really trans. They're a joke.

PAM: I think Jerry is a tranny-chaser. And I think he's resentful of it and wants to take it out on the community.

Soon we're informed that we're sitting smack in the middle of the space reserved for the "Feminism and the Gender Binary" workshop.

GEYL: I'll feminize your gender binary. If anyone quotes Judith Butler, I'll punch them.

## The Rally

There's that girl Mountain again, on the mike this time, letting everyone know that if her feminist separatist farming commune can let the trans women in, anyone can. "I always have said that if I didn't go to the festival each year I'd die," she tells the crowd. "Well, I didn't go, and I didn't die, and I'm not going until they change the policy!" Everyone cheers. Sadie's on the mike, revving everyone up by insisting that we're going to change the policy. I guess it's impossible to engage in any sort of activism with a fatalistic view, and who knows, maybe MWMF will surprise us all and roll out the trans carpet, but I just don't see it happening. I remember glimpsing Lisa Vogel in the festival worker area years ago, after Camp Trans had brought a protest onto the land. They'd been kicked off, of course, and a reiteration of the womyn-born-womyn policy was swiftly typed up, xeroxed, and distributed throughout the festival. Lisa was smoking, and she looked pissed. Someone told me that she saw it as a class issue and an age issue. Camp Trans was made up of a bunch of teenagers freshly released from liberal New England colleges, with their heads full of gender theory and their blood bubbling with hormones and rebellion. Lisa Vogel is loved the way that saints are loved by the women who attend her festival, and why shouldn't she be? She's provided them with the only truly safe space they've ever known. She's a working-class lesbian who built it all up from scratch, with her hands and the hands of old-school dykes and feminists, women who claim, perhaps rightly, that no one knows what it was like, what they went through, how hard they fought. It has taken a lot of work to create the MWMF that's rocking across the way, sending its disembodied female voices floating into our campsite. It's taken single-mindedness and determination. Lisa Vogel, I fear, is one severely stubborn woman.

Emily is speaking and she's saying things that could turn around some of the more stubborn festival women. Unfortunately, I don't think anyone has come over from the fest who wouldn't love to see the policy junked. Emily is preaching, as they say, to the choir. She's talking about her girlhood, how the girls all knew she was a girl like they were, and how powerful and life-saving it was to be recognized like that, your insides finally showing through. A young friend wished Emily would get a sex-change operation so she could come to her slumber party. It's a great response to the festival's insistence that trans women didn't have girlhoods. Anna speaks next. (Not Ana Jae — this is a brand-new Anna. You haven't met her yet.) She's got big, dark eyebrows and wide lips painted red; she's holding the mike, and she's come to lecture the lesbians. For dating trans men but justifying this shades-of-hetero behavior by saying, "He's not really a guy." Sacrificing trans men's maleness so that their lesbian identities can stay intact. Sheepishly explaining, "He's trans" — again invalidating the real masculinity so as not to be confused with a straight girl. For fetishizing, as a community, this sexy new explosion of trans men but remaining unwelcoming to trans women. It's all so true my frickin' eyes well up. I'd spent the first year and a half of my boyfriend's transition explaining to everyone — women on the bus, strangers in line at Safeway, people I sit next to on planes — that my boyfriend, he's transgender. So don't go thinking I'm some stupid straight girl, the confession implies. I'm QUEER. Okay? It tended to be more information than anyone wanted. Everyone's uncomfortable, but at least no one thinks I'm heterosexual, and that's what counts. Oy vey, as my Jewish friends say. And I know lots of lesbians who date trannyboys but freak out if a trans woman enters their space. It's all so fucked-up and heartbreaking and overwhelming. Or maybe I'm just really sleep-deprived from a night on bumpy ground, sleeping atop sticks and hard mounds of dirt. Before me are the Gainsborough Blue Boys, lying side by side on separate chaise longues, still in their wiggy tennis outfits. They clutch paper bags concealing what I assume are beers and make out. Seriously — who are they? I love them. I wipe my soggy eyes, grab Anna as she shuffles past with her boyfriend, and thank her for her speech. I confess my past as a shameful tranny-dating lesbian; I heap upon her how sad and scared I get when my dyke friends start talking shit about trans women. I want Anna — beautiful, strong Anna with the microphone — to absolve me and also solve all my social problems. She seems so capable. I think I overwhelm her. She gives me her contact information, including her phone number and e-mail address. "She loves being interviewed; it's her favorite thing," her boyfriend encourages. Of course she does; she's a genius. She walks away into the darkness, her beaded, sequined shoulder bag glinting in the night.

The rally is over, and everyone's dancing again. On the sidelines I find Carolyn, a writer and trans woman from Brooklyn. Carolyn must have found some way to construct a shower from rainwater and tree branches. Every time I see her, she looks really, really clean. Every night, before I sleep, I wipe a thick coat of grime from my body with some sort of chemical gauze pad called a Swash cloth. It's all I've managed to do, hygiene-wise, and I look mangled. Carolyn admits that others have commented on her cleanliness. "I don't know — I haven't showered for four days! I'm just lucky," she says modestly.

## I Had the Time of My Life

Two people — girls, trannyboys, genderqueers, I can't really tell in the light, so bright it turns them into silhouettes — are whirling across the dusty makeshift dance floor, doing a dance routine to a medley of songs from the movie *Dirty Dancing*. Here is my proof that this gender-smashing revolution is a generational thing: Someone walks across the stage holding a cardboard sign reading NOBODY PUTS BABY IN A CORNER and everyone roars. I have no fucking idea what they are talking about. I was a moody death rocker when *Dirty Dancing* came out. This was back before Hot Topic in the malls, back when goth was a slightly dressier version of punk and wearing black lipstick and ratting your hair into a tarantula was a uniform that conveyed information such as "I am opposed to the dominant culture and movies such as *Dirty Dancing*." My little sister loved *Dirty Dancing*, and I ragged on her for it mercilessly. Patrick Swayze? Come on. But I like watching these two spinning into each other, knocking each other down and crawling all over each other. At the very end of their act, after dancing close, they pull apart and draw the audience in, and everyone responds; they move into the brightness, becoming silhouettes that dance and raise their hands into the light and it's beautiful like a dark kaleidoscope, all the bodies coming together under the light. My eyes well up with tears again. Jesus. Chris asks me to dance, but I can't. I'm a mess. It's been such an emotional day, and I'm spent. A trans man is straddling the lap of a girl in a bright green dress, lap-dancing her on the folding chair. Two others are making out on the dance floor, and many bootys are being freaked. It's time for bed. I hike back to my tent, following the small spot of light my flashlight tosses into the weeds.

## Day Three

"I asked you to dance and you disappeared," Chris complains. We're on his patio. He's making real hot coffee on his camp stove, but I had to swear I would tell no one about this luxury, because he's almost out of gas. He starts talking about how confused he was about Camp Trans, how he thought it was a bunch of trans men trying to get into the women's festival, and he wasn't down with that. "You gain a few privileges, you lose a few." He laughs. "Go cry on your own damn shoulder; get over yourself." Once he realized it was about getting trans women some women-only privileges, he was down for the cause. He's glad he's here. "I'm so comfortable," he says. "My tree keeps getting closer." He means the tree he pees on. Maybe he saw *Sleepaway Camp II* as well and is scared of the portos, maybe he's lazy, or maybe it's just such a rarity to be a trans person who can take a piss in the woods without fear.

## This Just In

Excerpted e-mail forwarded from Carolyn, from the D.C. Metropolitan Police Department's Gay & Lesbian Liaison Unit (GLLU), received three days after returning from Camp Trans:

> WASHINGTON, D.C. In the past week, the transgender community has been shaken by three shootings, two of which resulted in the deaths of the victims.
>
> On 8/16/03. Bella Evangelista (Elvys Perez) was murdered at Arkansas Avenue and Allison Street, N.W. Antoine Jacobs was immediately arrested and has been charged with first-degree murder while armed. The case has been classified by the Metropolitan Police Department as a suspected hate/bias motivated crime (gender identity).
>
> In the evening hours of 8/20/03, a black male-to-female transgender individual was found near 3rd and I Streets, N.W., suffering from apparent gunshot wounds. The victim was transported to a local hospital, where she is in serious condition. The case has been classified as an assault with intent to kill.
>
> In the early morning hours of 8/21/03. Seventh district officers discovered the body of a black male-to-female transgender individual at 2nd Street and Malcolm X Avenue, S.E. The victim was unconscious and suffering from wounds by unknown means. Since there was no sign of life, D.C. Fire/EMS did not transport the individual.

Camp Trans is unraveling before my eyes. Cars and trucks are rolling out of the parking lot, which is just another part of the field we've all been living in. People wave out their windows as they pull onto the road. All day long the population shrinks. The planning meeting for Camp Trans 2004, which is happening beneath a tent, is repeatedly interrupted as vacating campers lavish goodbye

hugs on their friends. I am sitting back and listening to participants who raise their hands and offer compliments on what they
felt went well at this year's gathering, and what needs to be fine-
tuned for next year. Everyone is generally pleased, and the re-
newed focus on trans women's needs and overturning the policy
was a success. There are concerns about how white Camp Trans is,
but no one is naïve about seeking out token people of color to
make him- or herself feel better. Instead, a resolution is made to
make the event itself more welcoming to people of color, in hopes
that the gathering will organically diversify. Geyl suggests travel
scholarships for trans people who want to come but can't afford
the time off work or the travel expenses to the Middle of Nowhere,
Michigan. People are happy about trans women being in charge,
happy that there was essentially no rain in a region known for
violent summer thunderstorms, and want greater accountability
from women who say they are organizing within the festival gates.
There will be greater fundraising this coming year, though Camp
Trans did come out ahead by five hundred dollars. Incredible, really, since at the start of the week Ziploc baggies had been duct-
taped inside the portos asking for spare change each time you took
a whiz. It cost the camp eighty dollars each time those monsters
got cleaned.

Over at the welcome tent a few ladies from the festival have
strolled in. They're older, in their fifties perhaps, from Utah. Probably they live for the festival and have never spoken to a transsexual in their lives, but they've come over, minds open, "to see what
everybody's all 'ugh' about." Maybe because everyone at the welcome station is so burned out on this, the last day, or maybe because I'm sitting closest to the two women, I wind up answering some of their questions, or rather countering their concerns.
Their concerns are the usual ones: penises and girlhoods. So
many women have been traumatized by a penis, is it really fair to
force them to glimpse one at their annual retreat? I tell them that
women need to find a way to heal from their abuse without dis-
placing responsibility for it onto the bodies of trans women, who
are also likely to have been abused. That a roving detached penis

didn't abuse anyone, but men with penises did, and those men are not these women. I tell them that trans women did in fact have girlhoods, girlhoods as rough and confusing as any girl's. One tiny conversation and I'm drained and frustrated. And this isn't even my life.

Everyone is called to help dismantle what's still standing of Camp Trans. Intimidated by the architecture of the tents and lean-tos that need to be torn down, I busy myself gently untying the neon plastic ribbons that have been knotted, for some reason, around a rusting cage, which, for some reason, contains a stunted apple tree. Perhaps there's a hornets' nest in the crook of its branches. A large swath of our field has been roped off all week with that same neon plastic, to keep everyone away from a burrowing hornet encampment. That's being torn down now as well. I grab a trash bag and roam around the land, collecting debris. Part of what makes the Michigan Womyn's Music Festival is the land it takes place on. The trees are tall and cool; there's much grass and twining paths; the air smells fresh: It's nature, the real deal. And the women love it and care for it like a living thing, which it is. I try to arrange a similar mindset about cleaning up Camp Trans, but I don't feel connected to this rather lousy scrap of national forest. Maybe if the event keeps occurring here for twenty-eight years it will become imbued with the specialness and familiarity that haunts the woods across the road. I snatch the torn corner of a bag of Chex Mix from the ground, some empty water jugs, balls of toilet paper, bits of shredded trash bag that blew off one of the Fat-Tastics' pompoms. I pull from the ground tiki torches that had been guiding nighttime revelers to the Porta-Potties all week. I leave to decompose back into the land some carrots, some tofu dogs, some onion skins. There are bullet casings and smashed clay pigeons scattered throughout the weeds, left behind by whoever was here last.

Over by the portos is a structure made of tarps that all weekend I'd thought was someone's wicked punk-rock campsite. Tarps spray-painted with antipolicy slogans, tied and duct-taped to stakes driven into the ground. I'd had a brief fantasy that it was

Geyl's squatlike queendom. But as I pass it, Chris sticks his head out from the plastic and asks, "Did you know there was a shower here?!" He is delighted. The shower is a little pump with a thin hose attached; it looks like the pesticide tank an exterminator lugs around. You pump the top like a keg, click a switch at the end of the hose, and a fine stream of water mists all around you. It looks like a feeble shower, but a great way to cool off. Later I'll help Geyl and a person named Cassidy — butch girl? genderqueer? — tear the whole thing down, and have great fun squirting myself with all the leftover water in the little tank. I pull stakes from the ground and untangle knots of rope, listening to Cassidy tell the story of Blane, the man who rents out the portos we've been peeing in. Blane lives on five hundred acres of land and raises beefalo. Beefalos are a crossbreed of cows and buffalos, and Blane is proud that he has been able to breed out their horns. Beefalo is lower in cholesterol than regular beef, and after his doctor warned him that his was shooting dangerously high, he took to farming the animals. He feeds them corn that he also grows on his land, and the corn is grown in compost made from the slurry in the Porta-Potties. All of our crap will be distributed throughout a nearby cornfield. It's incredible, slightly sickening.

"The birds of prey have come for us," Geyl says, pointing a long finger up to the sky, where some large birds are indeed circling. I've been trying to find a place to sit and read, but every patch of shade I see is inhabited either by creepy daddy longlegs or by intimidating cliques of remaining campers. There's a girl doing yoga in a growth of weeds; her legs become visible, then her butt, her head. A car is flung open — all doors, the trunk — and people load their belongings. X's "White Girl" leaks from the stereo, soon to be overpowered by a car blaring Tiffany. I settle down in what's left of the dismantled welcome station and try to read, but I'm distracted by the heat, the mosquitos, the loud sex noises howling out from the woods in front of me.

I hitch a ride into nearby Hart with a boy named Billy. Billy drives his big red truck into Hart every day, three or four times, to dump trash, redeem bottles, and fetch more water. It seems nuts that this duty has fallen solely on his shoulders, but he's a trouper about it. Especially considering how trashed the bed of the truck has become — gummy with spilled booze and moldy produce — and that he's been living in that same truck bed for the past seven months, traveling around the country. A lot of the campers at Camp Trans are part of what I've heard referred to as "travel culture" and "youth travel culture." The anarchist hitchhiker, or the many groups of people who are not going home from here but traveling onward to distant states — New York, Chicago. Lots of people are heading to Tennessee, where a similar though less politically charged event will be taking place on a patch of land owned and inhabited by a group of pagan gay guys known as the radical faeries. Billy pulls in behind the nearest gas station and I help him dump clanking bags of unredeemable glass and wobbly boxes heaped with vegetables gone bad. He grabs a bottle of whiskey, sucks the dregs, and tosses it empty into the Dumpster. Next Billy dumps me at a Mobil station, while he fetches water, so I can call my boyfriend from a pay phone and grab some snacks. After a few days of nothing but tasteless nutrition bars, dry tuna, and cold canned chili, the weirdest snacks look appetizing. I buy a giant bottle of Coke, a pack of Pop-Tarts, and a bag of potato chips with a mysterious flavor — Mustard and Onion "Coney" Chips, the bag proclaims. They taste just like hot dogs.

Next is Dave's Party Store, where an affable, Pauly Shore–ish dude hands over twenty-five dollars in exchange for a worn trash bag of sludgy bottles, and a literally red-necked white guy tells the cashier, in deep ebonies, that he's going to join the traveling carnival. "That sounds like a great place for you," the woman says dryly. Back in the truck we listen to Lil' Kim and cruise to Camp Trans, past the music festival and its vast parking lot still stuffed with cars. There's Blane the Porta-Pottie guy, vacuuming the ultimate grossness out from the portos, then loading the empty toilets onto his truck and driving them away. Now we'll all be peeing on trees. I use my rusty can opener to peel the lid off another can of vegetarian chili and wander over to Chris's van. I find him inside, smoking pot with Andrew, a twenty-year-old trannyboy whose legend I'd already heard from Geyl, last night at the dance. How he's never met another tranny, ever, until arriving at Camp Trans yesterday. How he learned he was trans from watching the film *Boys Don't Cry*, in which the actress Hilary Swank (who later won an Oscar for her performance) portrayed the young trans man Brandon Teena, who was raped, then murdered when the boys he'd been hanging out with learned of his situation. Andrew lives in Lansing and caught a ride down to Camp Trans — which he'd just found out about — from a couple of anti–Camp Trans ladies on their way to the festival. They'd already stopped by earlier, to curtly inform him that they were staying at their festival a little longer, to hang out and catch the last concerts. "I don't want to go back with them at all," Andrew says, and soon he has arranged to catch a ride home with the nomadic Chris, who plans to continue meandering through the country in his surfer van for a few more months. Andrew is cute: He's got the buzz cut of a young recruit and eyes that shift icily between the palest blue and green. He is stroking the soft skin on his jaw tenderly. "Do I have a bruise?" he asks, half to pose an honest question and half to brag. I don't see any marks, but soon we're hearing about the wrestling match he was part of last night. He tells us how someone walked right up to him and said, "Can I kiss you?" He'd never been approached so bluntly by an admirer, and he's surprised that it didn't make him feel weird, threatened, or unsafe. He felt like he could say a friendly no and the person would have backed off. But since he felt so safe he said yes. Andrew has a girlfriend who is on her own vacation, and who, from the sound of it, is familiar with the heightened sex vibes of queer gatherings. When she heard he was off to Camp Trans, she said, "Don't even try to be monogamous — you'll be miserable." "What a great girlfriend," I compliment, impressed. Andrew is satisfied with last night's kisses and wrestling and is anxious to get back to Lansing and be with his very modern paramour.

## Adventure

Jess is complaining that she needs an adventure on this, the last night of Camp Trans, when all who remain are among the camp's

core organizers (Sadie's fled back to D.C.), a few people procrasti-
nating their long drives home, Chris, Andrew, and me. I have
found an adventure, but Jess does not approve. In fact, Camp
Trans does not approve. It is their policy to ask their campers to
please not sneak into the Michigan Womyn's Music Festival, but it
is this that I am setting out to do. To be fair, it's not exactly sneaking. Some exiting festies tore their rubbery blue bracelets from
their wrists and gave them away. I've got one, and so does Calwell.
Geyl has one, handed over to her by a woman who tearfully said,
"You deserve to be in there." True enough, but Geyl isn't going to
risk it. She gives the bracelet to a girl named Kelly, whose T-shirt
reads KING SHIT OF FUCK MOUNTAIN. "We really don't want
anyone going over there," Jess says earnestly. She is wearing a
black slip and has a fake blue rose in her orange bob. Last year
Camp Trans was accused of allowing, if not encouraging, bunches
of campers to sneak into the gates. The MWMF insist this is true
because the amount of food eaten was higher than it should have
been. "I don't know why they just didn't figure people were eating
a lot," Jess says with a shrug. So far, this year, no one has sneaked
over. Since we plan to do nothing but stroll through the woods,
and maybe find a party rumored to be going on at "the dump," it
doesn't seem like a drag on anyone's resources. Off we go.

Excerpt from "Welcome to the Festival!":

> Those Security Gals: The womyn in tasteful orange vests are here to
> answer questions, keep things orderly, and promote safety. Unfortu-
> nately, it has also become an increasing part of their job to deal with
> the girls who decide to try to sneak into the Festival in various places
> along the route. Please help in their effort to ensure everyone takes
> that basic first step and purchases a ticket to the Festival.

We enter the festival perimeter by strolling through an un-
manned (unwomanned?) checkpoint. The lean-to is there; the
chair is draped with a security vest, but no worker. Calwell especially likes feeling that we are being sneaky, even though we've got
the bracelets. Kelly is hoping to stay the night, maybe find a lady
with a tent to get lucky in. Calwell wants to find the party at

the dump, and I just want something to do. So we look for the dump. We do not find it. We find, instead, the RV campsite, where bunches of women are hanging out in luxury: Winnebagos and campers, patios set up with tables and mosquito netting. Someone even brought a birdcage containing a live bird. Other women have set up mannequins on their front lawns, or strung Christmas lights over their vehicles. No one is naked, but some women are topless. Hard as it is for some, the campers at Camp Trans are required to cover nipples and pubic hair at all times, the land being national forest and all. Which means lots of topless people with patches of duct tape — ow! — slapped on their nipples. We find the acoustic stage quite by accident. It is surrounded by hundreds of women, lined up on the cool grass before an elegant wood stage on which there's a white grand piano and an empty set of chairs. It feels so strange to be on the inside of this compound we've been locked in opposition against all week. It feels a little scary actually — which is odd, because I've been on this land before, and I don't really believe anything will happen to us, even if someone found out we half-sneaked in. It's hard not to have an affection for these women, comfortable, all hanging out with each other on a hillside. It's also hard not to be wary of them, to feel conflicted. I think of Geyl, Sadie, Carolyn, all the trans women I've met this weekend. You can call it unjust that they can't come in, call it wrong, unfair, but really more than anything it just seems absurd. We march out of the acoustic stage area and down a few roads. We get royally lost in the woods, the sky darkening around us. Good thing I brought my trusty flashlight. The three of us crunch along paths that wind through real wilderness, and we find ourselves in the infamous Twilight Zone, where the women who practice SM sex camp. We pass a campsite that is a collection of tarps stretched out and tied together, enclosing a large area. I can see a campfire burning inside the plastic barrier, butch women moving around, a bunch of chains rigged up to a tree. But that's all. It wasn't that long ago that the SM women weren't welcome at MWMF. Their presence was protested, boycotted, until this space on the outskirts of the festival was created for them so they could whip each other in peace without "triggering" the women who feel like it's just more of the patriarchy seeping in. The SM controversy perhaps peaked when the dyke punk band Tribe 8 was invited to play and was picketed by women holding signs accusing the performers of everything from domestic abuse to violence against children. I've heard a lot of people suggest that trans women be allowed to camp here, among the bondage practitioners and heavy partiers. At least they'd be inside the gates, but what if a trans woman doesn't want to camp amid such heavy sex play? I camped in the Twilight Zone my first year at the festival, and, like those around me, was drunk pretty much 'round the clock. There was puke in our neighboring bushes; beer cans, cigarette butts, and latex sex supplies littered the grass outside our tents; and we almost got kicked out for lighting fireworks. More than once, while stumbling around in search of a place to pee, I walked smack into the middle of pretty intense sex scenes. And each morning we were all awakened by the exaggerated sex cries of a woman camped down the path. To require anyone to camp in such an environment seems downright abusive.

It's calming to be away from Camp Trans. To be in such a political, tense environment for an extended period of time does some wear and tear on your head. Me and Calwell talk about being afraid of being judged, feeling like you could say the wrong thing and wind up ostracized and alienated. It's kept him quieter than normal. Same for me. "I'd like a safe space to fuck up," I say, and we laugh. A space where everyone recognizes that everyone is trying their best, imperfectly struggling, human. But perhaps that's not possible. Activism is, famously, "by any means necessary." People on both sides of this debate like to compare their stance to the struggle against racism, but it is true that, camping at Camp Trans these few days, I feel like I'm in the midst of the first swell of a new civil rights movement.

## The Fire, Last Time

Back at Camp Trans the final campfire roars, with Cassidy — somehow an expert on the various ways wood can grow — strategically loading branches into the flames. Chris is burning marshmallows on a long stick. Simon is shaving pieces of potato and garlic into an aluminum foil pouch to be roasted. Someone passes around cold pizza, someone else passes around a bottle of Boone's Farm. It's the first time alcohol has been visible all week, though many revelers have been visibly under its influence. Another of the national forest laws. Max, a trans man who is part of the posse responsible for reviving Camp Trans in 1999, is telling the story of the lesbian curse. Actually, he's acting it out with the help of others who stand in as various characters — trans campers and angry lesbians, mostly. Geyl acts as "rain," hovering over them and flicking her fingers. It is the story of how Max awoke in his tent to find a coven of festie women flashing mirrors at their campsite. They were angry witches putting a spell on Camp Trans, and they did succeed in scaring the crap out of Max. Simon tells a story of his first Camp Trans experience, and the action he undertook with a trans man named Tony, a sixteen-year-old trans girl named Cat, and the transsexual author and activist Riki Ann Wilchins.

## Simon's First Festival

"First Tony went on the land, to put the womyn-born-womyn-only policy to the test. He identified as a post-op trans man, with bottom surgery (I forget the kind). He was saying that his dick was made out of the skin on his arm — I think that's a rhinoplasty? — anyway. He said, 'Hey, if my trans women friends are still men because they were assigned male at birth, then I must still be a woman.' So he went into the fest and took a shower. He asked consent of the women showering, telling them what kind of body he had. They said okay, but because the showers were public, new folks came in and freaked. By the time the ticket-buying action happened the next morning, the rumor was that something like six non-op trans women flashed their erect penises at the girls' camp. Gross, eh?

"The ticket-buying action: At noon on Saturday, Riki led a ticket-buying action at the fest. A bunch of the Avengers [the Lesbian Avengers are a lesbian direct-action group that has prioritized fighting for the rights of trans women], myself included, bought tickets to the fest. The young trans woman who was with us also bought a ticket, though at the time she could have been 'read' other than a womyn-born-womyn. This was a great victory for us and there were certainly tears. Then the trouble began. A woman started walking in front of us, shouting, 'Man on the land!'

"We did have some support from festie-goers who walked with us. We got to the main area, and it was very overwhelming. We were asked if we wanted to have a mediated discussion in the kitchen tent. Before that discussion, women were just coming at us from all over, some to be supportive, some to yell at us, and some to stare. There was very little middle ground, and it was very hostile. So we started this 'mediated' discussion and the setup was such: We (us Avengers, maybe four of us, and Riki) were sitting on folding tables in the front, while seven rows of angry lesbians yelled at us, audience-style. I kid you not. People called us rapists, woman-haters, said we were destroying their space by just walking on it, that we had no respect for women, that we had no respect for rape survivors, etc. Three hours this lasted, and the mediation was so one-sided we didn't get out of there with any confidence that anyone heard what we had to say. That was my first festival."

I don't want to leave the circle, 'cause I know this is it. In the morning I will ride into Grand Rapids with a girl named Katina, a festie-goer who has spent basically all of her time over at Camp Trans, much to the dismay of the girls she's camping with. "You know how every time you leave Michigan, you think, I'm coming back next year?" she asks. "Well, this year it wasn't like that. I know I can't come back next year." Katina's got hair that's bound up in bunches of braids, the ends secured with elastics in different bright colors. She lives and works in Brooklyn, where she supplements her income selling Strawberry Shortcake dolls on eBay. Her trick is to search for the dolls right there on eBay, but to search for sellers who have misspelled the name of the toys, therefore getting fewer bids and selling their wares cheaper. After securing the dolls, Katina puts them back up on the site, with the proper spelling, and doubles her money. She's a smart cookie. Camp Trans is lucky to have her. All week she's been offering her cell phone, offering hummus and wine, and now she's driving me to the airport. I give her a big hug as I climb out of her car. We used to see each other at MWMF, hug each other goodbye, say "See you next year." And now we say it again.

# CONTRIBUTORS' NOTES

**Chimamanda Ngozi Adichie** was born in Nigeria in 1977 and grew up in the university town of Nsukka. An O. Henry Prize winner, she won the PEN/David Wong Award for short fiction and has recently completed an MA in creative writing at Johns Hopkins University. Her first novel, *Purple Hibiscus*, was shortlisted for the 2004 Orange Prize.

**Daniel Alarcón**'s fiction has been published in *The New Yorker*, *Virginia Quarterly*, *Glimmer Train*, and elsewhere. His first collection of stories, *War by Candlelight*, will be published by HarperCollins in April 2005. He lives in Tucson, Arizona.

**David Benioff** was born and raised in New York City. He adapted his first novel, *The 25th Hour*, into the screenplay for the Spike Lee film of the same name. His collection of stories, *When the Nines Roll Over*, was published by Viking in September 2004. He lives in Los Angeles, where he is at work on his next novel.

**Christopher Buckley** is the author of eleven books and the editor in chief of *Forbes FYI*. He is a graduate of Yale University and spent a year working on tramp freighters. He was a speechwriter for Vice President George Bush from 1981 to 1983, and he received the Washington Irving Medal for Literary Excellence. He lives in Washington, D.C.

**Ben Ehrenreich** grew up on Long Island and now lives in Los Angeles, where he works as a freelance journalist. He writes fiction whenever he can, and he recently finished a novel. His father is actually a very kind man.

**Eve Englezos** and **Josh[ua] Moutray** prefer canapés to appetizers, "erudite" to "really smart," and Latin to all other languages. They are also total dicks, despite what you've heard. Their self-published comic series, *icecreamlandia,* is a sure-fire, one-way ticket to fame and fortune. How odd that it has yet to receive widespread critical acclaim. Please, please 1) visit www.icecreamlandia.com; 2) view more of their work; and 3) acclaim it.

**Jon Gertner** is a contributing writer at the *New York Times Magazine,* where he often writes about business and science. A former editor at *Money* magazine and the *American Lawyer,* he lives in New Jersey with his wife and two children.

**Michael Hall** has written for the *Austin Chronicle,* the *Austin American-Statesman, Trouser Press, Blender,* and *Men's Journal.* Since 1997 he has been a senior editor at *Texas Monthly;* his December 2003 story "Death Isn't Fair" was nominated for a National Magazine Award. Hall is married and lives in Austin.

**Sammy Harkham** was born on May 21, 1980, in Los Angeles to a New Zealander mother and Iraqi father. He is currently spending his time editing and drawing comics for the somewhat annual comics anthology *Kramers Ergot* and his ongoing comics series, *Crickets,* which will debut early next year. A book version of *Poor Sailor* will be in print by the end of the year from Gingko Press.

**John Haskell** is the author of a story collection, *I Am Not Jackson Pollock* (2003), and the novel *American Purgatorio* (2005), both from Farrar, Straus and Giroux. His work has appeared in *Granta,* the *Paris Review, Conjunctions,* and *Ploughshares.* He contributes to the radio show *The Next Big Thing.* He currently lives in Brooklyn.

**Kaui Hart Hemmings**, a former Wallace Stegner fellow at Stanford, currently lives in San Francisco. Her fiction appears or is forthcoming in *StoryQuarterly, Falling Backwards: Stories of Fathers and Daughters,* and *Zoetrope: All-Story.*

**Thom Jones** is the author of three short story collections, *The Pugilist at Rest, Cold Snap,* and *Sonny Liston Was a Friend of Mine.*

**Tom Kealey**'s fiction has been published in *Glimmer Train, Alaska Quarterly Review, Prairie Schooner,* the *Black Warrior Review,* and other publications. He received his MFA in creative writing from the University of Massachusetts, Amherst, and he is a former Wallace Stegner fellow and current Jones lecturer at Stanford University. Kealey grew up in North Carolina.

**Robert Kelly**'s latest books are *Lapis* (a collection of poems of the past five years) and the long poem *The Language of Eden,* which explores the discourse of psychoanalysis. "How They Took My Body Apart and Made Another Me" is from a novel in progress. He teaches in the writing program at Bard College in upstate New York, where he lives with his wife, the translator Charlotte Mandell.

**David Mamet** is the author of the plays *Oleanna, Glengarry Glen Ross* (1984 Pulitzer Prize and the New York Drama Critics Circle Award), *American Buffalo, A Life in the Theatre, Speed-the-Plow, Edmond, Lakeboat, The Water Engine, The Woods, Sexual Perversity in Chicago, Reunion, The Cryptogram* (1995 Obie Award), *The Old Neighborhood, Boston Marriage,* and *Dr. Faustus.* His translation and adaptations include *Red River* by Pierre Laville and *The Cherry Orchard, Three Sisters,* and *Uncle Vanya* by Anton Chekhov. His films include, as writer, *The Postman Always Rings Twice, The Verdict, The Untouchables, Hoffa, The Edge, Wag the Dog,* and *The Winslow Boy;* as writer/director, *House of Games, Oleanna, Homicide, The Spanish Prisoner, State and Main, Heist,* and *Spartan.* He is also the author of *Warm and Cold* and *Bar Mitzvah,* books for children with illustrations by Donald Sultan, and three other children's books: *Passover, The Duck and the Goat,* and *Henrietta;* five volumes of essays: *Writing in Restaurants, Some Freaks, The Cabin, Make-Believe Town,* and *Jaffsie and John Henry;* two books of poems: *The Hero Pony* and *Cinaman; Three Children's Plays, On Directing Film, True and False, Three Uses of the Knife: On the Nature and Purpose of Drama,* and the novels *The Village, The Old Religion,* and *Wilson.*

**Gina Ochsner** lives and works in Keizer, Oregon, with her family. Her collection of stories titled *The Necessary Grace to Fall* was published by the University of Georgia Press. Ochsner is at work on a novel and another collection of stories.

**Lance Olsen** is the author of fifteen books of and about innovative fiction, including *Tonguing the Zeitgeist* (finalist for the Philip K. Dick Award) and, most recently, the novel *Girl Imagined by Chance* (Fiction Collective Two, 2002) and the short story collection *Hideous Beauties* (Eraserhead, 2003). Fiction Collective Two will release his next novel, *Nietzsche's Kisses,* in 2006. He lives somatically in the mountains of central Idaho and digitally at www.cafezeitgeist.com.

**Julie Orringer** is the author of *How to Breathe Underwater,* a collection of short stories. She was a Truman Capote fellow in the Wallace Stegner Program at Stanford, where she now teaches fiction writing. She received her MFA from the Iowa Writers' Workshop and her BA from Cornell University. Her stories have appeared in the *Yale Review,* the *Paris Review, McSweeney's, Ploughshares, Zoetrope: All-Story, The Pushcart Prize XXV* and *XXVII, The Best New American Voices 2001,* and *New Stories from the South: The Year's Best, 2002.* Her short story collection won the 2004 Northern California Book Award. She is now at work on a novel set in Budapest and Paris.

**Michael Paterniti** is the author of *Driving Mr. Albert,* which began as an article for *Harper's Magazine* and won the 1998 National

Magazine Award. He is a former executive editor of *Outside*, and his work has appeared in *Rolling Stone*, the *New York Times Magazine*, *Details*, and *Esquire*, where he is writer-at-large. He lives in Portland, Maine, with his wife and son.

**Paula W. Peterson** is the author of *Penitent, with Roses: An HIV+ Mother Reflects*, winner of the Bakeless Prize for Nonfiction from the Bread Loaf Writers' Conference, and *Women in the Grove*, a collection of stories. Her short fiction has appeared in the *Iowa Review*, *Nimrod*, *Carolina Quarterly*, the *Greensboro Review*, and other journals, and her stories and essays have been nominated for Pushcart Prizes. Peterson lives outside Chicago.

**Cheryl Printup** was born and raised in Venice, California, to an Apache/Seneca father and a Norwegian mother. She still lives in Venice with her musician husband and two sons. She earned her BA in English literature with a minor in American Indian Studies at UCLA — a book-learned city Ind'n (although she does make good fry bread). At UCLA she had the good fortune to study writing with Paula Gunn Allen and for two years worked with the poet and novelist Kate Braverman in a private writing workshop. However, the best education, she believes, was traveling the country in her 1963 Chevy Suburban; the most fascinating ideas come from graffiti in remote gas station restrooms. She is currently working on a book of short stories. When not writing, she teaches creative writing at a public school, watches her sons surf, and coaches basketball.

**David Sedaris** is a writer whose commentaries are heard on National Public Radio. He is the author of the bestsellers *Barrel Fever*, *Naked*, *Me Talk Pretty One Day*, and most recently *Dress Your Family in Corduroy and Denim*. He is a frequent contributor to *GQ* and *The New Yorker*. Under the name the Talent Family, he and his sister Amy Sedaris have written plays such as the Obie Award–winning *One Woman Shoe* and *The Book of Liz*. He lives in Paris and London.

**Michelle Tea** is the author of three memoirs, most recently *The Chelsea Whistle;* the illustrated novel *Rent Girl* (with Laurenn McCubbinn); and the poetry collection *The Beautiful*. She is the editor of the anthologies *Without a Net: The Female Experience of Growing Up Working Class* and *Pills, Thrills, Chills and Heartache: Adventures in the First Person* (with Clint Catalyst). In the 1990s she helped found the legendary Sister Spit open mike series and national tours. She presently lives in San Francisco, where she curates, hosts, and bakes cookies for the Radar Reading Series at the main library.

# NOTABLE
# NONREQUIRED
# READING
# OF 2003

STEVE ALMOND
What It's Like to Be a Man, *Antioch Review.*
GREG AMES
Playing Ping-Pong with Pontius Pilate, *The Sun.*

ALEC HANSLEY BEMIS
Mr. Fantastic, Superduper Star, *L.A. Weekly.*
AIMEE BENDER
I Will Pick Out Your Ribs (from My Teeth), *Land Grant College Review.*
RACHEL BLAKE
Elephants, *Open City.*
RYAN BOUDINOT
The Sofa, eyeshot.net.
CHARLES BOWDEN
Keeper of the Fire, *Mother Jones.*
DAVID BROOKS
Napoleon's Roads, *Kenyon Review.*
JOSEPH BRUCHAC
The Hawk in Prison, *Parabola.*

NELINIA CABILES
The Unreliable Memory of Fish, *Five Points.*

PASHA MALIA
  The Film We Made About Dads, sweetfancymoses.com.
TOM MARTIN
  Witness, *Ploughshares.*
MORGAN MCDERMOTT
  Fuel, *Speakeasy.*
JOE MENO
  Happiness Will Be Yours, *Other Voices.*

TAMMY OLER
  Blood Letting, *Bitch.*

LEWIS ROBINSON
  Officer Friendly, *Tin House.*
JIM RULAND
  The Previous Adventures of Popeye the Sailor, *Black Warrior Review.*

MARK SALZMAN
  The Writing Class, *American Scholar.*
GEORGE SAUNDERS
  Jon, *The New Yorker.*
JIM SHEPARD
  *Badlands* and the "Innocence" of American Innocence, *Believer.*
YEVGENY SHKLOVSKY
  A Cup of Coffee in the Café on Ostozhenka, *Agni.*
PATRICK SOMERVILLE
  Trouble and the Shadowy Deathblow, *One Story.*
VLADIMIR SOROKIN
  Hiroshima, *Grandstreet.*

JAMES TATE
  The Theory of Mowing, *Conjunctions.*
PAUL TOUTONGHI
  They Rise, They Rise, *Zoetrope: All-Story.*

TOM WHALEN
  Parents, *Hayden's Ferry.*

VARIOUS AUTHORS: FLORA BROVINA, PATRICK GRAHAM, WARD JUST,
DITH PRAN, JOEL TURNIPSEED, BRIAN URQUHART
  The Sky Was Falling, *New York Times Magazine.*

# THE B·E·S·T AMERICAN SERIES®

## THE BEST AMERICAN SHORT STORIES® 2004

**Lorrie Moore, guest editor, Katrina Kenison, series editor.** "Story for story, readers can't beat *The Best American Short Stories* series" (*Chicago Tribune*). This year's most beloved short fiction anthology is edited by the critically acclaimed author Lorrie Moore and includes stories by Annie Proulx, Sherman Alexie, Paula Fox, Thomas McGuane, and Alice Munro, among others.

0-618-19735-4 PA $14.00 / 0-618-19734-6 CL $27.50
0-618-30046-5 CASS $26.00 / 0-618-29965-3 CD $30.00

## THE BEST AMERICAN ESSAYS® 2004

**Louis Menand, guest editor, Robert Atwan, series editor.** Since 1986, *The Best American Essays* series has gathered the best nonfiction writing of the year and established itself as the best anthology of its kind. Edited by Louis Menand, author of *The Metaphysical Club* and staff writer for *The New Yorker,* this year's volume features writing by Kathryn Chetkovich, Jonathan Franzen, Kyoko Mori, Cynthia Zarin, and others.

0-618-35709-2 PA $14.00 / 0-618-35706-8 CL $27.50

## THE BEST AMERICAN MYSTERY STORIES™ 2004

**Nelson DeMille, guest editor, Otto Penzler, series editor.** This perennially popular anthology is a favorite of mystery buffs and general readers alike. This year's volume is edited by the best-selling suspense author Nelson DeMille and offers pieces by Stephen King, Joyce Carol Oates, Jonathon King, Jeff Abbott, Scott Wolven, and others.

0-618-32967-6 PA $14.00 / 0-618-32968-4 CL $27.50 / 0-618-49742-0 CD $30.00

## THE BEST AMERICAN SPORTS WRITING™ 2004

**Richard Ben Cramer, guest editor, Glenn Stout, series editor.** This series has garnered wide acclaim for its stellar sports writing and topnotch editors. Now Richard Ben Cramer, the Pulitzer Prize–winning journalist and author of the best-selling *Joe DiMaggio,* continues that tradition with pieces by Ira Berkow, Susan Orlean, William Nack, Charles P. Pierce, Rick Telander, and others.

0-618-25139-1 PA $14.00 / 0-618-25134-0 CL $27.50

## THE BEST AMERICAN TRAVEL WRITING 2004

**Pico Iyer, guest editor, Jason Wilson, series editor.** *The Best American Travel Writing 2004* is edited by Pico Iyer, the author of *Video Night in Kathmandu* and *Sun After*

# THE B·E·S·T AMERICAN SERIES®

*Dark*. Giving new life to armchair travel this year are Roger Angell, Joan Didion, John McPhee, Adam Gopnik, and many others.

0-618-34126-9 PA $14.00 / 0-618-34125-0 CL $27.50

## THE BEST AMERICAN SCIENCE AND NATURE WRITING 2004

**Steven Pinker, guest editor, Tim Folger, series editor.** This year's edition promises to be another "eclectic, provocative collection" (*Entertainment Weekly*). Edited by Steven Pinker, author of *The Blank Slate* and *The Language Instinct*, it features work by Gregg Easterbrook, Atul Gawande, Peggy Orenstein, Jonathan Rauch, Chet Raymo, Nicholas Wade, and others.

0-618-24698-3 PA $14.00 / 0-618-24697-5 CL $27.50

## THE BEST AMERICAN RECIPES 2004–2005

**Edited by Fran McCullough and Molly Stevens.** "Give this book to any cook who is looking for the newest, latest recipes and the stories behind them" (*Chicago Tribune*). Offering the very best of what America is cooking, as well as the latest trends, timesaving tips, and techniques, this year's edition includes a foreword by the renowned chef Bobby Flay.

0-618-45506-x CL $26.00

## THE BEST AMERICAN NONREQUIRED READING 2004

**Edited by Dave Eggers, Introduction by Viggo Mortensen.** Edited by the best-selling author Dave Eggers, this genre-busting volume draws the finest, most interesting, and least expected fiction, nonfiction, humor, alternative comics, and more from publications large, small, and on-line. This year's collection features writing by David Sedaris, Daniel Alarcón, David Mamet, Thom Jones, and others.

0-618-34123-4 PA $14.00 / 0-618-34122-6 CL $27.50 / 0-618-49743-9 CD $26.00

## THE BEST AMERICAN SPIRITUAL WRITING 2004

**Edited by Philip Zaleski, Introduction by Jack Miles.** The latest addition to the acclaimed Best American series, *The Best American Spiritual Writing 2004* brings the year's finest writing about faith and spirituality to all readers. With an introduction by the best-selling author Jack Miles, this year's volume represents a wide range of perspectives and features pieces by Robert Coles, Bill McKibben, Oliver Sacks, Pico Iyer, and many others.

0-618-44303-7 PA $14.00 / 0-618-44302-9 CL $27.50

HOUGHTON MIFFLIN COMPANY  www.houghtonmifflinbooks.com